THE NEW BOOK OF KNOWLEDGE ANNUAL

1977

HIGHLIGHTING EVENTS OF 1976

THE NEW BOOK OF KNOWLEDGE ANNUAL

THE YOUNG PEOPLE'S BOOK OF THE YEAR

Grolier

INCORPORATED
NEW YORK

MANAGING EDITOR	**JOHN RATTI**
ART AND PRODUCTION DIRECTOR	**BARBARA EFFRON**
ASSOCIATE EDITOR	**FERN L. MAMBERG**

EDITORIAL STAFF

EDITORS	**SUE R. BRANDT**
	PATRICIA ELLSWORTH
	JEROME Z. NEIBRIEF
	LEO SCHNEIDER
	JANET STONE
COPY EDITORS	**J. MICHAEL RAIKES**
	PATRICIA M. GODFREY
INDEXER	**VITRUDE DE SPAIN**
STAFF ASSISTANTS	**MAE BENETT**
	NILSA JIMENEZ
	JANET RAMLOW

ART AND PRODUCTION STAFF

PRODUCTION SUPERVISOR	**HARRIET L. SMITH**
LAYOUT ARTIST	**JACQUES CHAZAUD**
PICTURE EDITORS	**JOYCE DEYO**
	RICHARD A. GREENE

MANUFACTURING DEPARTMENT

DIRECTOR	**HARRY G. VERAS**
ASSISTANT DIRECTOR	**ANTHONY LEONARDI**

· · · · ·

YOUNG PEOPLE'S PUBLICATIONS DEPARTMENT

EXECUTIVE EDITOR	**WILLIAM E. SHAPIRO**
EDITORIAL CONSULTANT	**MARTHA GLAUBER SHAPP**

GROLIER INCORPORATED

SENIOR VICE-PRESIDENT, PUBLISHING	**HOWARD B. GRAHAM**
VICE-PRESIDENT AND EDITORIAL DIRECTOR	**WALLACE S. MURRAY**

CONTENTS

10 **OUR CHANGING WORLD**
12 January
14 February
16 March
18 April
20 May
22 June
24 July
26 August
28 September
30 October
32 November
34 December
36 The U.S. Presidential Election
41   James Earl Carter, Jr.
42 The Glorious Fourth
46   Around the Country
50   1876 Revisited
54   Operation Sail
56   Friendly Relations
60 Headline Highlights
61   Angola
62   Seychelles: A New Country
64   The Year After in Indochina
66   China Without Mao
67   Change in Italy and Sweden
68   Crisis in Southern Africa
70   Terror in Northern Ireland
72   Namibia
73   Terrorism
76   Lebanon
78   New Times for Portugal and Spain

80 **WORLD OF SCIENCE**
82 Mystery on Mars
84 A Cosmic Laser Concert
87 Ball Lightning
88 The Space Shuttle

90 The National Air and Space Museum
94 Calculators
95 Steps into Space
96 Identical!
100 Rockets to the Moon
101 The Concorde Controversy
102 Canadian Wonders
106 CB: Everybody's Talking
107 Biofeedback—A New Kind of Medicine?
108 When Was the Bronze Age?
110 Operation Nessie
112 A Gem of a Museum
116 1976: A Year of Disasters
118 Digging Up the Past
120 Grandmummy Tiy
121 Blackboard in the Sky
122 Mapping the World

124 **FUN TO MAKE AND DO**
126 Giant Dice
127 A Loch Ness Monster Maze
128 Coin Collecting
130 Apples of Amber
131 It Runs in the Family
132 Make a Present
134 Decorated Pencil Holders
136 Ojos de Dios
139 Where Have We Met?
140 Cover Your Books
142 Rock Necklaces
143 What's Wrong Here?
144 Come for Supper
146 Stamp Collecting
150 Printing from Nature

152 **LIVING HISTORY**
154 Found Masterpieces
155 Following the Cable

156	Haida Totem Poles
158	Saving Venice
162	Upper Canada Village
164	The Cones of Cappadocia
166	Deerfield—Past and Present
170	The Modern Pioneers
174	The Château Ramezay
176	Ghost Ships of Lake Huron
181	Ste. Anne de Beaupré
182	A Poster Portfolio
190	Celebrations of Water
196	Mother Teresa
197	Custer's Last Stand
200	**YOUTH IN THE NEWS**
202	Landsailing
206	A Medieval Festival
207	Young Headliners
210	Olympic Superstars
212	Fun and Games
214	Dig In!
216	Young Photographers
220	Boy Scouts
224	Girl Scouts and Girl Guides
228	**FUN TO READ**
230	Children Headed West
240	Live and Let Live
248	Poetry
252	Moby Dick—An Anniversary
256	Tom Sawyer's Birthday
260	Looking at Books
262	The Strong Voice
268	**THE ANIMAL WORLD**
270	Animals in the News
272	Westminster's 100th Dog Show
274	A Strange Little Whale

276	It's for the Birds
278	Operation Noah
279	Albino Animals
283	Why the Bear's Tail Is So Short
284	The Ibises of Biricek
286	The Beehives of Poland
288	Reigning Cats and Dogs
296	**WORLD OF SPORTS**
298	The 1976 Olympic Games
310	Baseball
313	Little League Baseball
314	Basketball
316	Football
319	Golf
320	Hockey
324	Ice Skating
324	Skiing
325	Swimming
326	Tennis
327	Track and Field
328	**THE CREATIVE WORLD**
330	Great Music for You
336	Magic in Molas
338	The Music Scene
344	Academy Awards
346	Animals in Art
352	Hundreds of Cats
354	Horses in Art
358	Fancy Duds
360	**INTERNATIONAL STATISTICAL SUPPLEMENT**
366	**INDEX**
383	**ILLUSTRATION CREDITS AND ACKNOWLEDGMENTS**

CONTRIBUTORS

ASIMOV, Isaac
Scientist; author, *The Bloodstream: River of Life; Breakthroughs in Science; Chemicals of Life: Enzymes, Vitamins & Hormones; The Human Body; Wellsprings of Life*   IDENTICAL!

BROOKS, Hugh C.
Director, Center for African Studies, St. John's University (New York); Fellow, African Studies Association   SEYCHELLES: A NEW COUNTRY

BUCTEL, George
Designer and illustrator of maps; map maker for *Reader's Digest* publications
Maps for WHEN WAS THE BRONZE AGE?
SAVING VENICE
Art work for STEPS INTO SPACE
IDENTICAL!

CLARK, Cecily
Poet; instructor, Brewster Academy
THE EDGE
NORTH

CRONKITE, Walter
CBS News Correspondent
OUR CHANGING WORLD

DAUER, Rosamond
Poet; author, *Bullfrog Grows Up; My Friend, Jasper Jones*   STONES
FROG

DAY, Wesley
Poet; picture editor; librarian
THE MECHANICAL LION
A CAT'S COMING
ARISTOTLE IN THE APPLE ORCHARD

DOWNEY, Rob
Photographer and designer
Construction and photography for
APPLES OF AMBER

ECHARD, Maribeth
Contributor to *Cat Fanciers' Federation Newsletter; All Cats* magazine
REIGNING CATS AND DOGS

GOLDBERG, Hy
Co-ordinator of sports information, NBC Sports; winner of New Jersey Sports Writer of the Year award   THE 1976 OLYMPIC GAMES
SPORTS

GRIMM, Michele and Tom
Writers and photographers; authors, *Basic Book of Photography; Hitchhiker's Handbook; My Brown Bag; What Is a Seal?; Can You Walk the Plank?*   LANDSAILING

HAHN, Charless
Stamp editor, *Chicago Sun-Times*
STAMP COLLECTING

HAIMOWITZ, Benjamin
Teacher, New York City Public School System; writer   HEADLINE HIGHLIGHTS

HARP, Sybil C.
Editor, *Creative Crafts* magazine
OJOS DE DIOS
PRINTING FROM NATURE

HONIG, Joel
Musician; music reviewer
GREAT MUSIC FOR YOU

KAVANAUGH, Ted
Director, ALPO Pet News Bureau
REIGNING CATS AND DOGS

KURTZ, Henry I.
Author, *John and Sebastian Cabot; Captain John Smith;* contributor, *History Today* and *American History Illustrated* magazines
THE U.S. PRESIDENTIAL ELECTION
OPERATION SAIL
FOLLOWING THE CABLE
CUSTER'S LAST STAND

MACDONALD, M. A.
Author, *The Royal Canadian Mounted Police;* co-author, *Growing Up*
GHOST SHIPS OF LAKE HURON

MARGO, Elisabeth
Author, *Taming the Forty-niner*
THE MODERN PIONEERS
CHILDREN HEADED WEST
RED SHIRLEY (poem)

MCVICKER, Charles
Illustrator; painter; member, Society of Illustrators and American Watercolor Society
Art work for LIVE AND LET LIVE

MISHLER, Clifford
Publisher, *Numismatic News Weekly*
COIN COLLECTING

PRICE, Harvey
Acting Chief Scout Executive, Boy Scouts of America
BOY SCOUTS

ROSENTHAL, Sylvia
Managing editor, *Disney's It's a Small World* encyclopedia; author, *Live High on Low Fat*
COME FOR SUPPER
MAGIC IN MOLAS

SHAW, Arnold
Author, *The Rockin' 50's; Honkers and Shouters: The Rhythm and Blues Years; The Rock Revolution; The World of Soul; The Street That Never Slept*
THE MUSIC SCENE

SKODNICK, Ruth
Statistician
INTERNATIONAL STATISTICAL SUPPLEMENT

STROUGHTER, Carol Brooks
Girl Scouts of the U.S.A.
GIRL SCOUTS AND GIRL GUIDES

SWAN, Susan
Illustrator, children's books and educational materials. Awards: Citation of Merit, Society of Illustrators 15th Annual Exhibition; A.I.G.A. Certificate of Excellence (1973)
Art work for TOM SAWYER'S BIRTHDAY

OUR CHANGING WORLD

At the end of 1976 there was peace in most of the world. This did not mean there were no problems. And there was always the danger of old disputes flaring up again. But at year's end, people in many countries felt able, for the first time in many years, to plan for a better future.

There was a truce in the bloody civil war between Christian and Muslim groups in Lebanon—and it seemed to be holding. The continuing struggle of blacks in southern Africa to gain their civil and political rights was out in the open in 1976, and being discussed constructively. Black and white leaders of Rhodesia were negotiating a timetable for black majority rule of Rhodesia, something that had seemed impossible a year ago. And the deep and complex problems between the races in South Africa were also being explored. In Northern Ireland, the bitter strife between Roman Catholic and Protestant groups continued, but there was a hopeful new force at work. A women's peace movement in Northern Ireland, made up of Roman Catholic and Protestant women, began to organize and to demonstrate. At year's end, they had drawn attention to Northern Ireland's plight and were acting as a conscience for both sides in the conflict. This movement provided a genuine glimmer of hope in an otherwise bleak situation.

And people in a number of countries sought orderly, governmental solutions to their problems. In November the people of the United States elected Democrat Jimmy Carter, a former governor of Georgia and a new face in national government, as president of the United States. Many people had high hopes that a new administration would find solutions to some of the economic and social problems of the United States. And in Britain, that country's Labour government tried to work out longtime economic problems. The British pound, once one of the world's most stable currencies, dropped drastically on the world market during the year, as serious inflation and trade problems continued in Britain.

Italy and Sweden voted in new governments in 1976. Sweden chose a middle-of-the-road government after years of Socialist leadership. Italy's growing Communist Party gained enough seats in Parliament to demand a voice in making Italian Government policy. Portugal had its first free elections in 50 years. Along with its neighbor, Spain, Portugal seemed to be on the road to democracy.

China, the giant of Asia, reached a turning point in its modern history in 1976. Chou En-lai, the nation's longtime premier, died in January. And in September an even more shattering event took place. Communist Party Chairman Mao Tse-tung, who had led China since 1949, died. Few people inside or outside China seemed sure what path the huge nation would take in the future. At year's end, Communist Party Chairman Hua Kuo-feng seemed to hold power as Mao's successor. But there were reports of public protests against the government in some areas. China was also shaken by severe earthquakes during the year.

But despite economic problems and tensions in many areas around the world, people were hopeful at the end of 1976. They looked forward to 1977 with great expectations.

WALTER CRONKITE

JANUARY

1 At midnight on New Year's Eve the Liberty Bell, symbol of American independence, was moved to a new home. The famous cracked bell was carefully taken from Independence Hall in Philadelphia and moved 100 yards (91 meters) to a steel and glass pavilion in Independence Square. More visitors will now be able to see it more easily. The bell, purchased from a London foundry in 1752, was rung at the first public reading of the Declaration of Independence in 1776.

8 Chou En-lai, 78, one of China's most important political leaders, died in Peking. He had been premier of the People's Republic of China since its founding in 1949.

11 General Guillermo Rodríguez Lara, president of Ecuador, was deposed in a bloodless coup. The three-man junta that came to power imposed a state of siege and martial law.

12 Agatha Christie, 85, British mystery writer, died in England. Dame Agatha, author of over 100 books, was the creator of Hercule Poirot, one of the most popular characters in detective fiction. Her books have been translated into 103 languages.

Visitors view the Liberty Bell in its new home in Independence Square.

Cuban Prime Minister Fidel Castro and Canadian Prime Minister Pierre Trudeau visit a textile factory during Trudeau's Latin-American tour.

17 The Communications Technology Satellite, a joint project of the United States and Canada, blasted off from Cape Canaveral, Florida. The communications satellite, the most powerful ever launched, was later placed in a stationary earth orbit.

20 President Gerald R. Ford named Anne Armstrong ambassador to Britain to succeed Elliot L. Richardson. The new ambassador would become the first woman to hold that post.

22 President Gerald R. Ford nominated Willie Julian Usery, Jr., secretary of labor to succeed John T. Dunlop.

23 Paul Robeson, 77, American singer and actor, died in Philadelphia. Condemned during the McCarthy era as a Communist, the black entertainer spent several years abroad before returning to the United States. One of his most widely praised roles was that of the Moor in Shakespeare's *Othello*.

23 Canadian Prime Minister Pierre Elliott Trudeau began an 11-day official visit to Mexico, Cuba, and Venezuela. The purpose of the trip was to stimulate trade with the three Latin-American nations.

FEBRUARY

4 A severe earthquake, which registered 7.5 on the 9-point Richter scale, struck Guatemala. More than 22,000 people lost their lives in the disaster, and about 74,000 were hurt. The quake was felt throughout the country as well as in neighboring Honduras and El Salvador.

13 General Murtala Ramat Mohammed, head of state of Nigeria, was assassinated in an attempted coup. He was succeeded by General Olusegun Obasanjo, chief of staff of the armed forces.

15 The 12th Winter Olympic Games came to a close in Innsbruck, Austria. About 1,100 athletes from 36 countries took part. The skiing events were among the most exciting. West German ski star Rosi Mittermaier, winner of gold medals in downhill and slalom events, was narrowly defeated in the giant slalom by Kathy Kreiner of Timmins, Ontario. In the final tally, the Soviet Union won a total of 27 medals, East Germany placed second with 19, and the United States came in third with 10.

Christl Haas, a 1964 Olympic star, lights one of the twin flames in the opening ceremony of the Winter Olympic Games in Austria.

Guatemalan families set up temporary shelters in the streets after their homes were destroyed by a severe earthquake.

20 SEATO (Southeast Asia Treaty Organization) was formally disbanded. The organization had been established on September 8, 1954. Its members then were Australia, France, New Zealand, Pakistan, the Philippines, Thailand, the United Kingdom, and the United States. These nations agreed to help defend each other against military aggression in Southeast Asia and the southwest Pacific.

21 Former president and Mrs. Richard M. Nixon began a week's visit to the People's Republic of China as the guests of the Chinese Government. During his visit, Nixon met with Hua Kuo-feng, the newly appointed acting premier.

22 Egyptian military forces took over the last of the Sinai desert territory that Egypt was entitled to receive from Israel. This was the final phase of the disengagement agreement provided for in the pacts signed by the two countries following the Middle East war in 1973.

23 President Gerald R. Ford named Robert Strausz-Hupe ambassador to the North Atlantic Treaty Organization (NATO) to succeed David K. E. Bruce.

25 President Gerald R. Ford named William W. Scranton U.S. representative to the United Nations. Scranton succeeded Daniel Patrick Moynihan.

MARCH

16   Harold Wilson, prime minister of Britain for a total of nearly eight years, announced his resignation. The move came shortly after the House of Commons had rejected one of Wilson's plans to fight inflation. (He was succeeded by James Callaghan, who was elected new head of the Labour Party on April 5.)

20   Patricia Hearst, the daughter of publisher Randolph A. Hearst, was convicted in San Francisco of robbing a bank and using a firearm to commit the robbery. She had been kidnapped in February, 1974, by a terrorist group called the Symbionese Liberation Army (SLA). Two months later she announced that she had joined the group. She was captured in September, 1975. (On September 24, 1976, she was sentenced to seven years in prison.)

22   Representatives of Israel and the Palestine Liberation Organization (PLO) engaged in debate in the Security Council of the United Nations for the first time. Until then, Israel had boycotted all meetings of the Council at which representatives of the PLO were present. The debate centered on protests by Arabs living in the Old City of Jerusalem and the West Bank.

Harold Wilson in a quiet moment, seen through the rain-splattered window of his car. This photograph was taken the day after Wilson announced he would resign as prime minister of Britain.

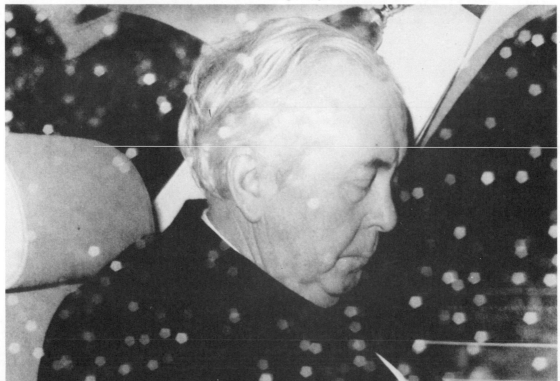

At a historic session of the U.N. Security Council, the Israeli Ambassador (*far left*) debates with the PLO delegate (*far right*).

24 Field Marshal Viscount Montgomery, 88, British World War II hero, died. Montgomery defeated the Germans and Italians in a decisive battle at El Alamein, Egypt, and later became deputy supreme commander of the North Atlantic Treaty Organization (NATO) forces under General Dwight D. Eisenhower.

24 Isabel Martínez de Perón, president of Argentina, was deposed in a military coup. She had become the first woman head of state in the Americas when she took office upon the death of her husband, President Juan Perón, in 1974. (Lieutenant General Jorge Videla was sworn in as the new president on March 29.)

24 President Gerald R. Ford called for a government-supported campaign to vaccinate the entire population of the United States against a virus strain related to swine influenza. The strain was believed to be similar to the one that had caused the death of 20,000,000 people in the epidemic of 1918–19. (A bill providing the funds for the national immunization was signed by the President on April 15.) On March 30, a limited vaccination program was announced in Canada.

APRIL

5 Howard Hughes, 70, American billionaire, died. Hughes was an eccentric industrialist, and his financial activities had been the subject of many legal controversies and federal investigations. He spent the last years of his life in seclusion.

13 The U.S. Treasury issued the first of some 400,000,000 $2 bills to mark the nation's Bicentennial. Two-dollar bills had not been printed since 1966. Like the old bill, the new bill (issued on Jefferson's birthday) has a portrait of Thomas Jefferson on the front. However, the reverse of the commemorative issue is different—it is a reproduction based on a painting of the signing of the Declaration of Independence.

This photograph was taken in Sublette, Kansas, on April 14, 1976. It shows the cracked soil of a thirsty wheat field caused by months-long drought conditions. The drought, which started during the summer of 1975 and continued throughout the winter, severely damaged the wheat crops of the area. It was estimated that the drought cut the total U.S. output of wheat for 1976 by as much as 10 percent.

Long lines form outside polling places in Lisbon, as Portuguese citizens wait to vote in the first free legislative elections in 50 years.

14 It was announced that Deputy Premier Khieu Samphan had been named chief of state of Cambodia (Kampuchea). He succeeded Norodom Sihanouk, who had resigned. Sihanouk, formerly the king of Cambodia, became chief of state in 1960. In 1970 he was overthrown when the country became involved in the war in Indochina. In 1975, Communist forces (the Khmer Rouge) took control, and Sihanouk again became chief of state.

25 Portugal held its first free legislative election in 50 years when voters went to the polls to cast ballots for members of the Legislative Assembly (parliament). The results of the voting gave the Socialists 107 representatives in the 263-seat body. The rest of the seats were divided among four of the remaining parties. The Socialist leader, Mário Soares, announced that his party would form a minority government.

28 Prime Minister Ian Smith named seven blacks to Rhodesia's all white Cabinet. They became the first black Rhodesians to serve as full and deputy ministers in the white minority government. Smith's move represented an easing of the traditional firm stand against allowing the black majority a meaningful voice in the government of Rhodesia.

MAY

6   A very strong earthquake hit northeastern Italy. The main quake, which registered 6.5 on the 9-point Richter scale, extended across the border into Yugoslavia. About 1,000 people were killed, and about 2,000 were injured. The towns of Gemona, Buia, and Maiano were the hardest hit. Gemona, a hill town dating back to the 11th century, was almost completely destroyed.

14   India and Pakistan agreed to resume diplomatic relations. Relations had been suspended when war broke out between the two countries in December, 1971.

19   Arnold Palmer, the famous American golfer, completed a record-setting around-the-world jet flight. Palmer, and two co-pilots and a time observer, circled the globe in 57 hours, 25 minutes, and 42 seconds. The time was more than a day faster than that of Arthur Godfrey and three others, who had established the previous record in 1966.

Golfer Arnold Palmer, just before leaving on his around-the-world jet flight.

Ellis Island in N.Y. Harbor, once the major point of entry for immigrants to the United States.

20 Typhoon Olga struck the northern Philippines. The typhoon caused floods that claimed the lives of 215 people and left 630,000 homeless. On May 24 the island of Luzon was declared a disaster area.

24 Two Concordes, British-French–built supersonic transports (SST's), landed at Dulles International Airport near Washington, D.C. The trips were the planes' first scheduled passenger flights between Europe and the United States. The planes, one from London and one from Paris, arrived two minutes apart.

28 The U.S. National Park Service officially re-opened Ellis Island in New York Harbor. From 1892 to 1954 the island had been the major point of entry for immigrants coming to the United States. Twelve million people passed through to the New World in that period. The island was closed in 1954. With the re-opening, guided tours allow visitors to see the historic buildings.

28 President Gerald R. Ford, in Washington, and Soviet leader Leonid Brezhnev, in Moscow, signed a treaty on underground nuclear explosions for peaceful purposes. The treaty limits the size of such nuclear explosions. It also provides that each country may make on-site inspection of such nuclear explosions in the other country.

JUNE

5   The 310-foot (94-meter) Teton Dam, on the Teton River near its junction with the Upper Snake River in Idaho, broke, causing great flooding. At least nine people lost their lives and 30 others were reported missing as a result of the heavy flooding. Thousands of homes and businesses were destroyed by the 15-foot-high (4.5-m-high) wall of water.

11   The United Nations Conference on Human Settlements (also known as Habitat) came to a close in Vancouver, British Columbia. About 4,500 delegates representing 134 nations had begun meetings there on May 31. The purpose of the conference was to explore ways to improve community life and living conditions around the world.

12   President Juan María Bordaberry of Uruguay was removed from office by the armed forces. (On July 14, Aparicio Méndez was appointed president for a 5-year term.)

20   Italians went to the polls to vote in certain local elections and for members of both houses of Parliament. The results of the most important election since 1948 showed impressive gains by the Communists. Although the ruling Christian Democratic Party retained the largest share of the vote, the Communists won 22 new seats in the Senate and 49 new seats in the Chamber of Deputies.

A town in Idaho is flooded as a result of the Teton Dam disaster.

A stranded traveler in Montreal during the Canadian pilots' strike.

23 The United States vetoed Angola's application for membership in the United Nations. Angola, a former overseas territory of Portugal, won its freedom on November 11, 1975. The vote on Angola's application in the 15-member Security Council was 13–1, with China abstaining.

27 Portugal held its first free presidential election in 50 years. General António Ramalho Eanes won a landslide victory. The new president asked Socialist leader Mário Soares to be his premier.

28 A nine-day strike by Canadian airline pilots, caused by a language dispute, ended. The pilots, who later had been joined by air traffic controllers, had begun the walkout in protest against government plans to increase the use of French at airports in Quebec Province. The strikers returned to work after the government announced plans to re-examine the proposal.

28 Seychelles, a group of about 90 islands in the Indian Ocean, became an independent republic. The islands, ceded to Britain by the Treaty of Paris in 1814, had been under British rule for 162 years.

JULY

2   The U.S. Supreme Court upheld the fundamental constitutionality of capital punishment. In an extremely important decision, the court ruled 7 to 2 that the death penalty does not always violate the Eighth Amendment, which prohibits cruel and unusual punishment.

2   North and South Vietnam were officially reunited as one country after having been divided for 22 years. The state of war that had existed between the two areas had ended when South Vietnam surrendered to Communist forces in 1975. Hanoi was declared the capital of the new country, the Socialist Republic of Vietnam.

4   The United States celebrated the 200th anniversary of the adoption of the Declaration of Independence with special observances throughout the country.

4   José López Portillo was elected president of Mexico in a landslide victory over the Communist Party candidate. López Portillo's 6-year term was to start on December 1.

4   Israeli rescue planes landed in Tel Aviv with 91 passengers and 12 crew members of an Air France plane that had been hijacked by pro-Palestinian guerrillas. In a daring operation, Israeli commandos in three transport planes had flown in to Uganda's Entebbe airport, where the passengers and crew had been held since June 28. Seven of the terrorists and three Israeli hostages died in the rescue.

20   Viking I, an unmanned U.S. spacecraft, completed its voyage to Mars and placed a robot Lander on the planet. Viking I had been launched on August 20, 1975. A few days after its arrival, the Lander began its search for chemical signs of life on Mars.

This fantastic picture of Mars shows a dune field that looks like a desert on Earth.

People seek temporary shelter in drainpipes after severe earthquakes shook the Peking area.

27 Russian chess grandmaster Viktor Korchnoi, the world's second-ranking player, asked for political asylum in the Netherlands. Korchnoi, who had earlier called for changes in international chess-tournament rules, had been censured by the Soviet Chess Federation and barred from international competition for six months.

28 An earthquake that registered 8.2 on the 9-point Richter scale caused serious damage in the heavily populated areas around and including Tangshan in the People's Republic of China. A second shock, registering 7.9, struck about 16 hours later. About 650,000 people were believed to have lost their lives in the two shocks, and thousands more were left homeless. The Chinese quakes were preceded by similar disasters in Indonesia. The first, the worst in Indonesia's history, struck Irian Jaya on June 26 and registered 7.1. The second, on July 14, registered 5.6 and hit the northern tip of the island of Bali. About 1,000 people died in the two quakes.

AUGUST

1 The Summer Games of the XXI Olympiad came to a close in Montreal, Canada. The star of the games was 14-year-old Rumanian gymnast Nadia Comaneci, the first person in Olympic history to be awarded a perfect score of 10 in gymnastics. The U.S. basketball team captured the gold medal it had narrowly lost in the 1972 Games. The U.S. men and the East German women dominated the swimming competition. In the final tally the Soviet Union won a total of 125 medals, the U.S. 94, and East Germany 90.

17 A severe earthquake struck Mindanao and neighboring islands in the Philippines. The quake registered 7.8 on the 9-point Richter scale. Over 3,000 people died, more than 650 were injured, and some 30,000 people were left homeless. Tremors were felt in Manila, about 500 miles (800 kilometers) from Cotabato Province, the hardest-hit area.

20 The fifth conference of nonaligned nations ended in Colombo, Sri Lanka. The meetings had started on August 16. In the final communiqué, representatives of the 85 member countries called on the rich nations of the world to give more of their wealth to the poor nations. Portions of the communiqué condemned Israel's Middle East policy, and called for independence for Puerto Rico and immediate black rule in Rhodesia and South Africa.

Billows of smoke and gas pour from the erupting La Soufrière volcano on Guadeloupe.

Soviet cosmonauts Boris Volynov and Vitali Zholobov, back on earth after a 48-day research program aboard an orbiting space station.

24 Two Soviet cosmonauts returned safely to earth after a 48-day research program aboard the orbiting Salyut 5 space station. The cosmonauts had blasted off aboard their Soyuz 21 spacecraft on July 6, and docked with the space station, which had been sent into orbit on June 22.

30 La Soufrière volcano on the French Caribbean island of Guadeloupe erupted. A series of very small eruptions had occurred a month earlier. Thousands of people had been evacuated from the area around the base of the mountain before the eruption.

31 Federal officials announced that the number of reported cases of "Legion fever" had reached 179. First signs of the mysterious illness had appeared shortly after an American Legion convention that took place in Philadelphia from July 21 to July 24. The Bureau of Epidemiology of the Center for Disease Control said that research into the cause of the illness would continue. (Eventually, 29 people died of the disease, and another 151 were hospitalized.)

SEPTEMBER

3 The Viking II Lander touched down on the plain of Utopia on Mars. The site of the landing was about 4,600 miles (7,400 kilometers) from where the Viking I Lander had touched down on July 20. The main purpose of the twin crafts was to test for signs of life on Mars.

6 A Russian pilot, defecting from the Soviet Union, landed his MiG-25 jet fighter on the Japanese island of Hokkaido. The aircraft, known as the Foxbat, can fly faster, higher, and farther than any other fighter in the world. The event made it possible for Japanese and U.S. experts to study the latest Soviet military aviation achievement.

9 Chinese Communist Party Chairman Mao Tse-tung, 82, died. Mao was a founder of the Chinese Communist Party and had been the leader of the People's Republic of China since its creation in 1949.

16 The general convention of the Episcopal Church voted to add to its canons (church laws) a provision that ordination to the priesthood apply equally to women and men. The vote at the meeting was intended to end the dispute over whether women should be allowed to become priests of the Episcopal Church.

The MiG-25 jet fighter, on a Japanese island. Known as the Foxbat, it is one of the latest Soviet military aircraft.

Mao Tse-tung, leader of Communist China since 1949, died in September.

20   Prime Minister Olof Palme of Sweden resigned after his party was defeated by a non-Socialist coalition, ending about 44 years of Social Democratic rule. Thorbjörn Fälldin, leader of the Center Party, was chosen to succeed Palme.

21   The 31st regular session of the United Nations General Assembly opened at U.N. headquarters in New York City. Hamilton Shirley Amerasinghe of Sri Lanka was elected to serve as Assembly president for one year. The newly independent republic of Seychelles became the 145th member of the body.

23   Two Soviet cosmonauts, Colonel Valeri F. Bykovsky and Vladimir V. Aksenov, returned to earth aboard their Soyuz 22 space capsule. They had spent eight days in earth orbit, photographing the earth's surface and conducting experiments on the conditions of life in space.

OCTOBER

4   Earl L. Butz, U.S. secretary of agriculture, resigned. The resignation came as a result of growing criticism of the Secretary, following reports of a racist remark made by him.

6   Seni Pramoj, premier of Thailand since April, 1976, was overthrown by a military coup. He was replaced two days later by Thanin Kraivichien. The new premier vowed to halt the spread of Communism.

10   American balloonist Edward Yost was rescued by a West German tanker after failing in his attempt to cross the Atlantic Ocean. Yost had lifted off from the Maine coast on October 5 and had stayed aloft for a record of almost 107 hours before his balloon ditched east of the Azores.

18   The U.S. Coast Guard announced that the cargo ship *Sylvia L. Ossa* was presumed lost at sea. The vessel, with a crew of 37, had disappeared two days earlier in the area known as the Bermuda Triangle in the Atlantic Ocean off the southeast coast of the United States. The area has been the scene of mysterious disappearances of ships and planes for many years.

26   The Transkei became the first of South Africa's nine black homelands to be given independence. About 3,000,000 blacks of the Xhosa people were assigned citizenship of the new republic by the government of South Africa. Almost half of them live and work outside the territory. The Transkei faced almost total diplomatic boycott because almost all foreign nations view it as an outgrowth of South Africa's racial policy of apartheid.

Rescued: Edward Yost, in the gondola of his ditched balloon.

Saul Bellow won the 1976 Nobel prize for literature.

THE 1976 NOBEL PRIZES

Chemistry: William N. Lipscomb, Jr., of the United States, for his studies of a class of compounds called boranes (fundamentally composed of boron and hydrogen). It is believed that boranes may eventually be useful in the treatment of cancer.

Economics: Milton Friedman of the United States, mainly for his theories on money, which have influenced government policies.

Literature: Saul Bellow of the United States, for his novels, which include *Henderson the Rain King, Herzog,* and *Humboldt's Gift.*

Peace: There was no Nobel peace prize awarded in 1976.

Physics: Burton Richter and Samuel C. C. Ting of the United States, for their discovery, made independently of each other, of a new type of subatomic particle, known as psi or J.

Physiology or Medicine: Baruch S. Blumberg and D. Carleton Gajdusek of the United States, for their independent studies that have led to a better understanding of infectious diseases. Their findings may be helpful in treating Parkinson's disease, multiple sclerosis, and hepatitis.

NOVEMBER

1 General Michel Micombero, president of the African country of Burundi since 1966, was deposed in a bloodless coup. Lieutenant Colonel Jean-Baptiste Bagaza became president.

2 Democrats James Earl Carter, Jr., and Senator Walter F. Mondale were elected by a narrow margin over the Republican slate of President Gerald R. Ford and Senator Robert J. Dole. The Democratic team carried 23 states and the District of Columbia, with a total of 297 electoral votes. Final election results for Congress: the House of Representatives—292 Democrats and 143 Republicans; the Senate—61 Democrats, 38 Republicans, and 1 Independent.

2 Alaskans voted to move their capital from Juneau to Willow South, about 70 miles (113 kilometers) from Anchorage, the state's most heavily populated area. The new site won out over Larson Lake and Mt. Yenlo.

12 Alexander Calder, 78, American artist, died. Calder was known for his mobiles (sculptures with parts that can be set in motion by air currents or by touching) and for his stabiles (large stationary metal sculptures). Many of his stabiles are in plazas and other open spaces around the world.

Happy winners: The newly elected U.S. president, Jimmy Carter, and vice-president, Walter Mondale.

Pomegranate, a mobile by American artist Alexander Calder. Calder died in November.

15 René Lévesque, candidate of the Parti Québécois, won an overwhelming victory in the race for premier of the Canadian province of Quebec. Lévesque founded the Parti Québécois in 1968 to promote Quebec independence from Canada. Although Lévesque represents the separatist movement, it is believed that his victory was the result of Quebec's weak economy and the poor leadership of his opponent. However, Lévesque stated that a referendum on separation would be held within two years.

23 André Malraux, 75, French literary and political figure, died. Malraux won an international reputation for his 1933 novel *Man's Fate.* He was also an art historian and archeologist, and a dedicated freedom fighter. He served as minister of cultural affairs under President Charles de Gaulle.

24 A severe earthquake, measuring 7.9 on the Richter scale, struck eastern Turkey. The area, the scene of many previous quakes, lies on the North Anatolian Fault, a rift in the earth's crust that crosses Turkey. About 3,600 people were killed, and some 150,000 people were left homeless.

DECEMBER

1   The newly independent country of Angola was admitted to the United Nations. The former overseas province of Portugal became the 146th member.

4   Benjamin Britten, 63, British composer, died. Among his best-known works are the operas *Peter Grimes* and *Death in Venice* and a mass, *War Requiem*.

15   Western Samoa was admitted to the United Nations. The Pacific island country had become independent in 1962. It had not applied for membership in those 14 years because it wanted to remain isolated from world affairs. The country became the 147th U.N. member.

15   The Liberian-flag tanker *Argo Merchant* ran aground on shoals off Nantucket Island, Massachusetts. A week later, high winds and heavy seas caused the hull of the aging vessel to break in two and spill its cargo of 7,500,000 gallons (284,000 hectoliters) of thick oil. The oil spill, which eventually spread over a vast area of water, was one of the

Pounding waves and raging winds broke the *Argo Merchant* in two. The tanker's oil cargo poured into the seas, causing an enormous oil spill.

largest in shipping history. It caused severe damage to the area's fisheries and left about 500 birds coated with oil.

16 The swine-flu vaccination program, sponsored by the U.S. Government, was halted. At least 94 people had suffered a form of paralysis, and an investigation was under way to try to find out if there was a link between the paralysis and the flu vaccine.

20 Richard J. Daley, 74, American politician, died. Daley, who had been mayor of Chicago since 1955, was one of the most powerful politicians in the United States.

24 Japan's parliament elected Takeo Fukuda premier. Fukuda, leader of the conservative Liberal-Democratic Party, succeeded Takeo Miki, who resigned after having been premier since December, 1974.

THE CARTER CABINET

President-elect Jimmy Carter completed his nominations of the members of his Cabinet and of the U.S. representative to the United Nations. The nominees would have to be approved by the Senate after Carter's inauguration on January 20.

Secretary of Agriculture: Bob S. Bergland, representative from Minnesota.

Attorney General: Griffin B. Bell, former judge of the U.S. court of appeals.

Secretary of Commerce: Juanita M. Kreps, vice-president of Duke University.

Secretary of Defense: Harold Brown, president of the California Institute of Technology.

Secretary of Health, Education, and Welfare: Joseph A. Califano, Jr., former aide to President Johnson.

Secretary of Housing and Urban Development: Patricia R. Harris, Washington, D.C., lawyer.

Secretary of the Interior: Cecil D. Andrus, governor of Idaho.

Secretary of Labor: F. Ray Marshall, professor of economics, University of Texas.

Secretary of State: Cyrus R. Vance, New York City lawyer.

Secretary of Transportation: Brock Adams, representative from Washington.

Secretary of the Treasury: W. Michael Blumenthal, chairman of the Bendix Corporation.

Representative to the United Nations: Andrew J. Young, Jr., representative from Georgia.

The Carters and the Mondales—the new first and second families of the United States.

THE U. S. PRESIDENTIAL ELECTION

"My name is Jimmy Carter and I'm running for president."

That was how James Earl Carter, Jr., began his acceptance speech when he received the Democratic Party's nomination to be its candidate for president in 1976.

It was a familiar phrase, and one that the former Georgia governor had often used in nearly two years of campaigning for the U.S. presidency.

When he had begun his quest for the nation's highest office, back in 1974, Jimmy Carter was unknown to most Americans. And so wherever he went on the campaign trail, he would extend his hand, flash the "Carter grin," and say: "Hi, I'm Jimmy Carter and I'm running for president."

By the time the Democratic National Convention met in New York, in July of 1976, Jimmy Carter's smile and soft, southern drawl were familiar to almost all Americans.

And after Election Day, in November, Jimmy Carter no longer had to tell people who he was. Everyone in the country knew that he had been elected the 39th president of the United States.

The presidential race had been too close for political experts to predict who would win. But Carter narrowly defeated President Gerald R. Ford, his Republican opponent. Carter received 297 electoral votes to Ford's 240. The popular vote was even closer: Carter, 50 percent, and Ford, 48 percent. (Eugene McCarthy and several other minor-party candidates received the remaining 2 percent of the vote.)

The 1976 election was the first time since the Civil War that a person from the Deep South had won the presidency. President Ford became the first incumbent president since Herbert Hoover (1932) to be voted out of office.

▶ THE PRIMARIES

Jimmy Carter's victory was the end of what President Ford called, in his speech conceding defeat, "our long and intense struggle for the presidency."

The struggle was indeed long and hard. The real campaigning began early in 1976 when both Ford and Carter entered the Republican and Democratic primaries.

The primary elections have been called elimination contests. The candidates who survive go on to the national conventions, which might be termed the semifinals. The conventions choose the finalists: the presidential and vice-presidential candidates. The candidates selected by the Democratic and Republican parties then compete against each other for the greatest prize in American politics—the presidency.

In 1976, candidates of both major parties entered thirty state primaries—nine more than in the 1972 presidential election. During the course of the primaries, which began in New Hampshire in February, twelve Democrats competed against each other. In addition to Carter, they included Senator Henry Jackson of Washington, Congressman Morris Udall of Arizona, Senator Frank Church of Idaho, Senator Fred Harris of Oklahoma, Governor Edmund G. Brown of California, and Governor George C. Wallace of Alabama.

Senator Hubert Humphrey of Minnesota, a favorite of the party regulars, did not enter the primaries but indicated he would accept the nomination if it was offered.

As the physically—and financially—exhausting marathon went on, one candidate after another dropped out. Carter's strength built up steadily, and he won 8 of the first 10 primaries. A "Stop Jimmy Carter" movement by backers of Senators Jackson and Humphrey failed. In June, Carter clinched the nomination with an impressive victory over Senator Church and Congressman Udall in the Ohio primary. The soft-spoken Georgian went to the National Convention with more than enough state delegates to win his party's endorsement.

The Republican primary fight was much closer. President Ford faced a major challenge from former California governor Ronald Reagan. Many Republicans preferred Reagan's hard-line conservative views to the more moderate approach of the President.

The result was a six-month running battle that seesawed back and forth. At times Reagan pulled ahead, and by mid-May he actually led Ford in total delegates. The President won most of the June primaries and appeared to have a narrow edge over Reagan. But as convention time neared, neither candidate seemed to have enough votes for a first-ballot victory.

▶ **THE CONVENTIONS**

The Democrats held their 1976 National Convention in New York City, from July 12 to 15. There was no doubt that Jimmy Carter would be nominated. When the first-ballot voting was completed, the "Jimmycrats" were jubilant. Their candidate had received 2,238 votes—over 700 more than the 1,505 needed for nomination.

Only one question remained unanswered. Who would be Carter's running mate? Carter kept his choice a secret until the last day of the convention. Then he announced his decision: Senator Walter F. ("Fritz") Mondale of Minnesota. The convention quickly approved Mondale as the party's vice-presidential candidate, and the ticket was dubbed "Grits and Fritz." (Hominy grits is a popular southern food.)

Most Democrats felt the ticket was well balanced. Carter was considered a moderate, and Mondale was known as a liberal who had supported strong civil rights laws and government reform measures.

The Republican National Convention proved the more exciting of the two. It was held in Kansas City from August 16 to 19. There was a down-to-the-wire fight for the nomination between President Ford and Ronald Reagan. When Reagan's name was put up for nomination, his supporters staged a noisy demonstration, cheering, whistling, and blowing horns. It was one of the longest demonstrations in the party's history.

But when the shouting was over and the voting began, the pro-Ford forces rallied enough votes to win the day. The final tally was 1,187 for Ford and 1,070 for Reagan—with 1,130 needed to win.

As a concession to Reagan supporters, Ford selected conservative Senator Robert J. Dole of Kansas as his running mate. And the Ford camp accepted a conservative party platform. (A platform is a list of statements ex-

37

pressing the party's views on various political issues.)

YOUTH IN POLITICS

Young people worked in the election campaigns, as they have in the past. They helped the candidates by distributing campaign literature, putting up posters, and encouraging people to vote.

A group of youngsters from a national news magazine called *Children's Express* made history. They became the first young people to be given full press status at the national political conventions.

The youthful reporters, aged 9 to 17, roamed about, snapping pictures and interviewing top political figures and other celebrities. They scored a big scoop at the Democratic convention when they predicted that Senator Mondale would be the vice-presidential candidate—a day before Carter's announcement.

President Ford's 24-year-old son Jack also made news as he campaigned for his father. The tall and handsome young man headed a Ford youth group called the "Presidentials,"

Peanuts and pineapples? That's the way it was at the conventions. The Democrats raised the peanut sign for Carter, and the Republicans paraded with pineapples for Dole.

which numbered about 1,200. Jack and his younger brother, Steve, both hit the campaign trail after the convention.

► CAMPAIGNING FOR PRESIDENT

As the campaign began, Jimmy Carter appeared to be on his way to an easy victory over his Republican rival. Political polls had shown Carter ahead of Ford by as much as 30 points. But as the campaign went on, Carter slipped badly in the polls, while Ford made big gains.

President Ford adopted a strategy of keeping a low profile. He spent most of the campaign at the White House, performing his presidential duties. This strategy was designed to give voters a feeling that Ford was in command. His supporters hoped the public would see their candidate as a dependable and trustworthy man who deserved re-election to the office he had inherited when President Nixon resigned. At the same time, Republicans accused Carter of not clearly stating his position on basic issues and of constantly shifting ground. The Republicans portrayed Carter as too inexperienced to be president.

The Carter forces countered by saying that Ford was a weak leader. They charged that the Ford administration's policies had produced a sagging economy, spiraling inflation, and high unemployment. In his campaign speeches, Carter focused on the nation's economic ills, for which he blamed the Republicans. He also spoke out in favor of a tax cut for middle-income families, a national health insurance program, and government programs to create jobs.

The Debates. The two presidential candidates met face-to-face in a series of three televised debates. (The last such debates were between John F. Kennedy and Richard Nixon in 1960.)

The first debate was held in Philadelphia at the end of September. Carter appeared nervous in the opening segment of this encounter, while the President seemed more poised and self-assured. Although Carter scored some points, most people felt Ford had won the first round.

In the second debate, held in San Francisco, Carter bounced back. He sharply criticized the Ford administration's foreign policy,

Jimmy Carter and Gerry Ford met face-to-face in three debates that were seen on national television.

stating that other nations had lost respect for the United States. Ford made a bad mistake when he answered a question by stating that the East European nations—such as Poland and Czechoslovakia—were not dominated by the Soviet Union. Many people of East European descent resented this remark, and Ford admitted he had made a mistake.

The third and final debate was held in historic Williamsburg, Virginia, a few days before the election. Carter again declared that Ford was a poor leader, and said that the American public was ready for a change.

Ford accused Carter of distorting facts and of being inconsistent on many of his positions. He asked the American people to use their votes to say: "Jerry Ford, you've done a good job. Keep on doing it."

▶ A CLOSE ELECTION

Over 81,500,000 Americans went to the polls on November 2, the largest number in election history. Still, only 55 percent of those eligible to vote did so. However, the turnout was larger than expected. It had been widely believed that many voters would stay home because they did not feel strongly about either candidate.

Carter was elected by a slim margin. President Ford actually won 27 of the 50 states. But the 23 states (plus the District of Columbia) that went for Carter had more electoral votes. The result was a 297 to 240 margin in

electoral votes for Carter—with 270 needed to win. (One elector from Washington, which had gone to Ford in the popular vote, cast his vote for Reagan.) Carter received 40,827,394 popular votes, and Ford got 39,145,977.

Carter's support came mainly from traditional Democratic strongholds. He was the first Democrat to sweep the South since the days of Franklin Roosevelt. (Virginia was the only southern state to vote for Ford.) Carter also got heavy backing from labor, city dwellers, and minority groups, all of which helped him carry key northern industrial states.

Ford, by contrast, won nearly all the western states. He scored heavily among white-collar workers and voters with high incomes. Although Ford was viewed as likable, honest, and well-meaning, he was considered by many to be a weak leader. The American people apparently felt it was time for a change.

Serious problems await the new administration. President Carter will face the difficult tasks of restoring public trust in government, rebuilding the economy, and aiding financially troubled cities. In foreign affairs, he will have to deal with troubled areas such as the Middle East and southern Africa, as well as U.S. relations with the Communist superpowers— the Soviet Union and China. It remains to be seen if President Jimmy Carter can meet these challenges.

HENRY I. KURTZ
Author, *Captain John Smith*

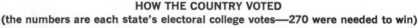

HOW THE COUNTRY VOTED
(the numbers are each state's electoral college votes—270 were needed to win)

JAMES EARL CARTER, JR.

James Earl Carter, Jr. (who has always preferred to be called Jimmy) has had an amazing career. He was born on October 1, 1924, in Plains, a small farming town in southwest Georgia. In 1976 he was elected 39th president of the United States. The story of his path to the presidency is a story of firm conviction and hard work—in the best American tradition.

Jimmy grew up in Plains, where his father managed the local grocery store and owned farmland. He was a good student and loved to read. His mother, Lillian Carter (who has always been a great influence in his life), encouraged his studies and reading. Jimmy's greatest wish from early boyhood was to go to the United States Naval Academy at Annapolis. He achieved that goal through hard work, entering Annapolis in 1943. He graduated near the top of his class in 1946.

After graduation, Carter married a girl from near his home in Georgia, Rosalynn Smith. They had four children, the youngest of whom, Amy, became a familiar figure during the presidential election campaign.

Carter spent seven years in the Navy, attaining the rank of lieutenant. For part of his naval service he worked in the Navy's nuclear submarine program. But when his father died in 1953, he felt he had to end his naval career and run the family farm.

Back in Plains, Carter worked hard and expanded into farm business activities. He became well known for enterprises involving a special kind of peanut. He grew relatively prosperous. But Carter also found time to become actively involved in church and community affairs.

In 1962 Carter decided to enter politics. He ran for the Georgia state Senate and won a seat in a close and bitterly contested election. He spent four years in the Georgia legislature. In 1966 he tried for the Democratic nomination for governor of Georgia. He lost the primary, but he made a good showing. He wouldn't accept defeat. In 1970 he decided to run for governor again. This time he won.

Carter brought many reforms to the organization of Georgia's state government. And he

The Carter family. Seated: Amy; the President's wife, Rosalynn; President Carter; Jeffrey's wife, Annette; and Jeffrey. Standing: James 3rd; James's wife, Caron; John and son, Jason; and John's wife, Judy.

appointed a number of blacks to state jobs. Carter's sympathy for the blacks goes back to boyhood and has remained an important factor in his political life.

In 1974 Jimmy Carter announced his intention of running for the presidency of the United States, even though he was unknown in national politics. "I do not intend to lose," he said.

He campaigned tirelessly, entering 29 primary contests and winning 17. He entered the Democratic National Convention with enough delegates to ensure his nomination.

The election campaign was tough and hard fought, and the election was relatively close. But Jimmy Carter had won, just as he said he would.

July 4, 1976: The biggest birthday party of them all was given in New York.

THE GLORIOUS FOURTH

On July 4, 1976, the United States celebrated its birthday for the 200th time. There were festivities around the country. The Bicentennial Fourth of July celebration was the climax of more than a year's preliminary celebrations. There was something special about this 200th celebration of the Fourth. More than ever before, it seemed to be a time for looking at the past and for looking toward the future.

On July 4, 1976, many Americans, as they stood watching fireworks displays whirling above them in the night skies, wondered about the past: What were Americans thinking about on the very first Fourth of July in 1776? And what were they thinking of when the country celebrated its Centennial in 1876?

▶ A QUIET BEGINNING

The most amazing thing about the first Fourth of July is that only a handfull of men in Philadelphia, in the British colony of Pennsylvania, knew what an important day it was.

All of the records that have come down to us tell us that the first days of July, 1776, were very hot in Philadelphia. We even know from records kept by Thomas Jefferson and other men in Philadelphia that the members of the Continental Congress were plagued by flies that flew in the unscreened windows. But it was too hot to close the windows.

Not only were the members of Congress and its committees working hard—they were very nervous. The task they were performing was difficult and dangerous.

A completely new and unusual thing was happening in Philadelphia. A group of the most distinguished men in Britain's North American colonies were drawing up a document at the direction of the Continental Congress. It was a document that would break America's ties with Britain forever. The document would be known as the Declaration of Independence.

As the members worked, some of them were aware of new British troop movements in America. British troops were massing on Staten Island, prior to an invasion of rebellious Long Island. Not only were the members of Congress about to defy the most powerful nation on earth, they were also in the middle of a revolutionary war they had no guarantee of winning. And if America lost the war, many of the men laboring at their desks in Philadelphia in that hot July weather would be hanged. From the British point of view, the Americans were committing treason.

The Declaration of Independence had taken a long time to write. All of the men assembled in Philadelphia suspected how important the step they were about to take would be. On June 11, the Continental Congress had formed a committee of five men, headed by Thomas Jefferson of Virginia. The job of that committee was to draw up the Declaration. On June 28, 1776, the committee submitted its first draft. The Congress debated and amended the document. Everyone was nervous. Tempers were high. On July 3, John Adams of Massachusetts wrote to his wife, Abigail, who was at home. He was convinced that on the previous day, July 2, Congress had been persuaded to accept the Declaration as it stood. He was so convinced that the work was complete that he told Abigail how he felt the Second of July (which he was sure would be the new nation's official birthday) ought to be celebrated:

"... with pomp and parade, with shows, games and sports, guns, bells, bonfires and illuminations, from one end of this continent to the other, from this time forward, forevermore."

But more additions and amendments had to be considered. The Declaration was not finally adopted until July 4. No member of Congress had been willing to be hasty. The men who had written the Declaration knew how important their actions had been. But when the Fourth finally came, they were exhausted. Copies of the Declaration had to be made and sent at once to the commanders of American forces in the various former colonies. And so that first Fourth of July was celebrated mostly with sighs of relief by the men who had taken the big step. The sighs were accompanied by the busy scratching of many pens writing out copies of the great document. Congress set July 8 as the official date for celebration in Philadelphia. And Philadelphia did, indeed, have the kind of display Adams had described to his wife. Troops marched in parade, church bells rang, and cannon were fired—although not too many times, because there was a shortage of gunpowder and it was wartime.

As messengers brought copies of the Declaration to the towns and cities of the new nation in July and August, the Americans began to realize that they were a nation—and a nation that would have to fight to remain free.

So the first Fourth of July celebration was not really held on the fourth. But it was a happy event, nevertheless. The Americans were a people standing on the brink of their own future.

▶ A NEW AGE

On July 4, 1876, most Americans went to watch a parade in the middle of the day and then stayed to hear a patriotic speech or two. The speeches were often delivered from platforms set up in front of Civil War memorials. Most American towns and cities had them. The memorials were often topped by statues of soldiers with rifles. In some parts of the country the statues wore Union uniforms; in other parts, Confederate uniforms. Many Americans had died a little more than a decade before.

Around suppertime, families got into their horse-drawn buggies and wagons and went out to the local park or fairgrounds. They usually took a big picnic hamper with them. Picnics had become an American Fourth of July tradition. After supper, they sat together and waited for the fireworks displays they knew would come. Fireworks had also become a traditional part of an American Fourth.

July 4, 1776: The citizens of the new nation learned of their independence very informally. In many towns and cities the Declaration of Independence was read aloud on street corners by special messengers, as you can see in this period print.

But the Americans had been through a terrible Civil War that had torn the nation apart. It was not the same country it had been in 1776. It was a country that still kept many old-fashioned traditions. But it was also a country that was growing up fast.

In July of 1876, the United States was a country with growing pains. There were no armies menacing American cities, and most of the members of Congress had no reason to fear the hangman's noose. But the country had problems. Industrialization and the building of the great railroads were happening fast —perhaps too fast. There were financial problems and unemployment and child labor and thousands of other things to be worried about. The country had grown so fast that there had been little time for careful planning.

But Americans on July 4, 1876, knew they had an exciting future before them—despite their problems. They could see the wonders of the new industrial age all around them. America, with its vast natural resources, showed every indication that it might one day move ahead of the great industrial nations of Europe. The most important and talked about event of 1876 was the Centennial Exposition held in Philadelphia, where the nation had been born. The Exposition featured all the new technological advances of the United States and the other industrialized nations. There were telephones and elevators and electric lights.

But among all the impressive machines and gadgets, one of the most popular items at the Exposition was a rather unimpressive looking

July 4, 1876: Philadelphia had time to plan a gala celebration of the nation's 100th birthday. This is what the festivities in front of Independence Hall looked like to an artist who was there. The United States was growing up.

length of steel cable. People by the hundreds and thousands flocked to see it—even though it could easily have been mistaken for an ordinary length of rope.

The piece of steel cable that everyone wanted to see was a piece of the cable that would be used for the greatest suspension bridge yet attempted. The Brooklyn Bridge, which was to link Manhattan and Brooklyn, was under construction. Some people believed it would never be finished. But many Americans saw The Great Bridge, as it was often called, as the symbol of a new America. The bridge roadways would be suspended by thick cables of steel from stone towers (which were already completed). The roadways were to carry pedestrians, carriages, and a steam railway over the East River. If by using steel cables, Americans could build the longest bridge in the world to carry the commerce of a great city over a rushing river—they could do anything. At least that's what many Americans hoped in 1876.

▶ THE FUTURE

Americans watching fireworks displays and special re-creations of historic events on July 4, 1976, knew that many of the promises of past Fourths really had come true. But, like the people in 1776 and 1876, they knew that challenges lay ahead. They knew that Americans had walked on the moon and would soon be headed for distant planets. But poverty, disease, and social injustice were not yet conquered. The challenge was still there—and the future.

AROUND THE COUNTRY

To celebrate the Bicentennial, many communities re-enacted famous events of the Revolutionary War. Here a rider representing Paul Revere pauses before a historic house, the Hancock-Clarke House, in Lexington, Massachusetts. He is warning John Hancock (or maybe Samuel Adams) that the British are coming. Both Hancock and Adams were staying at this house with the Reverend Jonas Clarke on the eventful night of April 18, 1775.

Half a million people watched the American Bicentennial Parade in Washington, D.C., on July 3. Here the float entered by the Bicentennial Council of the Thirteen Original States passes by. More than 50 bands, 60 floats, and 90 marching units took part in the colorful parade.

Is it real? Many people asked this question as they stared in wonder at the nation's towering birthday cake in Memorial Hall, Philadelphia. It was indeed a real chocolate layer cake. The eight-sided layers were covered with white icing and decorated with historical pictures in colored icings.

What was it like to go to school 200 years ago? Pupils in a Bremerton, Washington, school found answers to that question and created a colonial classroom as their Bicentennial project. Here a pupil, dressed in colonial finery, shows how well he can write with a quill pen and walnut-shell ink.

The Bicentennial Wagon Train, made up of covered wagons from around the nation, drew up in a circle at Valley Forge, Pennsylvania, for special ceremonies on July 4. Many of the wagons, like the Oklahoma one shown here, had traveled for weeks to reach the place where George Washington's ragged army had spent the winter of 1777–78. During the ceremonies President Ford signed a bill establishing the area as the Valley Forge National Historical Park.

Dressed in costumes of 200 years ago, pupils and teachers of the Woodward Township School (near Williamsport, Pennsylvania) marched to the music of fife and drum. Then they performed skits of Revolutionary War times. Similar Bicentennial celebrations marked the year in schools around the country.

The march of French troops, led by General de Rochambeau, from Rhode Island through Connecticut to New York in June, 1781, was a stirring event of the Revolutionary War. In this Bicentennial re-enactment of that event, Rochambeau jumps ashore at Hartford, Connecticut, after crossing the Connecticut River. From New York, French and American troops marched south for what was to be a great victory over the British at Yorktown, Virginia.

The Bicentennial Children's Museum at Fairfield University, Fairfield, Connecticut, was a favorite place for school trips in 1976. Many pupils from schools in the surrounding area spent a day there, pretending that they were back in Revolutionary War times. They dressed in colonial clothes, planned and performed skits, toured museum exhibits, and took part in craft activities, including colonial weaving, candle making, carpentry, and baking.

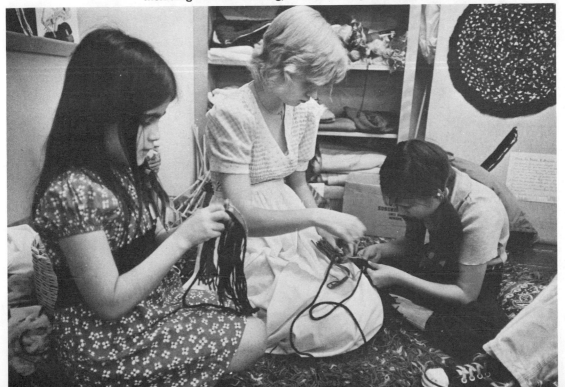

President Grant and the Emperor of Brazil turned the valves that put this mighty steam engine to work in Machinery Hall at the 1876 Exposition.

1876 REVISITED

The time was the early 70's. For the United States an important birthday was near. But, some people asked, what was there to celebrate? It was a time of economic depression. Many people were without jobs. A terrible war had divided the nation only a few years earlier. Reports of political scandals filled the newspapers. Political and economic problems were not new, of course, but something else was. Women were demanding increased rec-

ognition of their contribution to the life of the nation.

Was this the early 1970's, when the United States was approaching its 200th birthday? No, it was the early 1870's, when the country's 100th birthday was near. Some people may have thought there was little to celebrate, but many others disagreed. For one thing, there was the nation's mechanical inventiveness and all the marvelous new machinery being produced.

Why not celebrate with a great fair, at which the United States—and other countries, too—could show what they had accomplished in industry, agriculture, art, science, and education? In 1872, Congress approved plans for a world's fair, to be known as the Centennial Exposition. It was to be held in Fairmount Park, Philadelphia, from May 10 to November 10, 1876. The Exposition opened on time, complete with a Woman's Pavilion.

▶ THE CENTENNIAL EXPOSITION, 1876

More than 100,000 people gathered to see the parades, enjoy the music, and hear the speeches—made by President Ulysses S. Grant and other dignitaries—that were part of the opening ceremonies. Then they were free to explore the vast fairgrounds. There were several large buildings, or halls, and many smaller buildings, all filled with exhibits from 26 states and numerous foreign countries. A miniature railroad carried passengers around the grounds.

Many visitors went first to the Main Building, which was then said to be the largest building in the world. After listening to organ music and admiring the fountains, they could begin to be awed by the thousands of displays. These included almost every imaginable product of the United States—from carpets and tacks to bridges and Pullman berths (places to sleep on a train). Mingled in were fascinating exhibits from other parts of the world—ostrich feathers from southern Africa, Belgian wood carvings, shawls from India, Japanese lacquer ware, and much more.

In the Agricultural Building, visitors examined a surprising array of things—shiny new plows and reapers, horseshoes, baking powder, and stuffed animals. Horticultural Hall was filled with plants from around the world. Displays in the U.S. Government Building helped people understand the work of the many federal agencies. Of special interest were weather instruments, totem poles, statues of Indian chiefs, guns, and a marvelous rotary lamp used in lighthouses. Displays at the Woman's Pavilion included textile designs by women trained at the Massachusetts Institute of Technology, and exhibits from the Woman's Medical College of Pennsylvania.

But the chief attraction was Machinery Hall, where everyone stopped to stare in wonder at the towering Corliss steam engine. The Amer-

This brightly painted mortiser, a machine used to cut holes in wood, is decorated with grapes.

ican inventor George Henry Corliss had designed it for a special purpose—to provide power to run other machines on display in the hall. President Grant and Dom Pedro II, the emperor of Brazil, had turned the valves that set this mighty engine in motion. The machines on display seemed endless in number and variety. Many were brightly painted and decorated with colorful designs. There were fire engines, locomotives, sewing machines galore, and printing presses. There were amazing new inventions such as the typewriter and the telephone. And there were new machines used in making almost everything from bricks and watches to candy and chewing tobacco. Some of the machines turned out products before the visitors' eyes. And even after all this, there was still much to be seen at the Exposition.

Americans visiting the Centennial Exposition learned much about the decorative arts: they saw displays such as these fine enameled birds from China (*left*) and this elegant dressing case for a lady traveler (*below*).

Nineteenth-century steam-driven fire engines like this one were decorated with painted designs and were polished and shined to perfection.

▶ THE EXPOSITION RE-CREATED, 1976

In 1976, as a Bicentennial gift to the nation, the Smithsonian Institution presented *1876: A Centennial Exhibition.* This re-creation opened in May in the Smithsonian's huge old Arts and Industries Building in Washington, D.C. Before the exhibition, workers spent months restoring this century-old building to as nearly as possible the way it was when new. There visitors saw 25,000 objects of the Centennial period. Most of them were the same sort of things that had been shown in the 1876 exposition. They were pieces of life from 100 years ago, carefully restored and displayed in the exuberant style of the Centennial.

OPERATION SAIL

And all I ask is a tall ship and a star to steer her by . . . .
John Masefield

It was a sight to stir the heart and fire the imagination. A mighty flotilla of sailing ships —over 200 in all—parading into New York Harbor and up the Hudson River. Not since the early 19th century, when sleek-hulled Yankee clipper ships roamed the seven seas, had so many sailing vessels been gathered in one place. The event was Operation Sail, a seagoing salute to America's 200th birthday.

Shortly before noon, on July 4, 1976, the sailing ships moved under the Verrazano-Narrows Bridge and then past the Statue of Liberty, turning New York Harbor into a forest of masts and ballooning sails. Warships from 30 nations lined the route. As the fleet of barks, schooners, ketches, and sloops passed in review, the honor guard of modern warships fired a 21-gun salute.

On board the aircraft carrier USS *Forrestal,* President Gerald Ford and other dignitaries watched the parade of tall-masted ships. Nearly 6,000,000 people lined the New York and New Jersey shorelines. Millions of other people saw Operation Sail on television.

Leading the procession were 16 of the world's 20 remaining "tall ships" (square-rigged sailing ships whose masts tower at least 127 feet, or 39 meters, above the water). They came from many countries. There were Japan's *Nippon Maru,* Argentina's *Libertad,* West Germany's *Gorch Fock,* and Portugal's *Sagres II.* Largest of the tall ships was the Soviet Union's *Kruzenshtern,* a 378-foot-long (115-m) four-masted bark.

In years gone by, ships such as these, canvas sails billowing in the breeze, filled the harbors of the world. During the age of sail, they carried cargo and passengers to faraway lands. Today they serve another purpose. Most of them are school ships, used to train young men and women to become officers in their country's merchant fleets or navies.

In fact, Operation Sail was very much a young people's show. The tall ships were manned largely by naval cadets ranging in age from 14 to 25.

Life on board one of these training ships is anything but child's play, however. It's hard work. Cadets may be on duty up to 16 hours a day. No matter what the weather, they have to climb into the rigging to hoist sail. There are usually no machines to do the job; now as in the past it takes muscle power and teamwork. On some of the training ships, as many as 200 cadets have to pull together to raise and lower the giant sails.

What is it like to work high above the deck of a pitching and rolling ship? For some it may be frightening; but for others it's a great thrill. Said one Danish cadet: "You're up there standing on a rope. . . . You feel the wind, you smell the sea. It's a fantastic feeling. You're right in the middle of a big circle of water and can *see* the earth is round."

One British ship in Operation Sail, the *Sir Winston Churchill,* had an all-girl crew. Few of them had been to sea before, but they quickly learned the ropes. "Maybe it takes more of us," a girl crew member remarked, "but we can do anything on a sailing ship the boys can."

Many of the tall ships in Operation Sail took part in a series of races that began at Plymouth, England, where the *Mayflower* had set sail for the New World in 1620. Beginning on May 2, the ships raced to Tenerife, in the Canary Islands. Next they raced to Bermuda,

a voyage that took over two weeks. The third and final lap saw the young cadets competing to be the first to reach Newport, Rhode Island. The German bark, the *Gorch Fock,* won. Finally, on July 3, the vessels reached New York City. The following morning, they glided majestically up the Hudson, led by the U.S. Coast Guard's 295-foot (90-m) bark *Eagle,* which served as host ship.

It was a fitting way to celebrate the 200th birthday of the United States. Ships and the sea have played an important part in American history ever since Christopher Columbus and John Cabot first came to the New World in the 1490's. Millions of immigrants later came to America by ship. And today ships still bring the raw materials and other goods Americans need in their daily lives.

As the chairman of the Operation Sail committee put it: "Without the sailing ships and the valiant men who sailed them, we would not be celebrating the nation's bicentennial this year."

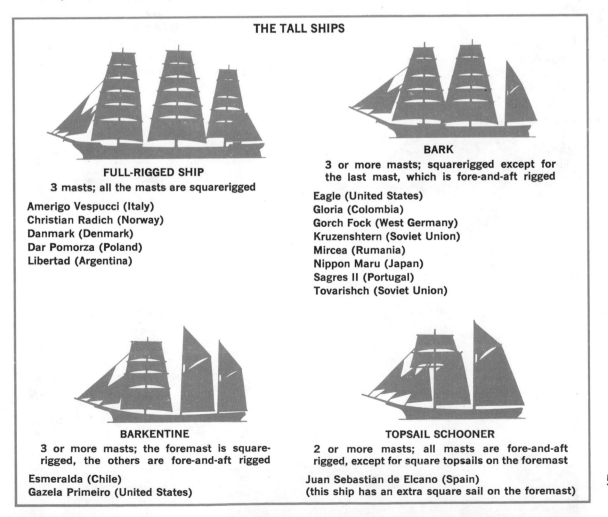

THE TALL SHIPS

FULL-RIGGED SHIP
3 masts; all the masts are squarerigged

Amerigo Vespucci (Italy)
Christian Radich (Norway)
Danmark (Denmark)
Dar Pomorza (Poland)
Libertad (Argentina)

BARK
3 or more masts; squarerigged except for the last mast, which is fore-and-aft rigged

Eagle (United States)
Gloria (Colombia)
Gorch Fock (West Germany)
Kruzenshtern (Soviet Union)
Mircea (Rumania)
Nippon Maru (Japan)
Sagres II (Portugal)
Tovarishch (Soviet Union)

BARKENTINE
3 or more masts; the foremast is square-rigged, the others are fore-and-aft rigged

Esmeralda (Chile)
Gazela Primeiro (United States)

TOPSAIL SCHOONER
2 or more masts; all masts are fore-and-aft rigged, except for square topsails on the foremast

Juan Sebastian de Elcano (Spain)
(this ship has an extra square sail on the foremast)

FRIENDLY RELATIONS

In 1976 more than 90 nations joined in saying, "Happy Birthday, U.S.A.!" Friendly greetings filled the nation's mailbox. Queens and kings, other dignitaries, and many thousands of tourists came to visit. So did theater groups, opera companies, dance troupes, and folksingers—to say nothing of ships from around the world, all sailing together. Gifts poured in. Several nations lent art treasures and historic items for special display. In a further expression of friendliness, a number of countries held exhibitions, festivals, or other events in honor of the Bicentennial of the American Revolution.

▶ **GUESTS AND GIFTS**

Queen Elizabeth II of Britain chose to begin her official U.S. visit on July 6 in Philadelphia, the city where the Declaration of Independence was signed. In a gracious speech, she told why.

I speak to you as the direct descendant of King George III. He was the last crowned sovereign to rule in this country, and it is therefore with a particular personal interest that I view those events which took place 200 years ago.

It seems to me that Independence Day, the Fourth of July, should be celebrated as much in Britain as in America. Not in rejoicing in the separation of the American colonies from the British crown but in sincere gratitude to the Founding Fathers of the great Republic for having taught Britain a very valuable lesson.

We lost the American colonies because we lacked the statesmanship "to know the right time, and the manner of yielding what is impossible to keep."

But the lesson was well learned. In the next century and a half we kept more closely to the principles of Magna Carta, which have been the common heritage of both our countries.

A month earlier Britain's Royal Air Force had flown a copy of the Magna Carta (Great Charter) from London to Washington, D.C., as a Bicentennial loan to the people of the United States. This is the famous document that the English barons forced King John of England to sign on June 15, 1215. The "principles of Magna Carta," which the Queen mentioned, were the guarantees of English liberties that it contained.

The 761-year-old document, which was lent for one year, is the oldest of the four remaining original copies of the Magna Carta. It was unveiled during special ceremonies in the Rotunda of the Capitol. The British also

With pomp and ceremony, an original copy of the Magna Carta is displayed in the Capitol.

sent a gold copy of the Magna Carta, which will remain permanently in the Capitol.

Another gift from Britain, the Bicentennial Bell, had arrived in Philadelphia before the Queen's visit. It was hanging in its special bell tower in Independence National Historical Park. In her speech the Queen spoke of the famous Liberty Bell, which is also in the park. The new bell, she said, was made by the same London foundry that had made the original Liberty Bell over 200 years ago. She quoted the words "Let Freedom Ring," written on the side of the Bicentennial Bell. Then she gave a signal for it to be rung.

During their six-day stay the Queen and Prince Phillip also visited Washington, D.C., New York, Boston, and other cities associated with Revolutionary War history.

Queen Elizabeth II made a leisurely voyage to the United States aboard the royal yacht *Britannia*. President Valéry Giscard d'Estaing of France roared across the Atlantic aboard a supersonic Concorde jetliner on his official Bicentennial visit.

In welcoming the French President and his wife on May 17, the people of the United States could not forget that they were welcoming representatives of their oldest ally. France entered the Revolutionary War on the side of the colonies and played an important part in the victory.

While he was in Washington, the French President addressed Congress, speaking in English. He also went to Mount Vernon, George Washington's home, to inaugurate a sound-and-light show on the life of Washington. The show was a gift of the French Government. This spectacular event was one of numerous Bicentennial contributions from the nation that had given the people of the United States a matchless gift—the Statue of Liberty —100 years ago.

The arrival of King Juan Carlos I and Queen Sophia of Spain early in June marked the first time that a reigning Spanish monarch visited the United States. After the King addressed Congress, the royal couple spent the next day presenting gifts and opening Bicentennial exhibitions in Washington, D.C. The gifts included a statue of Don Quixote and an equestrian statue of Bernardo de Gálvez, a Spanish commander whose victories against the British helped the cause of the American Revolution. The main exhibition was at the Smithsonian Institution. It was made up of paintings, books, and other items pertaining to Christopher Columbus, all lent by Spanish museums.

"Let Freedom Ring." The Bicentennial Bell is ready to be shipped from London to Philadelphia.

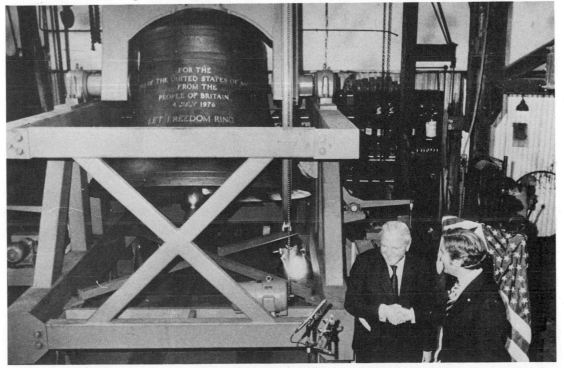

Spain presented the United States with a statue of Bernardo de Gálvez.

People from the U.S. and many foreign countries took part in the Festival of American Folklife. There were musicians, singers, dancers, and . . .

Members of Scandinavian royal families made informal Bicentennial visits. King Carl XVI Gustaf of Sweden spent a month touring the United States and visiting Swedish-American communities. Queen Margrethe II of Denmark, accompanied by her husband, Prince Henrik, opened an exhibition of paintings by Christian Gullager at the National Portrait Gallery of the Smithsonian Institution. Gullager was a Danish-born artist who migrated to America in 1788. He painted George Washington and other distinguished persons, as well as patriotic symbols of the United States. On a visit to Washington, D.C., Crown Prince Harald and Crown Princess Sonja of Norway gave President Ford their country's Bicentennial gift—a $200,000 check for a national sports center to be built in Minnesota.

Other distinguished visitors included Prime Minister Pierre Elliott Trudeau of Canada and Chancellor Helmut Schmidt of West Germany. The Canadian Prime Minister gave President Ford a handsome volume of Bicentennial photographs. The German Chancellor dedicated a planetarium instrument—a gift of his country—at the Smithsonian Institution.

More than 30 countries sent folksingers, dancers, musicians, and craftworkers to join Americans from every corner of the country in the Festival of American Folklife. The festival, sponsored by the Smithsonian, took place in Washington, D.C. It presented the foods, crafts, dances, and music of the many cultures that are part of America's heritage.

The Royal Danish Ballet and Britain's Royal Ballet gave performances in the United States. So did the Paris Opera, the Berlin Opera, and the La Scala opera company of Milan, Italy. Visiting orchestral groups included the Israeli Philharmonic, the Vienna Philharmonic, and the London Symphony Orchestra.

Switzerland sent a special Bicentennial greeting for the children of the United States. It was a fascinating collection of Swiss toys, to be shown in various U.S. cities for two years.

. . . craftworkers. Polish and Ukrainian Americans showed how to make *pisanki,* Easter eggs decorated by using wax and dye.

Switzerland sent a fascinating collection of toys, including these handsome wooden ones.

▶ FESTIVITIES ABROAD

One of the largest celebrations outside the United States was Denmark's Fourth of July Festival, held at Rebild National Park in Jutland. Some 30,000 U.S. visitors and Danes attended, with Queen Margrethe II heading the Danish delegation. Victor Borge, the Danish-American pianist and comedian, was the main speaker. The 1976 festival was a special occasion. But the Danes have held a Fourth of July celebration each year since 1912, shortly after Danish-Americans had bought land in the Rebild Hills and presented it to the Danish Government for use as a national park.

British museums devoted much time and effort to Bicentennial exhibitions. The Victoria and Albert Museum in London exhibited American art (paintings, glass, furniture, and textiles) of the period 1750 to 1800. The American Museum in Britain, near Bath, displayed American arts and crafts of the colonial period. Most interesting of all, perhaps,

was the exhibition entitled 1776, The British Story of the American Revolution, held at the National Maritime Museum in Greenwich. The museum had collected hundreds of paintings, documents, guns, military uniforms, and other items of the Revolutionary War period. These were arranged in more than twenty galleries in a most imaginative way. Visitors felt that they were taking a walk through history, sharing not only the events of the war but the grief and tragedy that it brought to many people.

In France the story of the Revolutionary War was the subject of a television series, much of it filmed in the United States. Vice-President Nelson A. Rockefeller traveled to Australia to attend U.S. Bicentennial events held there. In cities around the world, gift shops and street vendors offered Bicentennial souvenirs of every kind. And almost every country, large and small, issued stamps honoring the 200th birthday of the United States of America.

HEADLINE HIGHLIGHTS

ANGOLA

In 1976 Angola, in western Africa, faced the future. When it gained independence from Portugal in 1975 after 400 years of colonial rule, the new nation was already deep in a bitter civil war. And with civil war came intervention by other nations. However, in 1976, under the leadership of Dr. Agostinho Neto of the Popular Movement for the Liberation of Angola, Angola began its life as a nation. Not all of the old problems were solved, but there was hope for the future.

Angola has had a long history. In 1482 the Portuguese navigator Diogo Cão, looking for a good sea route around Africa to India, discovered the mouth of the great Congo River, bordering part of what is now northern Angola. Cão's discovery marked the beginning of Portugal's interest in Angola—although colonization went slowly. In 1575 the Portuguese began a settlement at Luanda, now the capital of Angola, and began their formal rule of the colony. When Angola gained independence in 1975, Portugal's once vast African empire came to an end. Portugal's other former African territories—Guinea-Bissau, Mozambique, São Tomé and Príncipe, and Cape Verde—had also become independent.

Angola lies on the western, or Atlantic, coast of Africa. It is a large country. With an area of 481,351 square miles (1,246,700 square kilometers), it is more than twice the size of France. Although its economy is still largely agricultural, with coffee the chief export crop, Angola also has great potential mineral wealth. There are deposits of iron ore and diamonds, and large offshore deposits of oil. The population is about 7,000,000. About 300,000 of the Portuguese colonists began leaving Angola as independence approached and the civil war began.

Angola won its independence through its own efforts and because of political problems in Portugal. Angola's armed struggle against continuing Portuguese rule actually began in 1961. Portugal sent thousands of troops, over the years, to keep the rebellion down. This lengthy period of fighting was a great drain on Portugal's economy. In 1974 a group of Portuguese military officers, angered by the endless years of fighting in Africa, overthrew Portugal's government. Angola and the other Portuguese African territories were promised their independence by the new rulers of Portugal.

Even before independence came, a struggle for political power had started among the three Angolan liberation movements. The Popular Movement for the Liberation of Angola, led by Agostinho Neto and supported by the Soviet Union and by Cuban troops, defeated its rivals.

Portuguese refugees fleeing the civil war are evacuated by airplane from Angola.

SEYCHELLES : A NEW COUNTRY

During the 15th century, explorers from Europe took to the sea in search of a route to India. The quest led to the discovery of many lands. In 1505, Portuguese sailors became the first Europeans to sight the islands of the Seychelles archipelago.

The group of almost 90 islands, strung out over about 600 miles (about 970 kilometers), lie in the Indian Ocean about 1,000 miles (about 1,600 km) off the eastern coast of the African continent. The islands have a combined land area of about 107 square miles (277 square kilometers). They form the independent country of Seychelles.

▶ THE LAND

About 45 of the Seychelles islands are formed of coral. These are mostly flat, with an occasional elevation formed by a coral reef. About 40 islands, formed by volcanic activity, are mostly granite mountains, with very little level land. The remaining few islands are uninhabited because they are so low and small that they are often completely submerged at high tide.

The largest island of the Seychelles group is Mahé, with an area of about 56 square miles (145 km²). Victoria, the country's capital and largest city, is on Mahé's northeast coast. The two other major islands are Praslin and La Digue. Many of the coral reefs, and even some of the volcanic islands, are sparsely inhabited because of the poor quality of their soil.

The Seychelles islands are located just south of the equator. The temperature is moderate to warm throughout the year. The coolest period occurs during the monsoon season, from May to September, when winds blow from the southeast. Rainfall is heavy, averaging about 90 inches (2,286 millimeters) a year in Victoria, and humidity is high.

▶ THE PEOPLE

Most of the 58,000 inhabitants of Seychelles are descendants of the original French settlers and the African slaves they imported. The present population also includes a few thousand Chinese and Indian merchants, some British civil servants, and a small number of Americans who work at a satellite-tracking station maintained by the United States Government.

About four fifths of the Seychellois (the people of Seychelles) live on the island of Mahé. Most of the remainder live on Praslin or La Digue.

The literacy rate of Seychelles is high. About 94 percent of the people are able to read and write. The language of the country is Creole, but most people also speak some French or English, the official languages.

Over 90 percent of the people of Seychelles are Roman Catholics. Most of the remainder are Anglicans.

▶ ECONOMY

For many years copra (dried coconut), cinnamon bark, and patchouli oil (used in the making of perfume) have been the chief exports of the Seychelles islands. But the income received from these products has not been great enough to pay for the necessary imports, and for many years the islands have been aided by sizable loans from Britain.

In 1976 the new government of Seychelles announced plans for strengthening the islands' economy. Efforts are being made to improve

---

FACTS AND FIGURES

REPUBLIC OF SEYCHELLES is the official name of the country.

CAPITAL: Victoria.

LOCATION: Western Indian Ocean. **Latitude**—3° 40′ S to 6° 05′ S. **Longitude**—53° 55′ E to 59° 10′ E.

AREA: 107 sq mi (277 km²).

POPULATION: 58,000 (estimate).

LANGUAGE: Creole, French, English.

RELIGION: Roman Catholic, Anglican.

GOVERNMENT: Independent republic within the Commonwealth of Nations. **Head of government**—president.

ECONOMY: Chief agricultural products—coconuts, cinnamon, vanilla beans, patchouli oil. **Industries and products**—tourism; fishing; processing of cinnamon, copra, and fish; guano. **Chief exports**—cinnamon, patchouli oil, copra, vanilla, guano. **Chief imports**—rice, sugar, cloth, foodstuffs. **Monetary unit**—Seychelles rupee.

the quality of the soil and increase agricultural production. Copra, still produced on almost all the volcanic islands, has shown a marked decrease in production in recent years. Many workers have left the copra plantations to seek better opportunities either in the larger towns of their own country, or in England and Australia. The government hopes to stem the emigration of copra workers by making the crop profitable once again.

The government also plans to increase livestock production, especially pigs and chickens, in order to help make the country self-sufficient in foodstuffs. Tea has been introduced, to be grown on the mountain slopes.

Efforts are being made to expand the small fishing industry. Rich schools of fish, especially tuna, are found in the waters around the islands, but very few are caught at present. Trawlers are being built to catch the fish, some of which could be exported and some processed into fish meal.

The few manufacturing plants are engaged in food processing or the processing of copra and cinnamon for export. The only other industries are a brewery, a cigarette factory, and a furniture factory.

In 1971 an airport was built to serve the growing tourist trade. Since then the number of tourists has quadrupled, and tourism has become the country's second largest industry. Recently a new port was built at Victoria.

▶ HISTORY

For more than 200 years after their discovery by the Portuguese, the Seychelles remained uninhabited. Toward the middle of the 18th century, Britain and France began to vie for power in the Indian Ocean, and in 1742 French settlers became the islands' first inhabitants.

In 1756, France laid formal claim to the islands and named them after Vicomte Moreau de Séchelles, the minister of finance in the court of King Louis XV.

The French developed a plantation system on the islands. African slaves were imported to cut timber, plant spice gardens, and pick coconuts.

Rivalry for a strong foothold in the area continued, and for the rest of the century the

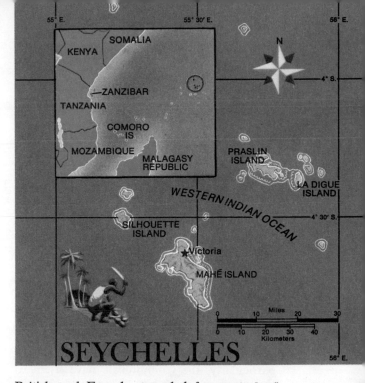

SEYCHELLES

British and French struggled for control of the Seychelles. In 1794 the British captured the islands, and in 1814 they were ceded to Britain by the Treaty of Paris. The islands were ruled by Britain as a dependency until 1903. In that year the Seychelles became a British Crown Colony.

In 1967 the Seychelles and Britain negotiated a new constitution—The Seychelles Order of 1967. The document granted the islands a governing council to carry out executive and legislative functions under a governor appointed by Britain. On June 28, 1976, Seychelles became an independent republic in the Commonwealth of Nations.

▶ GOVERNMENT

The two main political parties in Seychelles are the S.D.P. (Seychelles Democratic Party) and the S.P.U.P. (Seychelles People's United Party). The new republic's first president was chosen from the ranks of the Democratic Party, and the prime minister from the People's United Party. The constitution calls for elections every five years.

Although French occupation lasted less than 40 years, French influence is still strong. The legal code of Seychelles is based on the French system. Only the criminal laws are based on the British system.

HUGH C. BROOKS
St. John's University

THE YEAR AFTER IN INDOCHINA

For the three nations of Indochina, 1976 was the year after—the year after the Communists swept to victory. The three nations of the area of Southeast Asia called Indochina are Vietnam, Cambodia, and Laos. In 1975, after many years of war, Communist governments controlled all three countries.

Now that there is peace, Indochina's Communist rulers have turned their attention to repairing the damage caused by the years of war. A great effort has also been made to increase the production of rice, Indochina's major crop. Agriculture in Indochina was disrupted by the years of fighting. In Cambodia particularly, the Communists have used extremely harsh measures to increase rice production. Cambodia's new rulers have forced hundreds of thousands of people out of the cities and into the countryside to work in the rice fields. Many people have died after being forced to march great distances and do hard manual labor, often for the first time in their lives.

Although peace has come at last, these are hard times for the people of Indochina. Many have fled abroad since the Communist takeover. About 140,000 Indochinese refugees are now settled in the United States. Many thousands more are living in refugee camps in Thailand.

Communist governments came to power in Indochina after a very long struggle. For most of the first half of the 20th century, Indochina was ruled by France. In 1954, after an eight-year war against the forces of the Viet Minh, a Communist-led rebel movement based in North Vietnam, the French were defeated. After the French left, the United States tried to stop Communism from taking over all of Vietnam. With American support, non-Communist governments ruled South Vietnam, Cambodia, and Laos. North Vietnam was a Communist stronghold.

In the 1960's U.S. ground troops were sent to Vietnam to fight the Communists. Hundreds of thousands of American troops fought in Vietnam. American planes flew thousands of missions over Indochina. But the Communists could not be defeated. Finally, the United States decided to withdraw its troops. The last United States ground combat troops left Vietnam in 1972. American bombing missions in Indochina came to an end in 1973. The non-Communist governments of Indochina were not strong enough to rule without American support. They all fell to Communism in 1975.

▶ VIETNAM

Vietnam is the largest, in both area and population, of the three countries of Indochina. In fact, its population of about 44,000,000 people is the largest on the mainland of Southeast Asia. For a long time, Vietnam was divided between a Communist government in the north and a non-Communist government in the south. Vietnam was unified in April, 1975, when Communist troops entered the South Vietnamese capital of Saigon. This unification became official on July 2, 1976, when North Vietnam and South Vietnam formally became the Socialist Republic of Vietnam. Hanoi, formerly the capital of North Vietnam, became the capital of the new nation.

In 1976, the Vietnamese people were busy repairing the widespread damage done by long years of war. One visiting journalist said that Vietnam reminded him of a huge construction site, with bridges, railroads, and buildings being repaired everywhere.

The Communists also began another kind of reconstruction in Vietnam—the reconstruction of the minds and the way of life of the people of Vietnam. Children in South Vietnam found they had new school books. Millions of textbooks have been shipped to South Vietnam from North Vietnam since the Communist victory. Naturally, the new books reflect the Communist point of view. In addition, books, songs, poems, and movies that were formerly popular in South Vietnam are now banned there.

During the war in Indochina, many American political leaders had predicted that there would be mass executions if the Communists won. This does not seem to have happened in Vietnam. However, almost anyone who was a soldier or worked for the government of

Former South Vietnamese army officers do chores in a Communist "re-education camp."

South Vietnam or was an important person of any sort has had to spend time in "re-education camps." People sent to these camps spend many hours learning Communist doctrine. They may also be forced to do dangerous work with explosives or to do hard labor, such as cutting timber or building canals. In some camps, living conditions are harsh. There is a high death rate. In late 1976, experts in the United States estimated that between 100,000 and 300,000 people were still in these camps.

▶ LAOS AND CAMBODIA

Laos has re-education camps like those in Vietnam. It is estimated that there are between 40,000 and 50,000 people in the Laotian camps. The camps are controlled directly by the Communist Pathet Lao, who became the rulers of Laos in December 1975.

Some of the worst Laotian camps are in and around a great network of caves in the northeastern part of the country. The Pathet Lao used these caves as bases during their long struggle to win control of Laos.

The Communist rulers of Cambodia—now known as Democratic Cambodia or, in the Cambodian language, Kampuchea—have brought more sweeping changes to their country than any seen in the rest of Indochina. Hundreds of thousands of Cambodians have

been forced to migrate, often at gunpoint, from one part of their country to another. Sometimes they are moved into undeveloped areas to start up new farms. Sometimes they are moved to places where repair work is needed. For example, there has been a massive movement of people into northwestern Cambodia, where much war damage to dikes and irrigation systems had occurred.

Of Indochina's Communists, Cambodia's have proven to be the most extreme. The population of Cambodia is slightly more than 8,000,000—but hundreds of thousands of Cambodians have been executed or have died from disease and starvation since the Communist takeover in April, 1975. All private property has been abolished. Money has also been abolished. People either are provided with goods by the government or barter among themselves for what they need. The cities of Cambodia have been largely emptied. Pnompenh, the capital, now has a population of no more than 200,000 people—and possibly less. Before 1975 there were some 600,000 people in Pnompenh.

No one knows what the future holds for the people of Indochina. But they are peoples who have had more than their share of war and destruction. There are few people in the world who do not wish peace for them, and a happier future.

CHINA WITHOUT MAO

Three events shocked the Chinese people in 1976. In January the nation's longtime premier, Chou En-lai, died. Chou had been second in command to Mao Tse-tung for a number of years. In late July there were severe earthquakes in the coastal area near the country's capital, Peking. The earthquakes caused untold death and destruction. Finally, in September, came the greatest blow of all. Mao Tse-tung died. Mao was Communist Party chairman and leader of China's Communist revolution, and had been the nation's acknowledged leader since 1949.

Unlike the earthquakes the deaths of Chou and Mao did not come as a complete surprise to the Chinese. Both men were old, and they had both been ill for quite a long time.

Mao Tse-tung had not appeared in public since 1971. But his role in recent Chinese history had been so important that his death left the Chinese people dazed. And despite his long illness, Mao had never publicly named anyone to succeed him. His death thus left open the question of who would run China in the future, and how they would run it.

The importance of Mao and Chou to modern China is a result of two great accomplishments. They led the long revolution that brought Communism to China in 1949. And in the period from 1949 until their deaths, China went from a poor, war-torn country to a major world power.

Mao's special place in Chinese history goes far beyond the political role he played. Mao had made himself a kind of father to the Chinese people.

Whoever rules China as Mao's successor is sure to praise Mao and use his name to justify any course the government takes. But who will rule China now that Mao is gone? And what will the Chinese Government do in the future?

The first of these questions may already have been answered. In the weeks following Mao's death, Communist Party Vice-Chairman Hua Kuo-feng emerged as the leading figure in the Chinese Government. In his rise to power, Hua won out over a group that included four leading figures in the Chinese Government. This group was placed under arrest. One of the group was Mao's widow, Chiang Ching.

Hua had only recently become important in the Chinese Government. Most of his career was spent not in Peking, but in Mao's home province of Hunan. Hua did not enter the national government until 1971.

What kind of leader will Hua be? Will China, now that Mao is dead, continue its bitter feud with the Soviet Union? Will its recent friendly relations with the United States continue? Everyone will look for answers to these questions in the months ahead.

CHANGE IN ITALY AND SWEDEN

What was the most important election in 1976? Many people would say the presidential election in the United States. But there were also two very important elections in Europe. In 1976 both Italy and Sweden held national elections that broke old political patterns.

When the Italians went to the polls in the summer of 1976, no one was sure what would happen. The country was plagued with unemployment and inflation. As a result, the Italian Communist Party was growing stronger all the time. Could they actually win control of the government? The answer was No—but they came close.

The Christian Democrats, who have ruled Italy since 1946, kept control of the government by a slim margin. But they had to make a deal with the Communists to prevent a complete government deadlock. The Christian Democrats gave important jobs in Parliament to Communists. In return, the Communists agreed not to vote against the government on major issues; when they disagreed with the government position, they would abstain. In parliamentary government the ruling party loses power if a major vote goes against them. No one could be sure how long Italy's new government arrangement would work.

In Sweden the election issues were different from those in Italy. Sweden has a high rate of employment and the highest standard of living in Europe. Poverty has been all but abolished. Credit for this happy state of affairs usually goes to the Social Democratic Party, a socialist party that has governed Sweden for almost 44 years. But Sweden voted the Social Democrats out of office in 1976.

There seemed to be two major reasons for this surprising election result. The people were becoming concerned about the huge bureaucracy that had become part of their government. And they were also convinced that the Social Democrats had come to take their support too much for granted. So the Swedish electorate voted the more conservative Center Party into power. They had wanted a change and they got it.

Italian Communist leader Enrico Berlinguer.

Thorbjörn Fälldin, Sweden's prime minister.

Young people in Soweto, South Africa, stage a protest. Black people all over southern Africa are now demanding a real voice in their countries' governments.

CRISIS IN SOUTHERN AFRICA

In Rhodesia and South Africa, the two major countries of southern Africa, the great majority of the people are black. Most African nations have largely black populations. But unlike other black African countries, Rhodesia and South Africa are ruled by whites. And whites control most of the wealth of both countries. In the past 20 years, a period in which the rest of black Africa has gained self-rule, Rhodesia and South Africa alone have continued under all-white rule. The great question in southern Africa today is How long can this situation continue?

In Rhodesia, white control may be ending soon. During 1976, Rhodesia's white government promised to provide for black majority rule within two years. But in South Africa, Rhodesia's larger, wealthier neighbor, there was no shift from the government policy of apartheid—complete segregation, or separation, of the races. Even as thousands of blacks

rioted in 1976 to protest apartheid, the South African government seemed more determined than ever to continue its policies.

Although Rhodesia and South Africa both have minority white rule, there are important differences between the two countries—differences that make Rhodesia more likely to change than South Africa.

South Africa has a population of over 25,000,000 people. About 4,500,000 of these people (more than one sixth of the total population) are white. Rhodesia has a population of about 6,000,000 people. Only 270,000 of these people are white—less than one twentieth of the population. White Europeans have been in South Africa for a long time—more than 300 years, almost as long as Europeans have lived in North America. In Rhodesia, white settlement did not begin until the 1890's. And South Africa has been politically independent since 1910. Rhodesia declared its independence from Britain in 1965 and has never been officially recognized as independent by Britain or most of the other nations of the world.

▶ RHODESIA

Although Rhodesia's whites are few in number and relative newcomers to Africa, they were stubborn in maintaining control of their largely black country until recently. With its rich agricultural and mineral production, Rhodesia prospered in the years following its break with Britain. But in 1975, an important change came to southern Africa. Portugal withdrew from the neighboring territories of Angola and Mozambique.

As Portuguese possessions, Angola and Mozambique had shielded Rhodesia from black nationalism, which was spreading through most of Africa. Following Portugal's withdrawal, both Angola and Mozambique came under the control of black leaders with strong Communist leanings. Rhodesia's best rail routes to the sea go through Mozambique. Black-ruled Mozambique refused to let Rhodesia use these routes. Mozambique also became a sanctuary for black guerrillas fighting the Rhodesian Government. Aided by Mozambique and other black nations in southern Africa, Rhodesia's 10,000 or more black guerrillas were more active in 1976 than they had ever been before.

The increased guerrilla activity in Rhodesia worried South Africa and the United States, too. (South Africa did not want to risk a black revolt in neighboring Rhodesia, which might spread into its own territory.) Both the United States and South Africa urged the Rhodesians to negotiate with black leaders. Perhaps a way could be found to have black majority rule in Rhodesia without bloodshed.

In September, at the urging of the United States and South Africa, Rhodesia promised that it would accept black majority rule within two years. Representatives of the Rhodesian Government then met with four of the country's black leaders in Geneva, Switzerland, to discuss how black majority rule could come about while the rights of white citizens were protected. But even as the conference met, military equipment for Rhodesia's black guerrillas continued to leave the Soviet Union,

bound for guerrilla bases in Mozambique. However, there was much hope for peace in Rhodesia at the end of 1976. Both sides were talking to each other seriously—at last.

▶ SOUTH AFRICA

In 1976 the demand by South Africa's blacks for a share in their government increased sharply. In June thousands of young blacks rioted in Soweto, an all-black town near South Africa's largest city, Johannesburg. The young people attacked schools, shops, white-owned cars, and neighborhood welfare centers. Police bullets scattered the rioters. When it was all over, 176 blacks were dead. The rioting was set off by a government ruling that black schools teach in Afrikaans, the language spoken by many South African whites. But even after the government revoked its Afrikaans language policy, riots continued. Demonstrators throughout South Africa demanded civil rights for blacks.

Faced with these demonstrations, the South African Government made some concessions. For example, a law was passed in August permitting blacks to have full ownership of their houses, something that had not been possible before. In the past, blacks had been restricted to leasing houses. But basically, the South African Government continued its old policy of answering force with force. It gave no sign that it was willing to make major changes in its racial policies.

One of the unusual aspects of South Africa's apartheid policy involves the setting aside of nine areas of the country for all-black settlement. These areas are called homelands. According to the government's plan, these homelands will one day be self-governing.

On October 26, 1976, the largest of South Africa's black homelands became the first to accept independence. Called the Transkei, it consists of a large stretch of grassland along the Indian Ocean. But despite its officially independent status, Transkei remains dependent on South Africa financially, and in a number of other ways, too. Black leaders of most of the homelands oppose independence. They feel that it would be a bad bargain for South Africa's black people. These leaders would rather work for improvements in the status of blacks within South Africa as a whole.

The women of Northern Ireland march to protest violence in their homeland.

TERROR IN NORTHERN IRELAND

If you didn't know it was real, it would seem like a terrible nightmare—and a nightmare that didn't seem to end. At any time in the last few years you could pick up a daily newspaper and read about it. After a while, all the stories seemed to be a part of the same continuing story. "Pub in Northern Ireland Bombed." "Schoolchildren Injured in Sniper Cross Fire in Belfast." "Mass Funeral Held for Victims of Terrorist Bombs."

The fact is that incidents like this have been all too common in Northern Ireland. Since 1969, Roman Catholics and Protestants have been waging an undeclared war in Northern Ireland. It is not a war fought by armies with uniformed soldiers. It is fought by snipers, bombers, and murderers. No one is safe. Not even children. Northern Ireland had a bad year in 1976 and, what was worse, there was no sign that the trouble was letting up. As the struggle continued, the nations of the world became increasingly concerned about it.

Since 1969 more than 1,560 people have

been killed as a result of violence in Northern Ireland. Another 18,000 people—people of all kinds and all ages—have been wounded. Factories and stores and houses have been burned or bombed. More than $400,000,000 worth of property has been destroyed.

Why is this tragedy happening? Although the current undeclared war began in 1969, hatred between Roman Catholics and Protestants has a long history in Northern Ireland. It is the result of centuries of bitterness and conflict between the people of Ireland, who are mainly Roman Catholic, and the people of England, who are not. (The people of England are predominantly Anglican.) For centuries, Ireland was ruled by England. The Irish struggled against that rule. Finally, in 1921, an independent Ireland was formed. Today the Republic of Ireland and the United Kingdom (England, Scotland, Wales, and Northern Ireland) have officially friendly relations. But the old hatreds and disputes continue to rage in Northern Ireland.

Northern Ireland, or Ulster, as it is often called, occupies about a sixth of the land area of Ireland. Northern Ireland did not become independent with the rest of the island. This was, in part, because the majority of the population did not wish it. Most of the people of Northern Ireland are Protestants. English and Scottish Protestants had colonized Northern Ireland in the 17th century. They became the majority in the population and controlled the affairs of the country. The Ulster Protestants came to consider themselves different from the rest of the Irish people, who are mainly Roman Catholic. Thus, Northern Ireland, which now has some 1,000,000 Protestants and some 500,000 Roman Catholics, has chosen to remain part of the United Kingdom.

The Roman Catholic minority in Northern Ireland has not been happy with this situation. Many Roman Catholics would like to see it united with the rest of Ireland. Others are less interested in union with the Republic of Ireland than in gaining their full civil rights in Northern Ireland. Roman Catholics have long been discriminated against in jobs, housing, and politics.

In the 1960's, Roman Catholics formed civil rights groups to protest discrimination and to obtain rights equal to those of Ulster's Protestants. Demonstrations were held. Some Protestant groups met the demonstrations with violence. Although British troops were sent in to try to restore peace, old hatreds continually fueled the violence. And the Irish Republican Army (I.R.A.), a terrorist group long outlawed in both the Republic of Ireland and Northern Ireland, entered the picture with violent acts of its own.

In 1976 there were about 15,000 British troops in Northern Ireland to keep the peace. But the bloodshed continued.

And in 1976 the Ulster violence continued to spill into England and the Republic of Ireland. Some of it was the work of the I.R.A.; some, that of unknown terrorists. In London and in other parts of Britain, bombs were set off in subways, restaurants, and public buildings of all kinds. Letter bombs were sent through the mail. The terrorists said they were protesting British control of Northern Ireland. Terrorists also assassinated the British Ambassador to Ireland. In July Ambassador T. E. Ewart-Biggs and his secretary were killed. The car they were riding in was blown up near the ambassador's residence in Dublin, the capital of the Republic of Ireland, by a terrorist bomb.

No one can seem to agree on a way to put an end to the nightmare in Northern Ireland. One suggestion has been to reform the government. Although Ulster is part of the United Kingdom, it has traditionally been partially self-governing and had its own parliament. Protestants have controlled that parliament. If Roman Catholics had a fair share in the Ulster Government, political leaders of both sides might be able to work together to bring peace.

Other people believe that peace can never come under the traditional system. They argue that Northern Ireland should be united with the Republic of Ireland. And yet another group of people believes that the idea of a separate government for Northern Ireland should be done away with completely, and that Ulster should be totally integrated into the United Kingdom. In this way, all of the people of Ulster would have the political and civil rights guaranteed by the British constitution. Other people think that Northern Ireland should become a completely independent nation with a new constitution and a new government. Finally, there is a group of people who believe that Northern Ireland should be governed jointly by the Republic of Ireland and the United Kingdom.

So far, all attempts to solve Northern Ireland's problems have failed. But in 1976, despite bloodshed and violence, there was a hopeful development. A women's peace movement in Northern Ireland, with both Roman Catholic and Protestant members, held a march for peace. It was held in August and attracted 25,000 marchers. The movement was seen by many people as a reminder that the wish for peace is strong in Ulster. It may prove to be as strong as the hatred that has torn the country apart.

One of the August peace marchers summed it all up. She said, "We might be getting some opposition and there will be some hard times ahead. But we won't be stopped. You see we have love on our side, and that in the end is stronger than any bomb or bullet."

NAMIBIA

Another new African country appeared on the horizon in 1976. The new country, known as Namibia, is scheduled to become completely independent in 1978. Namibia is a former German colony. It has been administered by South Africa since 1920 as South West Africa. Guerrilla forces in Namibia have been at war with the South African authorities for the past ten years. And the United Nations and many African nations have long wished to see an independent Namibia. However, it was not until 1975 that South Africa agreed to begin discussions on independence.

Namibia is a large region on the southwest coast of Africa. It has an area of 318,260 square miles (824,290 square kilometers). For such a large area, Namibia has a small population. There are 900,000 people, about 100,000 of whom are white. There are distinct geographical regions—the Namib Desert along the coast, a central plateau, and part of the Kalahari Desert in the southeast. To the north of the Kalahari region is Windhoek, the capital. The climate is very hot and dry. Much of the land is arid and can only be used for limited agriculture and for grazing cattle, sheep, and goats. Diamond mining and fishing are important to the economy.

The largest black group in Namibia is the Ovambo people. These people have been active in the South West Africa People's Organization, the guerrilla movement that has led the fight for independence from South Africa.

The United Nations first appealed to South Africa to end its rule of Namibia in 1966. However, South Africa refused to take any steps in this direction until recently. Under the independence plan now being discussed, an interim government would be set up in Namibia in 1977. The South West Africa People's Organization, which the United Nations recognizes as the representative of the people of Namibia, insists that it should form the interim government.

The old and the new—traditional dress and modern automobiles—meet in Namibia.

Israeli commandos land at Entebbe in this television re-enactment.

TERRORISM

It was July 4, 1976, the 200th birthday of the United States. Far from the birthday celebrations, commandos from Israel had completed a mission as daring as any event in the American Revolution. Working under cover of dark, they had taken off from an Israeli airport and headed for Entebbe airfield in the African country of Uganda. Entebbe was some 2,500 miles (4,000 kilometers) from Israel. The commandos' mission was to rescue a large group of men and women being held prisoner in Uganda by terrorists.

Most of the prisoners were Israelis. Some were Jews from other countries. All of the prisoners had been aboard a flight from Tel Aviv, Israel, destined for Paris. But when the plane made a scheduled stop at Athens, terrorists boarded and hijacked the plane—took it over from its pilots and crew by force.

Terrorists are men and women who use violence or the threat of violence against people connected in some way with a government they oppose. The terrorists who hijacked the Israeli plane represented Arab groups opposed to the government of Israel. These groups believe that the state of Israel should not exist as a Jewish nation. They also believe that the land of Israel should be the homeland of the Palestinian Arabs, as it once was.

The terrorists forced the pilot of the plane to fly from Athens to Uganda, a country unfriendly to Israel. When they reached Uganda, the terrorists issued their demands. They demanded that terrorists for the Arab cause who were being held in jails in Israel and in other countries be released. The terrorists made it clear that if their demands were not met, their hostages—the people aboard the plane—would be killed.

For a while it seemed that Israel might have to give in to the terrorists' demands. What

73

choice did they have? But by July 3, one week after the hijacking, the Israelis had made up their minds. Israeli commandos flew, in great secrecy, to Uganda. Armed with machine guns and hand grenades, they were able to free most of the hostages and take them aboard planes bound for Israel. All but four of the hostages reached Israel safely. Three hostages died during the raid. One hostage, an elderly woman, was ill and in a hospital in Uganda at the time of the raid. No one knows what happened to her. The Israelis believe the Ugandans killed her.

The raid at Entebbe was the longest-range air rescue mission in history. The world marveled at what the commandos had done. But for all the skill and bravery the commandos displayed, their amazing raid was directed at only a very few people. A handful of terrorists had been responsible for the hijacking and it had taken an elaborate military plan to defeat them. The incident showed just how much trouble a few outlaws can create in the world as it is today.

▶ A REAL WORLD PROBLEM

Terrorism is a serious problem in many parts of the world, not just in Israel. Terrorism has many causes and is used for many reasons. Some terrorists belong to minority peoples within a country who are concerned about preserving their cultural traditions, want more say in their own affairs, or even wish complete independence. For example, some groups among the Roman Catholic minority in Northern Ireland have used terrorism in their efforts to gain freedom from British rule. The separatists among the Basque people of northern Spain sometimes use terrorism in their struggle for independence from the central government of Spain.

There are other terrorists who are involved in strictly political matters. They often wish to overthrow the governments of their own countries. There are many examples of political terrorist groups in Latin America.

There are other terrorists who are part of international revolutionary movements of various kinds. These terrorists try to stir up trouble anywhere they can to help bring about world revolution. Two of the people in the hijacking of the Israeli plane were "international terrorists." They were not Arabs or Palestinians. They were Germans.

And there are also terrorist movements that bring together people with different goals.

▶ WAYS AND MEANS

Most terrorists operate in one of three ways. One way is to kill officials of the governments they oppose. In recent years, a number of United States diplomats and other officials have been killed in various parts of the world by terrorists representing anti-American groups. A second terrorist method is even more frightening. It is random killing. Terrorists may set off a bomb in a restaurant. The people killed by the bomb may have nothing to do with the government the terrorists are opposing. Random killings spread fear and make people aware of the terrorist cause. The third kind of terrorist action involves taking hostages, holding people against their will and threatening to kill them if terrorist demands aren't met.

One favorite terrorist method of getting hostages is by hijacking airplanes. The Entebbe hijacking is a perfect example of this method. Another way to get hostages is by kidnapping individuals. A government official, a diplomat, or a businessman may be kidnapped and held as a hostage. For his return, the terrorists may demand money or the freeing of other terrorists from jail. In some cases, terrorist demands have been met and hostages have been returned unharmed. But unfortunately this has not always happened.

The most famous kidnapping attempt by terrorists took place during the Olympics of 1972. Anti-Israeli terrorists raided the quarters of the Israeli Olympic team in Munich, Germany, where the games were being held. Several Israeli team members were captured and held as hostages. Eventually, all of the hostages were killed. Because of this tragedy, the 1976 Olympic Games in Montreal were the most heavily guarded in Olympic history. Athletes at the games were actually outnumbered by the police and soldiers who were responsible for guarding them.

The taking of hostages creates very hard ethical problems for governments. Should a government bargain with terrorists to save the lives of hostages? If it does, the terrorists may

The Basques of northern Spain keep their way of life alive in processions like this one in Pamplona. The marchers wear traditional Basque red sashes and scarves.

be encouraged to strike again at a later date. Because of this possibility, some people believe that governments should never negotiate with terrorists. Other people believe it is impossible to refuse to negotiate when human lives are involved.

▶ **SOLUTIONS**

The control of terrorism is one of the most difficult problems faced by the nations of the world. Terrorism is nothing new, but many people feel that it has increased greatly in the last ten or fifteen years. Why? One major reason would seem to be the increase in air travel. It is easier to hijack a plane than it is to hijack a ship or a bus or a train. If terrorists can take control of a plane's cockpit, they have a very good chance of getting exactly what they want.

Because terrorism has become an international problem, representatives of governments have been meeting together to find solutions. Many nations are trying to set up international safeguards against hijacking. If you have taken a trip by jet, especially an overseas flight, you may have had your suitcase X-rayed for bombs or other weapons. And you may have been asked to walk across the path of an electronic metal detector, which would give a signal if you had any metal on your person. Or you might have been searched. But all countries do not take these precautions. And no matter how many precautions are taken, it is almost impossible to prevent all hijacking.

It will probably take the nations of the world, working together through the United Nations, many years to solve the problems of terrorism. But solutions must be found if people are to live in safety and dignity.

LEBANON

People used to speak of Lebanon as a political miracle. It was a Middle Eastern country with a population that was partly Christian and partly Muslim. Government power was shared by representatives of the two groups. Lebanon was also famous for what it wasn't —it was neither totally linked to the Arab world and its problems nor totally linked to the European world and its problems. And Lebanon had managed to stay more or less out of the long-standing dispute between the Arabs and Israel. Lebanon was unique.

But in 1975 the pressure of problems both within the country and in neighboring countries became too great. A bloody civil war erupted in Lebanon. It was a war that split the country and even split families. Instead of being an oasis in the midst of Middle Eastern conflicts, Lebanon became a battleground where all the region's conflicts were acted out in miniature. But by the fall of 1976 a new president of Lebanon, Elias Sarkis, had been installed. And a major attempt was being made at a ceasefire that would last long enough for the country to begin to function normally again.

Lebanon is on the eastern rim of the Mediterranean Sea. It has a border with Syria in the north and east, and with Israel in the south. Lebanon is a small country, with an area of 4,105 square miles (10,400 square

Three Palestine Liberation Organization (PLO) members in troubled Lebanon. The soldier in the middle is a woman. The PLO has been actively involved in the current troubles in Lebanon. This PLO group is celebrating a victory over a Syrian military unit in the Lebanese city of Saida.

kilometers). Its population numbers about 3,000,000 people. Lebanon is unique in the Middle East in having a large Christian population. Slightly less than half of its people are Christians. Most of the rest of the population is Muslim. Arabic is the official language of the country, although French and English are also widely spoken there.

Lebanon is a land of few natural resources. The economy is based largely on banking and trade, and the country depends on commerce for much of its prosperity. Its capital, Beirut, was long the financial and business center of the Middle East. Lebanon, in fact, has been the crossroads between Europe and Asia for centuries.

Away from the large, commercial cities, however, Lebanon is a land of farmers and shepherds. These country people live in small villages perched high in the mountains or nestled in the valleys.

Throughout its long history, Lebanon has been ruled by many powers—Assyria, Persia, Greece, Rome, Turkey. When the rule of the Turks ended after World War I, Lebanon was governed by France. Lebanon became independent of France in 1943. With the formation of the Lebanese republic, an unwritten agreement was arrived at: the president of Lebanon was always to be a Christian, and the premier and the speaker of the Chamber of Deputies (the Lebanese parliament) were to be Muslims. Seats in the Chamber of Deputies were apportioned among the various religious groups. With a few exceptions, this system worked well for many years.

Then why the civil war? The reasons for the civil war in Lebanon are varied. Lebanon is a country divided not only by religion but by culture and politics as well. Many Lebanese Christians are attracted to the West, to the United States and Western Europe. The Muslim community is drawn to the nearby Muslim world of the Middle East. At one time the Christians were in the majority in Lebanon and had a slightly higher proportion of representatives in the Chamber of Deputies. No census has been held for many years, but there are now probably slightly more Muslims than Christians in the population. The Muslims have therefore begun to demand a greater voice in the government. Hostility between politically conservative and politically radical groups complicated the situation.

There was also the issue of the Palestinian refugees living in Lebanon. They were Arabs who had left Israel. By the time the Lebanese civil war broke out, the Palestinians had become a powerful political and military force in Lebanon. In fact, they were involved in launching raids into Israel from Lebanon. The Palestinians opposed the moderate attitude of the Lebanese Government toward Israel. And when Palestinian terrorists would launch their attacks into Israel from Lebanon, the Israelis would counterattack by moving troops into southern Lebanon. With all of these problems, very little was needed to touch off a full-scale civil war.

When the war did break out, casualties on both the Christian and Muslim sides were heavy. An estimated 20,000 to 30,000 people were killed—including many civilians not engaged in the fighting. Many Lebanese were forced to flee their homes. Beirut was especially hard hit. In the house-to-house fighting that took place there, the once-beautiful international city was severely damaged. Business activities in the capital came to a standstill. Many Lebanese as well as foreign residents left the country.

A number of ceasefires and truces were arranged, but none lasted long. At the insistence of the Muslims, the President of Lebanon was replaced. Even the election of a new president failed to halt the fighting. In 1976 Syria, in an effort to separate the warring parties, sent troops and tanks into Lebanon. The Syrian move was also aimed at preventing the Palestine Liberation Organization, the largest of the Palestinian political groups, from taking over Lebanese affairs. It is believed that Syria's action really did prevent the Palestinians and the Lebanese Muslims from completely taking over the country.

After more than a year of war, there were signs of peace in Lebanon in 1976. The long-delayed inauguration of the new president, Elias Sarkis, in September was a hopeful sign. And continued efforts to maintain an effective ceasefire were also hopeful signs. But the future of Lebanon still remains unclear. Many people wonder if it will ever again have the unity and stability it once possessed.

NEW TIMES FOR PORTUGAL AND SPAIN

Two Western European nations that had long been ruled by dictators took important steps toward democracy in 1976. The two nations were Spain and Portugal, neighbors on the Iberian Peninsula.

The Portuguese dictatorship was overthrown in 1974. In 1976, after two years of rapid change and unrest, Portugal held free elections and got a new government. It was the first freely elected government to rule Portugal in 50 years.

Spain's long-time dictator, Francisco Franco, died in 1975. He had ruled Spain for almost 40 years. In 1976, Spain had a new government, which began to restore personal and political freedoms to the Spanish people.

▶ PORTUGAL STEPS AHEAD

With its free elections in 1976, Portugal took a giant step toward democratic government. This progress was particularly impressive because of the country's past problems. Between 1926 and 1974, Portugal was ruled by dictators. Then there were two years of military rule. Those two years were very hectic. Different military groups fought for control of the government. But many people in Portugal were determined to have a democracy—and they won out. In the 1976 elections, the Socialist Party received the greatest number of votes. The leader of the Socialist Party, Mário Soares, was sworn in as premier. Soares became the first freely elected leader of the Portuguese people in 50 years.

The new premier found himself faced with several serious problems. His most immediate problem was to see that the new government worked in an orderly way. During the previous two years everyone was so eager for change that many reform programs were started without proper planning. Another major problem facing Portugal's new government is the Portuguese economy. Portugal is basically a country of farmers and fishermen. But Portugal's farmers and fishermen have not been producing enough to feed the country. In fact, Portugal has had to import food from other countries. The new government will try to increase food production. And Portugal needs more modern industry. Too many of the country's 9,000,000 people do not have steady employment.

The future of Spain and Portugal is important to the people of the two countries and to their friends and allies. The United States and the countries of Western Europe are especially anxious to see Spain and Portugal become strong partners in the democratic world.

Mário Soares, Portugal's first freely elected leader in 50 years.

Spain's new monarch, King Juan Carlos I, with Queen Sophia and their children.

▶ SPAIN'S PROBLEMS

Replacing a dictatorship with a democracy is not easy. In Spain, the task is especially hard. There is still much bitterness and division among the Spanish people because of the Spanish Civil War, which was fought some 40 years ago. The rule of Francisco Franco was a direct result of that war, and he kept the memory, and the division, alive.

The Spanish Civil War, which played such an important part in modern Spanish history, began in 1936. At that time Spain had a new republican government. The Spanish Army began the war by revolting against that government. General Francisco Franco and other army officers involved in the revolt were known as the Nationalists. Their opponents, as the war spread, were called Loyalists. The Loyalists were a political alliance of Communists, Socialists, and Republicans. Both sides received support from outside Spain. The Nationalists were helped by the Fascist dictatorships of Italy and Germany. The Loyalists were helped by the Communist government of the Soviet Union. The Nationalists won the war by 1939, but about a million people died and much of Spain was left in ruins.

Before the 1930's Spain had been ruled by a king. Spain's last king, Alfonso XIII, reigned from 1886 to 1931, when he was deposed. In 1976, Spain again had a king—a king pledged to work for democracy in Spain. He is King Juan Carlos I, the grandson of Alfonso XIII. Franco, near the end of his life, chose Juan Carlos to rule Spain after his death.

The country of 35,000,000 people that Juan Carlos rules is quite different from the country his grandfather ruled. In his grandfather's day, Spain was a country of peasant farmers. Today, Spain has growing industries and a large middle class. And Spain has also become a popular tourist center. There was one major question facing King Juan Carlos when he became head of the Spanish Government. Could he help his country progress toward democratic government as rapidly as it had moved toward a modern economy? And could it be done in an orderly way?

There were a number of indications in 1976 that Spain was moving toward democracy. Under Franco, no political activity was allowed apart from Franco's own party. Now Spain has many political parties, although the Communist Party remains illegal. Under Franco's rule, many people were put in jail because of their political opinions. By 1976, most political prisoners had been released from jail. Other people opposed to Franco's rule had fled to other countries to avoid jail. These people were allowed to return to their homeland if they wished to. There were also many signs of increased freedom of speech and expression. Newspapers began to criticize the government freely—just as they do in democratic countries. Bookstalls were filled with once-forbidden books and magazines from all over the world.

But the strongest move toward democracy was the announcement that the first free elections in over 40 years would be held in 1977.

WORLD OF SCIENCE

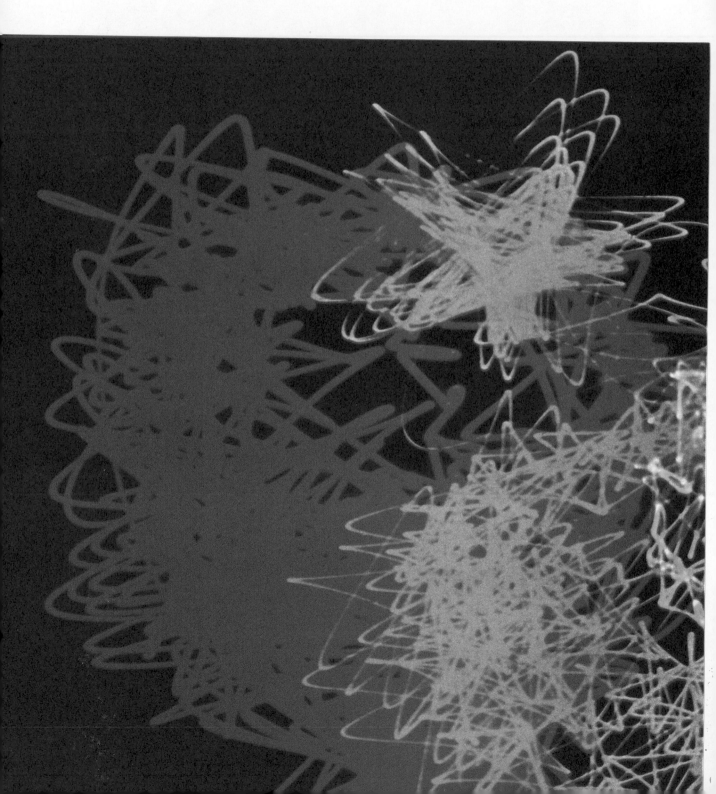

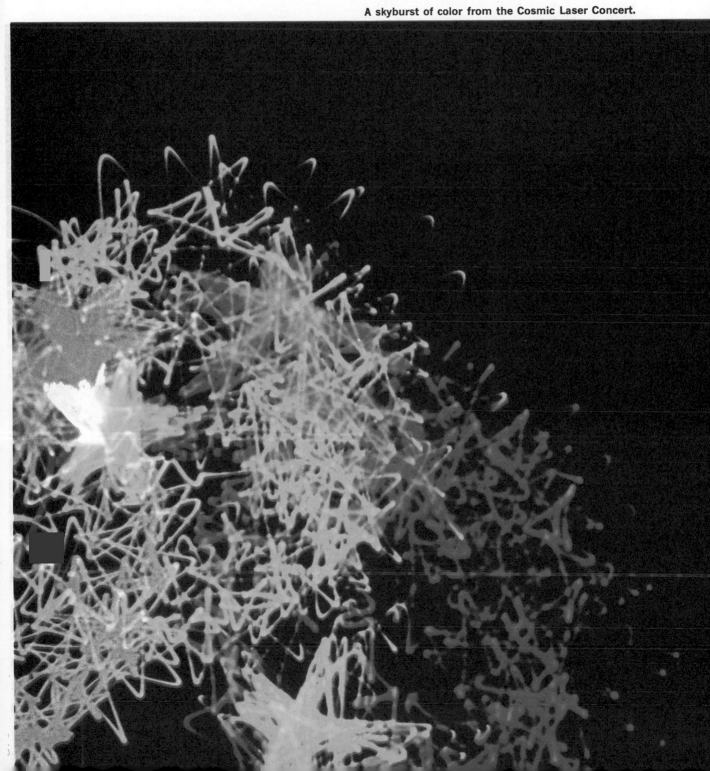

A skyburst of color from the Cosmic Laser Concert.

Photographed on Mars. *Above:* this strange bluish sunset is caused by atmospheric particles that both scatter and absorb the sun's light. *Below:* the orange-red color of the daylight sky is caused by atmospheric particles that scatter and reflect the sun's light. The orange-reddish material on the desolate, rock-strewn landscape may be limonite. (On Earth, this compound is one of the ores from which iron is obtained.)

MYSTERY ON MARS

For a long time, people have wondered if there is life anywhere in the solar system other than on Earth. Mars has always been a favorite for this kind of speculation. In recent years, space probes have detected a thin atmosphere around the planet, with very small amounts of carbon dioxide, water vapor, and some other gases. The plants and animals that we are familiar with could not exist in such an atmosphere. But there are simple micro-organisms—some bacteria, for example—that can survive in unfavorable conditions. Could organisms such as these be living on Mars?

In August and September, 1975, the United States sent space probes, Viking I and Viking II, to Mars. One purpose of the Viking missions was to learn whether any form of life exists on Mars. After their eleven-month journeys, the probes landed on the surface of the red planet, about 4,600 miles (7,400 kilometers) from one another. Each Lander performed its assigned experiments successfully. Yet several months after the landings, scientists could not give a yes or no answer to the question, "Is there life on Mars?"

How can we look for microscopic signs of life on a planet hundreds of millions of miles away? The equipment aboard the Viking Landers looked for Martian life by using chemical means, and the results were relayed back to Earth.

At every moment of its life, a living thing, even something as simple as a bacterium, is a busy chemical factory. Chemical substances (such as oxygen, water, sugar, and protein) are taken in by the bacterium. The chemical activity within the organism produces substances that are given off as wastes. So one way to detect living things is to look for certain kinds of chemical activity.

The Viking's "chemistry department" takes up about as much space as a schoolroom wastebasket. It is hard to believe that within this small space there are 40,000 electronic parts, three automatic biochemical laboratory chambers, a computer, radioactivity counters, ovens, and other devices.

Scientists on Earth radio-control the Lander's search for life. The search begins as a long arm on the Lander reaches out, scoops up a sample of soil, and drops it into openings on the top of the Lander. Automatic devices place a portion of the soil sample in each of the three laboratory chambers. Each laboratory performs a different test, looking for chemical signs of life in a different way.

Laboratory 1. On Earth, green plants make their food by a process called photosynthesis. They take in water and carbon dioxide, and, with the help of energy from the sun's light, combine these to make sugar or starch. Viking laboratory 1 provides the soil sample with the conditions needed for photosynthesis, or a similar food-making process, to take place. If micro-organisms in the soil sample make food, this laboratory should detect the chemical changes they cause.

Laboratory 2. What about organisms that do not make their food? Laboratory 2 moistens its soil sample with a nutrient liquid. (A nutrient is a food substance necessary for life.) The laboratory then keeps the soil sample at a temperature of 50° Fahrenheit (10° Celsius) for two weeks. If there are micro-organisms in the soil that make use of the nutrient, they should give off waste gases that the laboratory can detect.

Laboratory 3. Living things cause chemical changes in the atmosphere around them. This laboratory tests sample after sample of the atmosphere within the chamber. Changes in the amount and kind of gases in the chamber could be evidence that there are living things in the soil sample.

The Viking tests have not proved or disproved the existence of life on Mars. Two of the laboratory experiments indicated a possibility of micro-organisms in the soil. But in the third experiment, large amounts of oxygen were detected. The amounts were so large that scientists question whether they indicate life. Rather, they believe that there may have been a chemical reaction between the soil itself and the liquids used in the tests.

In November and December, 1976, the movement of Earth and Mars in their orbits put them on opposite sides of the sun. Communication between the Vikings and Earth was temporarily interrupted, leaving the question of life on Mars still a mystery.

A COSMIC LASER CONCERT

How would you like to be surrounded by light and color and music—all moving together and somehow connected, as if by magic? You can have the experience if you want to.

You might feel as if a great tidal wave of blue and green were washing over you to the accompaniment of a great symphony. Or you might see brilliant spots of yellow and orange and pink spraying out at you in time to an explosive rock beat.

Or, best of all, you might have the remarkable experience of seeing the patterns of a familiar piece of music take visible shape right in front of you, just as you have imagined them in your daydreams.

You can have all of these experiences and more if you visit a Laserium show. The full and official name of the show is Laserium: The Cosmic Laser Concert. By 1977 more than 2,000,000 people in Canada, the United States, and Japan had experienced Laserium.

It all started in 1970. A filmmaker named Ivan Dryer had completed a documentary film about laser beam experiments. It started him thinking about the creative potential of laser beam projections. And about the whole question of science and the arts. In modern times, science and the arts seem to have parted company. But once, in the days of the Italian Renaissance for instance, no one thought it particularly odd that a great painter like Leonardo da Vinci should also be fascinated by science and technology. When Dryer looked at the lovely sculptural shapes created with laser beam projections, he could see music—but music frozen, in mid-air. Why not join music and laser beam projections, he thought, and let one make the other even more beautiful? By 1973 the first Laserium show was ready.

The heart of every Laserium show is the laser, a device that sends out a powerful beam of light. The beam in the show is projected from a krypton-gas laser. Prisms break up the laser beam into different colors, and mirrors change the colored beams into different shapes. A Laserium show is often given in planetariums because the projections are especially effective on the vast domed ceilings most planetariums have. And planetariums often have excellent amplification systems, too. Such systems are important because music is so much a part of the Laserium experience.

When you first see Laserium, it will seem terrible that the fantastically beautiful moving patterns and designs disappear as soon as you've seen them. Color photographs can be taken of the patterns as they appear for an instant, but photos can't truly capture them. For part of the beauty of the designs and patterns of Laserium is movement and change—they change and flow from one second to the next. But after a while, you won't mind the fact that they go away. One beautiful shape or design leads to another, just as one passage of music leads to another. And soon you begin to be astonished by even more beauty.

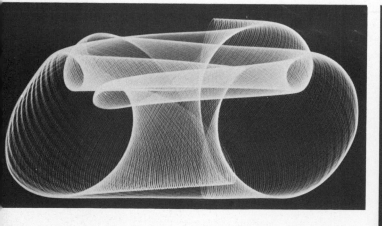

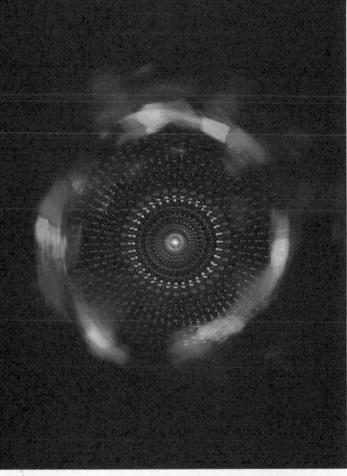

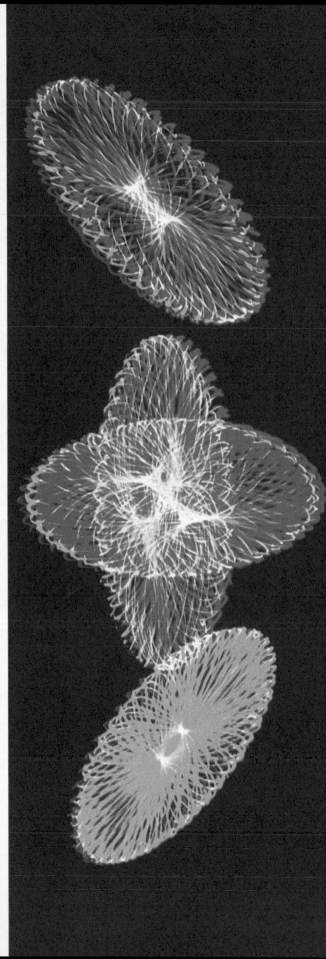

Patterns of color and . . .

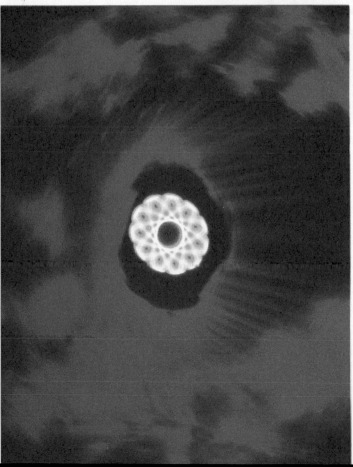

. . . swirling shapes explode at a Laserium show.

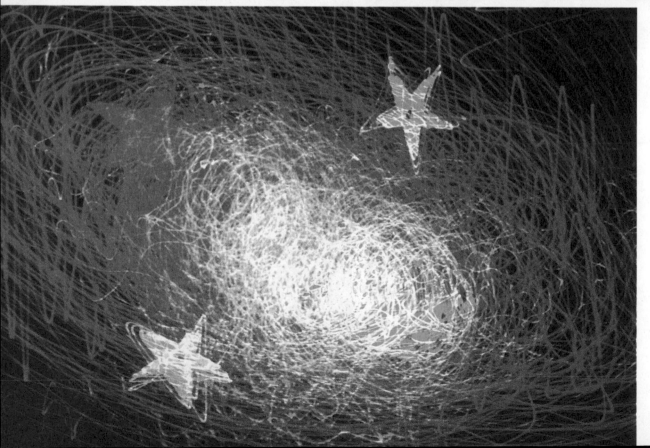

Ball lightning is shown in this 19th-century French woodcut.

BALL LIGHTNING

Flash! Flash! Flash! Brilliant streaks of light stab the air between earth and clouds. This is the familiar zigzag lightning of thunderstorms, moving at speeds of up to 20,000 miles per second (over 32,000 kilometers per second), and more. No wonder we speak of great speed as the "speed of lightning." But not all lightning moves fast.

Ball lightning, a rarely seen form of lightning, moves slowly enough to be watched by people nearby—if they are not too startled to watch anything at all. For example, the pilot of an Air Force plane reported that a ball of yellow light entered his plane through the windshield, then moved out onto one of the wings and disappeared.

Some ball lightning has been reported in connection with electrical equipment. In one case, an engineer in a powerhouse told of seeing a ball of fire come off a generator. It floated along a switchboard, and hit the ceiling of a room where a cat was asleep. The cat leaped up squalling, but did not seem to be harmed. The fireball fell apart and disappeared.

Recently, scientists working for the French Atomic Energy Commission conducted experiments to learn more about this mysterious form of lightning. They fired rockets to a height of 2,300 feet (700 meters) during thunderstorms. A long wire connected to each rocket conducted the electrical charge of the lightning to the ground. In some cases, fireballs appeared on the ground, but they lasted only a fraction of a second.

Why is the French Atomic Energy Commission interested in ball lightning? In France, as in other countries, scientists are looking for new sources of energy. The world seems to be quickly using up most of its traditional energy sources—wood, coal, oil, and natural gas. Scientists are now trying to harness the energy produced by the sun and wind. They are also trying to make use of nuclear energy.

One way of producing nuclear energy is by a process called fusion. In fusion, the nuclei of hydrogen atoms are united; this produces the energy. To get fusion to begin and to continue, the hydrogen gas must be heated to an enormously high temperature, so that it is in a state known as a plasma. But so far, scientists have found it difficult to complete the fusion process.

Some scientists suspect that ball lightning may be a plasma. If this is so, scientists would like to study it. The more we know about plasma, the better use we can make of it in the process of fusion, which, in turn, may supply us with another source of energy.

THE SPACE SHUTTLE

On September 17, 1976, the National Aeronautics and Space Administration (NASA) unveiled a new kind of spacecraft—the space shuttle. The space shuttle is designed to blast off from earth carrying up to 65,000 pounds (almost 30,000 kilograms) of cargo. It will be able to spend up to one month orbiting the earth. But the remarkable thing about the space shuttle is that it will then be able to return to earth, making a horizontal landing like an ordinary plane. In other words, it will be able to "shuttle" to and from the earth. Not surprisingly, the space shuttle looks like a rocket, a freight car, and a plane, all rolled into one. The first shuttle was named *Enterprise,* after the spacecraft on the popular "Star Trek" television series.

The purpose of the space shuttle is to lower the cost of space exploration in the future. Until now, every one of the hundreds of satellites in earth orbit was put there by its own rocket. A rocket assembly, with its huge engines, pumps, and masses of controlling equipment, costs many millions of dollars. Yet it is used only once. After it sends the satellite into orbit, the rocket assembly falls into the ocean and is lost. But the space shuttle will be re-usable. Each shuttle is expected to be used for about a hundred orbital flights.

NASA officials say that use of the shuttle may save up to $1,000,000,000 per year. However, some critics of the shuttle program believe that the cost of developing the shuttle, more than $7,000,000,000, will mean that more money will be spent than saved.

The entire space shuttle consists of an orbiter, rockets, and an external fuel supply. The orbiter is a 122-foot-long (37-meter) boxlike structure with stubby wings. It is about the size of a DC-9 jet airliner. The crew compartment at the front looks much like that of a plane. Behind it is the cargo compartment. Huge doors permit the whole roof of the compartment to open up, so that satellites or other large pieces of equipment can be loaded and unloaded.

At the rear of the orbiter are three rocket engines, which burn a mixture of liquid hydrogen and liquid oxygen. The liquid fuels are held in an enormous tank that is attached to the orbiter. Two solid-fuel booster rockets are also attached to the orbiter.

When the space shuttle is ready for launching, it will be stood on end, rocket engines pointing down. As the shuttle is launched, the solid-fuel rockets will burn, adding their thrust to that of the liquid-fueled rocket engines. The burned-out solid-fuel rockets will then be

The first space shuttle (actually just the orbiter). It is named *Enterprise,* after the spacecraft on the "Star Trek" TV series. Appropriately, at the shuttle's first showing were some of the "Star Trek" crew—Leonard Nimoy (Mr. Spock), George Takei (Mr. Sulu), and DeForrest Kelley (Dr. McCoy).

released from the orbiter, and parachutes will open to lower them safely into the ocean. There they will be recovered; they will be rebuilt and used again for more launchings. The tank that holds the liquid fuels will drop away when the shuttle comes near its maximum height, before it actually goes into orbit. This tank is the only part of the shuttle that will not be recovered for re-use.

Then just the orbiter will be left. The final push that sends it into orbit will come from small rockets at its rear. The orbiting height may be between 100 and 300 miles (160 to 480 kilometers) above the earth.

When the mission is over, the crew will slow down the orbiter, so that it will begin to fall toward the earth. Like other manned spacecraft, the orbiter must be protected from the enormous heat generated by friction with the air. Parts of the orbiter must endure temperatures of up to 3000° Fahrenheit (1650° Celsius); those parts are protected by layers of pure carbon. The rest of the orbiter is protected by thousands of bricks of an extremely light glass material. After the orbiter has been slowed to a low enough speed, it will be piloted to a landing like a glider.

▶ **WHAT SHUTTLES WILL DO**

One thing the shuttle will be able to do is carry satellites. Satellites now perform a wide range of activities. They monitor weather and pollution, study the earth's surface, relay telephone and television signals, and record scientific information. The space shuttle will be able to carry one or more satellites. As the shuttle goes into earth orbit, it will drop the satellites off, one at a time; the satellites will continue in the same orbit. The orbiting shuttle can also be used to launch a satellite that is to operate in a higher orbit. Such a launch will take only a very small fraction of the push that would be needed to launch the same satellite from the earth, and hence a very much smaller and less expensive rocket.

Today there is no way to service or repair a satellite in orbit, or to bring it back safely to earth. But the shuttle orbiter will be able to come alongside orbiting satellites. Service, repair, and recapture will be possible. It will no longer be necessary to replace old or faulty satellites by rocketing up expensive new ones.

The entire space shuttle consists of (1) the orbiter, (2) a pair of solid-fuel booster rockets, (3) the orbiter's external liquid-fuel supply, and (4) the three rocket engines at the rear of the orbiter, which burn a combination of liquid hydrogen and liquid oxygen.

NASA also expects to use the shuttle to carry manned scientific laboratory units into earth orbit. The lab, which will remain in the orbiter, will be able to stay in orbit for up to one month. After the orbiter returns to the earth, the laboratory unit can be removed from it. Then another laboratory unit with a fresh crew of scientists can be sent into orbit, using the same orbiter.

Tests of the shuttle system are expected to begin in the spring of 1977. It is hoped that by 1980, there will be two space shuttles operating on a regular schedule.

There is something else that is important about the space shuttle program: women are being encouraged to apply for this space mission, and there will probably be crews of male and female astronauts for the first time.

In the Milestones of Flight hall are two of aviation's most historic planes: the Wright brothers' *Flyer*, and Lindbergh's *Spirit of St. Louis*.

THE NATIONAL AIR AND SPACE MUSEUM

On July 1, 1976, the National Air and Space Museum opened in Washington, D.C. The opening ceremonies included an unusual kind of ribbon cutting. At the time of the opening, a Viking spacecraft was orbiting the planet Mars. The Viking sent a special radio signal to the museum. The signal triggered an electrical device that cut the ribbon.

The new museum is part of the Smithsonian Institution. It cost $41,500,000 to build. Like its cost, everything about the museum is on a large scale. It is three blocks long and a block wide, and some of its exhibit halls are as high as an eight-story building. It has a theater with a movie screen four stories high. The museum owns more than 250 aircraft, probably the biggest collection of aircraft in the world. The number of visitors expected is huge, too—over 7,000,000 every year.

Near the entrance to the museum is a huge hall called Milestones of Flight. It contains many exhibits that represent milestones, or

"firsts," in aeronautics and space exploration. A small but very popular exhibit is a rock from the moon, which visitors can touch.

Two craft in this hall catch every eye. One, suspended above the viewer, as if still on its historic twelve-second flight, is the *Flyer,* built by the Wright brothers. In this frail-looking machine, Orville Wright in 1903 made the first successful powered flight in a heavier-than-air craft. On the floor, not far from the *Flyer,* rests the command module of the Apollo 11, the craft that carried man to the moon for the first time.

In the 65 years that elapsed between these two events, there were other great "firsts" of flight. High above the visitor hangs the *Spirit of St. Louis,* in which, in 1927, Charles Lindbergh made the first non-stop solo transatlantic flight from New York to Paris. On the floor nearby is the command module of Gemini 4, from which the first American space walk was made.

One of the most interesting displays in the museum is this Apollo lunar module. Six such modules landed on various parts of the moon, each carrying two men.

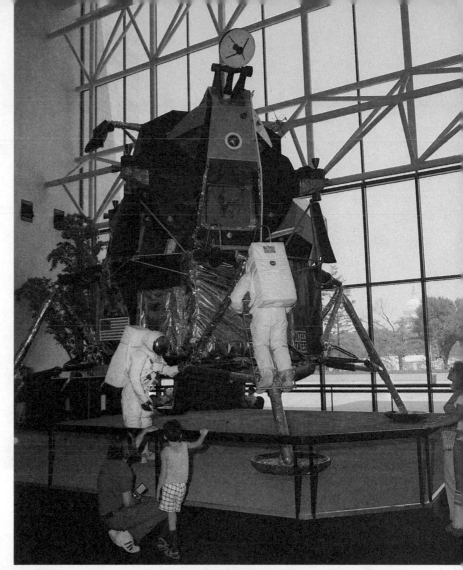

Robert McCall's *The Space Mural —A Cosmic View*. It depicts the past, present, and future of the universe.

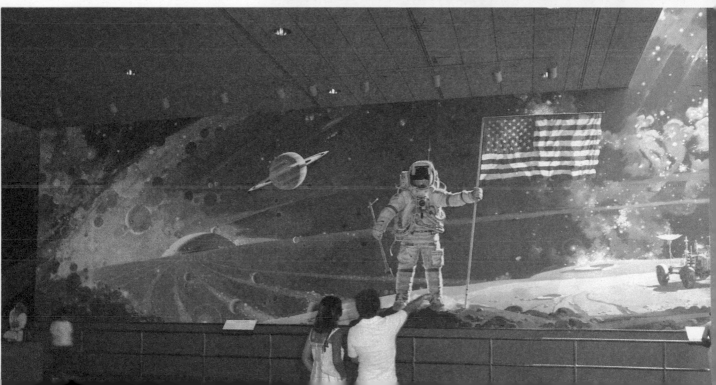

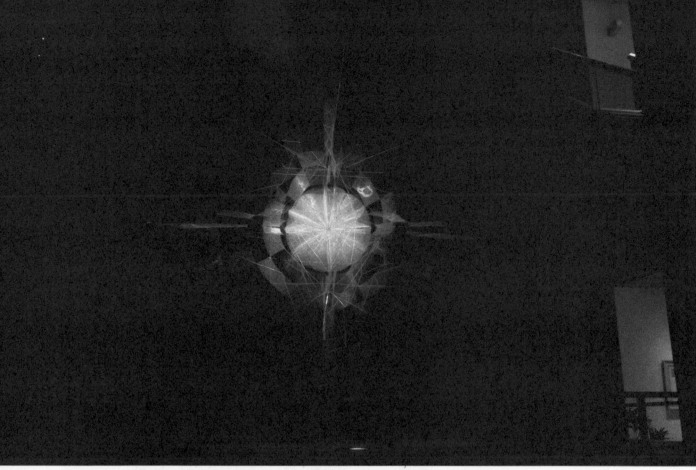

Richard Lippold's sculpture *The Sun* is on display in the Flight and the Arts gallery.

Rockets of all different kinds are in Space Hall.

Models of Robert H. Goddard's liquid-fueled rockets, forerunners of today's giant rockets, are in this hall. There, too, is the X-1, the first craft to fly faster than sound. There are also models of two small but historic spacecraft: Sputnik I, the first artificial satellite, launched in 1957 by the Soviet Union; and Explorer I, the first U.S. satellite, launched in 1958.

The history of air transportation is traced in another great hall. One of the earliest airliners, the Ford Trimotor, hangs there. There is also the world's most famous airliner, the Douglas DC-3. The DC-3's came into use 40 years ago. Many thousands of them were built, and some are still in service in various parts of the world.

Still another great hall is called the Space Hall. There you can see a Skylab Orbital Workshop, like the one in which U.S. astronauts and scientists spent months in earth orbit. This hall also has an Apollo and a Soyuz spacecraft, like those that met and docked in earth orbit in 1975. There, too, are many of the rockets that powered U.S. spacecraft.

Besides the exhibits in the great halls, there are many smaller galleries. One of these has an exhibit of balloons. Another gallery has the *Vin Fiz,* a Wright biplane that was the first to cross the continent, in 1911. It flew from New York to California in 49 days. If this seems a rather long time, keep in mind that *Vin Fiz* made 70 stops, including 15

crashes, on the way. Flying today is much less strenuous. In this gallery there is also a Fokker T-2 plane, which made the first nonstop transcontinental flight, in 1923, in a mere 27 hours.

Still another gallery is devoted to the military planes of World War II. It includes a simulated hangar deck of an aircraft carrier.

In the Gallery of Flight Technology are working models of engines and wind tunnels, and films and puppets that help explain the principles of flight and space flight.

There are more galleries for helicopters, space flight, and satellites. One gallery is given over to Life in the Universe. There is even a gallery called Flight and the Arts; it displays sculpture and other works of art.

The new museum also has a 250-seat planetarium called the Albert Einstein Spacearium. It has a 70-foot-high (21-meter) dome, on which visitors can see accurate projections of thousands of stars, star clusters, and nebulae, while listening to a narration in one of five languages—English, French, German, Japanese, or Spanish. The Spacearium's opening program commemorated the Bicentennial. It dealt with advances in astronomy in the United States since the American Revolution.

Near the Spacearium is a 485-seat auditorium. The first program held there was *To Fly,* a film showing an airborne tour of the United States. The breathtaking scenes were projected on the four-story–high screen, while loudspeakers surrounded visitors with sound.

CALCULATORS

Counting things is an everyday part of life. People learned thousands of years ago that they could count and do arithmetic more quickly and easily with the help of pebbles, knotted cords, their own fingers, or other devices. One simple, ancient counting device, the abacus, is still used in many countries.

About 300 years ago scientists began to build machines, called calculators, that worked with levers, gears, and other moving parts. The machines were cranked by hand at first, and later by electric motors. These calculating machines solved problems in arithmetic much faster than people could do them. But the machines were bulky, noisy, and far slower than today's electronic calculators.

The work of an electronic calculator depends on the flow of electrical currents. In the early models, transistors controlled the currents. A transistor may be as small as a pencil eraser, but thousands of them are needed in even the simplest calculator. So the early models were large and costly.

Small, low-priced calculators were made possible by the development of a device that is an improvement on the transistor. It is the integrated circuit, or IC. Some IC's, only ¼

inch (6 millimeters) on a side, can do the work of 6,000 transistors.

Hundreds of kinds of electronic calculators are available. There are desk models the size of this book, or bigger. For personal use there are mini-calculators, which fit comfortably in the hand. Other models are even smaller.

Every calculator has a keyboard. The operator presses the keys to feed a problem, say $6 \times 7 =$, into the machine. The answer, 42, appears almost instantly in the form of small lighted numerals in a display window on the calculator. Some machines also print both the problem and the answer on a paper tape.

All calculators can be used for doing addition, subtraction, multiplication, and division —the basic functions of arithmetic. Some schools are using calculators in the classroom. Once students have learned to do the basic functions with paper and pencil, they can save a great deal of time by working out problems on a basic calculator, which may be bought for less than $10. Shoppers find basic calculators useful for checking prices and taxes, totaling purchases, and keeping their checkbooks in balance.

A basic calculator can be used to solve any arithmetic problem. However, there are more advanced, more expensive calculators that can solve certain mathematical problems more quickly and conveniently. For example, calculators may be used to find square roots, to calculate profit and selling price, and also to figure interest.

One type of calculator can be used for quickly changing units of measurement from the system used in the United States to the metric system, or vice versa.

Some calculators can store numbers for use in future calculations. These numbers can be "forgotten," and others stored as they are needed. This ability is called memory.

Some scientists, accountants, and mathematicians use advanced calculators costing several hundred dollars or more. The user of such a calculator can preset or program it. The programmable calculator can quickly solve long, complicated problems that would have to be worked out in many time-consuming steps on a simpler calculator.

JAMES D. GATES
National Council of Teachers of Mathematics

STEPS INTO SPACE

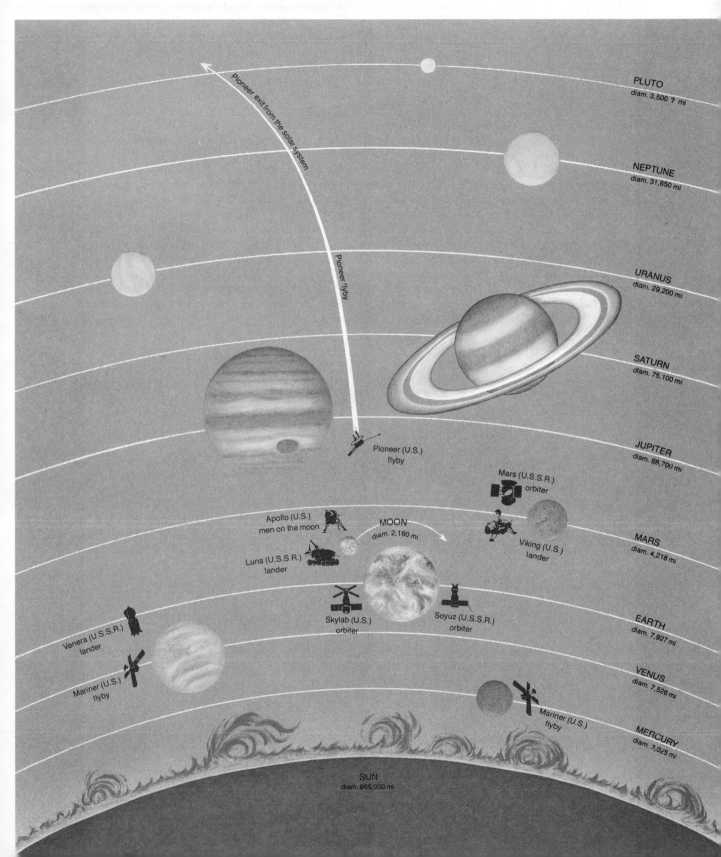

IDENTICAL!

A human being, like a fish, a frog, or a bird, begins life as a fertilized egg cell. This single cell comes into being when a sperm cell from the male parent unites with an egg cell produced by the female parent.

The central part, or nucleus, of the fertilized egg cell contains many thousands of genes. These genes determine what the new organism will be—how it will look, what its chemistry will be like, and so on. Half of those genes come from the father, and half from the mother. They add up to a new "mix," so that the baby frog or bird or person will not be exactly like any other frog or bird or person that has ever existed.

Fertilization requires a male and a female parent. It is part of the process called sexual reproduction. People learned thousands of years ago that the process could be used to improve the plants and animals they used for food. For example, the hardiest plants—those best able to withstand extreme heat, cold, or drought—were bred together, to produce plants as hardy as the parents, or even hardier. Unfortunately, the new "mixes" of genes sometimes produced plants that were not as hardy as either parent.

But there is a way to get new plants, generation after generation, without losing hardiness or any other desirable quality. This method is asexual reproduction. It requires only one parent, and it occurs in many plants naturally. It is also found in simple animals, but not in vertebrates (animals having backbones). There is no new "mix" of genes in asexual reproduction, because only one parent is involved. That means that the new individual is identical to the parent.

An example of asexual reproduction is seen in strawberry plants. Long stems called runners grow out of the plant, and lie on the ground. New plants develop from these runners. In turn, the new plants grow runners. In time, a whole field of strawberry plants, all

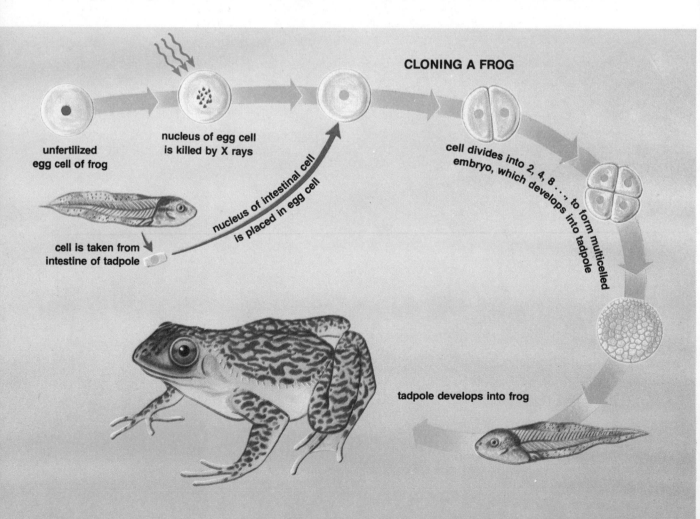

CLONING A FROG

unfertilized egg cell of frog

nucleus of egg cell is killed by X rays

cell is taken from intestine of tadpole

nucleus of intestinal cell is placed in egg cell

cell divides into 2, 4, 8 . . ., to form multicelled embryo, which develops into tadpole

tadpole develops into frog

identical, may grow where there was only a single plant.

Gardeners take advantage of another kind of asexual reproduction to get many begonia or geranium plants from a single plant. They cut up an old plant into pieces of stem and leaf, and plant the pieces. The cuttings grow into new plants, all identical to the original plant. If the old plant has especially handsome leaves or brilliantly colored flowers, the gardener knows that every one of the new plants will have them too. Runners, cuttings, and other asexual methods of reproduction are used to produce much of our fruit and vegetable supply.

Wouldn't asexual reproduction be even more useful if it could be used with vertebrate animals? Imagine what it would mean to our hungry world if we could produce millions of cows identical to one that gives unusually large amounts of high-quality milk. Or if we could turn out billions of chickens identical to an exceptionally meaty original! Recent work by scientists is taking this idea away from the world of science fiction. To understand what these scientists have done, we should first go back to see what happens to the fertilized egg.

As the fertilized egg cell begins to develop, its genes replicate (make exact copies of themselves). Now there are two identical sets of genes. The fertilized egg cell divides into two cells, and each one of these receives one set of genes. The two cells divide to form four cells, then eight, sixteen, and so on, making a growing mass of cells called the embryo. Before each division, there is a new replication of the genes. After a time, the embryo may be composed of millions of cells, all with identical sets of genes. And all these sets are identical to the set that was in the original fertilized egg cell!

In the early life of the embryo, all the cells look and act alike. Later on, the cells begin to change, or differentiate, so they can do special kinds of jobs. In this way we get muscle cells, nerve cells, liver cells, and so on, each kind fitted for its particular kind of work in the body.

▶ A QUESTION OF GENES

The genes dictate what a cell will become, but few of the thousands of genes in any cell ever get a chance to "do their thing." Let's focus on a particular cell. Certain genes in that cell cause it to develop into a muscle cell. Other genes in the same cell, which could have influenced it to become a skin cell or a nerve cell, were blocked, or put out of action. When the cell divides, the blocking of those genes continues, so two *muscle* cells are formed, then four *muscle* cells, and so on. Muscle cells, and no other kind, are formed from the original muscle cell.

What if the blocking of the genes could be avoided in some way? Could a muscle cell or some other body cell be taken from an individual—a frog, let's say—and be allowed to develop into the many kinds of cells needed to make up a whole new frog? If this could be done, the new frog would have exactly the same genes as the frog from which the body cell was taken. The two individuals would be identical! This production of a new individual from a body cell, with no change in gene makeup, is called cloning. Can it be done?

▶ POSSIBILITIES

Scientists have already cloned frogs. They solved the problem of the blocked genes by using a cell in which all the genes remain unblocked—an unfertilized egg cell. The scientists began by killing the nucleus (and the genes within) of the egg cell. One way they did this was by exposing the cell to X rays. They then took a cell from the intestinal lining of a young frog (or tadpole). The nucleus of this cell was taken out, and transferred into the unfertilized egg. In the transfer, the blocked genes in the nucleus of the intestinal cell were automatically unblocked. The stimulated egg began its division into numerous cells, each cell possessing the genes of the inserted nucleus. In the end a new frog was formed. Its genes were identical with those of the frog from which the intestinal cell had been taken. The new frog was the identical twin of the old one! If the cloning were repeated, over and over, a hundred frogs—or a million—could be formed, all with the same genes.

Cloned frogs may be only the first step toward clones of larger, more complicated vertebrates—mammals such as cows or sheep, for example. Certainly cloned mammals

Cloning has been suggested as a way of saving endangered species, such as the whooping crane. Only a few dozen of these huge birds are left. They nest in northern Canada in the summer, and fly south to Texas for the winter.

would be much harder to produce than cloned frogs, because mammalian eggs develop within the body of the female. But scientists have done enough work with mammalian eggs to know that it is not impossible.

Cloning has great advantages, but it has built-in risks as well. For one thing, a wide variety of gene combinations is valuable. Some combinations may be good in one way, while others are good in another way. If you concentrate on one particular combination, you might obtain some advantages while losing others. A cloned herd of cows might pro-

duce large quantities of rich milk. But it might also be exceptionally susceptible to some particular disease. If a single cow in the cloned herd caught that disease, all the rest would get it quickly and they might all die.

The most important use of cloned animals may be to provide more and better food for the people of the world, but other uses have also been suggested. The saving of endangered species is one of them. In the more than 3,000,000,000 (billion) years that life has existed on earth, many thousands of species have become extinct. In recent times, the rate of extinction, helped along by human activities, has become dangerously high. The case of the whooping crane is an example. Only a few dozen of these beautiful large birds are left. Conservationists are trying to protect them. But if anything goes wrong, all the birds could die. A clone of a few hundred of these birds would lessen the chances of sudden extinction.

There have even been suggestions that cloning could bring back an extinct species. Mammoths, long-haired elephant-like animals, roamed Siberia during the last ice age. The mammoths are now extinct, but sometimes dead specimens are found frozen in the Siberian soil. They are almost perfectly preserved, kept from decaying by the intense cold.

What if mammoths were found and thawed out—and some cells had a spark of life? Cloning such a cell might result in a baby mammoth. A few mammoths (at least one of each sex) produced in this way might eventually reproduce by natural means.

▶ THE HUMAN ELEMENT

Will it ever be possible to clone human beings? Many scientists think it likely. If human cloning became a reality, what advantages would it have? Would there be dangers as well?

Suppose geniuses in science, music, art, and other fields were picked for cloning in the hope that the world could benefit from an increase in the number of such people. Could we get, say, a thousand great scientists by cloning one great scientist?

We could not be sure. People are more than what their genes make them. They are also formed by their environment. The people around them, and the children they grow up with, are part of their environment. So are the books they read, and the things that happen to them. Individuals of a clone, starting out with identical genes, would grow up differently. Each would be a different person. developing in a different direction.

Perhaps most people would agree that some geniuses should be cloned. But a society must have non-geniuses, too. Which people would be chosen for cloning? Who would make these decisions, and by what right? How would "ordinary" people get along with people of the clones, who never had any real parents or family? What if some government decided to clone strong, gentle, stupid people to provide a large population of slaves? These and other risks and doubts have made many people hope that there will never be cloning of humans.

One valuable, and less risky, use of human cloning might be for producing body parts, rather than whole persons. As they learn more about cloning, scientists may learn how to block particular sets of genes. With such selective blocking, the cells of a clone might be directed toward developing into a heart, a kidney, or some other organ.

Doctors now have methods for transplanting major organs of the body. Thus, a heart from a person who has just died is set to beating within the chest of a person whose own heart is defective. In some cases, transplanted organs have worked well for years, but most transplants are not so successful. The reason for this is the way in which the recipient's body reacts to the presence of the transplanted organ. The body rejects the "foreign" organ in the same way it rejects "foreign" disease germs—by producing substances called antibodies. The antibodies attack the cells of the transplanted organ, and, after a time, put it out of action.

How might cloning solve the problem of rejection? Suppose that every person, soon after birth, had some 50 or so young, vigorous cells removed from the body in a very minor operation. These cells could be preserved for many years by freezing or by some other method. Then, if there were signs that a person's heart (or some other organ) was beginning to fail, one of the frozen cells could be cloned in the laboratory. The cell would be allowed to develop into the proper organ for transplanting into the body. There would be no rejection, because the body and the organ would have the same genetic makeup.

Every person, then, could have "spare parts," developed through cloning. And each of these parts, as it developed, could supply new cells for future cloning. Such a bank of spare parts could make it possible for human beings to live longer and healthier lives.

ISAAC ASIMOV
Scientist and author

ROCKETS TO THE MOON

On March 16, 1976, leaders in the field of rocketry gathered to watch a rocket launching at the Goddard Space Flight Center in Greenbelt, Maryland. The rocket took off, rose to a height of 100 feet (30 meters), and fell back to earth. The crowd of onlookers, among them people whose work had helped to send rockets to the moon, applauded and cheered. What was there about a five-second rocket flight that deserved cheers?

The occasion for cheers was the re-enactment of an event that had taken place 50 years before. On a cold afternoon in 1926, Dr. Robert H. Goddard, a professor at Clark University in Worcester, Massachusetts, flew the first liquid-fueled rocket. Only four people saw the original flight—Dr. Goddard; his wife, Esther; and two of Goddard's assistants from the university. Flame and white smoke shot from the 10-foot (3-m) rocket as the mixture of gasoline and liquid oxygen burned. With a roar, the rocket rose from its supporting frame, slowly at first, then much faster, to a height of 41 feet (12.5 m). It then arched over, and fell 184 feet (56 m) from its launching site. The flight lasted less than three seconds. So began the kind of flight that would one day reach the moon and distant planets.

Solid-fueled rockets are an old invention. They were first used by the Chinese as long ago as the 13th century. The solid fuel that propelled them was gunpowder. Goddard experimented with solid fuels, but found they were not right for the bold idea he had in mind. That idea, described in a report to the Smithsonian Institution in 1919, was to send a rocket to the moon. Gunpowder and other solid fuels were not powerful enough for the purpose. And the rate at which these solid fuels burned could not be accurately controlled. Goddard's solution to these problems was to build liquid-fueled rockets.

Many people refused to believe that Goddard's ideas would work. On January 13, 1920, an editorial in *The New York Times* questioned whether Goddard, a professor of physics, understood his own field. He had surprised many people by stating that a rocket could work in the vacuum of space. This notion seemed to contradict basic principles of physics as they were then understood. Forty-nine years later, in 1969, the *Times* apologized. The apology appeared in the paper during the flight of the Apollo 11 spacecraft. This craft, propelled by rockets through the vacuum of space, landed men on the moon.

Robert H. Goddard with the first liquid-fueled rocket (left). Half a century later, man had reached the moon with the help of liquid-fueled rockets like the Saturn 1B (right).

THE CONCORDE CONTROVERSY

The Concorde supersonic transport plane resembles a sleek, long-nosed bird in flight. It can cross the Atlantic Ocean in less than 4 hours, or about half the time of conventional passenger jets. It can travel so fast because it flies at about twice the speed of sound— 1,350 miles (2,170 kilometers) an hour. (A plane that travels faster than the speed of sound is called a *supersonic transport*—SST.)

The Concorde venture is a joint project of France and Britain. It took thirteen years of planning, developing, and building to produce the six Concordes that were flying in 1976. But in spite of its name—which means agreement or harmony—the Concorde has been a continuing source of controversy.

Its backers feel that the Concorde is an important technological achievement that could usher in a new age of supersonic air transportation. Its opponents say it represents a hazard to the environment, is noisy, wastes fuel, and is economically inefficient.

The Concorde's danger to the environment, and the noise it creates, are at the center of the controversy. Opponents claim that the Concorde's exhaust emissions would reduce the ozone layer of the atmosphere. (Ozone acts as a shield against a harmful excess of ultraviolet rays from the sun.) In addition, they say that the Concorde is considerably noisier than conventional passenger jets, which fly at less than the speed of sound. Advocates

of the Concorde say the danger is exaggerated, and that supersonic military aircraft have been flying for years without depleting the ozone layer. The noise, they argue, is about the same for supersonic and conventional jets.

The first scheduled passenger flights of the Concorde were made from London, England, to Bahrain in the Persian Gulf, and from Paris, France, to Rio de Janeiro, Brazil, in January, 1976. Concorde opponents strongly resisted flights to the United States. This caused diplomatic problems with the British and French governments, which threatened to refuse American passenger jets some landing privileges in their countries. The controversy finally went to the U.S. Department of Transportation to be resolved.

The Department of Transportation decided to permit a limited number of landings at Washington, D.C., and New York City for a 16-month trial period. The first American flights took place in May, 1976, between London and Washington, and Paris and Washington. Noise-control tests were inconclusive. Opposition to Concorde landings in New York, however, remained strong, and the supersonic transport had yet to make its first flight there.

Two sidelights on the issue: A Russian version of the Concorde, the TU-144, makes regular domestic flights. An American supersonic transport project was rejected by Congress in 1971.

Aurora borealis: beautiful northern lights reflected in an Alberta lake.

CANADIAN WONDERS

Canada is a large country. Sitting atop the North American continent, it has great forests, deep northern lakes, and a variety of climates and terrains. And like most vast countries, it has many natural wonders—some of them beautiful, some of them puzzling, and all of them interesting. Here are a few of Canada's most fascinating wonders.

▶ AURORA BOREALIS

Canadians, especially those who live in the far north of their vast country, are often treated to a natural wonder that is very beautiful to see—the northern lights. Although the northern lights can be seen in many places in the Northern Hemisphere, the displays are at their most beautiful in the far northern reaches of Canada. The northern lights are called au-

rora borealis by scientists. In the Southern Hemisphere the equivalent phenomenon is called aurora australis. ("Aurora" was the name of the Roman goddess of the dawn. Scientists call the northern and southern lights auroras because they can look like the most spectacular sunrises imaginable—except that they're usually seen at night!)

Auroras, wherever they occur, are caused by charged particles called ions, which emit tiny sparks of light. The ions are concentrated high in the earth's atmosphere, where they are created by particles from the sun. These particles come nearest to the earth's atmosphere in the polar regions. So the closer to the North or South Pole you live, the more likely you are to see the night skies aglow with beautiful colored lights.

▶ BONAVENTURE ISLAND

When you first see Bonaventure Island, which lies off Quebec's Gaspé Peninsula, you will probably think you're imagining things. The whole island will appear to be alive—and feathered. And, in a sense, it is. For almost any time you approach Bonaventure Island, it will be covered with birds, thousands of birds.

Bonaventure Island is a bird sanctuary. It attracts all kinds of birds, but its most numerous inhabitants by far are gannets. Gannets are lovely white seabirds, and Bonaventure is the ideal haven for them. They can perch on the island's rocky crags and ledges, and nest there, too. And when they're hungry, they can dive into the sea for fish, the favorite food of gannets everywhere.

Bonaventure Island: a place of safety for thousands of Canadian birds.

The tidal bore: a wall of water moving up New Brunswick's Petitcodiac River.

Magnetic Hill: the mysterious place where up is really down.

MAGNETIC HILL
TO APPRECIATE THIS
PHENOMENON PROCEED
TO SPOT INDICATED
BY WHITE POST
TURN OFF MOTOR
RELEASE BRAKES

Vancouver: a northern city with almost southern gardens and lawns.

▶ THE TIDAL BORE

The tides in the Bay of Fundy cause a number of strange and sometimes beautiful things to happen in the rivers that empty into the bay. When the tide comes in, a great wall of water called a tidal bore pushes up the Petitcodiac River, almost reaching the inland city of Moncton, New Brunswick. The tides in the Bay of Fundy are the highest in the world. The difference between high and low tide may be 50 feet (15 meters) or more.

▶ THE MAGNETIC HILL

Which way is up? Visitors who drive to a certain spot outside Moncton, New Brunswick, are amazed when their cars seem to coast uphill. The hill in question is called Magnetic Hill. The truth is, there's no magnet in the hill and it's not even much of a rise. But it is interesting. When you let your car roll "up" this hill, you are really rolling down. It sounds like something that might happen in *Alice in Wonderland*. But it is actually an optical illusion, a trick your eyes and your senses play on you. There is something about the pitch of this road in relation to the surrounding countryside that makes you feel as if you are going up when you're going down. It is like another experience you may have had.

Have you ever been in a train in a railroad station and looked out the window at another train, which was moving past you on the next track? I bet you had the feeling, if only for a few seconds, that your train, too, was moving. That is another example of an illusion, a trick played on you by your senses.

▶ LUSH VANCOUVER

Take a look at this photograph. Where would you say it was taken? In the southern part of the United States? Near the capital of a Latin American country? Surprisingly, this is a photograph of Queen Elizabeth Park, which is situated on a hill overlooking the handsome city of Vancouver, British Columbia. And Vancouver is quite far north, as you'll see if you check its location on a map. It's almost as far north as Alaska and the legendary world of dogsleds and fur parkas.

The truth is that moist, mild winds from the Pacific Ocean bring moderate temperatures and a great deal of rain to the coastal parts of British Columbia. In these areas, lush gardens and parks like this stay green almost all year long. In neighboring Alberta, which lies inland and is cut off from the moist Pacific winds by mountains, you're suddenly in the north, with little chance of having your rose bushes bloom in January, as they do in Vancouver.

CB: EVERYBODY'S TALKING

"There's a skating rink east of the hole in the wall. Good numbers." This strange-sounding message is no mystery to people who talk and listen on Citizens Band (CB) radio. Translated, the message says, "The road on the east side of the tunnel is slippery. Best regards, and take care."

For many people who are on the go, CB radio has become a substitute for the telephone. A stranded motorist calls for help on the CB set in his car. Fishermen swap information about where the big ones are biting. One driver warns another about dangerous road conditions. But mostly, people talk to other people to pass the time.

By the end of 1976, some 12,000,000 "good buddies" (male CB users) and "good ladies" (female CB users) were filling the air with their code-like conversations in the United States and Canada. Perhaps the best known of the good ladies was Betty Ford, wife of U.S. President Gerald R. Ford. The popularity of CB is growing at a tremendous rate, and there are hundreds of CB clubs. Some experts believe that soon there will be as many CB sets as there are TV sets. One reason for the popularity of CB is its low cost. Some sets may be bought for less than $100.

A typical CB radio set is about the size of this book, or smaller. It is called a transceiver because it both transmits and receives messages. Large transceivers, called base stations, are usually set up at a fixed location, such as a home or an office. Smaller sets, called mobile units, are installed in autos, trucks, boats, and planes. A base station has a maximum range of about 20 miles (over 30 kilometers). Mobile units have shorter ranges.

Operating a transceiver is easy. There is a volume knob to raise or lower the sound coming from a speaker or earphones. There is a microphone with a button that is pressed down when one is talking, and released when listening. A dial, like the tuning dial of a TV set, is turned to bring in any one of the 40 channels used for CB. When you choose a particular channel, say channel 16, everyone within range whose set is tuned to that channel can hear you. Those whose sets are tuned to any other channel cannot hear you.

There are many CB users but only a few channels. Because of this, conversations should be limited to five minutes, to give others a chance to talk. Some people pay no attention to this, so there is a good deal of breaking in and interference. Like any other invention, CB can be put to good uses and bad ones. Among its best uses, CB can help prevent accidents, and help people who are sick or injured or in some other difficulty.

A 23-channel mobile CB transceiver.

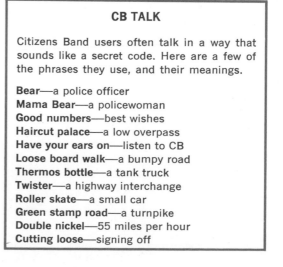

CB TALK

Citizens Band users often talk in a way that sounds like a secret code. Here are a few of the phrases they use, and their meanings.

Bear—a police officer
Mama Bear—a policewoman
Good numbers—best wishes
Haircut palace—a low overpass
Have your ears on—listen to CB
Loose board walk—a bumpy road
Thermos bottle—a tank truck
Twister—a highway interchange
Roller skate—a small car
Green stamp road—a turnpike
Double nickel—55 miles per hour
Cutting loose—signing off

BIOFEEDBACK—
A NEW KIND OF MEDICINE?

What is this young woman doing? Listening to beautiful sounds? Wrong! She is demonstrating how to get rid of a headache, with a method called biofeedback.

Many headaches arise from the tensions of everyday life. People worry about many things —being late for an appointment, failing a test, losing a job, or not having enough money. An overtightness of some muscles, called muscle tension, usually comes along with tension headaches.

Researchers have found that many tension headaches can be relieved if the patient is taught to relax the muscles of the forehead. The electrodes on this young woman's forehead sense the tightening, or contraction, of these muscles. The electrodes are connected to the boxlike machine, called an electromyograph (EMG). When there is even the tiniest contraction of her muscles, the EMG sends the patient this information, or feedback, by causing clicks in her earphones. By concentrating on preventing the clicks, the patient learns to relax the muscles of her forehead.

Soon after scientists began working with feedback in the 1960's, it became clear that some long-held ideas about the body's activities would have to be changed. We can control many activities of our bodies—bending, walking, chewing, and so on. These are called voluntary activities. Other activities, such as the rate at which the heart beats or the strength of the blood pressure, were thought to be involuntary—beyond our control.

But the biofeedback experimenters showed that many people could be trained to control "involuntary" activities. The key to this training is feedback—being made aware of what is happening within the body. For example, an electronic instrument may be set up to monitor a person's heartbeat. The instrument sounds a tone that rises if the heart beats faster, and falls if the beat slows. By listening to the changing tones, some people can learn to control their heartbeat rate. After a time they may be able to do this without the help of the instrument, although they are unable to explain how they do it.

In the same way, people can control their blood pressure and body temperature with biofeedback training. Others have learned to increase the production of one type of brain wave (alpha waves) or change the amount of digestive juice made by the stomach.

There is much excitement about using biofeedback in treating illness. In experiments, patients who have high blood pressure have learned to regulate their pressure without the use of drugs. Patients suffering from irregular heartbeat have learned to control the rate themselves. Biofeedback therapy promises to be valuable in other diseases too. But there are hard questions that must be answered first. Will biofeedback work with enough patients to make the treatment worthwhile? Can the patient successfully continue the therapy at home without supervision? The biofeedback researchers are working hard to find the answers.

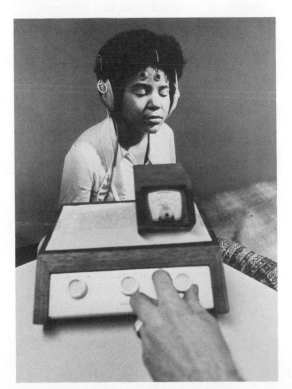

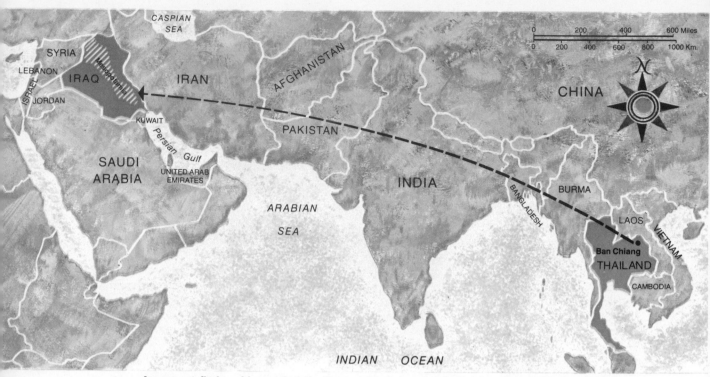

Are recent finds evidence that the Bronze Age began in Thailand and spread to Mesopotamia?

WHEN WAS THE BRONZE AGE?

Archeologists recently made some surprising discoveries in northeastern Thailand. Their finds may upset some long-held beliefs about where and when the Bronze Age began.

As ancient civilizations developed, the people learned to make the tools and weapons they needed from the materials they found. At first, they used the handiest material of all—stone. The people who used stone tools and weapons are said to have lived in the Stone Age. But people are curious and want to make their lives easier. In time, Stone Age people learned to make and use bronze. This metal is much better than stone for making strong, durable tools and weapons. After the Bronze Age, people moved on to the Iron Age—they discovered how to use iron ore, and they found it better for their needs than bronze. One of the ways in which scientists can judge the advance of a particular prehistoric civilization is to find out which metals its people used to make the things they needed.

Until now, most archeologists have believed that the Bronze Age began about 5,000 years ago in Mesopotamia—an area located in what is now the modern country of Iraq. The archeologists also thought that the making of bronze must have spread from Mesopotamia to other parts of the ancient world. These beliefs are now being challenged by new discoveries.

In the early 1960's, archeologists working in Ban Chiang, a village in northeastern Thailand, were testing pieces of broken pottery they had found scattered around the village. They were amazed when their dating tests showed that some of the pottery was nearly 6,000 years old. The National Museum of Thailand and the University of Pennsylvania organized an expedition and began digging at Ban Chiang. They found a treasure of ancient artifacts (as scientists call articles made by humans). The artifacts near the surface were about 2,000 years old. But as they dug deeper their finds got older and older. At a depth of

22 feet (7 meters) some objects as old as 5,600 years were uncovered. At first, the scientists were so surprised that they thought their dating tests were not working correctly. But more and newer dating tests were made, and the extraordinary findings were announced in 1976.

Pottery, stone, and glass objects were found at Ban Chiang and other sites in the area, as were many tools, weapons, and ornaments made of metal. Among the artifacts was a 5,600-year-old spearpoint, which may be the oldest bronze object known. There were also skeletons of people and of animals.

How do the findings at Ban Chiang challenge the theory that the Bronze Age began in Mesopotamia and spread from there? First, dating tests show that some bronze artifacts from Ban Chiang are older than those from Mesopotamia. The second reason has to do with the makeup of bronze, which is an alloy —a mixture—of copper and tin. Almost no tin is found in Mesopotamia. But Thailand has rich deposits of tin and copper. Can it be that the Bronze Age began in tin-rich Thailand and spread to Mesopotamia? The digging now going on at several new sites in northeast Thailand may help to answer that question.

Artifacts unearthed at Ban Chiang: pottery, bronze bracelets, and a bronze spearpoint.

Scientists of the Loch Ness expedition lower an elapsed-time camera into the lake. The camera will automatically take a picture every 15 seconds.

OPERATION NESSIE

In 1976, scientists tried to find out if there really is a Nessie, the monster that is said to live in a lake in Scotland called Loch Ness. They used electronic and photographic equipment, and even a computer, in the most elaborate search so far for the Loch Ness monster. In fact, scientists even gave the legendary creature a real scientific name: *Nessiteras rhombopteryx*. This name is derived from Greek words meaning "Ness marvel with a diamond-shaped fin."

The legend of the monster in Loch Ness seems to have begun in A.D. 565 with St. Columba, an Irish monk. He is said to have been present when a fierce monster killed one man "with a most savage bite," and was just about to kill another. Columba firmly ordered the animal to be off, and the frightened monster is supposed to have retreated into the lake.

For more than 1,400 years, stories of the monster in Loch Ness have turned up regularly. Many people have claimed that they have seen its dragonlike form, swimming in the lake. Hazy photographs taken at various times seem to show something in the lake.

In 1969, Dr. Robert H. Rines of Boston led the first of a series of annual scientific expeditions to Loch Ness. In 1972 and in 1975, instruments detected underwater movements by large objects of some kind. And more fuzzy photographs of "things" in the lake were taken. The 1976 expedition, sponsored by the Academy of Applied Science and *The New York Times,* prepared to follow up these clues.

Underwater photography seems to be the best tool for tracking the monster—but it has a serious drawback. The waters of Loch Ness are murky. In some places the lake is more than 700 feet (over 200 meters) deep. Underwater lights cannot penetrate very far under such conditions. And without light, it is not easy to take clear photographs.

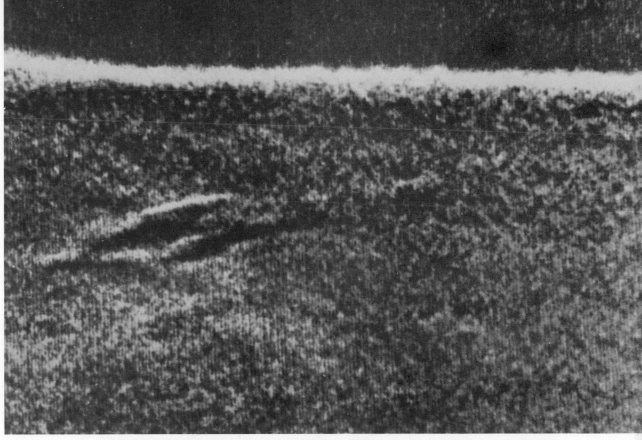

This fuzzy picture, made during the 1976 expedition, shows something in the waters of Loch Ness. The object is about 40 feet (12 m) long. Could it be a living thing?

The 1976 expedition established a base in an area where many of the supposed sightings of the monster have occurred. A floating platform was anchored 300 feet (90 meters) from shore. Frames extending down into the water were attached to the platform. These frames held cameras and lights below the surface. Control and power cables connected the cameras with the scientists' headquarters in a house on the shore.

Several kinds of cameras were used. One, a television camera, was connected to a television monitor at headquarters. The television camera was kept on at all times. There was always a person on duty at the monitor, too. This person was to switch on the other cameras if anything appeared on the monitor. One of the other cameras was a Polaroid. There was also a pair of stereo cameras, which are capable of taking pictures that can be viewed in three dimensions. Still another camera, called an elapsed-time camera, ran continually, taking a picture every 15 seconds.

The scientists also used sonar in their hunt for Nessie. Sonar makes use of pulses of sound waves. These sound waves were sent down into the water from an underwater intrument towed by a boat. The sound waves bounced back to the instrument whenever they hit a solid object—the bottom of the lake, a school of fish, a sunken log, or a monster. The instrument measured the length of time it took the sound waves to return. This told the operator how far down the object was.

The photographic results of the 1976 expedition were disappointing. However, the sonar operations did detect a large object on the lake bottom. Could it be the carcass of a monster? Perhaps, but it could also be a sunken boat or some other large object. Dr. Rines and other scientists plan to resume the hunt in 1977. Besides using the photographic and sonar equipment, the scientists expect to send down divers. No one is willing to give up the hunt for *Nessiteras rhombopteryx*—better known as Nessie.

A GEM OF A MUSEUM

Can you imagine walking into a museum and finding yourself at the entrance to a cave? And not just any old cave—but a cave whose walls are lined with glittering treasure! No, you have not been carried by some magic carpet into the land of *The Arabian Nights*. You have found this wondrous place just by making an expedition to the new Hall of Minerals and Gems, which opened in May, 1976, in New York City's American Museum of Natural History.

The shivery sense of excitement and mystery you feel at the Hall's entrance—as if you were walking into an underground cavern with hidden secrets waiting at every turn—never leaves you. For even though the Hall is not actually a cave, the rooms have been designed with curving walls, and are built on different levels to suggest a cave's sloping ground and many niches and ledges. Dim lighting and earth-toned carpeting on the walls and floors add to the feeling of being in the original home of the earth's mineral treasures.

The walls of the first room you enter are studded with meteorites. These are the "shooting stars" that fall to earth from outer space.

Farther on, in the other rooms, is every sort of rock and gem imaginable. They range from a huge 4½-ton block of copper ore to a tiara made of 1,040 diamonds given by Napoleon to the Empress Josephine.

Some famous jewels hold center stage in the gem room. These include the Star of India sapphire, the deLong Star Ruby, and the Patricia and Schettler emeralds. Lining this room's outer walls are brilliantly lit glass cases displaying such beautiful semiprecious stones as opals, garnets, amethysts, and tourmalines.

A number of very large exhibits are not glass-enclosed, but are right out in the open—and visitors are urged to touch them. You can run your hands over a gigantic topaz from Brazil. You can sit down on a stool made of petrified wood. And, best of all, you are invited to slide down a 2½-ton slab of jade from Poland if you have a mind to.

The planners of the Hall of Minerals and Gems give you every bit as much fun and adventure as you could hope for. Visiting it is almost as thrilling as seeking and finding all these rocks and jewels for yourself. The gem museum itself is a rare and wonderful gem.

The orange-yellow color of this 100-carat sapphire from Ceylon is called padparadschah, or lotus flower. It is a very rare color for sapphire, which is typically blue.

This 215.85-carat black opal, found in Australia, is called the Harlequin Prince. (A harlequin opal has many brilliant colors and is of high quality.)

When you wander through the cave-like atmosphere of the Hall of Minerals and Gems, you will find many treasures—like this case of magnificent minerals.

Above: The famous Star of India (a star sapphire) was mined in Ceylon centuries ago. It is a little larger than a golf ball and weighs 563.35 carats.

This 9-inch-high (23-cm) statue of Kuan-yin, the Chinese goddess of mercy, is carved from chloro-melanite, an unusual, deep green variety of jade.

Left: Nothing is definitely known about the history of the 107.46-carat Rojtman Diamond. It is noted for its beauty and purity.

The Schettler Emerald was mined in Colombia and engraved in India, where it was worn as a head ornament by a Hindu prince some 300 years ago.

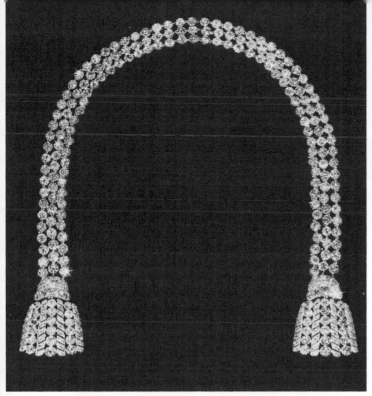

The Bicentennial Diamond Necklace was made in England in 1776, and contains about 500 diamonds. It is believed to have been ordered by King George III for the Duchess of Marlborough.

Dogs were a typical subject of Chinese art. This handsome one was carved from translucent rose quartz within the past hundred years.

This altar vase was probably once used in Chinese Buddhist ceremonies in the 18th century. It is made of jadeite, and carved with intricately entwined dragons.

This fragile elephant and the globe it is carrying were carved from flawless clear rock crystal by a Japanese craftsman.

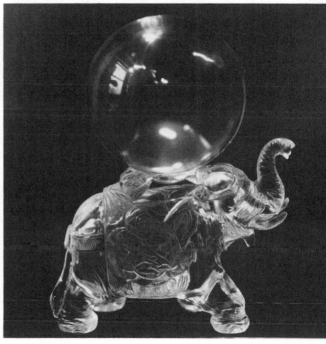

1976: A YEAR OF DISASTERS

Earthquakes, great storms, and other natural disasters occur every year. But 1976 will be remembered as a year in which natural disasters were widespread and severe.

▶ **MAJOR EARTHQUAKES**

The most terrible event of the year was the earthquake that shook China in July. Two enormously powerful shocks, measuring 8.2 and 7.9 on the 9-point Richter scale, shook the area near Peking, the capital of the People's Republic of China. Tangshan, an industrial city about 100 miles (160 kilometers) from Peking, was almost completely destroyed. At least 650,000 people were killed by the Chinese earthquake, and many more were left homeless. For weeks after the major quake, millions of people in this densely populated area of China slept in the streets. They feared they would be trapped in collapsing buildings if further quakes came while they slept.

The disaster in China was the worst in a grim series of earthquakes that had begun in Guatemala in February. More than 22,000 people lost their lives in Guatemala. In May an earthquake in northern Italy killed about 1,000 people. As a result of the quake, Gemona, an ancient Italian hill town, was almost completely destroyed. Two quakes, one in June and one in July, together killed over 1,000 people in Indonesia. In August, the southern portion of the Philippine Islands was struck by a tsunami. Tsunamis are giant waves —commonly called tidal waves—stirred up by underwater earthquakes. More than 3,000 people were killed in this disaster. In early November a series of five earthquakes hit, first in China, then in the Philippines, Japan, Iran, and Greece. In late November an extremely severe earthquake, measuring 7.9 on the Richter scale, struck eastern Turkey. About 4,000 people were killed.

Many earth scientists believe that the great earthquakes of 1976 were not separate events. They believe they were all connected. They base this belief on the theory that the outer crust of the earth is made up of a number of large, flat plates that rest on a lower layer of the earth called the mantle. The material of the mantle shifts, but it shifts very slowly, carrying along the plates of the crust. At the point where two moving plates meet, their edges usually slide past one another. But the edges sometimes catch, and block the motion. This causes enormous pressure to build up. The pressure finally causes a sudden slippage of the plates. This sudden motion is what we call an earthquake.

Earthquakes are most likely to occur where edges of the plates that make up the earth's crust meet. One such area, called an earthquake belt, stretches through Japan, China, and Southeast Asia to the Mediterranean Sea. Many of the places that were struck by terrible earthquakes in 1976 were in this earthquake belt.

Scientists are not just learning more about what causes earthquakes. They are also learning more and more about how to predict when and where they will occur. To the trained earth scientist, the tilt of the land, the level of underground water, and many other measurements are vital clues. American scientists successfully predicted a small earthquake in California in 1976. Chinese experts had predicted a major quake in the area of Peking, too. Unfortunately, they were unable to predict exactly when the quake would occur.

In addition to earthquakes, there were other major disasters in the world in 1976. In the northern Philippines, typhoon Olga caused floods that killed more than 200 people.

One event that could have been a major disaster seemed to have turned out well. La Soufrière, a volcano on the Caribbean island of Guadeloupe, became unusually active in July. It blew out gases and great batches of glowing rocks. In August there was an explosion within the volcano. Fortunately, thousands of people living near La Soufrière had been moved to safer places. But in spite of the eruptions and the many small earthquakes they triggered, there was no great damage done. The residents of Guadeloupe hope that their famous volcano will calm down soon— and stay that way.

This Englishman may have been thinking of breaking the law by fishing in this reservoir, but in the summer of 1976 it wouldn't have done him much good.

▶ DROUGHT IN BRITAIN

In Europe one of the worst droughts of the 20th century ruined crops in many countries. Some of the hardest-hit areas in Britain had no rain for nearly five months.

In fact, Britain faced a major drought disaster until well into the fall, when the familiar rain pattern of the islands began to come back. For Britain, it was the worst drought since the British began keeping records of their weather, in 1727. Meteorologists estimated that it was probably the worst drought in 500 years.

The ruined field crops and parched grazing lands were a severe blow to Britain's farm economy and to the British economy as a whole. And shrinking water reserves, especially in London and other large cities, became alarming. However, the lack of rain was a severe emotional blow to the people of Britain, too. All their lives they had heard bad jokes about how wet their homeland was. There were countless stories about mists and fogs and endless rainfall—and very little sun. The British had learned to live with their odd climate and even to like it. Britain became famous for manufacturing good raincoats and umbrellas. And people bought them all over the world. (The theory being that if anyone knew how to make a raincoat or an umbrella, the British did.) But for Britain to be without rain seemed almost unbelievable—in addition to being inconvenient.

One of the most conspicuous victims of the drought was the legendary Thames River, which usually flows charmingly through pretty villages, majestically through London, and rapidly on to the sea. The Thames had become a trickle in the villages, was less than majestic in London, and had very little water, relatively speaking, to carry on to the sea. And another odd thing was happening. The Thames was leaking. Scientists discovered, at the height of the drought, that on one particularly hard hit stretch of the river, water was being drawn off the river by the parched fields surrounding it. This is exactly the reverse of the way things should be. Rivers normally drain water off the land. But land isn't normally as dry as the land was along the Thames in 1976.

1976 was, indeed, a year of disasters.

DIGGING UP THE PAST

A tablet found in Ebla, an ancient kingdom.

The foundations of one of Ikhnaton's temples.

All the world's a place for archeologists to seek out the past. Among their recent findings have been clues to a great empire in the Middle East, a temple in Egypt, a lost civilization in Colombia, and a statue of the Buddha in India.

▶ EBLA

Egypt and Mesopotamia (which today is in Iraq) were the great centers of commerce and culture in the ancient world. In late 1975, archeologists digging in northern Syria uncovered evidence of another great kingdom, called Ebla, that rivaled the civilizations of Egypt and Mesopotamia. At its height, 4,300 years ago, Ebla had a population of more than 250,000.

Thousands of cuneiform tablets have been found in Ebla. These are flat pieces of baked clay containing an ancient form of writing. They tell of the trade carried on by the kingdom, and of Ebla's conquests of other ancient cities. Some of the words and names on the tablets are similar to those used by the ancient Hebrews. The language of the Eblaites may even be one of the oldest of all the Semitic languages.

▶ THE TEMPLE OF IKHNATON

The ancient Egyptians worshiped thousands of gods until the reign (1366–1349) of the pharaoh Ikhnaton (Akhnaton). Ikhnaton decreed that only a single god, the sun god Aton, was to be worshiped. He built eight temples in Aton's honor. After Ikhnaton's death, the Egyptians again began to worship many gods, and the eight temples were destroyed. Because Ikhnaton is an important figure in the history of religion, archeologists have been searching for the temples for many years.

In 1976 the foundations of one of these temples were uncovered at Thebes, in upper Egypt. There was also a stone block identifying the structure as part of the temple Gem-Pa-Aton. About a hundred pieces of relief, a kind of sculpture in which the designs are raised off the surface, were also found.

Great stone statues carved by the Agustinianos.

A statue of the Buddha found in India.

▶ THE AGUSTINIANOS

The village of San Agustín lies high in the Andes mountains of South America. It looks like any other village in southern Colombia—until you are shown the Forest of the Statues. More than a hundred great stone statues of gods, men, and animals are there. They were carved thousands of years ago by a mysterious people, whom archeologists call the Agustinianos.

It is believed that the Agustinianos came to the area in the 6th century B.C. and stayed for about 2,000 years. But no one knows where the Agustinianos came from and why they disappeared—all long before the Spaniards came to the New World. Over the years, the statues were covered by forest and disappeared from sight. About 50 years ago archeologists began uncovering this lost civilization.

In addition to the statues, they found ceremonial fountains, tombs, and burial mounds. And they are still searching, hoping to uncover more of the lost world of the Agustinianos.

▶ KAPILVASTU

The teachings of the Buddha are the basis of one of the world's great religions, Buddhism. The Buddha lived more than 2,500 years ago in India. It is believed that he spent the first 29 years of his life in the ancient Indian city of Kapilvastu.

In 1976 a statue of the Buddha was found in ruins believed to be those of Kapilvastu. Among other finds made by archeologists was a large soapstone casket. An inscription on the lid of the casket is said to identify the contents as the ashes of the Buddha.

119

GRANDMUMMY TIY

Do you know what a mummy is? Now, of course, we are not talking about your relative. We are asking about the other kind of mummy—the kind that is kept in museums.

A mummy is a dead body—usually of an ancient Egyptian—that has been preserved by a complicated method and wrapped with strips of linen. Ancient Egyptians believed that if they were to find comfort after death, their bodies and the things they used in their life had to be preserved.

When a dead body was placed in its tomb, all sorts of useful items were placed there with it. These included clothing, furniture, cooking utensils, and food. Royal tombs contained especially valuable items.

Through the centuries grave robbers have carried off nearly all the treasures from the old Egyptian tombs. But in 1922 one tomb was found whose burial chamber had never been robbed. This was the tomb of King Tutankhamen, who died about 1343 B.C. at about the age of 20. It is from this tomb, and the magnificent belongings found in it, that we know what Egyptian royal tombs were like. People have even come to feel they know the pharaoh who died so young, and they continue to use the nickname given him at the time of the tomb's discovery, King Tut.

Besides the furnishings of this tomb, which included a gorgeous throne covered with gold and ceramic, a locket was found containing a twist of a woman's hair. An inscription on the locket said the hairs were from the head of Queen Tiy (pronounced "tee"), King Tut's grandmother. This locket became one of the major clues in a detective story, for Queen Tiy herself had long been a missing person. The mummies of most of her royal relatives had long ago been found and placed on display in the Cairo Museum in Egypt. But Queen Tiy's mummy was not among them.

In 1976 Queen Tiy was discovered. Actually, her mummy had been found way back in 1898, but it had not been recognized, because the busy grave robbers had stolen her identification. For years Queen Tiy's mummy was thought to be that of an ordinary woman. Then in 1976 an American scholar, who was studying a photograph of this mummy, noticed something odd. He noticed that one of her arms lay across her chest in a way usually seen only in the royally born. Could this be Queen Tiy? he asked himself.

To answer this question required the work of experts. First the mummy itself, which was in Egypt, had to be examined. X rays were made of her skull and facial bones. These X rays were compared with X rays that had been made earlier of Queen Tiy's mother, Thuyu, and Queen Tiy's grandson, Tutankhamen. The "mystery mummy" seemed to fit into the family bone-structure pattern.

But the final identification came when a few hairs from the locket from King Tut's tomb were sent to the United States for electronic chemical analysis. This amazing new technique, which bounces beams of electrons off hair, is rather like fingerprinting, since the chemicals in hair differ greatly from person to person. In the case of Queen Tiy, the technique proved beyond a shadow of a doubt that the hairs from the Queen Tiy locket (from King Tut's tomb) and the hairs of the "mystery mummy" were one and the same in chemical composition. After more than 3,300 years, Queen Tiy was to join her royal relatives once again.

A piece of hair is clipped from what is believed to be Queen Tiy's mummy. (It was later compared with hair found in King Tut's tomb.)

BLACKBOARD IN THE SKY

In India, a year-long experiment with television via satellite ended in July, 1976. During that year, millions of farm people in thousands of remote villages became TV fans. Most of them had never even seen a television set before the experiment began.

The project was named *S*atellite *I*nstructional *T*elevision *E*xperiment, or SITE for short. The satellite that was used, called the ATS-6, was lent to India by the United States. Launched in 1974, ATS-6 had first been used to bring TV to remote villages in Alaska and in other parts of the United States.

When the broadcasts in India were being planned, teams of researchers talked with people in various parts of the country. They learned what the villagers' needs were, and what they wanted most to hear about. It was decided that each day there would be 1½ hours of morning programs for children in school, and 2½ hours of evening programs for adults.

The school programs for children became known as "The Blackboard in the Sky." One immediate effect of the programs was a sharp lowering of the school dropout rate, which is very high in India. The broadcasters also found that most of the adult villagers were more interested in information about farming and health than they were in entertainment. The TV programs became so popular that after the experiment had ended, the government began building more ground transmission stations. These stations would take the place of the satellite in bringing television to an information-hungry nation of more than 600,000,000 people.

What use is a satellite in transmitting TV? Television and radio signals travel in straight lines. They do not bend with the curvature of the earth, so they are not received well over long distances. One way to overcome this problem is to build a network of ground stations to relay signals over shorter distances. Another solution to the problem is to use a communications satellite like the ATS-6. The satellite is rocketed to a height of 22,300 miles (35,880 kilometers) above the earth. There it is turned to go into orbit around the earth, exactly over the earth's equator. At that height the satellite takes 24 hours to circle the earth. But the earth rotates on its axis once every 24 hours. As a result, the satellite remains over the same spot on the earth.

Television and radio waves are beamed to the satellite from big antennas on the earth. The satellite amplifies (strengthens) the waves, using electricity generated by its panels of solar cells. The waves are beamed back to earth in a cone-shaped pattern that covers a large part of the earth. In this way, many places scattered over great distances, or hidden by mountain ranges or other obstacles, can receive strong TV signals.

After finishing its Indian assignment in July, ATS-6 was moved back to the Western Hemisphere, to a spot over Ecuador. There it was to be used again for broadcasts to the United States and to Latin America.

Thanks to satellite transmission, these people in a village in India are able to watch TV.

MAPPING THE WORLD

● Do you think the map below looks tilted? That's because you are used to maps that show 48 of the states and the District of Columbia neatly level on the page. On such maps the states of Hawaii and Alaska are usually stuck in somewhere near California and Mexico—not because that is where they are, but because that is where there is space to print them. And usually those two states are the wrong size, compared with the other 48.

Now the U.S. Geological Survey has produced a more accurate map. In this map (below) Alaska and Hawaii are shown in the same scale as the other states, and in the right location. The new map should make the people who live in Hawaii and Alaska feel better, and it may make the rest of us take note of some interesting facts. For example, look at the meridians and parallels (lines of longitude and latitude):

1. Which state is the farthest south?
2. Which state is the farthest west?

3. Which state lies partially in the Eastern Hemisphere?

ANSWERS:

1. Hawaii; 2. Alaska; 3. Alaska, because a few of the islands in the Aleutian chain are west of the 180th meridian, and are thus in the Eastern Hemisphere.

● Look again at the new map made by the U.S. Geological Survey. What is the smallest number of colors that can be used to color the states, so that no two adjacent (touching) states will have the same color?

A map maker can tell you that this map—or any other map, no matter how many areas it has—can be fully colored with only four colors. The map makers have known this for a very long time, but no one was able to prove mathematically that it was so until 1976.

Attempts to work out the map-coloring proof began more than 120 years ago. A graduate student at University College in London had observed that only four colors were used to show all the counties of England on a map. He wondered whether four colors would be enough to color every map. For more than a century, many leading mathematicians tried to work out the proof.

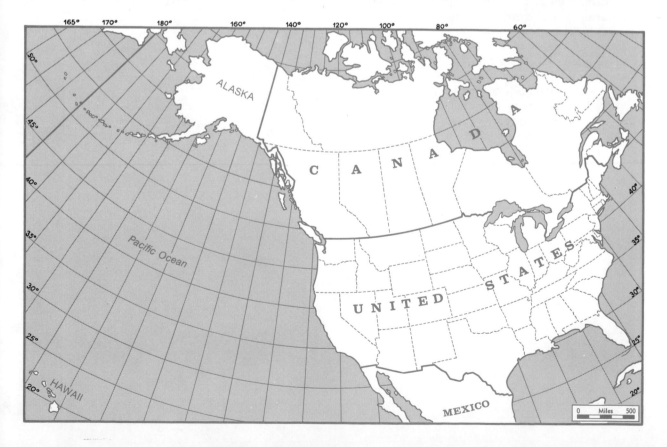

A view of part of the U.S.—Canada border, made by the Landsat satellite.

Partial proofs were worked out, but it was not until 1976 that two professors at the University of Illinois presented the complete proof. They used about 1,200 hours of computer time to do the enormous number of calculations needed. In addition, the two mathematicians and some of their children put in many hours checking parts of the work. The proof is difficult to follow. However, you can see for yourself that four colors are really enough to color the new map of the United States. Do this:

1. Trace the map on a piece of tracing paper.
2. Use four colors of crayons to fill in all the states and provinces on your map. Remember that no two adjacent states or provinces may have the same color. If you wish, you can use the numbers 1, 2, 3, and 4 to stand for the four different colors.

You can also test your knowledge of geography by labeling the states and provinces.

● This view (above) of the earth was taken by a Landsat satellite from a height of 570 miles (920 kilometers). It shows a part of the border between the United States and Canada.

The U.S.—Canada border is the straight line that is running across the middle of the picture. The Canadian provinces of Alberta and a corner of Saskatchewan are above the border, and below it is Montana in the United States. The broad line twisting across the border is the Milk River.

The 49th parallel forms the border between the two countries for a distance of nearly 1,300 miles (about 2,000 km). Like the equator and all the other parallels of latitude, the 49th parallel is an imaginary line. But how does an imaginary line show up in a photograph? This happened because most of the land on the U.S. side is under cultivation, and much of the land on the Canadian side is not. And so two distinct areas, with a boundary line, can be seen.

A Landsat satellite can do much more than merely spot the difference between cultivated and uncultivated land. With the help of a computer, it produces maplike pictures that tell experts a great many things about the land. In this photograph, for example, the red squares and rectangles are fields on which crops are growing, and the light blue ones are fields lying fallow (uncultivated). The roundish areas of bright red are mountains covered with vegetation. Experts looking at pictures made by Landsat can tell what kinds of crops are growing in an area, or even in a single field. They can judge the health of the crops and the moisture of the soil, and can tell where there is water pollution.

The first Landsat was launched by NASA in 1972. (It was then called ERTS, for Earth Resources Technology Satellite.) The second Landsat was launched in 1975. Together the two satellites continue to provide information of enormous value to governments and planners all over the world.

FUN TO MAKE AND DO

This tapestry of the New York City skyline was created by art classes of the Hunter College Elementary School. About 40 boys and girls, from third to sixth grade, took part. Each child stitched a separate building. Then the whole work was put together by their teacher. Notice the children's names embroidered as the whitecaps in the water.

GIANT DICE

MATERIALS:
Two square cardboard boxes
White glue
Tempera paints or felt-tipped pens

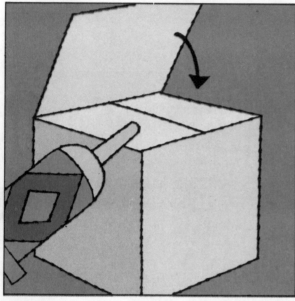

Glue down all the flaps of the boxes.

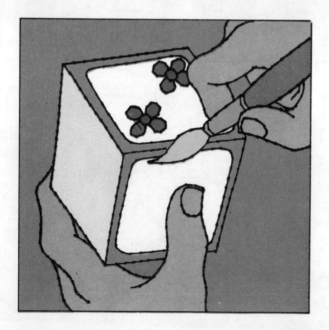

Paint the sides of the boxes. This will provide a background for your pictures. Paint the dice with pictures instead of dots. You can use flowers, butterflies, or anything else you can think of. Just remember that the six must be opposite the one, the five opposite the two, and the four opposite the three.

A LOCH NESS MONSTER MAZE

Place a sheet of tracing paper over this maze of Nessie. Begin at the arrow below and try to find your way out of the maze (to the arrow on your right). If you come to a blind alley, try a different route and a different-colored pencil. Answer on page 383.

COIN COLLECTING

Two events of 1976—the U.S. Bicentennial and the Olympic Games—gave a strong boost to topical coin collecting. Those events inspired many countries to issue commemorative coins. Topical collecting (collecting by subject or theme) has long been popular among stamp collectors. They have been able to choose from among many international stamp issues on a single subject—such as animals, art, history, or sports. Some coin collectors have been interested in topical collecting, too. But until recently there have not been enough issues on a single theme to inspire broad interest.

A major international coinage program began in 1968. At that time countries around the world issued coins to commemorate the Grow More Food theme of the United Nations Food and Agriculture Organization (FAO). Since then, more than 200 coin issues from some 75 countries have been dedicated to that theme, and additional issues are planned. The FAO program set an example that was followed by coin issues honoring International Women's Year (1975). Another program, sponsored by the World Wildlife Fund, began in 1974. This four-year program was dedicated to endangered species of wildlife. The number of multinational coin series honoring the Olympic Games has grown steadily since 1952, when Finland issued commemoratives for the XV Olympiad in Helsinki.

▶ INTERNATIONAL COIN ISSUES, 1976

To honor the U.S. Bicentennial, Poland issued coins commemorating two famous Poles who had fought on the American side in the Revolutionary War. They were Thaddeus Kosciusko and Casimir Pulaski. A number of Bicentennial coins came from the Caribbean area and Central America. An eight-sided gold coin from the Netherlands Antilles (Dutch West Indies) shows the *Andrew Doria,* a ship of the Continental Navy that sailed to those islands in November, 1776, flying an American flag. It saluted the Dutch flag and received a salute in return. That event lives

in history as the first salute by a powerful nation (the Netherlands) to a flag flown by a U.S. naval vessel. The Turks and Caicos Islands issued a pair of coins with portraits of King George III and George Washington. Haiti offered coins showing the siege of Savannah, Georgia, in 1779, in which French and Haitian troops aided the Americans. Nicaragua issued a pair of coins. One shows the Liberty Bell. The other portrays Betsy Ross sewing the first American flag and the astronaut Neil Armstrong placing the first U.S. flag on the moon.

U.S. Bicentennial coins: from Poland, the Netherlands Antilles, Turks and Caicos Islands, Haiti, Nicaragua, and Western Samoa.

Coins from Western Samoa, in the South Pacific, show Paul Revere making his famous ride. The nearby Cook Islands provided a gold $200 commemorative with portraits of Benjamin Franklin and Captain James Cook. A portrait of George Washington appears on a pair of coins from the Isle of Man, in the Irish Sea.

U.S. $2 bill.

In 1975 the United States issued coins—quarter, half dollar, and dollar—with Bicentennial designs. The new $2 Federal Reserve note issued in 1976 has a Bicentennial theme—a portrait of Thomas Jefferson on the face and an adaptation of John Trumbull's painting *The Declaration of Independence* on the back. This new U.S. $2 bill was meant to be a permanent denomination of U.S. currency, replacing a $2 bill last produced in 1966.

Big things also happened in Canadian coinage in 1976. Canada put the finishing touches on its 30-piece coinage tribute to the Summer Games of the XXI Olympiad, held in Montreal. This coinage program, which began in 1973, ended in 1976 with eight silver $5 and $10 coins depicting fencing, boxing, soccer, field hockey, and the Olympic flame, village, stadium, and velodrome (a track for cycling). As a climax, there was a $100 gold piece in

Olympic coins: from Canada, Austria, Western Samoa, and Yemen.

two sizes, each with a different gold content. This was the highest-denomination coin ever issued in North America. It shows the Greek goddess Athena and a victorious athlete.

Austria produced a series of four commemoratives for the Winter Games, held at Innsbruck. Coins honoring the Summer Games also came from Poland, Western Samoa, and Yemen.

RECORD PRICES FOR RARITIES

Price records continued to be broken in 1976. In May a special Canadian silver dollar of 1911—one of a few coins struck in that

Canadian 1911 silver dollar coin.

year but not issued for circulation—sold at auction for $110,000. This was a record for a Canadian coin. Also in May a specimen of the famous U.S. 1913 Liberty nickel sold for $135,000. In January a great hoard (407,000) of cartwheels (U.S. silver dollars) was sold for $7,300,000—the richest sale in numismatic history.

CANDY CURRENCY

Because Italy's mint was unable to produce enough coins in low denominations, many Italians ran out of small change in 1976. But they were resourceful. They substituted a piece of candy for the 10-lira coin (value

This special bag of candy was used as a 10-lira coin in Italy.

about U.S. 1 cent). Other substitutes for small change included postage stamps, bandage strips, matches, and single cigarettes.

CLIFFORD MISHLER
Publisher, *Numismatics News Weekly*

APPLES OF AMBER

Long ago,
during the Renaissance, fine
ladies and gentlemen would sometimes carry
small balls of sweet-smelling substances in their
pockets or on chains around their necks. The wealthier
might have special ball-like cases, often shaped like apples or oranges, to hold the perfume. These cases were made of gold, silver,
crystal, or ivory. Both the perfume and its jeweled case were called a
pomme d'embre ("apple of amber"—"amber" probably meant sweet-smelling
ambergris). In England this became a "pomander." Today, you can have a simple
pomander to hang in your closet or tuck in a drawer to keep your clothes smelling
nice. Or give a pomander as a present to someone you like. Here's how to make one.
You will need an orange—a thick-skinned eating one, not a thin-skinned juice orange.
You will also need lots of cloves, enough to cover nearly the whole orange. You must also
have adhesive tape and some colored ribbon the same width as the tape. At a drugstore in
your neighborhood, you should be able to buy a dram of oil of roses or lavender. Also try
to buy an ounce or two of powdered orris root—it adds to the scent and will help preserve
your pomander. But you can manage without it. Lastly, you will need one old woolen or cotton
glove—the one that fits the hand you do things with.
Now you are ready to begin. Soak a couple of teaspoonfuls of cloves in the oil of roses or
lavender. While they are soaking, take the adhesive tape and wrap it around the orange, from
the navel on top, down around the bottom, and back to the navel again. Now put on your
glove and start pushing the cloves into the orange skin wherever it is not covered by the
tape. Don't forget the cloves soaking in oil—push them in along with the plain ones.
Keep on doing this until the orange skin is covered with cloves. Then, if you have the
orris root, sprinkle the clove-studded orange with it. (If you can't finish all at one
time, lay your half-finished orange on a piece of newspaper in a cool, dry place out
of the way until you can get back to it.)
The last thing to do is to wrap the ribbon around the pomander, right over the
adhesive tape you put on earlier. Make a loop in the ribbon at the top of
the pomander, and hang it in your closet. If you are going to tuck it
into a drawer, leave your pomander out in a cool, dry place for a
few days before putting it with your clothes. And if you are
giving it as a gift, wrap it in some colored tissue paper. What a nice surprise your little,
handmade, scented ball
will be!

IT RUNS IN THE FAMILY

The numbered column lists well-known mothers. The lettered column lists, in jumbled order, their well-known children. Match the numbers and letters so the mothers go with their children.

1.	Maria Theresa	A.	Jacob and Esau
2.	Anne Boleyn	B.	Princess Caroline
3.	Nancy Hanks	C.	Mrs. Mark Phillips
4.	Bathsheba	D.	Marie Antoinette
5.	Elizabeth II	E.	Liza Minnelli
6.	Sarah Delano	F.	Elizabeth I
7.	Queen Isabella	G.	Mrs. Patrick Nugent
8.	Rebecca	H.	George VI
9.	Mary of Teck	I.	Abraham Lincoln
10.	Princess Margaret	J.	Solomon
11.	Judy Garland	K.	Lady Sarah Armstrong-Jones
12.	Lady Bird Johnson	L.	Catherine of Aragon
13.	Princess Grace	M.	Franklin D. Roosevelt

Answers: 1-D; 2-F; 3-I; 4-J; 5-C; 6-M; 7-L; 8-A; 9-H; 10-K; 11-E; 12-G; 13-B

The numbered column lists well-known fathers. The lettered column lists, in jumbled order, their well-known children. Match the numbers and letters so the fathers go with their children.

1.	Powhatan	A.	Mary, Queen of Scots
2.	Abraham	B.	Absalom
3.	Henry VIII	C.	Virginia Dare
4.	John Adams	D.	Caroline and John
5.	Richard M. Nixon	E.	Isaac
6.	John F. Kennedy	F.	Theodosia Alston
7.	David	G.	Alexander the Great
8.	Columbus	H.	Pocahontas
9.	John White (grandfather)	I.	Jemima
10.	Philip of Macedon	J.	Elizabeth I
11.	James V	K.	Julie Eisenhower
12.	Aaron Burr	L.	John Quincy Adams
13.	Daniel Boone	M.	Diego

Answers: 1-H; 2-E; 3-J; 4-L; 5-K; 6-D; 7-B; 8-M; 9-C; 10-G; 11-A; 12-F; 13-I

MAKE A PRESENT

WOOD COLLAGE PAINTING

WHAT TO USE:

Piece of wood or plywood (scrap, usually free, from lumberyard is fine)

Scraps of pictures from magazines, newspapers, etc.

Self-adhesive picture hook

Glue, shellac, sandpaper, scissors, brushes, dust cloth, newspapers

WHAT TO DO:

1. Spread newspapers on your working surface. Dust the piece of wood with a dust cloth. If the edges of the wood are rough, smooth them with sandpaper. Dust the edges too.

2. Cut out and arrange scraps of pictures in a pattern pleasing to you —overlapping, sideways, upside down, or whichever way. Do not neglect to use printed words from magazines or newspapers if they fit your design or if you have a special motif you want to emphasize in the picture. For instance, if the person you are going to give the gift to likes golf, work into your collage the names of golf champions, scores of games, tournaments or whatever. This will show that you really thought of the person to whom you will give the picture.

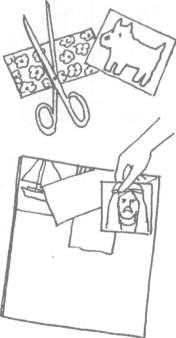

3. After you are satisfied with the design, glue the pieces of picture onto the wood. Let the glue dry completely.

4. Cover your design with shellac and let the shellac dry. Repeat shellacking procedure if you want a really high-gloss finish.

5. Secure a self-adhesive picture hook to the back of the finished picture, about 2 inches (5 centimeters) from the top and in the very center of the picture.

GIFT-WRAPPING PAPER

WHAT TO USE:
Roll of white shelving paper
Stamp pads of various colors
Potato, carrot, cabbage, onion,
empty thread spool, pencil, bottle cork,
gum eraser, newspapers, stapler

WHAT TO DO:

1. Spread plenty of newspapers on your working surface.

2. Cut an onion, potato, carrot, or cabbage in half. It is the texture and the natural design of the vegetable that make your printed design interesting and unusual.

3. Unroll the shelving paper a little at a time. Press whatever objects you decide to print with—the vegetables just mentioned, plus bottle corks, thread spools, gum erasers, etc. —on the stamp pads, then on the paper. Print the design in whatever fashion pleases you. Keep printing slowly until the whole roll of shelving paper is covered with designs.

4. Let the paper dry and then reroll it until you are ready to wrap your gifts in it. Mark the present "Open Before Christmas" or Hanukkah, Easter, Passover or whatever other holiday you may be celebrating.

DECORATED PENCIL HOLDERS

MATERIALS:
A tin can
Yarn
Felt fabric
White glue
Paintbrush
Scissors

A good way to keep your pens and pencils together is to put them in colorful containers. You can even make your own. Here are two ways to make pencil holders, by decorating tin cans with felt fabric or with yarn. The very first thing you must do is to let the can soak in water until all labels are removed. When it is clean, dry the can well. Now you are ready to go ahead and decorate the can. Just follow the directions on these pages.

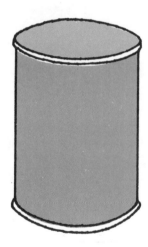

As you apply glue to the can, a little at a time, carefully wrap yarn around it.

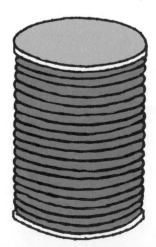

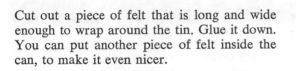

Cut out a piece of felt that is long and wide enough to wrap around the tin. Glue it down. You can put another piece of felt inside the can, to make it even nicer.

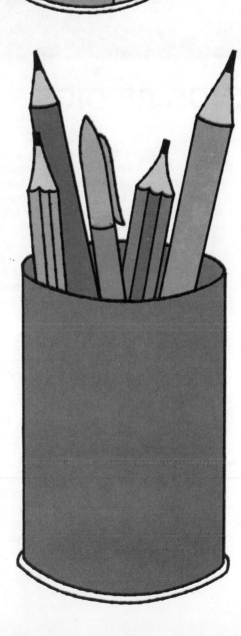

135

OJOS DE DIOS

Ojo de Dios (pronounced O-ho-day-DYOS) means "eye of God" in Spanish. This is the name that the Indians of Mexico and the U.S. Southwest give to the colorful woven designs that they make for their homes to bless their families and keep away evil spirits.

An ojo de Dios is made by crossing two sticks, and then weaving yarn or another fiber around the crossed sticks, making a diamond pattern. The result is so attractive that many people are now buying or making ojos to hang as decorations in their homes.

An ojo can be very large, up to 2 feet (over 60 centimeters) across, or tiny enough to hang from a chain as a pendant. It can be made with elegant metallic thread or with heavy, colorful yarn. The peoples who first created ojos wove them of reeds and other natural fibers, and of course they can still be made from such materials.

Ojos are easy to make. And once you've learned the basic method, it is possible to try some other, more unusual ways of working with them. For instance, you can make them as decorations for special holidays, using the colors of the season. An orange and black ojo would make a very different Halloween decoration and perhaps ward off ghosts! Or give a baby a pastel colored one, or a whole group of small bright ojos to be hung as a mobile over the baby's crib.

Almost everyone enjoys looking at these ancient symbols of good fortune, and presenting one as a gift is a nice way of saying "Good Luck."

▶ **MATERIALS**

> ¼-inch dowel, cut into two 12-inch-long pieces
> Several balls of yarn of different colors
> White glue

Almost any kind of stick can be used to make your ojo—dowels, tree branches, tongue depressors, popsicle sticks, or toothpicks. The type and size of stick you use will be determined by the kind of ojo you are making and by the size you want it to be. A good stick for a first project is a ¼-inch (about 6-millimeter) dowel, cut into two 12-inch-long (30-cm) pieces.

Yarns of various colors and thickness can be used. If a thick yarn is used, the ojo can be made very quickly. You may want to mix textures as well as colors. If you have some nubby yarn around the house, it can be woven into the ojo for a more interesting pattern.

In planning your ojo, you may want to draw a sketch of it in color first. Simply draw a diamond shape on a piece of paper. Then with colored pencils or crayons fill in the shape with the colors you've selected. Experiment with color, trying out different colors next to each other until you hit upon the design you like best.

Bright colors are usually the most effective in an ojo, but you can combine these with more subtle colors. Be guided by your own taste. Do you like fall colors? You may want to use orange, rust, and yellow yarns in an ojo. If you have one favorite color, try combining different shades of it. You might use bright blue, navy blue, light blue, and turquoise, for instance. Don't forget that white, when placed next to other colors, can often give a vivid effect. Tweedy yarns are very pretty, too, especially when combined with solid colors in an ojo.

▶ MAKING YOUR OJO

Now you are ready to start winding.

Figure 1: Cross the two dowels at their centers. Then take the yarn that you have selected for the center of the ojo; use it to lash the dowels together with a slipknot. Wind the

Figure 1

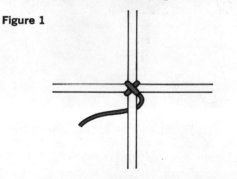

yarn tightly for a few turns in an X shape around the point where the dowels meet in a cross. Do not break off the yarn.

Figure 2: Now, with a pencil, lightly number each of the dowel ends from 1 to 4, counterclockwise. Hold the crossed sticks so that the number 1 is at the bottom. Pick up the yarn and wrap it twice over dowel arm 1 —bring it from left to right over the front, then around the back, and finally over the front again. Pull it tight, winding it so that it

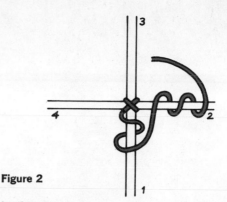

Figure 2

is close to the center. Now carry the yarn up over the front of dowel arm 2; wrap it twice around the dowel. Do the same around dowel arms 3 and 4—up over the front, and around twice. Then come back to dowel arm 1. Continue wrapping in this manner until the center of the ojo is as large as you want it to be, ending on dowel arm 1.

This is what to do if you want to change colors. Finish wrapping the color you are working with on arm 1. Cut the yarn and glue the end down to the dowel. Allow the glue to dry for a few minutes before starting the next color, on dowel arm 2. Begin the new color by winding tightly over the yarn end for several wraps so that it is secure. Start wrapping the new color, beginning with dowel arm 2, working counterclockwise, and ending on dowel arm 2 when you have completed that color.

The next color will begin on dowel arm 3, the following one on dowel arm 4, and so on. You can wrap the entire ojo in this way.

Figure 3: You can get a dimensional effect in your ojo by wrapping one or more colors backward. This is done by winding the yarn

Figure 3

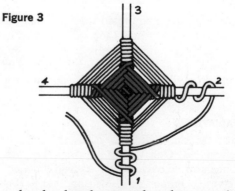

under the dowel arm rather than over it. Attach the yarn and wrap it around the dowel from the back.

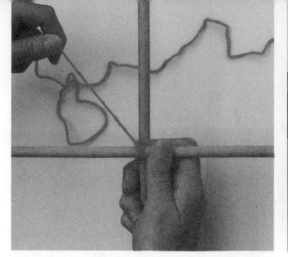

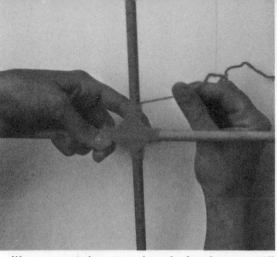

Cross dowels at their centers; lash them together and wind yarn for a few turns in an X shape.

Wrap yarn twice around each dowel arm, until center of ojo is as large as you want it to be.

To change colors, cut yarn and glue the yarn end down to the dowel. Then start next color.

To get a dimensional effect, wrap the yarn backward—under the dowel arm rather than over.

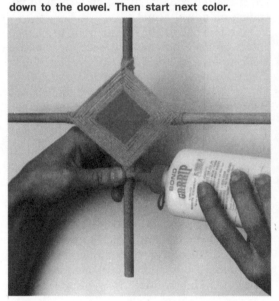

After you have completed the last color on your ojo, attach a small loop of yarn to the end of one of the dowel arms to hang it by. The ends of the dowels can be left plain, can be painted or gilded, or can be wrapped with yarn, gluing the ends in place.

▶ OJO VARIATIONS

There are many other ways to vary the pattern of an ojo. One way is to wrap the yarn only once around each dowel, instead of twice. This gives a tighter look. Still another variation is to use both single and double wrapping in one ojo, changing the pattern as it happens to please your eye.

A fancy ojo might have tassels attached to the end of each dowel. Wrap yarn loosely around your hand, about six times, and cut it off from the ball. Slip the looped yarn off your hand and tie the loops together in the center with a short piece of yarn. Apply glue to the end of the dowel and glue it to the center, where the yarn is tied. Bend the loops down so that they hang below the dowel. Then snip the looped ends and fluff them out.

Whether you're superstitious or not, the ojo de Dios will add a bright spot wherever you hang it.

SYBIL C. HARP
Editor, *Creative Crafts* magazine

WHERE HAVE WE MET?

Do you know these characters from books you have read? Try to match each character with the book in which he or she appears and the author of the book.

CHARACTER	BOOK	AUTHOR
A Henry	1 Great Expectations	m Jim Kjelgaard
B The Boy	2 The Little Prince	n Lewis Carroll
C Puck	3 Alice's Adventures in Wonderland	o Fred Gipson
D Manolo	4 Shane	p Charles Dickens
E Little Arliss	5 A Midsummer Night's Dream	q Marjorie Kinnan Rawlings
F Elsa	6 Shadow of a Bull	r Antoine de Saint-Exupéry
G Pip	7 The Yearling	s William Armstrong
H The rose	8 Born Free	t William Shakespeare
I Jody	9 Old Yeller	u Stephen Crane
J Danny	10 Sooner	v Joy Adamson
K The Mad Hatter	11 The Red Badge of Courage	w Maia Wojciechowska
L Bob	12 Big Red	x Jack Schaefer

Answers: A,11,u; B,10,s; C,5,t; D,6,w; E,9,o; F,8,v; G,1,p; H,2,r; I,7,q; J,12,m; K,3,n; L,4,x.

COVER YOUR BOOKS

MATERIALS:

The book to be covered

Soft or medium cardboard

Two pieces of fabric, such as linen; thin felt; or denim or other heavy cotton

Needle and thread

Strips of elastic

Glue

Utility knife

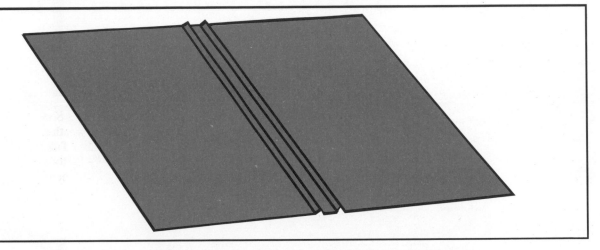

Cut out a piece of cardboard slightly larger than the book you want to cover. Using a utility knife, score lines down the center of the cardboard. Do not cut through the cardboard. Fold to make creases as shown in the picture. This will help your covered book open and close easily.

Cut out a piece of fabric larger than the cardboard. Glue it to the cardboard; turn over the edges of the fabric and glue them down as shown. (This picture shows the strips of elastic. In the next step you will see how to use them.)

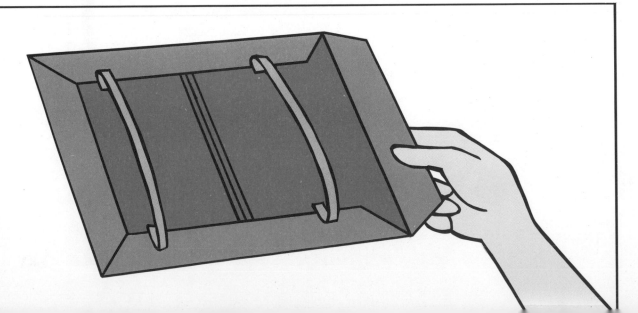

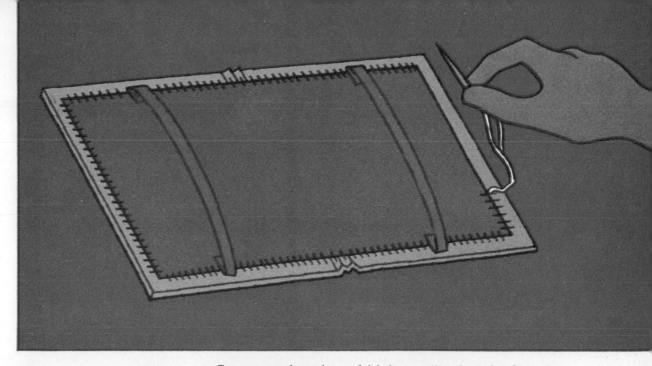

Cut out another piece of fabric, smaller than the first. Sew this piece to the inside of the cover, stitching it to the other piece of material. Do not sew through the cardboard. Take two strips of elastic. Sew them to the cover at top and bottom. You will slip the existing covers of your book under them.

If you wish, you can decorate the outside of your cover with other bits of colored material.

ROCK NECKLACES

Did it ever occur to you that you could take a rock and make it into a piece of jewelry? You can—and it's a lot of fun to do, too. Start with a little imagination, and a small smooth rock. Paint a design on it with tempera paint. Coat the entire rock with varnish or clear nail polish to keep your design permanent. Put white glue around the sides of the rock and press yarn onto it. Glue a loop of yarn to the back, and use a long piece of yarn as a chain.

Your rock necklace is ready to wear!

WHAT'S WRONG HERE?

The people who live in this house are not being careful with energy. How many ways can you find in which energy is being wasted? (Answers are on page 383.)

COME FOR SUPPER

Wouldn't it be fun if, after a Saturday afternoon movie or a school football game, your friends came to your house and you served them a meal that you had actually cooked yourself? Here's a simple supper menu that you can prepare for them. Everything, including setting the table, can be done before you meet your friends in the afternoon. Then, when you get home in the evening, the last-minute putting-together and heating will be quick and easy.

This delicious menu will serve six hungry people.

CHILI CON CARNE

3 tablespoons of shortening (butter, margarine, or oil)
1 large onion, chopped
2 pounds of lean ground beef
1½ cups of tomato sauce
½ cup of catsup
1 teaspoon of salt
1 tablespoon (or more) of chili powder
1 20-ounce can of kidney beans, drained

1. Heat the shortening in a heavy skillet. Add the chopped onion, and cook until the onion is limp and golden. Add the meat, and stir constantly until it becomes brown and loses its raw look.
2. Transfer the meat and onion mixture to a large saucepan, and add tomato sauce, catsup, salt, and chili powder. Stir. Taste to see if you want to add more chili powder.
3. Cover and cook over a low flame for 25 to 35 minutes.
4. Add the drained beans and cook an additional 15 minutes. This dish can be refrigerated, and then reheated at serving time.

HERBED GARLIC BREAD

1 loaf of Italian bread
1 garlic clove, peeled and cut in half
3 tablespoons of softened butter or margarine
1 teaspoon of parsley flakes
½ teaspoon of freeze-dried chives
Aluminum foil

1. Rub the crust of the bread all over with the garlic clove.
2. Slice the bread into 2-inch slices, but don't cut all the way through.
3. Combine the butter or margarine with the parsley and chives. Spread lightly on each slice of bread.
4. Wrap the bread in a sheet of aluminum foil and crimp the edges of the foil tightly together. (Do all this in advance. Then follow step 5 when you are ready to serve.)
5. Place in a preheated 350° oven for 20 minutes. Then place the bread (foil and all) on a long platter and fold the foil down around the loaf.

MIXED SALAD

2 cucumbers, washed and thinly sliced
1 green pepper, washed, cored, and sliced in thin rings
1 bunch of radishes, washed and thinly sliced
1 large head of lettuce, broken into bite-sized pieces

1. Prepare the salad ingredients and place them in a large bowl. Cover with plastic wrap and refrigerate until serving time.
2. When you are ready to serve, toss the salad lightly with just enough of your favorite salad dressing to moisten the ingredients, but not enough to drown them.

BROWNIES

¼ pound of butter or margarine (1 stick)
1 cup of sugar
2 squares of bitter chocolate, melted
¾ cup of unsifted flour
2 eggs
1 teaspoon of vanilla
1 cup of walnuts, in pieces

1. Preheat the oven to 350°
2. Mix the butter and sugar together until smooth and creamy.
3. Add the melted chocolate and mix well.
4. Beat in the flour until the batter is smooth.
5. Add the eggs and vanilla and beat until smooth. Mix in the nuts.
6. Pour the mixture into a greased 9-inch-square baking pan. Bake for about 25 minutes. Do not overbake. When cool, cut into 16 squares.

These brownies may be made in advance and frozen. They will still be delicious days later. Just take them out of the freezer a few hours before you are ready to serve them.

STAMP COLLECTING

Rising prices affected stamp collecting around the world in 1976. More stamps were issued than ever before. One reason was that many countries had raised their postal rates and needed new stamps in higher denominations. The number of collectors increased, and many new stamps were issued to meet their needs. The price of valuable stamps rose as people sought to buy them as an investment.

But higher prices and more stamps did not make news in 1976. Collectors have been aware of these trends for some time. What did make news was the outpouring of stamps around the world to honor a single anniversary or other event, such as the Bicentennial of the American Revolution or the 1976 Olympic Games.

▶ **BICENTENNIAL STAMPS**

The United States has been issuing Bicentennial stamps over a five-year period, beginning in 1972. The first of the 1976 series was a strip of three commemoratives based on a painting, *The Spirit of '76,* by Archibald M. Willard. Next came a sheet of 50 stamps, each showing the flag of one of the 50 states. Sharp-eyed collectors were quick to notice that the flag of one of the states—Tennessee—had been printed upside down. Because the whole issue was printed with this error, it was shared by all collectors.

Four souvenir sheets were issued for IN-TERPHIL 76, the international philatelic exhibition that opened in Philadelphia on May 29. They were the largest such sheets ever issued in U.S. postal history. Each one reproduced a painting of an important event of the Revolutionary War. The four paintings were *The Surrender of Lord Cornwallis* and *The Declaration of Independence* by John Trumbull; *Washington Crossing the Delaware* by Emanuel Leutze; and *Washington Reviewing His Ragged Army at Valley Forge* by William T. Trego. Each sheet contained five stamps of one denomination (13, 18, 24, or 31 cents). The stamps were outlined by perforations so that they could be torn from the sheets and used individually for postage. Fi-

nally, to commemorate its actual 200th birthday—July 4, 1976—the United States issued a strip of four stamps. The four, taken together, showed all of Trumbull's *Declaration of Independence.* (The left third of this painting had been omitted from the souvenir sheet.)

Stamps commemorating the U.S. Bicentennial came from almost every country. Canada and the United States joined in issuing a stamp honoring Benjamin Franklin. Before the Revolutionary War, Franklin had served as a deputy postmaster general of an area that included some of the American colonies and Canada. Later, he became the first U.S. postmaster general. The Canadian–U.S. stamp showed a bust of Franklin against an early map of North America. Britain, Ireland, France, and the Cook Islands also chose Franklin as the subject of Bicentennial stamps.

Besides famous people, other subjects of stamps included U.S. symbols, soldiers and ships of the Revolutionary War period, and great moments of U.S. history, past and present. The stars and stripes of the U.S. flag, together with the Bicentennial star, were used in imaginative ways on stamps from Israel, Chad, the Netherlands, Belgium, South Korea, and other countries. The Cayman Islands used the seals of the original thirteen states and the U.S. Great Seal as symbols on a set of commemoratives. The islands of the Caribbean seemed to specialize in colorful stamps showing Revolutionary War soldiers, weapons, drums, and ships. Some countries chose historical subjects that showed the links between themselves and the United States. Denmark, for example, issued four stamps with ships that sailed between it and America, beginning with Viking times.

▶ **OTHER ANNIVERSARY ISSUES**

Anniversaries—100th, 200th, and even 500th—seemed to dominate the stamp world in 1976. Nations around the globe joined in honoring the 100th anniversary of the invention of the telephone by Alexander Graham Bell. The United States issued its Bell commemorative on March 10. On that very day

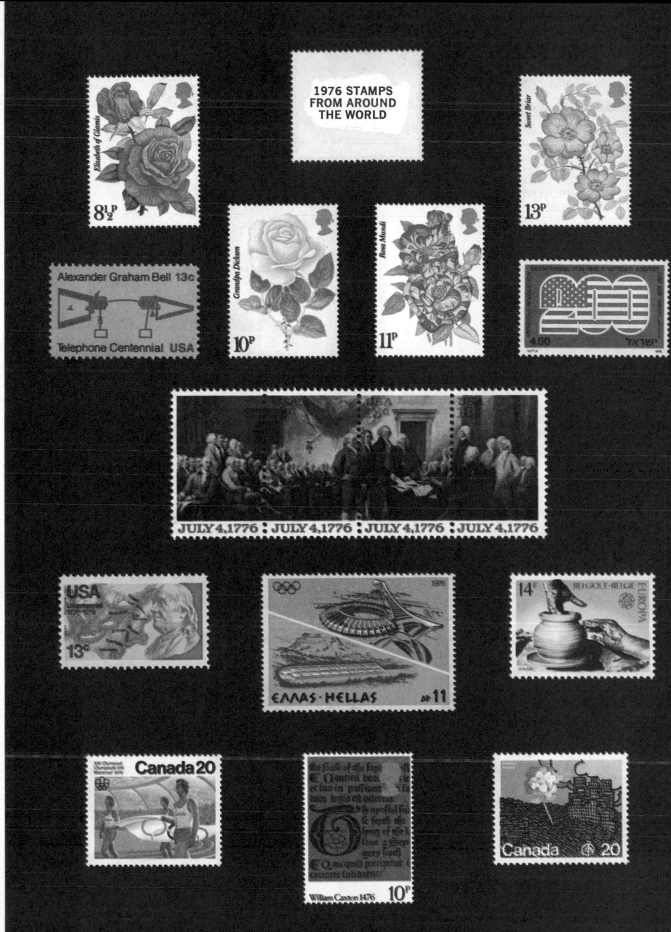

1976 STAMPS
FROM AROUND
THE WORLD

A TOPICAL
COLLECTION
OF SPORTS STAMPS

—100 years earlier—in Boston, Massachusetts, Bell had transmitted the first understandable words by telephone. The U.S. stamp reproduced the drawing that Bell had filed with his application for a patent. Stamps from many other countries showed the first telephone instrument, a picture of Bell, or modern applications of the telephone.

There were several other 100th anniversary stamps. From Britain came four colorful stamps depicting roses, to mark the 100th anniversary of the Royal National Rose Society. One of the roses shown was the Elizabeth of Glamis, named after Queen Mother Elizabeth. The United States issued a stamp commemorating the 100th anniversary of the founding of the American Chemical Society. Another U.S. stamp honored the 100th anniversary of the birth of a heroic young nurse, Clara Maass, who gave her life in the struggle to conquer yellow fever. During experiments in Cuba in 1901, she allowed herself to be bitten by a mosquito that was suspected of carrying the deadly fever, and she died.

The 500th anniversary issue came from Britain. It consisted of four handsome stamps honoring William Caxton, who introduced printing into England in 1476. One stamp shows two styles of type that Caxton used in printing. Two other stamps are examples of woodcuts (of a knight and a chess player) used to illustrate books printed by Caxton; and the fourth shows an early printing office.

▶ OLYMPIC STAMPS

The 1976 Winter and Summer Games produced an array of colorful stamps. Canada —the host country for the Summer Games, held in Montreal—began issuing Olympic stamps in 1973. Among the Canadian stamps issued in 1976 was a dramatic set of three showing Olympic ceremonies—the carrying of the flame, the flag ceremony, and the victory ceremony held after the final contest in each event. Greece, where the games originated, issued a series of stamps showing both the ancient and the modern ways of competing in certain sports. The United States issued a block of four Olympic stamps. Two commemorated the Summer Games; and two, the Winter Games, which were held in Innsbruck, Austria. Stamps from many other countries featured almost every kind of Olympic event.

Canada was also the host country for the Olympiad for the Physically Disabled, or "Wheelchair Olympics," held at Etobicoke, Ontario, in August. To mark this event, Canada issued a stamp showing a contestant in a wheelchair competing in archery.

▶ OTHER STAMPS FROM AROUND THE WORLD

Both Canada and the United Nations issued stamps commemorating a conference that was held in Vancouver, British Columbia, to consider the problems faced by people in urban areas. The conference was called the United Nations Conference on Human Settlements; it was also known as Habitat. The Canadian stamp showed a very crowded city, with a rose springing from the pavement as a symbol of hope. The U.N. stamp featured a globe, surrounded by a design that represented houses. Many countries issued stamps commemorating the World Health Organization's theme for 1976, the fight against blindness.

Handicrafts was the theme in 1976 of the popular Europa series, issued each year by member nations of the Conference of European Postal and Telecommunications Administrations. Most of the countries chose ceramics as examples of their handicrafts.

Stamps showing birds and other wildlife, trees, flowers, and fish were abundant and colorful. Native trees appeared on stamps from Montserrat, Anguilla, and Singapore. Native birds adorned stamps from Ascension Island and the island of Saint Lucia. Several countries used the conservation of endangered species as a theme for stamps.

▶ A TOPICAL COLLECTION

The Olympic stamps of 1976 offer many interesting choices for the girl or boy who has already started a collection based on sports and games—or who wishes to begin such a topical collection. Other stamps of 1976 on this subject include one from Austria showing the game of bowling at ninepins and another from Greenland depicting a form of arm wrestling. The game of chess was the subject not only of one of the Caxton stamps but of stamps from Nicaragua and Israel.

CHARLESS HAHN
Stamp Editor, *Chicago Sun-Times*

PRINTING FROM NATURE

When you let nature design a craft project, you can be sure that you are working with the best possible artist. Each piece will be an "original," for nature never repeats herself.

The shapes of nature are all around us, from the blades of grass growing along the road to the huge trees found in the woods and parks. And these are available to everybody who wants them.

What can you do with nature's shapes? What designs can you make? The possibilities seem to be almost endless, but one of the easiest and most rewarding kinds of craft projects is to print with natural objects. You will be surprised at the many different designs you can get with just a few different kinds of leaves or grasses. Nature prints can be used to decorate stationery, place mats, and book covers. They can be applied to fabric, too, for wall hangings, clothing, or linens.

The materials needed for your first nature printing project are very few, and they can easily be bought in an art supply or craft shop or in a department store. You will need to buy some block-printing ink, a small brayer (roller), and block-printing paper or heavy newsprint. Block-printing ink comes in a variety of colors and is available in both oil and water base. If you buy oil-based ink, you will need either mineral spirits or turpentine for cleaning up. Items that you will need but can probably find around the house are newspaper, and a slick surface—such as a metal or glass baking pan or a piece of linoleum tile.

For a beginning project, it is best to make some simple prints of just one or two leaves. When you discover how easy it is to do, you will want to try some more complicated designs of several leaves and a variety of colors. To start, however, let's try decorating some notepaper.

If you live in the country or suburbs and it's not winter, finding leaves and grasses for nature prints is no problem, for they are all around you. If it is winter or if you live in the city, it may not be so simple to find leaves and other natural materials to print with. In that case, try looking inside the house. Most people have houseplants, and these often have very attractive leaves; indoor plants are a part of nature, too. A healthy ivy or fern usually grows very fast and would probably never miss a few leaves if you should pick them (but be sure to ask the plant's owner first!).

Now you are ready to start designing. Spread newspaper over your working area and lay a piece of newsprint or block-printing paper on it. Squeeze some printing ink onto a slick surface and roll your brayer back and fourth in the ink until the ink is spread over the surface, and covers your roller.

Now take one of the leaves you have selected and place it right side up on the newspaper. Carefully run the brayer all over the leaf and the stem until they are thinly covered with ink. Be careful not to apply the ink too freely; allow some green to show through here and there.

Decide where on the paper you want your printed leaf to appear. If you print on a corner of the sheet of paper, it can later be trimmed and folded into notepaper. Pick up the leaf by the end of the stem and place it inked side down on the paper. Once the leaf has been laid on the paper, it mustn't be moved. Take a second sheet of paper and place it over the leaf, taking care that the leaf doesn't move. Now gently rub back and forth on the paper, over the leaf, with the back of a large spoon. Remove the paper and lift the leaf. The printed image should be a definite leaf pattern that shows veins and texture. If the printing is too solid and shows no texture, you have used too much ink and should try again, using less.

Let the ink dry completely before printing on the same paper again. If you lay the covering sheet over wet ink, it will cause the ink to smear.

You might try printing some similar leaves in different colors, perhaps overlapping them for a collage effect. You may also want to experiment, printing with shells, pebbles, or bits of bark. Whatever you use, you will find that when you work with nature, you can design with confidence.

SYBIL C. HARP
Editor, *Creative Crafts* magazine

Spread newspapers; squeeze ink onto slick surface. With roller, apply ink to leaf and stem.

Place leaf, inked side down, on the block-printing paper. Once placed, do not move the leaf.

Take a second sheet of paper and very carefully place it over the leaf.

Using the back of a large spoon, gently rub back and forth on the paper, over the leaf.

Remove the paper and lift the leaf. You should have a leaf pattern that shows veins and texture.

This is some of the beautifully designed notepaper you can get by printing from nature.

LIVING HISTORY

Posters through the ages have captured the spirit of the times by recording events in politics, the arts, sports . . . . This 1896 Belgian poster announces a photography exhibit.

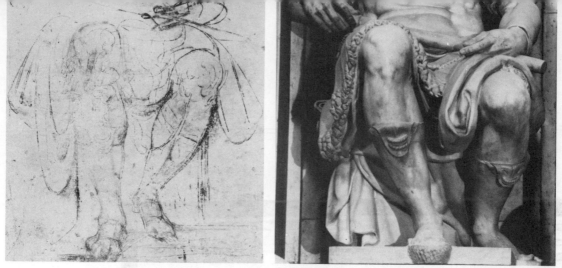

A drawing (*left*) found on the walls of a room beneath the Medici Chapel looks much like part of a statue by Michelangelo (*right*) in the chapel.

FOUND MASTERPIECES

They worked carefully, chipping and scraping away layers of whitewash that had covered the walls for some 400 years. To their surprise, they were uncovering what seemed to be charcoal drawings. Their astonishment grew as they uncovered sketches of feet and legs, heads, and full human figures.

The place was a small basement room beneath the Medici Chapel in the church of San Lorenzo in Florence, Italy. The time was late autumn, 1975. The director of the chapel stood by the workmen, pondering an important question: Were the drawings made by the great sculptor, painter, and architect Michelangelo? Michelangelo had worked in the church between 1520 and 1534. He had designed the chapel as a memorial to the Medici family, who long ruled Florence. The marble sculptures on the tombs of Medici dukes in the chapel were among his many masterpieces.

The basement room, long unused, had been discovered when the director was seeking a possible rear exit from the Medici Chapel. One of the caretakers remembered a trapdoor in a storeroom off the chapel. It led to a basement that might have an opening at street level. When the trapdoor was opened, the director clambered down a stairway to the dark cellar. Immediately he was curious to know whether the whitewash on the walls concealed charcoal drawings from the days of Michelangelo. There were such drawings in a small room upstairs off the chapel. Their existence had been known for some time. But they had never been fully uncovered until the chapel was cleaned and restored in 1975 for the 400th anniversary of Michelangelo's birth. The director believed that some of those drawings were by Michelangelo. Many art experts disagreed, and the upstairs drawings attracted little public attention.

But there was to be great interest in the newly found drawings—more than 50—that covered the walls of the basement room. The director studied them, had them photographed, and compared them with finished works by Michelangelo. One drawing of feet and legs was much like the feet and legs of the statue of one of the Medici dukes in the chapel. Brief announcements of the discovery were made early in 1976. In April the photographs of the drawings were published in an art magazine, with an article about them by the director of the chapel. He was convinced that most of them were drawn by Michelangelo. Some art experts agreed. Other scoffed at the idea. The debate may go on for years.

Museum collections contain many drawings made on paper by Michelangelo. But the drawings in Florence could be the first charcoal wall drawings by Michelangelo ever discovered.

FOLLOWING THE CABLE

In 1849 an enterprising young man named Paul Julius Reuter began to use carrier pigeons to send messages between France and Germany. At that time there was no main telegraph line between the two countries, and so there was no way of sending messages quickly between Paris and Berlin. That is, there was no way until Paul Reuter came along with his pigeons. With the Reuter birds on the wing, Reuter clients in Berlin and Paris were able to receive stock exchange prices many hours before they were known to other investors.

After the telegraph lines were completed, the German-born Reuter closed down his pigeon post and moved to London, England. It was there, in 1851, that he founded the international news agency that bears his name—Reuters.

At first the agency provided its clients with only commercial and financial news. But by the late 1850's, Reuters had widened its coverage to include general news—anything from wars to royal weddings.

Reuter built up his news agency by using modern technology. In his day that meant "following the cable"—the telegraph lines. Wherever a telegraph line went up or was laid down, a Reuters correspondent would soon be there to file news stories.

But even when there was no telegraph line, quick-witted Reuters reporters often scooped their competitors. When President Abraham Lincoln was assassinated in 1865, the Reuters American agent hired a tug, overtook a mail boat bound for England, and tossed his story aboard in a metal canister. As a result, Reuters beat the other news agencies by over a week in reporting Lincoln's death to people in Europe.

Since those early years, when Reuters operated out of two small rooms in London's financial district, the agency has grown rapidly. In 1976, as Reuters celebrated its 125th anniversary, it could boast of being one of the top three worldwide news agencies. (The others are The Associated Press and United Press International.)

Today, Reuters has some 1,000 correspondents covering the news all over the globe. Its dispatches are sent to newspapers and other clients in 155 countries and territories. Reuters news reports are even flashed on some home TV screens—in those homes that receive cable TV programs. The Reuters agency is always "following the cable."

HENRY I. KURTZ
Author, *Captain John Smith*

This is a caricature of Paul Julius Reuter, at the height of his fame. It appeared in a British magazine in the late 1800's.

MEN OF THE DAY, No. 55.

These fallen and decaying Haida totem poles are sad reminders of a vanished way of life.

HAIDA TOTEM POLES

If you were asked to think of a symbol for the North American Indian, what would enter your mind? A teepee? Some wampum? A totem pole? Do you know that one of these symbols, the totem pole, is a very great form of art? One that is majestic, mysterious, and dying.

The people who made totem poles—they made other wonderful wood carvings, too—were the Indians of North America's Northwest Coast. The finest totem poles of all were carved and painted by the Haida people, most of whom live in the Queen Charlotte Islands of British Columbia, Canada.

The heyday of Haida art lasted from the mid-1700's or earlier until the late 1800's. In those days this highly cultured seafaring people was proud and wealthy and was ruled by great chiefs. In summer the Haida men took enough seals, sea otters, whales, and fish from the seas around the islands to last all year, while the women gathered a good supply of shellfish, seaweed, roots, and berries. In the winter months they had the leisure time to fashion their remarkable canoes from cedar trees, build their large sloping-roofed houses from cedar planks, and carve their totem poles.

Their settlements hugged the coves of the rain-lashed Queen Charlotte Islands, and a forest of totem poles rose in front of each circle of houses. The carvings on the totem poles are stylized animal and human figures. These figures were usually the clan symbols of the "house chief" and his several wives. They were arranged so as to tell the family history or some mythological story.

The totem poles were of four kinds. A pole anywhere from 40 to 60 feet (12 to 18 meters) high was raised as part of the front wall of each house. In fact, you entered the house through an opening that was part of the totem pole's design. The great chiefs also had shorter totem poles that supported their houses from inside. The two other types of totem poles honored the dead. There were tall, slender memorial poles, and shorter poles supporting rectangular chests that contained the dead person's remains.

Today most of the old Haida villages are ghostly places, their houses gone, their totem poles falling into decay. The people have moved away to more sheltered settlements where they work at such modern tasks as fish canning. And the best-preserved of the totem poles have been removed to parks and museums on the mainland. A once-vigorous culture has died. And although skilled Haida wood carvers are making excellent copies of the old totem poles, the spark that fired the original blaze of creativity has been put out by the modern age.

An echo of the Haida past: this totem pole is at the University of British Columbia, in Vancouver, Canada. It was carved in 1960 by a Haida Indian. It is a reproduction of a pole that was carved a hundred years earlier. Remember when you look at totem pole figures that the animals and people are not meant to look as they do in real life.

Dogfish tail
The dogfish is a small shark. The tail of one crowns the totem pole, and its back fin pokes through the forehead of the "watchman" below.

Three watchmen
Two of these figures face left and right near the pole's top; the third, below them, faces forward.

Dogfish face
The fierce dogfish holds the tail of a small **killer whale** in its teeth.

Eagle
Symbol of a major Haida clan.

Sculpin
A small local fish. The sculptor has given it horns for the eagle to grasp with its talons.

Killer whale
The whale's flippers enclose a **small human figure**. This figure occupies the space where the doorway was in the original pole.

SAVING VENICE

Venice the Serene—that's what Italians call the fabulous city in the Adriatic Sea. They call Venice serene because it seems to float unmoving and majestic in its lagoon. But the city has been the cause of great international concern for the last ten years. The stillness—and the serenity—was an illusion all along, it seems. Scientists discovered that Venice was undoubtedly sinking steadily, if slowly, into the waters of the Adriatic.

People began to realize how much trouble Venice was in after a severe flood hit the city in the fall of 1966. During the flood, the tide rose nearly 6½ feet (2 meters) above normal. Floods had been recorded in Venice as far back as A.D. 885. In fact, Venice had always flooded somewhat, even in good times, about 25 times a year. But the flood of 1966 was truly bad, and it seemed to have been the beginning of a cycle of greater flooding. In 1971 alone, water covered the pavements of the city almost 100 times.

As a result of the 1966 flood, a careful study was made of the city's problems. The study made it clear that in addition to being damaged by water, the city's historic palaces and public buildings were being eaten away by polluted air. The preservation and restoration of art works damaged by pollution has been an on-going operation in Europe for many years. But Venice's problem was acute. The air was particularly destructive because it combined salt air with chemical fumes. The fumes came from the oil used to heat the city and from fuels used in nearby industrial plants.

The air pollution of Venice has been an easier problem to deal with than the flooding. The Italian Parliament recently set aside funds

When the tides of the Adriatic run high in Venice even the Piazza San Marco, the famous square in the heart of the city, begins to go under water.

to help Venetian home-owners change their heating systems from oil to a non-polluting gas. The government also set aside about $150,000,000 for restoration of the city's historic buildings and the sculpture that decorates them.

But Venice's greatest problem is flooding —flooding that has damaged and continues to damage the foundations of buildings. Flooding in Venice has several causes.

First, world ocean levels, generally speaking, have been rising at a rate of 6 inches (15 centimeters) per century for the past 20,000 years. This is caused by the melting of glaciers.

Second, more water is now being swept into Venice's lagoon. Venice is protected from the open sea by a 38-mile-long (61-kilometer-long) sand spit, or barrier, called the Lido— "the beach." There are three shipping channels that cut through the Lido. These channels

have been deepened and widened over the years to allow heavier traffic of ocean steamers. This means that more water is now flowing into the lagoon through these channels.

And, third, thousands of acres of mud flats and marshlands that for centuries acted as sponges to absorb excess water in floodtime were landfilled and attached to the mainland for industrial development.

And there is one additional reason for Venice's floods growing more severe. The city is actually lower than it used to be. This is because the water cushion that buoys up the 118 tiny islands on which the city is built has been flattened out. Beginning in 1930, over 20,000 artesian wells were drilled to supply fresh water to the industries of the city and to the increased population of the nearby suburbs, Mestre and Marghera. These wells drained away water from the water cushion. As a re-

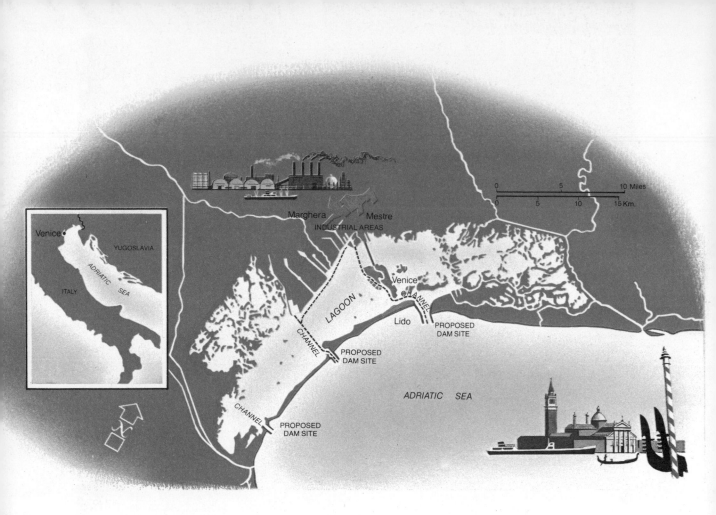

sult, the city began to sink. In fact, it is estimated that between 1930 and 1973, Venice sank 5 inches (13 cm).

For the past ten years, the Italian Government has been trying to stop the sinking by capping Venice's artesian wells. Fresh water for the suburbs is now brought in from the Alps by a newly constructed aqueduct. After three years of careful measuring and testing, scientists have proved that the city has stopped sinking.

The government's next project for Venice is to dam the channels through the Lido. In this way, the city would be protected, but the vital sea traffic could continue. Two types of floodgate have been proposed. One floodgate would be permanent, with a system of locks. It would take five years to build and would cost roughly $80,000,000. The other type of floodgate would be, in fact, a huge, inflatable, rubber-coated nylon tube. This giant tube would lie flat—and out of sight—on the seabed in normal tides. However, whenever the danger of flooding arose, the tube would be pumped full of seawater and would partly rise above the surface. Three of these giant tubes could be built for $50,000,000—considerably less than the cost of the more conventional floodgate and lock system. Another advantage of the rubber dam is that it could be built in just two years. The Italian Government was to attempt to reach a decision in 1976 on what kind of floodgates to build.

The attempts to save Venice have already caused some problems for the city's suburbs. The government has stopped industrial development of the area, including landfill projects in Mestre and the proposed filling of thousands of acres of marshland in Marghera. But many people feel that any sacrifice is worth it to save one of the most unusual and beautiful cities in the world.

The statues and carvings that decorate the buildings of Venice are safe from water but you can see that they are being eaten away by harsh, polluted air.

Many Venetians believe their city could be saved from damaging floods if rubber dams like this one were placed at the entrances to the lagoon.

Costumed villagers and a rattling stagecoach give an impression of the past.

The lady of the house is baking her own bread.

UPPER CANADA VILLAGE

When the St. Lawrence Seaway was built in the 1950's, several communities in the Canadian province of Ontario were drowned by the widening of the St. Lawrence River. Most of these communities had fine old buildings from Ontario's early days, and about 40 of these buildings were saved from eight of the drowned towns. They were moved to a partially wooded tract of land near Morrisburg, Ontario, where no village had ever stood before. The buildings, which included two churches, a hotel, a tavern, a stable, several shops, three early factories, and fifteen houses, were carefully arranged on newly laid out streets. In this way Upper Canada Village was born.

Now a visitor can walk along the streets of Upper Canada Village and never suspect that it is both old and new at the same time. The

Graceful old village buildings are mirrored in the quiet waters of the lake.

The whir of the spinning wheel is heard again.

feeling of old Upper Canada (as Ontario was called from 1791 to 1867) is very strong here because the most historic buildings from the drowned villages are now in one place.

One of the main attractions is the Loyalist farmhouse, a spacious stone building. The Loyalists were people from the American colonies who opposed the American Revolution. Many of them found a haven in Canada, which, like them, chose to remain loyal to the English king. They were among the first settlers of Upper Canada (Ontario).

Many old crafts are kept alive in Upper Canada Village. The waterwheel is turning in the woolen mill, and soft blankets are being made in another factory. The sound of the blacksmith's hammer and anvil is heard, and the smell of fresh-baked bread fills the air around the bakeshop. Even more important, the village is inhabited—at least in the daytime—by people decked out in 19th-century dress. They practice the crafts and greet the visitors, and make them almost believe they have made a time-machine trip into Ontario's past.

The cones of Cappadocia look like rock formations on a remote planet.

This cone was hollowed out and used as a house.

The inside of a cone church is ablaze with art.

THE CONES OF CAPPADOCIA

Throughout human history, people have built their houses in many shapes and out of many different materials. Some of the most unusual houses in the world are found in Cappadocia.

"Cappadocia" is an old name for an area in Turkey. The unusual dwellings there are caves—not natural ones, but caves that people have hollowed out. But the most interesting fact is that these caves have been cut out of the strange and spectacular rock formations that are found in Cappadocia. These formations have been described in many ways: chimneys, cones, steeples. What do they look like to you?

The origin of these cones lies far back in prehistoric times. This area of Turkey is part of a high plateau ringed by mountains. Some of the mountains are volcanoes, and at some time in the past they erupted and covered the land with layers of ash and lava. As this volcanic material cooled and became rock, cracks appeared in it. Over the centuries, wind and rain, heat and cold, enlarged the cracks. Rain and melting snow formed streams that wore away still more rock. "Islands" of higher rock were left, and these were nibbled at by the wind until they stood as they do today—cones and columns, towers and pinnacles, some clustered, some rising singly. They are mostly yellowish beige, mauve, or gray in color.

This natural landscape is a startling sight. But something has been added to nature's work; the hand of man has been at work too. No one is sure when the inhabitants of this land first got the idea of hollowing out dwelling places in the cones, but it may well have been in ancient times. Some scholars, however, think that the very first cave dwellers were Christian monks. In about the 4th century, Christianity came to Cappadocia. For the next 700 years Cappadocia was part of the vast Byzantine Empire (the Eastern Roman Empire). It is believed that during this period the monks discovered the cones of Cappadocia. They began hollowing out rooms to live in and chapels to pray in, sometimes in a small cone, sometimes in a large cone or a whole cluster of cones.

The traditions of Eastern Christianity call for paintings on the walls and ceilings of churches and chapels. Many of these wall paintings, or frescoes, can still be seen inside the cones of Cappadocia. Some are representations of Christ, saints, or angels. Others depict Byzantine rulers.

In the 11th century the area was conquered by the Turks, whose religion is Islam. There was no sudden change in the lives of the people in the cones. Churches, monasteries, and houses (built by the local inhabitants) continued to be cut out of the rock. But slowly the number of Christians dwindled, and Turkish peasants moved into abandonded cave houses and cut new ones.

In the early 18th century, reports of the cones of Cappadocia began to reach Western Europe. Soon scholars interested in Byzantine art began to study the church paintings. In the middle of the 20th century, the Turkish Government began to take steps to protect the cave dwellings and churches. Some of the houses were unsafe, and people could not live in them. The local people have strengthened other caves by shoring up walls with brick and by putting glass in the windows. New caves are still being cut. The Göreme Valley, where many of the cones are, has been declared a special tourist zone by the Turkish Government, and there are guided tours.

A few years ago, an American couple spent a month "cave-keeping" in one of the empty cave dwellings. The dust of ages covered the cave floor, but they coped with it by spreading a large plastic tarpaulin on the floor and then laying their rugs over it. They made use of some modern conveniences, such as a stove fueled with bottled gas and gasoline lanterns to light their rooms. But they ate local produce and piled cushions made of locally woven fabrics on the benches cut in the rock that served as sofas.

The Turkish Government hopes that as Cappadocia becomes more widely known, tourists will come to see the caves. With the money the tourists bring, the truly unique cones of Cappadocia can be preserved.

DEERFIELD—PAST AND PRESENT

Americans have just celebrated their Bicentennial. The commemorations and celebrations around the United States have probably given many Americans a much stronger sense of their own past. Yet there have always been people in the United States with a special interest in the past. The people of a unique small town in western Massachusetts called Deerfield, for example, live quite happily with their own past. Let's take a walk through Deerfield—past and present.

▶ A WALK THROUGH TOWN

Walking down The Street, as the main street of Deerfield is called, you will notice right away what a pleasant place it is to be in. There are no ugly buildings—and no parking lots. The town is very old, but it doesn't seem like a museum. You won't find guides dressed up in colonial costumes. There are no horse and buggy rides to take. And although a dozen of the thirty old houses along The Street are museums, the town's newer buildings keep it from looking unreal or artificial. As you walk past the colonial houses, past the Civil War monument, past the late 19th century houses with their long windows, and past the school building erected in 1954 you get a special feeling. Deerfield is not a memorial to the past. It is a lovely town where the layers of time have settled quietly and naturally. Everything blends with everything else.

A great deal of planning and effort and skill really were required to make Deerfield the place it is today. The natural look and feeling of the town didn't just happen. Nor is the town really so quiet and sleepy as the huge elms and maples that line The Street and surround the houses make it seem. The old town is, in fact, alive with young people. It is the home of Deerfield Academy, one of America's best-known preparatory schools, and of two other private schools for younger children.

The teenagers at Deerfield Academy have always agreed that Deerfield is an ideal place to study American history. Reminders of history are all around you. And the students at the academy are entitled to free admission to the town's fifteen museums for their entire time there. A student who is interested in American history can live with the artifacts of pre-Revolutionary New England.

▶ THE PAST

The land on which the village of Deerfield stands was bought from the Pocumtuck Indians in 1667. Shortly thereafter, the first British colonists arrived, The Street was laid out, and the name "Deerfield" was adopted for the settlement. From the time of its settlement until 1746, Deerfield suffered repeated Indian attacks. The worst of these attacks was the famous Deerfield Massacre of 1704.

The Marquis de Vaudreuil, the French governor of Canada, wanted to prevent a peace treaty between the British and the Abnaki Indians. He therefore encouraged the Indians to raid a British frontier settlement. He offered the Indians the support of French troops in their efforts. The Deerfield settlement was chosen as the target.

Before dawn on February 29, 1704, 200 French soldiers and 142 Indians crossed the frozen Deerfield River and crept toward the settlement. Deerfield was guarded by a high wooden stockade. The French and Indians moved across the snow-covered fields in short rushes so that the sound of their feet would seem like the wind to any colonial sentry who was awake. A few of the Indians scaled the high stockade and dropped, unheard, into the compound. They surprised and murdered the sentinel before he could sound the alarm. Then they opened the stockade gates to the French troops and Indian braves who waited outside. The invaders poured into the compound with shrill war cries that woke the people of Deerfield.

The attack, which lasted five hours, nearly destroyed Deerfield as a settlement. Of its 268 inhabitants, 49 were murdered and 112 were taken prisoner. Those taken prisoner were marched 300 miles (almost 500 km) to French-held Canada. Twenty of the Deerfield captives were either killed or died of starvation on the march. Of those who reached Can-

Just look at this elegant old door and you will know a lot about Deerfield. This is the front door of the Dwight-Barnard house, which was built in 1725. But a number of the houses in Deerfield have doors like this. Open any one of them and you will discover America's past.

This 1816 house is where Deerfield's printer and binder lived and worked.

Fall has come to New England and there are fallen leaves around the stone that marks the grave shared by the victims of the famous Deerfield Massacre.

This 1797 classroom was used by generations of Deerfield students.

ada alive, only 61 eventually returned home to Deerfield. One of the captives, a girl whose mother had died of exhaustion during the month-long trek through the snow, grew up among the Indians and eventually married one of her captors.

For two years after the massacre, Deerfield was little more than a military outpost. But the prisoners returned in 1706, and a few new houses were built. The community tried to pick up where it had left off, despite the continued threat of Indian attack. It was not until 1735, when a treaty was made by Governor Belcher of the Province of Massachusetts Bay and representatives of the Six Nations of the Iroquois, that there was relative peace.

Beyond the exciting story of the Deerfield Massacre, which has been retold many times (including once in a movie), there is little today to remind you of that cold morning so many years ago. There are a few mementos, a door with a hole hacked in it by tomahawks, the burial mound in the old cemetery—the common grave of 48 murdered settlers, men, women, and children.

Although the old days of Indian attacks and sentries on the stockades are the most romantic part of Deerfield's history, they are not the whole story. The people of Deerfield, like those of other New England towns, were involved on both sides in the American Revolution. Deerfield attained great prosperity when the railroads were built. And Deerfield men fought in the Civil War. The town also had a period of decline toward the end of the 19th century. The young people of the town were no longer content to stay at home and follow in their fathers' footsteps as farmers or craftsmen. They began to go to Springfield—or even Boston—to find jobs in the mills and factories that were springing up everywhere.

▶ PRESERVATION

Through all its troubles and changes Deerfield survived—and it survived without losing the good things of its own past. Deerfield's survival has more to it than the New England Yankee's reluctance to throw anything out. It has survived because there has been a consistent effort made to preserve it. As early as 1847 an appeal was made to raise money to preserve the Old Indian House. It was called

that because the Indians had held hostages in it after the massacre. The appeal failed and the house was torn down. But Deerfield had made the first attempt to preserve its own past —and it would allow very few old buildings to be torn down in the future.

In 1870, George Sheldon, an early Deerfield historian, took an important step in preserving the town's past. He founded the Pocumtuck Valley Memorial Association. In the 1880's the Deerfield Summer School of History and Romance was founded. People went there to learn about colonial life in America. By the end of the 19th century several groups had been founded to revive colonial crafts.

The houses that line The Street in Deerfield remain the most important thing about the town. Deerfield's houses are not modern reproductions—as many of the houses in Williamsburg, Virginia, are. They are real. The only museum building in Deerfield that is not authentic is the Old Indian House. It was reproduced in 1929, replacing the original, which the town had failed to save in 1847. However, not all of the houses on The Street were built on the sites they now occupy. Some of them were moved there from the area around the village, or from as far away as Springfield, 30 miles (almost 50 km) to the south. The Hall Tavern, an 18th-century tavern that Emerson and Thoreau both visited, was moved from the Boston Stage Coach Road in Charlemont, Massachusetts, a town farther north along the Deerfield River.

The restoration of most of the town's old buildings was begun in the 1940's as a private project. The project grew into a foundation, which is now known as Historic Deerfield, Incorporated. In 1962 the United States Government recognized the importance of Deerfield. It is now Old Deerfield Village National Historic Landmark.

Deerfield is an especially wonderful place for the townspeople and the students who live there. But it's also a very nice place to visit, even for a little while. The town has a charm not easily forgotten. Leaving it is like waking from a dream. In the dream, you found a small American town that had miraculously survived from the past into the present.

RICHARD TEDESCHI
University of Massachusetts (Amherst)

A farm in the hills of northern California is the ideal of many new pioneers.

THE MODERN PIONEERS

Perhaps you know what a shakuhachi is. I have to admit that when I lived in New York, a city where people of many cultures live and exchange information and ideas, I didn't know. I wouldn't have known if you ate it, danced it, rode it, or stepped on it. I had never even heard the word "shakuhachi" until I moved to a little country town on the edge of northern California's redwood country.

And I was in for some other surprises when I moved. I am a native Californian. I have long been interested in the history of the early California pioneers and gold prospectors. But I never really understood what their lives were like until I arrived at my new home.

I went back to California, in part, to enjoy the country. I had missed the outdoors in the years I had spent in the city. But I didn't really look forward to small-town life as I remembered it. I had grown up in a small California town and had spent most of my youth wanting to escape from it. When I was a teenager, I yearned for the freedom and excitement of the big city.

But to my surprise I discovered that country towns really are changing. And my new hometown in northern California was certainly no exception.

The majority of the people in the town still live in the usual way. But a new kind of person has begun to settle in the town and the surrounding countryside, too. Old timers call them "the hill people."

▶ NEW WAYS—OLD WAYS

The newcomers in my town think of themselves as people trying to search out a new way of life. They know all about native herbs, health foods, unusual religions, t'ai chi ch'uan (an ancient Chinese exercise system), experimental poetry—and shakuhachis! But these people do have a real love of the land and of nature. And the way they choose to live is much like the way the pioneers who came to California in the 1840's lived. If one of those early settlers walked through the hills near my new home town, he would probably feel right at home.

The young settlers are creating what might be called an alternative life-style in the wilderness. Their wilderness is usually a few acres of hilly, tangled woodland and meadow with a creek flowing through it. It is usually several miles from the nearest village. Here, if they're lucky, a modern pioneer family will build their own cabin, grow their own food, keep their own flock of goats for milk, and make everything, or almost everything, they need—just like the 19th-century people on the frontier.

If the new pioneers come from the San Francisco Bay Area, they pile everything they own into a van or pickup truck (the modern version of the covered wagon) and head north. Some are bound for Mendocino County. Others go still farther north to Humboldt County. Some people veer eastward into the Sierra Nevada mountains—the mother lode country of Gold Rush days.

Mendocino County, where I live, lies entirely in the Coast Ranges. The countryside is incredibly beautiful. It has mountains, valleys, creeks, and a rugged stretch of the Pacific coastline. Although the county covers an area of 3,500 square miles (almost 9,100 square kilometers), it has a present population of only about 56,000. A fifth of these people live in one town, Ukiah, the county seat. That means there's a lot of country still open for settlement. But like many other wild, lovely regions, the county is economically depressed. Because of this, many old timers fear the steady tramp of desert boots and sandals headed north. They are afraid the county's economy may not be sturdy enough to support the young pioneers.

Too often, the pioneers find the soil of their meadows rocky and poor. Hillsides are difficult to till, and it is hard to grow many crops. People advertising land for sale often promise an "all-year creek" on the land as part of the deal. More often than not, in northern California, it won't be an all-year creek. In fact, by August it may well be as dry as the Mojave Desert. The pioneer must then dig a well—but is there any water under all that rock? Sometimes there isn't.

And then there is the problem of the shelter the modern pioneers build for themselves. Many of them work very hard, building cabins with their own hands from trees they cut on their own land—just as the early California

pioneers did. But the early pioneers didn't have to cope with building codes and building inspectors. No matter how hard the builders have worked, their cabin may be declared "unfit for human habitation" if it doesn't live up to the modern building code. (And sometimes the shelters the pioneers put up for themselves aren't even cabins; sometimes they put up a tepee or a yurt or a geodesic dome of some kind.) Because of their troubles with the building inspectors, the new settlers in my area banded together into a group called United Stand. The aim of the group is to work for changes in the building code.

But even people who cut down trees to build their own houses need to buy nails. And not all the settlers manage to grow all the food they need, especially in the first year or two. In addition to living off the land, the new settlers, like the pioneers before them, need money. They must get jobs. And in a rural area with a depressed economy, finding jobs can be difficult.

▶ BACK ON THE TRAIL

But aren't we really getting off the trail of the mysterious shakuhachi? Not really. The young craftsman who finally explained the shakuhachi to me is also the person who helped me see how the pioneer dream was really working, after all, for some of the people trying to live an alternative life-style. When I first saw him, I thought he looked like Abe Lincoln. Same long, black beard, tall, lanky frame, and big, capable hands. But his hair was much longer and bushier than Lincoln's, the gold-rimmed spectacles were a different shape—and I never saw Lincoln pictured in overalls. It turned out that his name was Monty. Monty Levenson.

"Where are you from?" I asked.

"Brooklyn." Another ex–New Yorker! After the usual small talk about the problems of cities and the beauty of the redwood country, I asked him the crucial question: "How does anybody make a living here?"

"It can be tough," he said. "Some don't. But some people are nurses. Others work for the local health food store. Some people are singers, rock musicians, craftsmen. People do odd jobs, even work in lumber mills—we find ways. Personally, I'm doing fine."

"What do you do?"

"I make shakuhachis," he said. "I make them by hand, in a shop in back of the lawyer's house. I advertised them for sale in *The Last Whole Earth Catalogue,* and I have two months' worth of orders to fill right now."

"Terrific. But what on earth is a shakuhachi?"

"Why, it's a Japanese flute. You mean you've never heard one?"

I had to confess I hadn't.

"Come to the concert Saturday night. Koga Masayuki will be playing my shakuhachis."

▶ CONCERT—COUNTRY-STYLE

The concert was held in the county museum. As I edged through the crowd, I noticed that most of the people were young. Some of the long-haired young women were elegant in saris or caftans; others wore faded blue jeans. Nobody wore an ordinary dress. A bearded young man in a red flannel shirt and high boots leaned against a museum case containing a model of a 19th-century general store, complete with miniature kerosene lamps and a

These are the mysterious shakuhachis. They are actually handmade Japanese flutes.

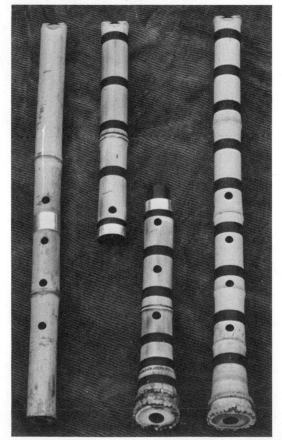

tiny potbellied stove. Except for his hair, tied back in a ponytail, the young man looked like a California forty-niner come to town to stock up at a general store just like the one in the case. Beside him, his wife cuddled their baby in a voluminous, hand-knitted shawl. Beneath it, her lavender calico granny dress flowed to the floor. She needed only a sunbonnet to pass for a 19th-century pioneer.

All the folding chairs were taken, so I moved to the back and sat on the floor. Soon I realized that I was in the nursery section. On the floor to my left were half a dozen blanket-wrapped infants, arranged in a neat row. Their mothers leaned against the rear wall of the hall or sat in the last row of chairs. The older children sat on their parents' laps or on their fathers' shoulders, so they could see better.

Soon the audience quieted down and the lights dimmed. A slender, black-clad figure stepped forward on the tiny stage and bowed. From the group of shakuhachis that lay on a cushion before him, he selected a small one, lifted it to his lips, and tested the sound. He did not hold the instrument to one side, as you do a traditional Western flute. He held it vertically, in front of his chest.

The shakuhachi, he told us, was invented hundreds of years ago. He would begin, he said, by playing music that had first been played on the shakuhachi in medieval Japan.

He began a kind of birdsong melody, starting high, sliding slowly down the scale like quicksilver slipping along a blade of grass. I closed my eyes. It was a wild sound, not like any I had ever heard before. Its unfamiliar minor scale, its sudden shifts from a liquid purity to a blurred, velvet tone, the unexpected blending of notes, made the music seem very strange indeed.

But who can describe sound? In my mind's eye I saw the sound turn into quick, flashing images—waterfalls, the sun blazing through dark trees, a shower of falling stars.

It was easy to feel dislocated in time and space. You could close your eyes and slip with the shakuhachi along the misty mountain paths of ancient Japan. Or you could open them and imagine you were back on the frontier, where mining-camp mothers brought their babies to square dances, and scenes like the ones here in the museum—both in and

The new pioneers get together at Adam's house to have fun and swap stories.

out of the exhibit cases—were common. Then, when the soloist played modern experimental music on his flute, you began to imagine the distant reaches of the future and science fiction.

▶ **A HOUSEWARMING**

A few weeks later, I got to see some of the new pioneers in their own home setting. Through my friend Monty—the one who made shakuhachis—I was invited to the housewarming of a man called Adam. Adam had just finished building his new house. A jouncing jeep ride along a canyon and up a sort of horse trail brought us to Adam's place. The house, which was two stories in back and one story in front, was perched on the very edge of the mountaintop. It was spacious and sturdily built, with broad stairs—not a ladder—leading to Adam's upstairs studio. A round stained-glass window, set under the peak of the roof, cast a kaleidoscope of flickering, colored light on the crowd in the main room below.

About 200 people were able to come to the party. Children were everywhere, clinging to their mothers' long skirts, playing tag in the forest of grown-ups' legs, or sliding down a pile of lumber left out in the yard.

On the western deck, bongo drums were playing and people were dancing. Somebody started to play a wild, happy tune on a shakuhachi. The people sitting above us, dangling their feet from the balcony, began to improvise a kind of song or chant.

Two children bounded in with bags of wildflowers. They threw some of the flowers in the air and distributed others for us to wear in our hair and on our clothes. A long table was loaded with salads, fruit, cookies, and baked dishes. Each guest had brought something to the party. Long lines of hungry people began to form.

Now, on the other deck of the house, fiddles tuned up and an impromptu square dance began in the yard. Down the road, a volleyball game was in progress.

Amid all of this sound and activity, some people just sat on one of the decks in the sun, wrapped in their own inner silence, and looked out over the valley below. From there you could see no town, no road, no sign of modern American civilization. This is the way it must have seemed to the very first pioneers who came to northern California. Or it might have been like this in ancient Japan, the land of the shakuhachi. Or perhaps these happy people had discovered a brand-new world.

ELISABETH MARGO
Author, *Taming the Forty-niner*

173

Walk into this house in Montreal and recapture the great days of New France.

THE CHÂTEAU RAMEZAY

In Montreal, there is a neighborhood that in the dimness of twilight looks like another world. That other world is the past—the 1600's and early 1700's, to be exact, when Montreal was part of the French colony of New France. This neighborhood is known as Old Montreal, and its streets are narrow and cobblestoned and—at night—are bathed in the warm glow of gas lamps. Old Montreal has a romantic, slightly haunted atmosphere.

A proud landmark of this historic district is the Château Ramezay, built in 1705. The man who caused this sturdy yet graceful building to be raised on a knoll with an open view to the St. Lawrence River was Claude de Ramezay, the eleventh governor of Montreal.

The Château, made of gray fieldstone, looks somewhat like a French manor house. It was built not only as a home for Ramezay, his wife, and their sixteen children, but also as the seat of government for Montreal. The doors of this comfortable mansion were always open. Soldiers, merchants, explorers, and Indians were all welcomed here by the Governor.

After Ramezay's death and the cession of Canada to Britain, the house eventually be-

came the residence of Montreal's English governors, and remained so until 1849. For a brief interlude of seven months in 1775 and 1776, however, an American army occupied Montreal and used the Château as its headquarters. At this time Benjamin Franklin, Charles Carroll of Carrollton, and Samuel Chase (all signers of the Declaration of Independence) stayed at the Château while they tried to persuade the French Canadians to join the revolt against the British.

The doors of the Château Ramezay are open to the public today, much as they were in the time of Claude de Ramezay. The Château serves as a museum where historical exhibits of many kinds can be seen—from General James Wolfe's sash to a dagger that belonged to the Indian chief Tecumseh. The Château's guides, dressed in the costume of 1700, show visitors how people of that time wove cloth on a loom and used a saddler's bench. They even offer them bread and other foods made with colonial utensils. Claude de Ramezay would be happy if he could see the warm welcome that is still being extended to visitors in his grand old house.

Look at the deep window ledge. The walls of the house were built thick to keep out the cold.

A mother might have woven a rug at this loom while her baby slept in the cradle.

You could spin wool by the fire while dinner cooked in the deep fireplace.

GHOST SHIPS OF LAKE HURON

Lake Huron lies open to the wind. Its vast waters and the ferocity of its storms have led many writers to describe it as an inland ocean. Nineteenth-century navigators complained of its "monstrous waves" and the "wind that blew a perfect hurricane." Some shelter from the winds and storms can be found among the Canadian islands of the lake's North Channel and in the curved stretch of Georgian Bay. Yet the inside channels with their many reefs, banks, and submerged rocks can also be treacherous, even to experienced navigators.

Over the years, the high winds, pounding waves, and hazardous rocks of Lake Huron

The *Griffon*

have combined to spell doom for hundreds of unlucky vessels. The ships that have survived the treacherous waters have been sturdily built, and have had skilled captains and crews —and a great deal of luck. The men that sailed Lake Huron had many a story to tell of their adventures. Here are four such stories.

▶ THE "GRIFFON"

Probably the first sailing ship ever to enter the upper Great Lakes was the *Griffon*. The *Griffon* was a small, squarerigged vessel with a length of about 65 feet (almost 20 meters). It was built in 1679 on the Niagara River. The man who had it built was the great French explorer Robert Cavalier, Sieur de La Salle.

On August 7, 1679, the *Griffon* was launched. With La Salle and over thirty men aboard, the ship made a hazard-filled journey through Lake Erie and Lake Huron to the Straits of Mackinac, where the Indians had a gathering place known as Michilimackinac. The Straits were also the gateway to Lake Michigan. The year before, La Salle had sent fifteen men to Baie des Puants—now Green Bay—on Lake Michigan. This party was to collect the furs brought in by trappers and wait at Michilimackinac for La Salle's arrival.

Now, when he reached Michilimackinac, La Salle learned that some of these men had deserted and fled to Sault Ste. Marie, about 50 miles (80 km) away. He was furious. He ordered his lieutenant, Henri de Tonty, to go to Sault Ste. Marie and arrest the deserters. When Tonty failed to return in three weeks, La Salle felt he had to send the *Griffon* and its valuable cargo of beaver and buffalo pelts back to the Niagara River. Winter was coming. Manned by a skeleton crew, the *Griffon* sailed off—and was never seen again.

La Salle expected that the *Griffon* would deliver its cargo of furs and then return to Michilimackinac. He waited anxiously until March. The ship didn't come. La Salle then returned on foot through hundreds of miles of dense wilderness to his base on the Niagara River, without finding any trace of the ship or its crew. Sometime later, Jesuit priests reported that goods and fittings from the *Griffon* had washed ashore near their mission on Georgian Bay.

There were many rumors about the fate of the *Griffon,* then and later. Storms, Indians, rival fur traders, a mutiny by its own crew, and even the Jesuits themselves were blamed for the ship's disappearance and presumed destruction. Today, thanks to the Vail family of Tobermory, Ontario, the mystery seems closer to a solution than at any time in the last 300 years.

The Vail family has lived and worked on Lake Huron since 1833. Through most of that time they kept secret the existence of an old wreck lying in a harbor on Russel Island, at the tip of the Bruce Peninsula. Since 1955, when experts were brought in to examine the weathered timbers and metal bolts of the old keel and ribs, many people have come to believe that the *Griffon* has been found at last.

Harrison John MacLean, a Canadian newspaperman who has long been interested in the old wreck, has drawn certain conclusions about the fate of the *Griffon.* MacLean believes that the ship was driven off course toward Georgian Bay by a lake storm. He believes that somehow or other Indians boarded the ship and forced the crew to maneuver the *Griffon* into the harbor on Russel Island. There the Indians must have set fire to the ship, which then sank. The crew either escaped or were killed by their captors.

The government of Ontario is now trying to obtain pieces of the wreck. If tests show that the wood fragments are the correct age to be part of the *Griffon,* the wreck will be put on exhibit at Fathom Five Provincial Park, near Tobermory, Ontario.

▶ **THE "NANCY"**

In 1789, 110 years after the launching of the *Griffon,* a fine sailing schooner 80 feet (24 m) in length was built for a Montreal fur-trading company. It was called the *Nancy.*

Over the next 23 years, the *Nancy* traveled between trading posts on Lake Huron, Lake Michigan, and Lake Erie. When the United States declared war on Britain in 1812, the schooner was taken over by the Canadian Government for use as a troop transport ship.

The *Nancy*

Canada was still a loyal British colony. The *Nancy*'s first major war service was to carry troops to attack the American city of Detroit.

After the British captured Detroit, the *Nancy* continued to transport troops and supplies across the Great Lakes. In 1813, when the British Fleet of the Upper Lakes was captured in the Battle of Lake Erie, the *Nancy* alone escaped. Returning from a journey to Mackinac, the ship was almost trapped in the St. Clair River, between Lake Huron and Lake Erie. Both banks of the river were in American hands. When he was called on to

The *Ploughboy*

surrender, Alex Mackintosh, the captain of the *Nancy,* said he would blow his ship up rather than surrender it. Despite the fact that the Michigan militia were on both riverbanks, Mackintosh decided to make a run for it. Although the *Nancy* was struck repeatedly by gunfire, Mackintosh and his crew got the ship out of the river and back into Lake Huron.

After being repaired and refitted at Sault Ste. Marie, the *Nancy* was ready for war again. This time Lieutenant Miller Worsley was in command. The American fleet had entered Lake Huron. Worsley was ordered to keep the *Nancy* away from them, as far up the Nottawasaga River as possible. The Nottawasaga runs behind sand dunes parallel to Georgian Bay for several miles before it enters the bay. Although the schooner lay about 2 miles (3 km) upstream, it was close to the shore of the lake.

Three armed American ships headed toward the *Nancy.* A blockhouse on the shore was protecting the ship. The Americans began trading shots with the Canadians in the blockhouse. The Americans were by far the stronger force. They had 500 men and 24 cannon.

There were only 23 men in the blockhouse, and they had only one cannon. The blockhouse was soon set afire by the American cannon blasts. The *Nancy* was moored so close to the blockhouse that the flames spread to the ship. It burned and sank. Lieutenant Worsley and his men escaped in small boats.

But the *Nancy* didn't just sink beneath the surface of the river to be forgotten. An island actually formed around the charred wreck of the ship. In 1927 the remains of the *Nancy* were found and raised. Today they form the central exhibit in a museum on the island.

▶ THE AGE OF STEAM

With the advance of the 19th century, steamers gradually replaced sailing ships on the Great Lakes. People began to settle on the northern shores of the lakes. A way had to be found to transport goods and building materials and people from one settlement to another. Because the country to the east of Georgian Bay is rocky and studded with lakes, it was almost impossible to build roads there. Lake steamers seemed to be the best form of transportation. Lake ports like Owen Sound

The *Waubuno*

and Collingwood at the south end of Georgian Bay became important links with the outside world.

One of the Royal Mail steamers that put in at Collingwood was the *Ploughboy*. Built in 1858, the *Ploughboy* was a side-wheeler, and was 135 feet (41 m) long. On Friday, July 1, 1859, a large and distinguished group of people came by railroad to Collingwood. They boarded the *Ploughboy,* which sailed shortly after midnight. The group was composed of Conservative members of the Canadian Parliament and some of their important political supporters. Many of the men had their wives and children along. John A. Macdonald, who was then attorney general for Upper Canada, was among them. Evidently the expedition, which was bound for Sault Ste. Marie, was a pleasure trip. However, with so many government and political figures aboard, it's hard to imagine there wasn't a good deal of business discussed, too.

Soon after the *Ploughboy* left Collingwood, a gale came up. Nevertheless, after stopping at Owen Sound, the ship proceeded into the storm. In late afternoon, when the *Ploughboy* was almost abreast of Lonely Island (which lies at the entrance to Georgian Bay), dangerous mechanical difficulties developed, and the engine had to be shut off.

Unfortunately, the *Ploughboy* had no mast or sail. It was helpless and at the mercy of the waves. No one lived on Lonely Island, and the rockbound mainland was also deserted. The nearest help was at Owen Sound, and that was 75 miles (120 km) away. One of the ship's lifeboats was fitted out with a makeshift sail, and six crewmen volunteered to go to Owen Sound for help. Another steamer, the *Canadian,* was scheduled to be in port and might be able to help them.

The wind continued to increase in violence. The *Ploughboy* was blown back toward the rocky shores of Cabot Head on the Bruce Peninsula. Anchors were let go in the faint hope that they might catch hold, although the navigation charts showed that the water was too deep for anchoring. The anchors did slow the drifting, but it became clear just after midnight that the *Ploughboy* would probably be wrecked on the shore. The captain told the passengers to prepare to face death.

About two-thirty in the morning, when the ship was no more than its own length from the shore and everyone on board was prepared to jump for his or her life, the anchors took hold. The ship remained in that position through Sunday. On Sunday evening, the steamer *Canadian* came into view. They were saved. By noon of the next day the *Canadian* had towed the *Ploughboy* into Collingwood.

Twenty years later, the *Waubuno,* another wooden side-wheeler, proved less fortunate than the *Ploughboy*. The *Waubuno* had been built in 1865. By 1879 it had been considerably weakened by years of facing Great Lakes weather. Its engines were no longer considered strong enough to battle a gale. Therefore, the *Waubuno* was put on a route where there was less than 30 miles (50 km) of exposed water.

A rival steamship company had put another steamer, faster than the *Waubuno,* on the same route. The new steamer was called the *Magnettawan*. Captain Burkett of the *Waubuno* and his crew were indignant at the unequal competition for passengers and freight. Tradition says that the crew of the *Waubuno* was determined not to be outsailed.

On Friday, November 21, 1879, the *Waubuno* was at Collingwood, heavily loaded with passengers and freight. There was a high wind. The captain was waiting for the wind to slacken before setting out. Sometime late Friday night the wind finally did fall off a little. Without waiting for some of the passengers, who had decided to spend the night at a hotel ashore, Captain Burkett left port. Thereafter, the only person who saw the *Waubuno* afloat was a lighthouse keeper on Christian Island. Saturday brought a blinding snowstorm. About noon on Saturday, lumbermen working on the Moon River heard a ship's whistle which they recognized as the *Waubuno*'s. Although it sounded like a distress signal, they decided that the steamer was saluting someone on an offshore island.

The *Magnettawan,* which had ridden out the snowstorm near Christian Island, reached Parry Sound at noon on Monday. The *Magnettawan's* crew was surprised not to find the *Waubuno* there before them. Afraid that the ship might have gone aground in a shallow channel, the steamship company sent out a tug to look for the *Waubuno*.

The tug found a lifeboat and some wreckage, but there was no sign of passengers or crew. Further search revealed that islands for miles north and south of an uncharted reef called Haystack Rocks were strewn with wreckage—apples, bags of flour, chests of tea, bales of dry goods and clothing, pieces of furniture.

The following March an Indian named Pendonquot found the *Waubuno*'s hull, bottom up, in a sheltered bay a few miles south of Haystack Rocks. The vessel had not struck rocks. It had probably capsized—turned over. The weight of the freight and the ship's engines had taken the crew and passengers to the bottom. No bodies, human or animal, were ever found, although every one of the steamer's life preservers was eventually found along the lakeshore. Whatever had happened, it had happened suddenly.

For decades nothing more was learned of the fate of the *Waubuno*. However, in the late 1950's, divers found the site of the mysterious disaster. It seems that the ship had indeed rolled over, broken up, and then dumped its contents out in a broad swath along the floor of the deep, open bay. Among the relics the divers recovered were the ship's safe and two of its anchors. Today one anchor sits as a memorial in the town square at Parry Sound. The other, along with the *Waubuno*'s rudder, can be seen at the dock of Sans Souci, a nearby village.

A ghost ship is usually understood to be one that has disappeared without explanation. The *Griffon* and the *Waubuno* fit this description. But a ghost is also said to be a spirit that survives beyond its time—often, in order to give a message to the living. The *Nancy* and the *Ploughboy* fall into this category. They and their crews provide an example for everyone of courage and determination. The men of the *Nancy* did more than their share to protect Canadian freedom. The political leaders aboard the *Ploughboy* played a vital role in shaping the modern Canadian nation.

Therefore, all four ships deserve to be remembered for the bravery they called forth, for the hopes they carried, and for the gallant service they rendered.

M. A. MACDONALD
Author, *The Royal Canadian Mounted Police*

STE. ANNE DE BEAUPRÉ

The United States was not the only one celebrating an important anniversary in 1976. During the year the village of Ste. Anne de Beaupré in Quebec, Canada, welcomed some 2,000,000 visitors to a special celebration at its famous shrine of Saint Anne.

The occasion was the 100th anniversary of the proclamation of Saint Anne, mother of the Virgin Mary, as the patron saint of the province of Quebec. The proclamation, made by Pope Pius IX on May 7, 1876, was especially pleasing to the people of Quebec. Devotion to Saint Anne had begun with the earliest settlers of the province. Many of them migrated from Brittany, a region of northwestern France, where Saint Anne is often referred to as "The Holy Grandmother of Brittany."

There are many shrines to Saint Anne. But the one at Ste. Anne de Beaupré is her chief shrine, not only in Quebec but in all of North America. It is on the banks of the St. Lawrence River, about 20 miles (over 30 kilometers) northeast of the city of Quebec. It began with a simple wooden chapel built in 1658 for farm families. At that time the settlement was called Petit Cap ("little cape") because of a small cape, or point of land, nearby that jutted into the river. Because fields of grass stretched inland, providing pasture for the farmers' cattle, the name was changed to Beaupré ("beautiful meadow").

Among those who worshiped at the first chapel were sailors, giving thanks to Good Saint Anne for narrow escapes from drowning. Other worshipers reported that they had been cured of crippling rheumatism and other ailments. News of such happenings spread, and people journeyed to the shrine in ever-increasing numbers. Some of the Huron Indians, who lived in areas bordering the St. Lawrence, made their first organized pilgrimage in 1671. They traveled in birchbark canoes and spent several days worshiping at the shrine.

Today the Shrine of Ste. Anne de Beaupré is spread over a large area. The main building is the magnificent white granite Basilica

Angel Sounding a Trumpet: a statue in the museum at the shrine of Ste. Anne de Beaupré.

(Church) of Saint Anne, with a huge statue of the saint between the twin steeples. Surrounding it, in a parklike setting, are other religious buildings, a museum, and information centers and accommodations for visitors.

181

Posters are everywhere. In New York City (*above*) the style is giant framed posters. Paris (*below*) still favors 19th-century kiosks.

A POSTER PORTFOLIO

You may not know it, but you receive messages and information every day of your life through a very old-fashioned means of communication. It is older than television or radio or the movies or the telephone—or the Pony Express! Every time you walk out of your house to go to the store for your mother or to go to school, you are probably influenced in some way by this form of communication. What is it? It's the poster—and it really is one of the oldest forms of communication. After many centuries, it's still very much alive.

Posters are sheets of heavy paper or cardboard, very often quite large, with information printed on them. Sometimes posters are used to sell a product to you. Sometimes they're used to give you a message or explain an idea to you. And sometimes they are used to announce an event. One reason this historic form of communication is still used is that it's so easy. A well-designed poster can communicate a message to you in a few words or just by using a picture.

Posters have a long history. Some people believe they can be traced back to announcements the people of ancient times wrote in chalk or paint on the walls of houses. For many centuries, public announcements were written on boards, or on pieces of paper called handbills—and they were written by hand. When the printing press was invented, in the 15th century, announcements could be printed quickly and in large quantities. As printing presses were built which could handle larger sheets of paper, large notices and announcements could be printed. These were the direct ancestors of our large modern posters.

The poster as we know it today—brightly colored and eye-catching—could not exist without the development, in the mid-19th century, of economical methods of color printing. A French painter, Jules Chéret, is usually credited with being the father of our modern posters. He designed and then printed on his own press the first colored poster. He did it in 1866.

The introduction of commercial color printing caused a poster boom around the world. First of all, it made it possible to design really striking and effective posters. Secondly, the possibility of using color drew many of the best artists of the day into the field of poster design. Artists had been interested in book illustrations but in the mid-19th century they were almost never able to use color in their illustrations. Posters presented endless opportunities for working with color. In fact, posters were not just advertising notices; they became a real medium for artistic creation.

Color also gave posters a tremendous advantage, as far as advertising was concerned, over the newspapers and magazines of the 19th century. Newspapers sometimes printed red headlines to announce an important event, but they didn't run color advertising. Color prints did sometimes appear in magazines, but they were expensive and often had to be inserted by hand. They were rarely used for advertising. So, for a while, posters had the whole field of color advertising to themselves.

Following Chéret's lead, the French painter Henri de Toulouse-Lautrec (1864–1901) began designing posters for clubs, restaurants, and theaters. His bold style and brilliant color-

A Mucha poster for a Sarah Bernhardt play.

sense made him enormously popular in his own day. Today, if a person owns a Toulouse-Lautrec poster, they have it carefully framed and under glass. His posters are very valuable and highly prized as works of art.

Another 19th-century painter who became a famous poster artist was a Czech named Alphonse Mucha (1860–1939). Mucha went to

A turn-of-the-century poster by Will Bradley announced the appearance of the Thanksgiving issue of a popular literary magazine. Bradley's designs were in the international style of art called art nouveau.

Paris and specialized in designing posters for theatrical presentations. He would often include portraits in costume of the famous actresses of the day. Sarah Bernhardt, the great tragic actress, was one of Mucha's favorite subjects.

In England and the United States, posters became a popular means of advertising new books and magazines. Artists like Aubrey Beardsley (1872–98) in England, and Will Bradley (1868–1962), Maxfield Parrish (1870–1966), and Edward Penfield (1866–1925) in the United States, became famous for their literary posters.

In the 20th century, photography entered the world of posters in a major way. When it became possible to print black and white—and later, color—photographs on posters, new worlds opened up. An advertiser could have a photograph of his product on a poster. An art gallery or museum could announce an exhibition with a poster that included a photograph of a painting or a sculpture.

Photography did not replace graphic art in the poster world. It became one more technique for making posters more effective and attractive. One of the unusual things about the history of the poster is that it has been like a big snowball rolling toward the future, collecting ideas and techniques as it goes.

This handsome 19th-century French poster advertises shoe polish.

As far as many people are concerned, circus posters have always been the most exciting posters of all. This one was used by the Barnum & Bailey Circus in 1908. They seem to have specialized in trained animal acts. The dog standing on his head on an elephant's back (*center*) is certainly an impressive performer.

James Montgomery Flagg, a well-known American artist, designed this poster. It was a direct appeal to the young people of the United States to aid their country by buying savings stamps. The United States had entered World War I.

ГРАМОТА-
ПУТЬ К
КОММУНИЗМУ

This Soviet poster dramatically proclaims "Literacy—the road to Communism." The Communist regime of Russia, after the 1917 Revolution, used posters to encourage Russian peasants to learn to read and write. The posters were so striking and simply designed that even poor readers could get their message.

▶ GOVERNMENTS AND POSTERS

Because posters could reach many people in a direct and simple way, governments began to use them. In World War I and World War II, all the participants used posters, and they used them for many purposes. There were patriotic posters to encourage people to enlist in the armed forces and fight for their countries. There were posters to encourage people to buy war bonds or make other contributions to the war effort. There were posters cautioning people against giving away military secrets. And there were propaganda posters in both wars, issued by both sides.

Some of the propaganda posters were designed to make the enemy appear brutal or cruel. Others were designed to make the ene-my seem ridiculous, and therefore easy to defeat. This was often done by having an artist draw an unkind and often funny cartoon of the leader of an enemy nation doing something foolish.

After Russia was torn by revolution in 1917, the new Soviet government had leading Russian artists design posters encouraging the people to work for their country.

Sometimes governments use posters to remind citizens of serious matters other than wars. Posters are printed to encourage people to be immunized against dangerous diseases. Recently, posters printed in the United States, Britain, and the rest of Western Europe have been used to remind people to conserve fuel, which has been in short supply in many places.

BOOKMAGIC

BOOK WEEK/NOVEMBER 8-14,1976

Every year Children's Book Week in the United States is announced by a colorful poster. This one was designed for 1976 by Uri Shulevitz, a leading illustrator of books for children.

▶ POSTERS AND YOU

Many young people do more than look at posters. They collect them. In recent years, shops have sprung up in many parts of the United States and Canada, and in Europe— shops selling posters of special interest to young people. In most cases they are inexpensive. There are posters featuring almost life-sized photographs of popular rock music groups and other performers. And there are posters featuring huge portraits of movie stars. In fact, you can even have a photograph of yourself or a friend printed on a poster if you want to.

Young people have been especially interested in collecting posters of sporting events. New posters are designed each time the Olym-pic Games are held, and these posters are distributed all over the world. The amazing flotilla of sailing ships—Operation Sail—that assembled in New York Harbor to celebrate the Bicentennial of the United States was the subject of posters.

Even advertising posters, originally designed to sell a product, are interesting to collect. Some of them have been designed by the world's leading graphic artists.

The most important thing about posters is that they're still with us, despite the changes in the means of communication over the years. The more beautiful or amusing they are, the happier we are to see them and to accept the message they present. For some reason, it is hard to forget a really good poster.

Montréal 1976

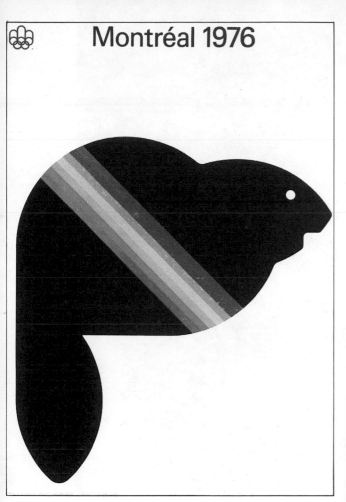

This is one of the striking posters designed for the 1976 Olympic Summer Games, held in Canada. It proudly carries a stylized figure of a beaver, Canada's national animal.

This poster announced Operation Sail, the flotilla of sailing ships that visited New York Harbor on July 4, 1976, in celebration of the 200th birthday of the United States. The tall ship on the poster is the West German bark *Gorch Fock*, a participant in the flotilla. The *Gorch Fock* is sister ship to the U.S. Coast Guard bark *Eagle*. The *Eagle* actually led the parade of tall ships on the Fourth.

A Moorish fountain in one of the walled gardens of Granada in Spain.

The Trevi fountain in Rome is a true masterpiece of the Renaissance.

This step fountain cooled a garden in the ancient Roman city of Pompeii.

CELEBRATIONS OF WATER

There is probably no country in the world without a fountain—without some device that shoots water into the air or throws it down from a height, merely so people may have the pleasure of seeing it rise or fall. Nor has there been a time in recorded history when there were no fountains to provide the spectacle of moving water that is so fascinating to watch. People love to look at water. On an idle Sunday's stroll, we head for water—a pond or lake, a cool fountain in the park, or the river, where we stare down from a bridge at the slow eddying of the water. We never tire of it.

Water and fire fascinate people. We can stare, nearly hypnotized, at an open fire. And we are pleased and a little excited when, walking in the woods or through a meadow, we come upon a natural spring bubbling up—as if by magic—from a hole in the ground. It is suddenly quite easy to understand how primitive man came to worship water. No life is possible without it; yet, like fire, water can also destroy life.

It is in this primitive impulse to worship water—or at least to recognize it as a gift of the gods—that fountains have their origin.

▶ **THE ANCIENT WORLD**

The ancient Greeks believed that natural springs were guarded by spirits who dwelt in them. There were springs that were believed to cure ailments—there still are in some parts of the world—and there were even springs where future events might be predicted. The most famous of the ancient springs where prophecies were made was at Delphi, in the shrine of the great oracle. The sacred spring at Delphi was channeled into the Temple of Apollo. There the Pythia—a kind of fortune teller—drank from the spring before making her prophecies.

Because so many people came as pilgrims to the sacred springs of ancient Greece, it became necessary to cover them up—to enshrine them—in order to preserve their purity. The earliest known covered spring in Greece was the Callirhoë in Athens. The shrine there was built about 500 B.C. The covering of the shrine was a simple one—a carving of nine lions' heads spewing the water of the sacred spring out of their mouths. Soon every city or town in Greece had an architectural fountain dedicated to a specific god or goddess.

While continuing the tradition of sacred fountains, the practical people of ancient Rome, with their genius for city planning, turned their efforts to the task of supplying water to the inhabitants of the growing capital. A complex network of aqueducts, constructed over a period of roughly 500 years, brought water from outlying areas to fountains in every part of the city. In many ways, this system was like our modern method of bringing water through pipelines from reservoirs or rivers and lakes to the faucets in our own houses. By A.D. 410 there were eleven aqueducts carrying water to 1,212 public fountains in the great city of Rome.

But fountains do more than provide water for the necessities of everyday life. They have another practical use that was well known to the Romans and skillfully developed by them. Fountains are a kind of air conditioner. The evaporation of water by heat causes a drop in temperature. We find relief in summer beside a pond or lake because, in part, of this interaction between the water's surface and the hot air. But a lake covers a large area and has a large surface; a fountain does not. However, a fountain's vertical motion can have the same cooling effect as the broad surface of a natural body of water. Sometimes the distance the water falls—and therefore its effectiveness in cooling—can be extended by causing it to fall diagonally. The Romans often built stepped fountains—fountains where the water was

made to fall in interrupted stages down a stepped tile surface into a small pool. You can still see fountains like these in the ruins of the ancient Roman city of Pompeii.

▶ **THE MIDDLE AGES**

Fountains have always been used for cooling in the countries of the Mediterranean. But it was in Spain in the Middle Ages that some of the most exceptional uses of fountains were made. The most famous were located in the courtyards and gardens of the Alhambra, the Moorish palace-fortress in the city of Granada.

The Moors brought to Spain some of the architectural ideas and designs of the Middle East. Many of the courts of Moorish Spain were planned according to a traditional Persian design called *char-bagh*—meaning "four gardens." Such a court was intersected by narrow channels and had a fountain at the center. In fact, this kind of Persian design seems to be the very model of the enclosed garden that was repeated all over Europe in the Middle Ages. A rectangle is divided into four equal parts by channels of water that, for the people of the Middle Ages, might represent the four rivers of paradise. These, in turn, flow out from a common source—or "fountain of life" —at the center of the rectangle. Not only is this design rich in religious significance, it is also very practically suited to hot, dry climates, where the soil of gardens needs to be irrigated and the air to be cooled.

However, the actual fountain design of the Middle Ages was not exceptional—although the gardens of which they were a part often were. Exceptional fountains seem to be built at times in history when life is centered on big cities—big cities with large central plazas. For the most part, that wasn't the case in the Middle Ages, a time when people usually lived in small, enclosed communities. But Roman life had been centered on one great city, which had had exceptional fountains. When the Goths attacked Rome in A.D. 537, they cut the aqueducts that fed the fountains of the city. The Romans then had to drink the water of the Tiber River, as their ancestors had done.

▶ **THE RENAISSANCE**

But the great city of Rome rose again in the Renaissance, and with it the fine art of foun-

Jets of water rise from vast reflecting pools at Versailles, outside Paris.

tain building, which had been so much a part of old Rome. Rome began to have splendid fountains again because of three popes of the period, all of whom had lived in Florence. Florence was the birthplace of the new art and architecture of the era. The popes of the Renaissance were determined to make the papal city, Rome, the rival of Florence in beauty and magnificence. Their first step was to repair the aqueducts. Then they, and other powerful patrons, brought the major architects, painters, and sculptors of the age to work in Rome. The result was the modern city of Rome, more or less as we see it today—a city of late Renaissance magnificence, a city filled with fountains.

Most of Rome's 55 major fountains and fountain groups (some with four fountains to a group) date from the Renaissance. The people of the Renaissance were fascinated by ancient Greek and Roman subjects. Because of this, many of the Renaissance fountains of Rome included mythological figures, especially those associated with water: figures of Neptune (the Roman sea god), sprites, shells, and dolphins, and figures representing the principal rivers of the world. And all of these fountain designs were filled with vitality and ener-

gy. The figures—even when the water isn't playing—still appear to be in motion.

People all over Europe became fascinated by Italian gardens and fountains. The rulers of the rest of Europe wanted something equally exciting for their palaces, castles, and villas. However, the fountains changed a bit in each country that built them. For the Italian fountains were very much shaped by Italian taste and the special characteristics of the Italian landscape. The dramatic, almost violent look of many Italian fountains was made possible, in part, by the hilly terrain of much of the Italian peninsula. Water could cascade hundreds of feet down sculptured stairs and be shot up by writhing stone dragons into a pool whose surface was in constant motion.

This kind of "Italian effect" was impossible to achieve in France, for instance, especially in the low-lying area around Paris, and in the Loire Valley, where most of the great châteaux of the 16th and 17th centuries were built. The flat terrain of these areas, and French taste, led to a different style of fountain. French fountains were serene and majestic. The most famous examples of these French fountains are those in the vast palace of Versailles, outside Paris.

Visitors are invited to jump right into this modern fountain in Portland, Oregon.

The Tilting Fountain of Liverpool, England, is a fascinating piece of moving sculpture.

At Versailles there are ornamental pools—vast, placid sheets of water set into the main axes of the landscaped grounds. These pools reflect the huge, elegant buildings and the sky. Jets of water rise from the surface of the pools. Unfortunately, there was never enough pressure to keep them all playing at the same time. Even when the king was in residence, only the fountains nearest the palace could play at once. Nevertheless, they offered a splendid spectacle—and still do—with their great sprays of water resembling the fans of strutting peacocks.

Like Renaissance Rome and its villas, Versailles inspired many imitations. Fountains in the style of those at Versailles continued to be built for another 200 years. But for fountains that were truly new and different, it was necessary to wait for a new and different kind of art.

▶ MODERN TIMES

People are still building great fountains. The Tilting Fountain of Liverpool, England, is one of the most fascinating modern fountains. It was completed in the late 1960's. Like a good deal of modern sculpture, it is kinetic—that is, it moves or can be made to move. Crescent-shaped "buckets," attached to vertical metal poles, are held at various heights above a pool. When the buckets fill, the weight of the water in them causes them to capsize. The buckets flip, dumping their contents into the pool. The effect of the numerous buckets, each separately flipping and filling and suddenly flipping again, is delightfully giddy.

The waterfall in Lovejoy Plaza in Portland, Oregon, was built in 1966. It is a fine example of another new idea in fountain design. Although very simple, the design of this fountain is intended to suggest natural rock formations. It looks a little like something that might be found in a Japanese garden, and is quite a departure from the whole Western fountain tradition. There are no symmetrical forms or sculptured human figures here. And, like the Tilting Fountain, it uses a technique that is popular in much modern sculpture. We are invited to "experience" the fountain. We are encouraged to enter it, walk through it, even climb it—if we like. In fact, the only limitations put on your experience of the Lovejoy fountain is how wet you're willing to get.

Really exuberant fountains are like fireworks. They play with one of the elements of nature. But whether fountains are exuberant or quiet, whether they trickle quietly in a secluded garden, explode joyously in a public square, or pour forth life itself like the sacred fountains of 25 centuries ago, they are all celebrations of water.

RICHARD TEDESCHI
University of Massachusetts (Amherst)

In the 18th century Czar Peter the Great of Russia had this huge fountain built at the summer palace outside his capital city of St. Petersburg. Czar Peter's capital is now called Leningrad, but his fountain still plays.

MOTHER TERESA

At the age of 12, she knew she had a vocation, or calling, to help the poor. At 15, she knew she wanted to work as a missionary in India. She was stirred by the accounts of Roman Catholic missionaries from Yugoslavia who were working in India. What she did not know was that through her service to "the poorest of the poor" in Calcutta, India, she would become famous in her lifetime as the saintly Mother Teresa of Calcutta.

Mother Teresa's original name was Agnes Gonxha Bojaxhiu. She was born to an Albanian family in Skopje (now in Yugoslavia) on August 27, 1910. At 18 she left a comfortable and happy home to join a community of Irish nuns, the Sisters of Loreto, who had missions in India. After receiving training at Loreto institutions in Ireland and India, she became a teacher—and later the principal—in a school at the Loreto mission in Calcutta. From the beginning she was aware of the teeming slums surrounding the well-kept buildings of the mission. There lived the poorest of the poor—abandoned children and homeless people of all ages, many of them starving and many sick or dying. In 1948, Mother Teresa received permission to leave the convent and devote her life to them. Some of her former students, daughters of prosperous Calcutta families, joined her. In 1950 she founded a new religious order, the Missionaries of Charity. At first she worked in the streets, tending the sick and dying, feeding the hungry, and teaching children in an open-air school. But gradually she was able to find buildings for use as shelters. One of the most famous is the home for dying destitutes in Calcutta.

As the order grew and more members were trained, Mother Teresa was able to carry her work beyond the slums of Calcutta and other cities of India. Today the Missionaries of Charity operate children's homes, medical stations, havens for the dying, and leper colonies around the world. And Mother Teresa —in her coarse white sari, bordered by three blue stripes—has become one of the best-known and most beloved figures in the Roman Catholic Church. She has received many honors, including the Pope John XXIII Peace Prize in 1971. The Nobel peace prize was not awarded in 1976; but Mother Teresa had been among those honored by a nomination for it.

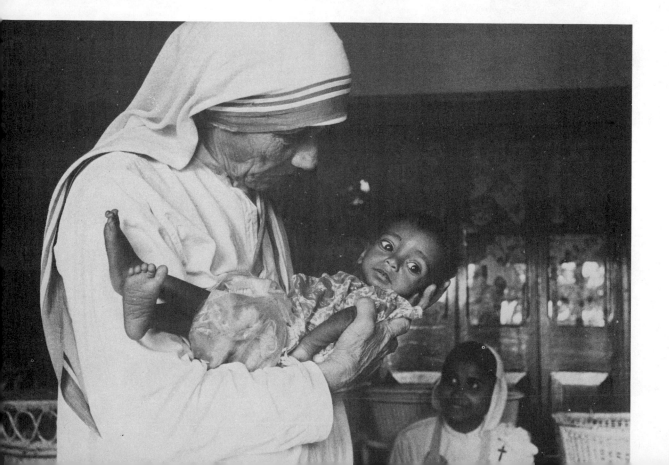

CUSTER'S LAST STAND

Our hearts so stout have won us fame,
For soon 'tis known from whence we came,
Where'er we go they dread the name
Of Garry Owen in Glory.

    From "Garry Owen," the regimental
    march of the 7th Cavalry

It happened a hundred years ago. Trumpets blared and a band played "Garry Owen" as jaunty cavalrymen trotted out of Fort Abraham Lincoln, Dakota Territory. It was May 17, 1876. The 7th Regiment of United States Cavalry, 600 strong, was marching off to join other troops gathering for a campaign against the Indians. At the head of the column, decked out in buckskin jacket and trousers, rode the 7th Cavalry's famed commander, Lieutenant Colonel George Armstrong Custer.

Five weeks later, on June 25, 1876, Custer and more than 200 of his troopers lay dead on a ridge near the Little Bighorn River, in what is now Montana. Dashing, colorful George Armstrong Custer—hero of numerous Civil War battles and Indian fights—and his entire detachment had been wiped out in a battle with Sioux and Cheyenne Indians.

News of the Custer disaster stunned the United States, which was then celebrating the centennial of its birth. Sensational accounts of "Custer's Last Stand" quickly appeared in the press. One newspaper carried the banner headline:

> MASSACRED . . . CUSTER AND 261 MEN . . . NO OFFICER OR MAN OF 5 COMPANIES LEFT TO TELL THE TALE.

In Philadelphia, where government officials had gathered for the Centennial celebrations, high-ranking army officers at first refused to believe reports of the "massacre." They did not think it possible that a crack regiment of U.S. Cavalry could be whipped by Indians. But dispatches from army commanders out west soon confirmed the newspaper stories.

In fact, the Battle of the Little Bighorn turned out to be the worst defeat suffered by the U.S. Army in its wars against the Indians.

A hundred years later, two ceremonies were held to mark the centennial of the Custer fight. On June 24, 1976, about 500 people gathered at the Custer Battlefield National Monument in Montana for an official U.S. Government ceremony.

The following day, Sioux and Cheyenne Indians held a celebration of their own. At a ranch not far from the Custer battlefield, they staged a victory dance to commemorate the defeat of "Long Hair" Custer. (The Indians gave him that nickname because he usually wore his reddish blonde hair shoulder-length.) As one Indian remarked, "One hundred years ago our people didn't have time to hold a victory celebration."

In the century since Custer charged to fame and glory, popular attitudes toward the Indians and the battle have changed. No longer are the Indians spoken of as "savages." They are regarded as native Americans who fought to defend their land and way of life—just as American colonists had fought for their independence from the British, and for possession of their land, a hundred years before.

Historians no longer view Custer's Last Stand as a "massacre." It is seen as a battle between two armed foes, which the Indians won because there were more of them and they fought more skillfully. Nor is Custer so highly thought of as he once was. Some authorities consider him a reckless glory-hunter and a poor field commander who committed serious blunders.

Nevertheless, Custer remains one of the most famous figures in American history. Over the years the Custer legend has grown. Novelists, artists, historical writers, poets, and Hollywood filmmakers have added to it. The fascination of Custer is due mainly to the controversy and mystery that surround his last battle.

That battle was the result of a chain of events dating back to 1874, when gold was discovered in the Black Hills of Dakota. Gold-hungry prospectors flocked into the Black Hills. The area had been given to the Indians by the Treaty of 1868. The Black

This is the legend: a 19th-century lithograph shows a neatly uniformed Custer, pistols blazing, holding off an attack by Indians on horseback. Custer's men, even the casualties, seem to be dressed for a parade.

This is how it was: a modern painting called *Here Fell Custer*, based on recent historical research, recaptures the horror of Custer's Last Stand. The soldiers couldn't stand, and most of the Indians moved in on foot.

Hills were sacred to the Indians, and the invasion of white prospectors angered them because it seemed to threaten their way of life.

They began to leave their reservations and band together for war. Government orders to return to the reservations were ignored. Troops were then sent to round up the Indians.

Several columns of soldiers moved against the massing Sioux and Cheyennes from different directions, hoping to trap them. Custer's column struck the trail of a large group of Indians and followed it to the valley of the Little Bighorn. His orders were to await reinforcements before attacking.

Instead, Custer marched directly against the main Indian camp and attacked it on his own—a day before the reinforcements were supposed to arrive.

Just why Custer did this remains a mystery. His critics claim that the headstrong officer willfully disobeyed orders because he wanted all the credit for defeating the Indians. But Custer's defenders say he acted properly. He believed the Indians would try to escape, and attacked to keep them from slipping away.

Whatever his motives, this much is certain: Custer badly underestimated the Indian strength at the Little Bighorn. He expected to find about 1,000 Indian braves in the camp. Actually there were 3,000 to 4,000 Sioux and Cheyenne warriors under Sitting Bull and his war chiefs Crazy Horse and Gall.

Shortly after noon, on June 25, Custer divided his command into three detachments. Two detachments were sent to encircle the south end of the Indian camp. Custer, meanwhile, marched north to strike from the rear.

No one will ever know exactly what happened to Custer. Not one of the soldiers who rode into the Little Bighorn Valley with him lived to tell about it. But although there were no white survivors, there were thousands of Indians who survived the fight.

According to their accounts, Custer was attacked from all sides before he reached the village. Hundreds of hidden warriors swarmed out of gullies and ravines, driving the soldiers up the slope of a low hill. Here Custer and his remaining troopers made their last stand. In less than an hour, all the soldiers were dead.

The two other 7th Cavalry detachments were also surrounded and pinned down. But they held on until another column of troops rescued them two days later.

The Indians won their greatest victory over the white man on that bloody day in June of 1876. But George Armstrong Custer also won a victory of sorts. When he and his cavalrymen charged into the valley of the Little Big horn, they rode into American folklore. Custer's Last Stand remains a part of the living legend of the Old West.

HENRY I. KURTZ
Author, *Captain John Smith*

YOUTH IN THE NEWS

Cheri, by Clark Federer, 18, of Amarillo, Texas: A 1976 Scholastic Photography Award winner.

LANDSAILING

Sherri Comer is a teenage champion sailor who never gets wet. She is one of many young people who enjoy an unusual hobby and sport called landsailing. Her land yacht has three wheels. When she gets aboard it, Sherri fastens her seat belt and puts on goggles. Then she's off with the wind, zipping across a dry desert faster than a sailboat can skim through water.

Traveling over land under sail power is nothing new. But landsailing has only recently become popular as a racing sport. Everyone can do it—regardless of age or sex. Sixteen-year-old Sherri Comer helped prove that in 1976 by winning the women's division competition at the third America's Landsailing Cup Regatta. She was the youngest competitor in an exciting event that lasted several days at Superior Dry Lakes in the Mojave Desert, midway between Los Angeles, California, and Las Vegas, Nevada.

"There were ten women racers," Sherri said, "and judges watched how each of us performed on the course during daily competition. They counted points against you for being overtaken or making errors, like cutting inside a turn." Sherri captured the first-place "Ms. Regatta" trophy with a low score of 8½ points. Her closest challenger finished with 19¼ points.

Another winner in the 1976 landsailing regatta was Randy Jackson. Randy, who was twelve years old, won first place in the junior division. He beat a previous junior champion, Linda Beach, who was fifteen. Linda said they were still friends. "Land sailors race for the fun of it," remarked Linda. "This is really a family sport."

▶ LEARNING THE SPORT

Good wind and flat, open surfaces are what land sailors like. Dry lake beds are perfect. This is why much of the landsailing done in the United States is done in the western deserts. In Europe, land sailors race at low tide over wide, sandy beaches on the coasts of Belgium, France, the Netherlands, and West Germany. Abandoned airplane runways are also popular spots for land sailors. A number of abandoned World War II airfields in England are used for landsailing.

And young American land sailors have found other places to sail, too. They use empty parking lots at stadiums and shopping centers, and large school playgrounds. In fact, there is at least one American school where land-sailing is being taught; it is part of a marine activities course. At the Rancho San Joaquin Intermediate School near Irvine, California, a man named Alan Lukei instructs students in canoeing, kayaking, rowing, and sailing. Since there was no place near the school to launch a boat during class time, Mr. Lukei hit on the idea of using a landsailer. It enables the students to learn the basic techniques of handling a sail efficiently so as to capture and control the wind's full power.

The school's landsailer has a simple frame of metal pipe, three rubber wheels, a plywood deck big enough for two riders, and a sail made of Dacron. The student-pilots steer by moving a tiller that controls the front wheel. And they pull on a rope to adjust the tension on the sail. To stop the boat, the sailor releases the rope so that the sail loses wind. But there's also a handbrake for extra safety.

There are many names for these craft—"landsailer" is one of the more common ones. But some people call them sand sailers, or land yachts, or sail cars. They're even called dirt boats. Many of the machines are homemade. However, those that are designed or built professionally are often given special names, such as Desert Dart and Friendship.

▶ AN OLD TRADITION

People began harnessing the wind to sail on land at least 2,200 years ago. That's when the Chinese are believed to have made the first crude sailing vehicles to carry warriors into battle.

In more recent times—in the 1830's—some practical Americans fastened sails to railroad cars. It seemed to these clever businessmen that wind-powered passenger service might be quite inexpensive. But when the trains were tested it was a very windy day. In fact, gusts of wind blew the cars—with the people aboard—off the tracks. The idea of sail-powered, commercial land transportation was soon practically abandoned.

Champion land sailor Sherri Comer handles her craft expertly in the Landsailing Cup Regatta.

Later in the 19th century, when miners headed west in the California Gold Rush, some enterprising men attached sails to their covered wagons while they were crossing the vast prairies.

Frontier tales are also told about a man called Windwagon Smith. Smith interested some Missouri citizens in investing their money in a company that would haul freight in wind-powered wagons. Once he had raised the money, Smith actually built a wagon with sails and took other prospective investors for rides in it. But one day his wagon—loaded with possible investors—blew over. The passengers were first frightened and then angry. Windwagon Smith quickly sailed out of town.

In Europe, landsailers were used primarily for sport. In Belgian seaside resorts real sailboats were hauled out of the water and outfitted with pairs of bicycle wheels. Then these odd-looking sand yachts were raced along the beaches. In 1910, the first landsailing competition was held, with contestants from Belgium and France. But the new sport failed to gain really widespread popularity.

▶ NEW POPULARITY

Two landsailing expeditions across Africa's Sahara desert helped arouse interest around the world in landsailing as a sport. In 1967 and again in 1972, land sailors from eight countries spent a month racing with the wind across 1,800 miles (2,900 km) of desert sand in northwestern Africa. One of the adventurous skippers who took part in the Sahara expeditions was Don Rypinski of Newport Beach, California. He revived landsailing activities in the United States by forming the North American Landsailing Association (NALSA) in 1969. Five years later, NALSA sponsored the first America's Landsailing Cup Regatta.

Don thinks international racing contests help make landsailing more popular every year. But he also hopes it will continue as a true family sport. He believes that anyone can build a landsailer.

▶ TRIM NEW CRAFT

As interest in landsailing increases, more sophisticated ideas in design are being developed. Some landsailers are modeled after the sleek, scientifically conceived iceboats that race across the frozen lakes of Europe and the eastern United States in the winter. But the most recently designed landsailers, often built of fiberglass and wood, feature a pivoting mast with a rigid wing that is designed to catch the wind. When winds are so strong that they might tear an ordinary cloth sail, this unique mast makes it possible to go landsailing without using a sail at all!

In 1976, an American-built Friendship landsailer, equipped with both a wing mast and a cloth sail, set a world speed record of 88.6 miles per hour (142.6 km per hour).

Despite such speeds, landsailers are remarkably safe, as Sherri Comer knows. Before becoming the 1976 women's champion, Sherri practiced in high winds at El Mirage Dry Lake in Southern California's Mojave Desert. Sudden gusts would fill the sail, lifting a rear wheel of her landsailer several feet off the ground.

"It's a funny feeling when you're racing along at 50 miles per hour and suddenly you start going up in the air," said Sherri. "You have to react fast by releasing tension on the mainsheet rope so the sail will slacken and let some wind escape. That brings the wheel back to the ground."

Because of a landsailer's tall mast and wide rear axle, pilots and riders wear seat belts that prevent them from hitting the ground if the machine tips over. When racing, they also wear windbreakers, and helmets with visors or goggles, to protect their skin and eyes from windburn and blowing sand.

When visitors come to their first landsailing race, they sometimes think they've stumbled on a terrible accident: When they reach the race site they often see many of the machines lying on their sides. But an oldtimer is sure to calm their fears. That is the way landsailers are parked. If they were left upright and unattended, they might well sail off by themselves.

"Wind is the only power you need," said one young land sailor. "You don't have to buy any fuel because there isn't any engine, and that means there's no pollution from a smelly or noisy exhaust. And landsailing is so quiet you can really enjoy the ride."

MICHELE and TOM GRIMM
Authors, *Hitchhiker's Handbook*

A student land sailor really has her hands full! She controls the sail with the rope in her left hand and steers with the tiller in her right hand.

They're lined up for the start of an exciting race. The competition is held on an emergency aircraft landing strip in Fountain Valley, California.

A MEDIEVAL FESTIVAL

Bright banners wave in the summer breeze. Brave knights compete in jousting events, and skillful jugglers perform astounding feats. Lovely ladies sing medieval ballads, and troubadors play strange, ancient instruments.

These are some of the wonderful sights and sounds that can be enjoyed one day each year in the courtyard of the Cloisters, a branch of the Metropolitan Museum of Art, in New York City. The occasion is the Community Medieval Festival, an event that attracts thousands of visitors, both young and old.

The Festival is the result of many weeks of planning and preparation. In the spring, about 150 young people from the city's elementary schools are selected to serve as "apprentices" for several exciting weeks before the Festival. During the Middle Ages, apprentices were people who were learning their trade by working for a master craftsman for several years. The young "apprentices" chosen to work for the Medieval Festival learn to design banners, make shields, and sew costumes under the supervision of adult volunteers and members of the museum's staff.

As if by magic the courtyard of the Cloisters, and the nearby apple orchard and tournament field, are gradually transformed into a town of the Middle Ages. The day's events begin with a procession that forms in the courtyard and makes its way to the tournament field. Thousands of visitors join the dancers, jugglers, knights, and ladies as they parade to the tournament field.

The day is filled with exciting activities. Children play games that are 600 years old—like pin the tail on the unicorn. In gaily decorated stalls there are demonstrations of such medieval crafts as calligraphy and work in enamel and stained glass. Vendors sell medieval foods. Singers, dancers, and tumblers entertain the crowds. Fierce dragons and noble unicorns stand guard at castle walls. Archers, fencers, and jousting knights give demonstrations of medieval sports. And a theater troupe even performs medieval mystery plays.

For one exciting August day, the medieval world is re-created—with the help of young people—in the heart of a 20th-century city.

YOUNG HEADLINERS

This is actress Tatum O'Neal (with Walter Matthau) in *The Bad News Bears.* Thirteen-year-old Tatum made history in 1976. She was on the American movie industry's list of ten top box-office attractions—and she was the only female on the list. Tatum had won a 1974 Academy Award for her performance in *Paper Moon*—a film she made when she was 10.

It was a big year for 15-year-old Mark Kleiman of New York City's Stuyvesant High School. In June he won the U.S. Mathematical Olympiad with a perfect score. This qualified him to compete in the International Mathematical Olympiad, which was held in Austria in July. Mark didn't disappoint his fans. He was one of the nine first-place winners in the contest, which drew competitors from 17 countries.

Determine (with proof) all integral solutions of
$$a^2 + b^2 + c^2 = a^2 b^2$$

She may just look like an attractive teenager to you—and she is that—but Becky J. Schroeder, a 14-year-old high school sophomore from Ohio, is also an inventor. In 1976 she was awarded her third patent. She got her first when she was 12. Becky's patents are all connected with the unique sheets she is displaying here. Becky has invented luminescent backing sheets. By using a sheet beneath a page of printed matter or a sheet of regular paper, you can read and even write in the dark.

A Pennsylvanian named Mark Keck was certainly one of the most successful farmers of 1976. He stuck a seed in the ground, and the pumpkin shown with him here was the result. In fact, Mark's pumpkin was so big you might consider it a whole crop in itself. It was 80 inches (203 centimeters) in circumference.

In July, 18-year-old Kornelia Ender of East Germany had a great deal to be proud of. She won five medals in swimming in the Montreal Olympics—four gold medals and one silver. The young German star announced her retirement from active competition later in the year. She wants to continue her education, since she would like to be a doctor one day. And she is engaged to be married to Roland Matthes, who is also an East German swimming champion.

Score one for the women's movement! In August, Joan Ferdinand, 14, of Canton, Ohio, became the second girl in history to win the All-American Soap Box Derby. The Derby is held annually in Akron, Ohio.

OLYMPIC SUPERSTARS

The Olympic Games of 1976 produced stars —and superstars—in many different sports. But few shone as brightly as a pixieish 14-year-old Rumanian gymnast and a radiant 19-year-old figure skater from the United States.

ON THE BARS...

▶ **NADIA COMANECI**

On the first day of competition in the Summer Olympics in Montreal, a 14-year-old gymnast soared and spun as lightly as a bird above, between, below the uneven parallel bars. Thousands of people in the stadium and millions more at television sets watched in stunned silence. Nadia Comaneci was unbelievable, perfect! There was frenzied applause. Then all eyes turned to the scoreboard.

Would the judges give the tiny Rumanian gymnast a near-perfect 9.99? No, a score of 1.0 appeared. But announcers hurriedly explained that the electronic scoreboard was programmed to record scores only as high as 9.99. Nadia had a perfect 10.00. Never before in Olympic history had such a score been given in gymnastics. Nadia went on to earn seven perfect scores—three in team competition, two in individual all-around competition, and two on individual pieces of apparatus (uneven parallel bars and balance beam). She ended up with three gold medals, a silver, and a bronze.

Nadia quickly became a superstar of the Olympics. Reporters scurried to supply information about her. Her name is pronounced NAH-dee-ah ko-mah-NEECH. Her height is about 5 feet (150 centimeters), and her weight, 86 pounds (39 kilograms). She was born in an industrial town in Rumania. She had spent more than half her life training for the days of triumph at Montreal.

But Nadia's parents did not have to find coaches for her or pay for her training. While in kindergarten, she was discovered by a government scout who goes to the schools looking for children who do well in gymnastics. At the age of six she entered a special school, where she received expert coaching and also studied the usual school subjects. She loved gymnastics and practiced at least four hours a day, six days a week. She also likes to bike, swim, and collect dolls. Nadia's fans had a chance to see more of her later in the year when she made a world tour with her teammates and appeared in a U.S. television special, "Nadia—From Rumania with Love."

What is ahead for Nadia? "She is still very young," her coach said. "But in four years, she will be 18. We consider 18 the perfect age to give the most she can give." Was he thinking of the 1980 Olympics in Moscow?

▶ DOROTHY HAMILL

At the Winter Olympics in Innsbruck, Austria, 19-year-old Dorothy Hamill skimmed, leaped, and spun her way to a gold medal in the figure skating competition. Each time she glided onto the ice, she gave a performance that dazzled the crowd in the stadium, as well as millions of television viewers.

Dorothy excelled especially in the freestyle program. Experts compared her leaps to those of the ballet dancer Mikhail Baryshnikov, one of her idols. They also praised her spins, calling them "high-speed yet delicate rotations within rotations." Everyone was charmed by her costumes, which were in shades of red, her favorite color, and by her radiant smile. But it was her shiny brown hair, which flowed with her movements and then fell back neatly into place, that had everyone talking. Her striking hair style became known as "the wedge," and girls everywhere began to copy it.

As casual as she may have looked in the Olympics, Dorothy often had to overcome stage fright and the jitters on her way to stardom. And there were many wins on her way to Innsbruck. She had already won the U.S. figure skating championship three years in a row (1974–76). Twice she had won second place in world competition (1974–75). But she was little known outside the skating world. Between appearances on the ice, she told reporters how she began her skating career at the age of about eight on a pond near her home in Riverside, Connecticut. "The others could skate backwards but I couldn't," she said. "I wanted to learn, so my mother got me group lessons. I progressed quickly, we switched to private lessons, and by the time I was 10, I was in my first competition."

For the past several years, Dorothy said, she had seen little of her Connecticut home. She had lived in Denver, Colorado, and other places—wherever she found the kind of expert coaching that she needed. When training for major competition, she practiced seven hours a day, six days a week.

In March, after the Olympics, Dorothy won first place in the world figure skating competition in Sweden. She then returned to a tumultuous "welcome home" celebration in Riverside. Shortly afterward, she retired from amateur competition. She said that she was going to become a professional skater. Her fans look forward to seeing her as the star of the Ice Capades.

...AND ON THE ICE

This is the logical conclusion of the Lap Game: the moment when everyone is sitting on everyone else's lap—more or less. It all started when an anchor person lay down on the ground, knees up. Madness followed.

In Orbit, the trick is to keep the big Earth Ball in the air. Here you see the outside team hitting the ball with their hands. You can't see the inside team. They're lying on the ground in the center, kicking with their feet.

FUN AND GAMES

Just imagine this! One day, on your way home from school, you happen to notice a large group of young people in a vacant lot. There are 25 or 30 of them, and they are all smiling or laughing. They've formed a big circle, and they all seem to be sitting on each other's laps. Yes, that's right, there really are 25 or 30 happy people sitting on each other's laps in the middle of a field.

Should you call the police? Should you call a doctor? Should you keep what you've seen to yourself for fear your parents will think you've lost your mind? No. The best thing you could do is see if there's room in the circle for one more. It's fun. In fact, it's a new game called the Lap Game.

It seems that the days of hide-and-seek, red rover, and tag are over—at least as far as some young people are concerned. The new games are mostly for groups of people, and they really are just for fun. There are no winners, there are no losers. The new games usually involve a group of people performing a humorous, or unusual, or difficult feat by working together.

The new games are fun—but they're more than fun. Educators like them as well as young people do. The new games can teach valuable lessons and skills. They prove that there can be real fun in games without serious competition. They also help young people work off excess energy and even forget their anger if they are upset about something. And the new games are so informal that participants can forget about complicated rules and just learn to be at ease with their bodies.

What better way to spend a summer day than fencing with your best friend? —using Styrofoam-covered boffers, of course. When someone is hit, boffers make a cracking sound but there are usually no injuries, not even to the boffers.

Planting a community garden can be a lot of fun—with delicious rewards.

DIG IN!

Hoes made soft sounds as they scraped the ground. Eager hands carefully lifted small seedlings from pots while others patted soil around newly planted seeds. All the workers seemed to be concentrating intently on what they were doing. What was going on? These youngsters were planting a community garden!

The land they worked on belongs to the Denver, Colorado, Botanical Gardens. But before any seeding was done, plans had been a long time in the making. The youngsters had to draw lots for their plots and decide what to plant where. Should they plant flowers as well as vegetables? (Of course. Some, like marigolds, are great natural pesticides.)

Sounds like fun? You bet! And you and your friends can do the same thing in your community. Maybe somebody has already organized a community garden. OK. Join up, or better yet, start another one. Look around. Are there any good-size pieces of land near you that nobody is using? Check your town hall, church, or garden club to see whether they know of any available land. With the owner's permission, you, too, can turn that plot into a community garden. Once the plot is found, start planning everything you will plant, and when. Find an expert to help you.

Once your seeds are in the ground, sit back and watch—work a little, too. Before long that bare ground will begin turning into a lush green island full of delicious fresh food. And you will have grown that food yourself.

That's the way it was in Denver. After a few weeks, small green shoots began to appear.

"Hey, my radishes are coming up!"

"Boy, my peas look great. Bet they'll be sweeter than yours—you'll see!"

"No way! My green beans are going to taste best!"

"I'll give you some of my buttercrunch lettuce if you'll give me some of your tomatoes when they get ripe later on."

It was hard to resist the temptation to pull some of the things up and see how they were growing, but the young Denver gardeners were patient. They hoed and watered and weeded, and often stood around just plain admiring their work.

Finally it was harvest time—a fat, tasty squash; ripe red tomatoes; crisp beans and parsley. Yummy vegetables and tasty makings for salads. Mouths watered. What feasts they would have!

Then, at summer's end, the youngsters created funny "creatures" to win prizes, and everyone shared in an enormous feast of all the goodies they had grown.

Dig in! What you dig up will be delicious!

Once you have a piece of land, you are ready to start your garden. Plant, hoe, water, and weed—soon you'll see a beautiful area of green growing all around you. Then at last it will be time to harvest, and get those yummy vegetables out of the ground and into the kitchen. And then, if you like, turn some of the vegetables into funny "creatures" and see who can make the best one!

215

YOUNG PHOTOGRAPHERS

Young people are curious about the world around them. Everything seems new and invites them to a great journey of discovery. A camera can be the perfect companion for a talented young person who sets out to discover the world. And the photographs young people take allow us all to go along on their journeys with them. Everything becomes exciting—a fall leaf, stately swans, a reflection in a pond, the patterns made by city lights at night. This is a selection of prize-winning photographs from the Scholastic Photography Awards contest of 1976. The contest was sponsored by the Eastman Kodak Company.

Untitled, by Peter Battersby, 14, Bellevue, Washington.

A Carnival Excursion, by Ron Levinson, 17, Highland Park, Illinois.

Untitled, by Larkin Duff, 17,
Seattle, Washington.

Indianapolis at Night, by Scott Shoemaker, 14,
Indianapolis, Indiana.

Autumn Rest, by Arnold Geller, 14, Cranston, Rhode Island.

Encased, by Lee Connor, 17, Seattle, Washington.

Break Thru, by Jim Schnepf, 17, Shawano, Wisconsin.

Multiple Horseman, by Donald Knight, 17, Seattle, Washington.

Quebec Venturers get ready to cast off for an exciting sailboat regatta.

BOY SCOUTS

It was a big year for world Scouting. By 1976 there were 14,200,000 boys, young men, and uniformed adult leaders enrolled in Scouting associations in 110 countries. More than 4,270,000 of these Scouts and leaders are in the United States and Canada.

Although Scouting methods are a little different in each country, Scouts everywhere have important things in common. They all pledge themselves to good citizenship, service to others, and physical, mental, and moral fitness.

▶ INTERNATIONAL SCOUTING EVENTS

In 1976 the largest international gathering of Boy Scouts was held in Melbourne, Australia. It was the 11th Australian National Jamboree. It began on December 21. About 10,000 Scouts from nations around the world attended.

There were other major international events, too, in widely scattered countries. In Canada, a Canadian Provincial Jamboree was held in Alberta. There was a month-long Scout Friendship Caravan in Israel. And the Caribbean nation of Trinidad and Tobago was host to a patrol camp.

Scouts and their leaders traveled a lot in 1976. More than 2,000 Scouts and leaders from a number of countries visited the United States during the U.S. Bicentennial year. They stayed in the homes of American Scouts. The visitors were able to play an active role in local Bicentennial celebrations and Scouting activities wherever they stayed. Many of the American Scouts who acted as hosts to visitors in 1976 will be visitors themselves in 1977. They will visit Scouts in Europe, Japan, Taiwan, and Latin America. Both the visits to the United States in 1976 and the overseas visits planned by American Scouts in 1977 are part of an international program called Scout Friendship Exchange.

Scout leaders had a special exchange of their own in 1976. More than 100 leaders from 24 countries were counselors in Scout summer camps in the United States. American Scouts continued to support the World Friendship Fund, which aids Scouting throughout the world. Contributions to the World Friendship

Fund help provide Scouting equipment, uniforms, books and pamphlets, and training for leaders in many countries.

ADVENTURES IN SCOUTING

Members of the Boy Scouts of America participated in thousands of local celebrations of their country's 200th birthday. They marched in parades, joined in local festivals, and worked on special service projects to improve their communities.

The most important national event in American Scouting was the Eagle Scout Bicentennial Celebration in Washington, D.C. Over 700 Eagle Scouts from every part of the United States participated. While they were in Washington, the visiting Eagle Scouts gave demonstrations of Scouting skills and acted as guides for summer visitors to the city. The Eagle Scouts themselves were also able to visit historic sites in and around Washington. The Boy Scouts of America will continue Bicentennial activities through August, 1977.

Scouting in the United States continued to work for conservation of natural resources in a variety of ways. In a campaign called Project SOAR (Save Our American Resources), Cub Scouts, Scouts, and Explorers worked on many projects aimed at conserving energy resources. Thousands of packs, troops, and posts collected wastepaper, metal, and glass. The chief purpose of the collections was to save energy. Less energy is needed to recycle waste than to make new products from raw materials, and it saves natural resources.

Another SOAR program involved the outdoors and wildlife. Cub Scouts, Scouts, and Explorers planted gardens and carried out projects to improve wildlife habitats. They planted shrubs to provide food and shelter for birds and small animals. They also set out bird feeders and nesting boxes for birds.

Almost 90 percent of the local Scout councils in the United States had SOAR activities in 1976. Many Scouting groups set up long-term conservation programs. These programs included litter prevention and erosion control along roadways and waterways.

MOVING ALONG

The Boy Scouts of America have three basic programs. There is Cub Scouting for boys 8

This New Jersey Explorer is trying his hand at teaching in a grade-school classroom as part of the Exploring Careers in Child Care program.

Canadian Beavers learning how to make—you guessed it—a beaver poster.

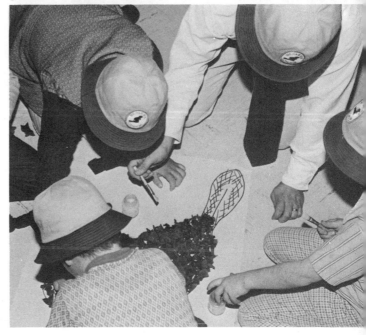

Co-educational volleyball (*left*) and men's soccer (*above*) were two of the events in the National Explorer Olympics, held in Colorado.

to 10 years old; Scouting for boys 11 to 17; and Exploring for young men and women of 15 to 20.

In Cub Scouting, there was an increase in the number of summer day camps and in the number of boys attending them. Most of the camps used recreation facilities run by local communities and industries. They provided a wide variety of sports as well as other outdoor activities.

In Scouting, changes were made in the program by which Scouts earn progress awards. The requirement that a Scout earn a merit badge to become a Tenderfoot was eliminated. In other changes, more requirements in outdoor and camping skills were added to the list of things a Scout has to accomplish to earn higher progress awards—Second Class through Eagle.

In 1976, Scouting also had a program called All Out for Scouting. About 200,000 boys and troop leaders took part. The activities and events in the program involved the development of outdoor skills and of Scouting's patrol system.

Exploring had two major national events in 1976. In March, 2,000 presidents of Explorer posts met in Washington, D.C., for the sixth national Explorer Presidents' Congress. Activities included seminars in leadership and careers, visits with government leaders, and many social events.

In June, the fourth biennial National Explorer Olympics was held at Colorado State University, Fort Collins, Colorado. The events were organized in co-operation with the United States Olympic Committee and other sports groups. There was competition for men and women in swimming, diving, gymnastics, track and field, archery, orienteering (a form of cross-country racing), cycling, basketball, field hockey, team handball, volleyball, golf, tennis, weight lifting, water polo, marksmanship, table tennis, chess, and public speaking. Additional men's events included soccer and wrestling.

The three highest-scoring teams in the National Explorer Olympics were invited to attend the 1976 world Olympic Games in Montreal, Canada. The winning teams formed the United States Youth Camp delegation at Montreal. The winning teams were from Post 169 of Temple City, California; Post 89 of Austin, Texas; and Post 604 of Oklahoma City, Oklahoma.

Other important Explorer events in 1976 covered a wide range of interests. Among the events were the National Explorer Sailing Championship in New Orleans, Louisiana; Invitational Canoe Races in Arkansas; and ski conferences in Minnesota and Utah.

Explorers and older Scouts who belonged to Florida Gateway High Adventure Base had an exciting new adventure in 1976. It was a scuba-diving program and it took place in the Bahamas, a favorite spot for scuba divers from all over the world. The Florida base is one of six high adventure bases run by the Boy Scouts of America. There are others in Maine, Minnesota, Wisconsin, New Mexico, and on the Kentucky-Tennessee border.

The National Eagle Scout Association (NESA) added 10,000 new members in 1976. It is Scoutings's top honor organization. NESA is made up of both young men and older men who have earned Scouting's highest award, the Eagle Scout progress award. In August, NESA held its second biennial convention, in Washington, D.C.

The National Council of the Boy Scouts of America met in New York City in May. They re-elected Arch Monson, Jr., of San Francisco as president. Harvey L. Price, formerly the Los Angeles Scout executive, was appointed Acting Chief Scout Executive. He succeeds Alden G. Barber in the highest professional position in the Boy Scouts of America.

And in 1976, the American Scouting movement made some changes in their famous three-leaf (fleur-de-lis) symbol. The new design keeps the basic symbol and adds, below it, the words "Scouting/USA." The new symbol will be used to mark all Scout camps and offices, and will appear on all official books and pamphlets.

HARVEY L. PRICE
Acting Chief Scout Executive
Boy Scouts of America

A lesson in scuba diving is part of the Boy Scouts of America's high adventure program.

GIRL SCOUTS AND GIRL GUIDES

There are now almost 7,300,000 people in 94 countries around the world who are active in Girl Scout or Girl Guide groups. The World Association of Girl Guides and Girl Scouts (WAGGGS) is the international body that helps Girl Scouts and Girl Guides from Argentina to Zambia to work toward their common goals of peace and better understanding among all peoples.

▶ WORLD ASSOCIATION

The World Association of Girl Guides and Girl Scouts (WAGGGS) was founded in 1928 to bring fellowship and unity of purpose to Guide and Scout organizations all over the world.

WAGGGS has worked with the United Nations and its specialized agencies for many years. Through the UNESCO Cooperative Action Programme, WAGGGS receives grants for a number of its own projects. In 1976 these included a literacy project in Ecuador and leadership projects in Argentina and Peru.

WAGGGS also helps member organizations to have a voice in international discussions of special interest to girls and women. WAGGGS sent delegates to the International Women's Year Conference, which was held in Mexico in 1975.

▶ ACTIVITIES AROUND THE WORLD

Wherever they are, Girl Guide and Girl Scout groups try to learn the needs of their communities, so that they may better help to meet them. In 1976 special attention was given to education in nutrition and to literacy projects.

Liberian Girl Guides hope to improve their country's village gardens. They have started by working in one village. They plan to give information about good nutrition to the villagers and show them how to plant a garden in which they can grow the food they need for good health. The Liberian Girl Guides have prepared a list of good foods available in Liberia. They will use the list to teach villagers good sources of protein, vitamins, and iron. The Guides will begin by working with

A Girl Guide counselor from Ghana models her uniform for American campers.

village mothers. Then they will encourage the mothers to teach the other villagers what they have learned.

Girl Guides in Pakistan have also been doing valuable community work. There were severe floods in Pakistan in 1973. At that time the Pakistani Guides began to work in small villages that had been damaged by the floods. They saw that the villagers needed to improve the way they ate. The Guides decided to start their own project. They chose a village of about 700 people. By 1974 they had begun teaching the villagers how to balance their diets, using foods they already knew how to grow. They also helped them improve their farming and gardening methods.

However, as the Pakistani Guides worked with the villagers, they began to see how one problem—poor nutrition—was connected with many other problems the villagers had. In the village they had chosen, the Pakistani Guides also became involved in helping to wipe out malaria, in improving the village water supply and drainage system, in holding classes to teach people to learn to read and write, and in teaching the villagers how they could increase their incomes.

Two years ago the Girl Guides Association of Panama launched a project called *Plato Completo* ("full plate"). The Panamanian Guides wanted to help the people of one of the poorest sections of the city of Santiago. The goal was to improve the health of the community in every way possible. Improving nutrition was a major goal of the program. The Guides set up an adult community center. At the center classes were offered in subjects the women themselves felt they wanted to study. The subjects included reading and writing, family education, nutrition, cooking, poultry farming, first aid, dressmaking, knitting, and handicrafts.

Poultry farming was a popular course because it helped families eat better and it helped increase their incomes. Many Santiago housewives were soon able to raise enough chickens to feed their families—and have enough left to sell.

Improving nutrition and preventing hunger are not just concerns of developing countries. There is important work in these areas for Girl Guides and Girl Scouts of industrialized nations, too.

In the United States, for instance, the Girl Scouts of Suffolk County, New York, started a new food project in honor of their country's

A Brazilian girl learns to write in a class taught by Girl Guides.

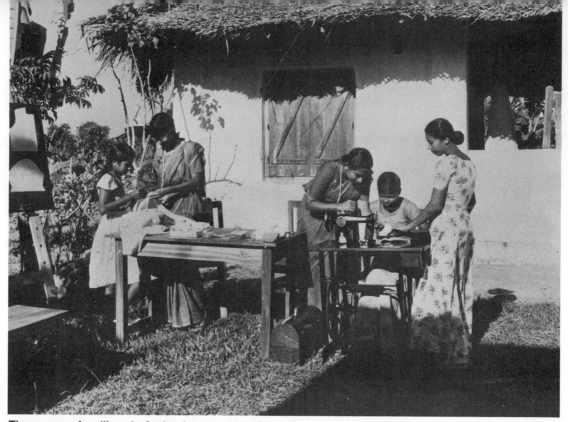

The women of a village in Ceylon learn to sew with the help of Girl Guides.

Bicentennial. The project is called Gardening for the Hungry at Home and Abroad. The Scouts in this project planted gardens using both modern and American colonial gardening methods. They then sold some of the produce from the gardens and used the money they earned to buy seed peanuts for Sangam, a WAGGGS center in India. The produce they didn't sell to raise money was delivered to emergency food-distribution centers in Suffolk County. The girls also collected surplus crops donated by other community gardeners in their area. This food was then distributed to poor people who needed it.

In 1976, eleven new Girl Scout gardening sites were started in Suffolk County. In fact, Gardening for the Hungry has grown so fast and reached so deeply into so many Suffolk County communities that the project is expected to continue long after the other Bicentennial celebrations are over.

While Guides and Scouts in some countries battle the problem of undernourished bodies, Guides and Scouts in other countries fight the problem of undernourished minds—illiteracy. Because 60 percent of the illiterates in the world are women, Girl Scouts and Girl Guides in many countries can play a vital role in the war against illiteracy.

In India, the older Rangers went into 50 villages in a campaign against illiteracy. They lived with the women of these villages while they taught them arithmetic and reading and writing. This helped the women sell their produce at the market without being cheated. They became eager students. Soon they wanted courses in hygiene, nutrition, and many other subjects.

Guides in Papua New Guinea are supervising lessons by mail for children who are primary and secondary school dropouts. In Turkey, Girl Guides are running literacy programs for adults and also have special courses for children who cannot go to school. Senior Guides in Denmark are producing their own materials for teaching children to read. They make word games, picture cards, and flash cards. They are especially interested in working with the children of migrant workers living in Denmark, who often do not know Danish.

When Girl Guides in El Salvador decided to start a literacy project, they went where the people were—into the open-air markets that most Latin American towns and cities still have. Every working day, Girl Guides in the capital city, San Salvador, went to two large markets to teach the women there to read and write. The project has proved so successful that two more markets in the city have been added to the program. More than 200 women a year learn to read and write in this program.

Girl Scouts of the U.S.A. is the largest national organization in WAGGGS. In addition to their wide variety of activities in the United States, the American Girl Scouts are involved in many international exchange programs. The American organization also coordinates programs for Girl Scouts and Girl Guides from other countries who come to the United States for special projects.

Girl Guides and Girl Scouts from other countries who visited the United States in 1976 also helped celebrate the American Bicentennial. A large Bicentennial event sponsored by the Girl Scouts of Philadelphia, Pennsylvania, drew 70 international participants.

In 1976, Canadian Girl Guides had a unique opportunity to share in an international experience right in their own backyard. The United Nations Conference on Human Settlements, also known as Habitat, was held in June in Vancouver, British Columbia. The Canadian Girl Guides Association helped in planning the conference. Girl Guides of all ages learned about the topics being discussed at the conference. Older Girl Guides began planning continuing community projects, based on things they had learned at the Habitat conference.

The Canadian Guides are working hard to bring handicapped girls into their programs. In most of the provinces of Canada, advisers with special knowledge of the problems of the handicapped are working with Guide leaders. Brownie and Girl Guide handbooks in braille are now being distributed to every school for blind students.

International friendship is not just an empty slogan for Girl Guides and Girl Scouts around the world. On February 22 they have Thinking Day. This is the day on which Girl Scouts and Girl Guides all over the world re-dedicate themselves to world fellowship.

CAROL BROOKS STROUGHTER
Girl Scouts of the U.S.A.

Girl Scouts in Suffolk County, New York, in one of their successful Bicentennial gardens.

Canadian Rangers visited Belgium in 1976 as part of an international exchange program.

FUN TO READ

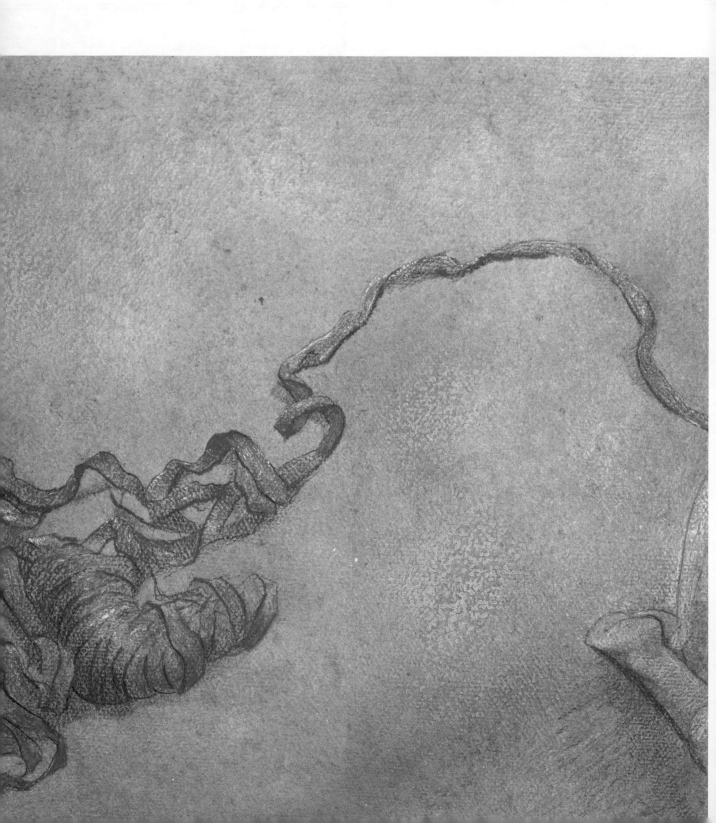

One of the most beautiful and unusual new books of 1976 was *A Special Birthday*, by Symeon Shimin. It is a story told without words—the charming illustrations say it all.

A lithograph of the period showing the vast and impressive land the Sager family saw when their wagon train reached the Rocky Mountains.

Children Headed West

This is a true story about some children who were part of the great movement of pioneers headed into the American West in the 19th century. One of the children, Catherine Sager (known to her family as Katy), later wrote a detailed account of the exciting and tragic adventure she shared with her brothers and sisters. Parts of this story are based on Katy's account.

"Daddy, when can we go to Oregon?" Katy Sager was folding her best calico dress before packing it away in a chest with the rest of her clothes.

"Soon, Katy," her father, Henry Sager, said. "We'll start just as soon as your Ma gets done packing and I load the wagon. We'll head for Capler's Landing."

"But Capler's Landing isn't Oregon! It's just up the river."

"That's where we'll meet all the other folks who'll be in our wagon train, Katy. Capler's Landing is where we leave the Missouri River behind us. The trail west begins beyond the Missouri."

"But when will we really be on the trail?" Katy was getting tired of waiting for their great adventure to start.

"April, I reckon. That's when we'll really get going." He squinted at the rain-swept fields. "As soon as this weather clears, we'll start west on the trail. And then there'll be no more ice and snow for us, Katy! It almost never snows in Oregon. It's green all year round. And they say everything you plant out there grows so fast you have to scamper to get out of its way."

Katy liked that idea. Oregon had begun to seem like heaven to her. She went back into the little cabin where they'd been living. Her father had sold their farm and his blacksmith shop to raise the money for their covered wagon, their team of oxen, and the supplies they would need for the journey—and there was a little money left over to start their new life in the West.

"Daddy says we can leave for Oregon as soon as we're packed," Katy told her mother. "Let me help so we can finish right away."

Naomi Sager, Katy's mother, straightened up wearily. She had been examining the contents of her cedar chest. Naomi was expecting a baby soon. She found it hard to concentrate on the hard and almost hopeless task of deciding which of her precious belongings she would take with her and which would have to be left behind. There wasn't room for much in a covered wagon; everything you took had to have a purpose.

"Oh, dear, what's the rush, Katy?"

"Don't you want to go to Oregon, Mama?"

"I suppose so," Naomi said. But at the same time she really wished they could wait until the baby came—or, better yet, wait until next year when the baby would be older and not so much of a care. But her husband Henry was possessed with the idea of reaching the rich land of Oregon. He had determined that they would go now, this spring of 1844, and no later. And the boys were just as determined as their father. Now even Katy had Oregon fever, as everyone was calling the urge to move West.

"If you want to help me, see what the little ones are up to," she told Katy. Elizabeth and Matilda Sager were supposed to be watching their little sister Hannah Louise—but they could still be mighty scatterbrained.

Finally, Henry Sager did load his wagon. He and Naomi got aboard with their six children. Katy, at nine, was the oldest girl. John was thirteen and Francisco (who was called Frank) was eleven. Then there was Elizabeth, who was seven; Matilda Jane, who was five; and Hannah Louise, who was just three. They were all off for the Promised Land. It was not soon enough for Henry Sager; it was too soon for Naomi.

Off to Oregon

By mid-April, the 48 wagons of the people from around St. Joseph, Missouri, who had planned to make the trip West together were gathered at the appointed meeting place on the west bank of the Missouri River—Capler's Landing. The Sagers were among them. The whole company elected Captain Cornelius Gilliam to be their leader on the perilous trail. Gilliam had as his assistant a man named Michael Simmons. The wagon train was then divided into four companies of twelve wagons each, with a commander for each company. William Shaw was commander of the company that the Sagers were to travel in. Shaw was a close friend of the Sager family and a strong leader. The Sager children called him Uncle Billy.

In addition to the caravan the Sagers were traveling in, there were three other large caravans of emigrants moving along the trail to Oregon in that spring of 1844. Often, the caravans stayed within a few days of each other. But the wagon train leaders had learned from the experience of the Great Migration of 1843, in which a thousand people had traveled west, that it was better for large caravans to keep at a considerable distance from each other. In dry weather you literally had to "eat the dust" made by the wagon train ahead of you if the trains weren't spaced far enough apart.

A pioneer family cooked beside the trail after a hard day's journey.

In the beginning of the Sagers' journey, the problem didn't prove to be dust; it was mud. For six weeks rain poured down nearly every day. It was a year of great floods. Wagons struggling across raging streams were often in danger of being swept away by the current.

At one point the Sagers' wagon train camped by a river that actually did overflow its banks. Many of the wagons were flooded. The whole group had to move back a day's journey on the trail to escape the torrent. Everything in the Sagers' wagon was soaked. The sun seldom came out long enough for them to dry the bedding. Even Katy and the boys, shivering under damp blankets at night, began to think the Oregon adventure wasn't so much fun after all. And Henry Sager, who had never driven a team of oxen before, had trouble with his animals until Uncle Billy showed him the rather rough trick of throwing a few rocks at the team to hurry them along.

But when the sun finally did come out, Katy romped on the prairie and picked wildflowers, while John and Frank, her brothers, kept a sharp eye out for buffalo and took turns learning to drive the oxen. Then it began to seem to Katy as if every day on the trail was like a marvelous picnic.

Another Sager

On May 30, in the midst of a downpour, the drenched wagons reached the Nemaha River, near present-day Seneca, Kansas. Women came hurrying to the Sagers' wagon, and the children were bundled off to stay with friends in other wagons. Katy was old enough to know what all the unusual activity meant. She'd been through it all back home—but never on the Oregon Trail!

The next morning Aunt Sally Shaw, Uncle Billy's wife, told Katy the news.

"It's a girl. Your mother's ailing, so keep the children quiet and good."

Another girl. Frank and John Sager had wanted a brother. But their new sister did have the distinction of being the first baby born in their wagon train.

The wagons waited in the rain while the women cared for Naomi Sager. The river was badly flooded, so no one even attempted to cross it until noon. Even then, the Sagers' wagon didn't move.

Katy was worried. Her mother was in great pain, she knew. Mama had to get well so they could go on. How long would the wagon train wait for them?

The men controlled their impatience to move on as well as they could. Finally, on June 3, the train began moving again. The Sager wagon was moving with it. But every bump was agony for Naomi, who was still very ill. Naomi had begun to fear that she would never be well again.

Buffalo and Bad Luck

On July 7, they reached the wide, muddy Platte River. There were many stories about the characteristics of the Platte. It was sometimes said that the river was "too shallow to swim, too thick to drink." Not until their arrival at the Platte did the rain stop. A few days later, another major event took place. Someone looking out over the plains shouted:

"Buffalo!"

There they were, tremendous herds of the shaggy beasts. Yelling and shooting off their rifles, the men saddled up their horses and galloped off madly in pursuit of the buffalo. These people knew how valuable buffalo hides were and how useful for food and every other imaginable purpose the carcasses would be. They had learned this lesson from the Plains Indians. Katy was sure the men had lost their minds when she saw them dashing off so wildly. The whole caravan came to a complete standstill and the hunters didn't return until nightfall.

Quarrels began to break out the next morning. Some of the emigrants wanted to move on right away. They were disgusted by the blind killing of the animals and by the carcasses littering the ground. However, other pioneers considered the buffalo too valuable a treasure to pass up. They insisted on staying another day to hunt. Finally, the leader, Captain Gilliam, did agree to a day's delay—but no longer. The wagon train waited for the hunters to finish their work.

It was not quite the same wagon train that got moving after the buffalo hunt. The debate over killing the buffalo had brought to the surface many disagreements that had developed among the settlers during the journey. The wagon train was now divided into conflicting factions. The conflicts among the pioneers grew so fierce that Gilliam and his assistant Simmons, both of whom had been elected by the whole caravan back in Missouri, were forced to resign their commands. Now the caravan had no single leader. Each company in the wagon train became independent under the command of its own leader. That was good for the Sagers since they trusted their leader Bill Shaw (Uncle Billy) completely.

One day the wheels of the Sager wagon ran up on a ledge alongside the trail. The wagon tipped over. Horrified, Henry Sager dug through the confusion of all their worldly possessions to rescue his family. Katy's dress was nearly torn off, but she was unhurt. But Naomi lay unconscious under the twisted canvas of the wagon's roof. By the time the men had gotten the wagon back in an upright position and had repacked it, Naomi had regained consciousness. She moaned a bit as they lifted her back into the wagon. And then she felt the wagon jolting along the trail again.

Katy often rode with her father on the high front seat of their wagon. The wagon moved so slowly that when she got bored with sitting, she could jump down and explore the prairie near the trail. She found unfamiliar and fascinating flowers and rocks. Sometimes she would try to follow a stray prairie dog to his hole. On July 30, Katy made her last carefree jump from the wagon. As she jumped down that day, her long dress caught on an ax handle that was sticking out of the wagon. She fell. Before her father could stop the team, one of the wagon wheels had rolled over her leg.

Elizabeth, one of Katy's younger sisters, screamed. When Henry Sager was finally able to halt the oxen, he jumped down off the wagon. Katy's leg was badly twisted.

There was no doctor in the Sager's company of wagons. However, a friend rode back to the company behind them to fetch Dr. Dagon, a German physician who was traveling west as part of the caravan. Henry was desperate because Katy was in pain and he couldn't be sure how long it might take for the doctor to reach them. (The other company might well be several miles behind them.) Finally, he decided to set Katy's leg himself. There was no doubt that it was broken.

When Dr. Dagon did come galloping up, he knelt by Katy and examined her leg.

"Why you did as good as I could myself!" he told Henry.

The doctor picked the little girl up and carried her to a bed in the back of the Sager wagon. Her mother, Naomi, was in the wagon, as well as the new baby. The doctor soon discovered that the baby was ill, too. He offered to ride along with the Sagers to make sure they were taken care of.

Katy tried not to cry with the pain of her leg. Now there were three of them ailing, she thought. Would they ever get to Oregon?

Camp Fever

On August 1, the wagon train left Fort Laramie (in present-day Wyoming). It would still take them two months to reach their destination in the Blue Mountains of Oregon. And there was the danger that snow would catch them in the mountain passes along the way. Fall wasn't far off. The caravan continued on its way. Many of the emigrants were worried.

They had reason to worry. An epidemic broke out before the end of August. The emigrants called the disease "camp fever." No one knew what it was or how to treat it. They only knew that people died of it. Soon after the wagon train had crossed the Continental Divide at South Pass, Henry Sager felt the first symptoms of camp fever—sore throat and nausea. He continued to drive his team until his fever was so high he could no longer sit upright on the driver's seat of the wagon. Friends put up a tent for the sick man beside the Green River (in present-day Wyoming) and carried him to it.

When his friend Bill Shaw came into the tent, he saw tears running down Henry Sager's cheeks.

"I'm dying, Bill," he said. "Promise to take care of my family. Take them to Marcus Whitman's mission in Oregon."

Shaw promised to do what his friend asked. Henry Sager did die, and he was buried beside the trail on August 29.

Dazed with grief, Naomi at first refused an offer from Dr. Dagon to drive her wagon the rest of the way to Oregon. She respected the physician but he was the first "foreigner" she had ever known. She wasn't sure she should trust her life and the lives of her children to a stranger. Instead, she hired a young American in the company to drive for her. However, he promptly stole the one musket the Sagers owned and disappeared. Then Naomi had to accept Dr. Dagon's help. And he proved to be a true and loyal friend to the whole family.

Heartbroken, fearing her sons John and Frank might also have camp fever, worried about her baby, who wasn't strong, and about Katy's broken leg, Naomi still fought furiously to stay alive. But as the wagons followed the winding course of the Snake River, the mountain nights began to grow bitterly cold. Naomi was still weak from the birth of her child and from the illness that had followed. She couldn't fight off camp fever any longer herself. Late in September she gathered her children around her and begged them to stay together as a family. Then she, too, died. The seven Sager children were orphans adrift in the vast American wilderness.

As it turned out, the Sager children were adopted by the whole wagon train. John, who suddenly became the man of the family at thirteen, helped Dr. Dagon drive the wagon. His brother, Frank, and his four sisters rode in the back of the wagon. The women of the company took turns helping the girls with the baby. And the Shaws and many other families shared their food with the Sagers.

At one point the Sagers' wagon collapsed while they were crossing the Snake River. There was talk of abandoning the wagon and splitting the family up, distributing the children among several families in the wagon train. But Uncle Billy Shaw got the men to cut the damaged wagon in half, making a kind of cart of it. The children continued on in their cart. They were still together. Finally, they reached the Blue Mountain country of Oregon.

The Whitman mission as it looked when the Sager children got there.

The wagon train halted at a point where a side trail branched off to the already-famous mission established by Dr. Marcus Whitman near the site of present-day Walla Walla, Washington. (The present-day states of Oregon and Washington were both included in the Oregon territory of the mid-19th century.) Dr. Whitman and his wife, Narcissa, were Protestant missionaries to the Indians. They were among the first American settlers in the Oregon territory. Remembering his promise to Henry Sager, Bill Shaw rode the 40 miles (65 kilometers) to the mission to ask the Whitmans to give the Sager children a home. He told Narcissa Whitman of Naomi Sager's dying wish that her children should stay together.

Narcissa Whitman had lost her only child five years before. She already had four foster children at the mission. Could she and Marcus take care of seven more? But then Narcissa thought of the little Sager baby who was sick and without a mother. She couldn't refuse Bill Shaw's request.

Late in October, Dr. Dagon and Bill Shaw brought the cart loaded with children—all Sagers—to the Whitman mission.

"Your children have come," Shaw told Narcissa. When she reached the cart, Narcissa found the little girls searching madly for their bonnets. Seeing her, the girls froze, huddling together. They were barefooted as well as bareheaded. Some of the children cried, perhaps from nervousness, perhaps from relief at finding a home at last.

"We thought . . . she was the prettiest woman we had ever seen," Katy Sager wrote later, describing her family's first meeting with Narcissa Whitman. Katy went on to tell what an odd spectacle she and her brothers and sisters were when they arrived at the mission. She said that they were "dirty and sunburnt . . . . and John had cropped our hair, so it hung in uneven locks."

The first thing Narcissa did after welcoming her new family was to scrub the children and trim their hair properly. The baby was filthy and looked half-starved when she was handed over to Narcissa. She sucked hungrily on the bottle that had been prepared for her and then slept soundly in a warm cradle. Marcus Whitman decided the baby should be named Henrietta, in honor of her real father, Henry Sager.

Katy, still lame from her fall, clung close to Narcissa. She had reached Oregon at last. But how different it all was from her dream! Her parents were dead and the new life at the mission seemed so strange, despite the kindness of the Whitmans. As she wrote afterwards, she "shed many tears in solitude" that first autumn.

The Promised Land

If this story were fiction, it would have ended happily with the arrival of the Sager children at the mission. But this is a true story of pioneer days. Life in the West was hard for people of all ages.

For a while, life at the Whitman mission was pleasant enough for the Sager children. Narcissa was a stern mother, but she was loving. And Katy herself later admitted that the free life of the trail had made her, and her brothers and sisters, quite wild. Eventually, most of the children adjusted to life at the mission. But Frank Sager, the rebel among them, always resented the Whitmans' discipline. He particularly disliked a teacher the Whitmans had hired to run a school for their foster children. Evidently the teacher was an old-fashioned disciplinarian and was in the habit of beating the children when they didn't obey. When their first spring in Oregon came, Frank Sager, who was then twelve, ran away to make a life of his own in the frontier West. By fall he was back home at the mission. Luckily for Frank, a kinder teacher had taken over the school.

The Sager children worked hard. They were used to that. They helped Narcissa with the household chores and they helped Marcus Whitman work his fields. In spite of the time taken up by their chores, by school, and by the religious life of the mission, there were some things they did just for fun. Narcissa took the children on picnics in the woods and taught them the names of trees and wildflowers. And each of the girls had her own flower garden. The Walla Walla River, which ran near the mission, became the Sager children's favorite place of all for a good time in the summer months. The older children learned how to swim and the younger ones played on the river bank. The children thrived and grew tan and sturdy.

Marcus Whitman was a physician as well as a religious missionary. Among the Cayuse Indians of the area, a medicine man, or doctor, was traditionally rewarded with gifts and honors when his patients got well. However, if a patient died, the medicine man was blamed for it. In fact, the family of a person who had died had the right, among the Cayuse, to kill the medicine man who had been treating their dead relative. Marcus Whitman knew he walked a tightrope when he treated Cayuse patients. But as a doctor and a religious man, he had no intention of refusing to treat anyone who needed help.

Whitman's problems at the mission were multiplied by the harsh winter of 1846–47. It was one of the most severe winters in the history of the West. Snow came early and stayed late. Many of the cattle owned by the Cayuse people froze to death. It began to seem to the Indians that the powerful white medicine man who lived among them, Dr. Marcus Whitman, must somehow be responsible for their sufferings. To make matters worse, Whitman was so busy during that dreadful winter rescuing white emigrants stranded on the Oregon Trail by the bad weather that he didn't have as much time as usual to work closely with the Indians. They resented his neglect. Then, in the fall of 1847, word came to the mission that an epidemic of measles had broken out among the wagon trains on the Oregon Trail. Measles was a white man's disease. For the Indians, who had no natural resistance to it, it could be fatal.

Whitman worked day and night treating emigrants, Indians, and members of his own mission household who had contracted measles. (By then, the population of the Whitman mission itself had risen to about seventy people.) Among the Cayuse the death toll mounted alarmingly. Some estimates indicate that half the Cayuse people in the area died of measles within two months.

Meanwhile, a renegade white named Joe Lewis was stirring up trouble with the Indians. Lewis had been thrown off a westbound wagon train in a bitter dispute. As a result he was determined to make trouble for the white settlers in Oregon, whom he had come to hate. Lewis went among the Cayuse, pointing out that white children usually recovered quickly from measles while Indian children often didn't. Perhaps, Lewis suggested, the white doctor's "medicine" was really poison.

The Cayuse leaders, frantic with worry over the fate of their people, reached what was, for them, the inevitable conclusion. The white medicine man, Marcus Whitman, had to die if any of the Cayuse were to survive.

On November 29, 1847, the Indians attacked the Whitman mission without warning. They killed some people. They held others hostage. Thirteen people died at the mission—twelve men and boys and one woman. Marcus Whitman and John and Frank Sager died. Narcissa Whitman was the one woman killed. She died gallantly defending a terrified group of women and children.

The Cayuse held the survivors of the massacre captive for a month. Hannah Louise Sager, who was ill before the attack started, died during the captivity. Finally, Peter Skene Ogden of the powerful Hudson's Bay Company was able to persuade the Indians to let him ransom their hostages.

The Indians traded their fifty or so captives for 62 blankets, 63 cotton shirts, 12 rifles, 600 loads of ammunition, 12 flints, and 37 pounds (nearly 17 kilos) of tobacco.

On December 29, a wagon train of survivors left the mission. When they reached the Columbia River, there were boats waiting to take them downriver to the settlement that was to become Portland, Oregon. There Ogden turned the Sager children over to the provisional governor, George Abernethy. Their old friend Uncle Billy Shaw was also on hand to greet the Sagers. The Governor himself looked after them until foster homes were found for them.

So in 1848, Katy, Elizabeth, Matilda, and little Henrietta Sager were separated, and each was sent to a different foster home. Times on the frontier were hard, and no one could take them all. The Sager family was finally settled in Oregon. But they could never be, as their father Henry Sager had dreamed, all together in the Promised Land.

a historical adventure by ELISABETH MARGO

Live and Let Live

Horace Tailington was a mouse of some distinction. He lived in one of the finest old houses on Washington Square in New York City. His place of business was in the Washington Market, near the Hudson River. Horace was in cheese. In Horace's day, many of the wholesale cheese dealers of the city were located in the market district.

Horace came of a long line of English gentlemice. His forebears had sailed to New York aboard a clipper ship out of Plymouth. Tailington family tradition had it that the original American Tailingtons had enjoyed absolutely first-class accommodations on their journey. They had been snugly berthed—all the way across the Atlantic—in a Chinese Chippendale sideboard destined for the house of the governor of New York.

The Tailingtons had originally settled in a modest but comfortable merchant's establishment off South Street, quite close to the exotic sounds and smells of the East River docks. Five-hundred-times (or so) great-grandfather Godolphin Tailington, who had founded the American line of the family, had been in cheese too, although he had also dabbled a bit in the grain market. However, as the Tailingtons' fortunes improved, they joined the general movement of society uptown. They finally settled on Washington Square. The entrance to their comfortable residence was hand-chiseled into the solid cherry baseboard in the front parlor of Number 50 Washington Square.

Horace was an exceptionally well-organized mouse. He had always possessed that quality and had a reputation for it. If you asked any of his friends over at the Wedge of Cheese Club what Horace was like, the first word they would say would be "organized," and then the other, usual things, such as "jolly good fellow," "proud tailed," "fast on his feet," and even "quicker than a cat's whisker!" But "organized" was always the average mouse's first reaction to hearing Horace Tailington's name. When the mice down at the Wedge of Cheese gathered to sing club songs, it was always Horace who sang lead securely and on key, no matter how many off-key squeaks there were from younger members. And when they twined tails in comradely fashion as they sang "Auld Lang Syne" at the end of every club meeting, it was Horace who could be counted on to bind all the interlocked tails together with a double, pretzel-shaped flourish of his own tail.

And Horace's home life and business life were equally well organized. His beloved wife, Brie, with Horace's support and good counsel, kept a magnificent household running smoothly. The four children, their daughters, Daventry and Wensleydale, and their sturdy little sons, Stilton and Cheshire, were well brought up and got to school on time every day. And Tailington Unlimited, Horace's cheese company, was as well run as his household.

Horace Tailington was, in effect, a middle-mouse. His well-trained and disciplined crew of cheese runners knew the cheese warehouses of the Washington Market inside and out. Through an intricate network of tunnels that linked the whole market district, Horace's runners brought neatly gnawed squares of cheese—all kinds from many parts of the country and the world—to the show-rooms of Tailington Unlimited. And the purveyors of cheese to the mice and even the rats of the city all came to Horace's establishment for their wholesale supplies. The dealers catering to the mouse trade chose the more special and delicate cheeses. However, those doing business with the rats bought the least distinguished cheddars. Rats undoubtedly had coarser tastes.

All in all, Horace Tailington's life was a good one. And he was the best-organized mouse in New York. But all that ended quite abruptly one fine day in spring. Horace had walked at a leisurely pace from his house on Washington Square to his place of business near the river. It was a fine day, and so he whistled softly between his rather prominent front teeth, as mice will do when they're content. And as he walked he twirled his blackthorn walking stick, sent to him by a distant cousin in Ireland. Horace didn't have a care in the world, because he had organized his life so successfully. But when he neared the familiar front hole of Tailington Unlimited, he saw a sight that stunned him. In front of his own business establishment was the biggest, most disreputable, reddest, most spoiling-for-a-fight tomcat he had ever seen. And that tomcat's considerable bulk was without doubt barring anyone from entering.

"I beg your pardon," said Horace, standing quite erect and glaring the tom straight in the eye, "but this is my place of business. Will you please let me pass? I have half a dozen shipments of cheese coming in today and little time to spare."

"You're not going anyplace, mouse," said the cat. "I'm here to see you don't."

Horace thought he would try another approach to the big red tom.

"What's your name, my good fellow?"

"Rake O'Mouser—and what's it to you, mouse?"

"Well, Mr. O'Mouser," said Horace (with a bit of a shudder at the horrid implications of that last name), "who sent you to guard my doorway? It seems a boring task and certainly nothing you would do for the pleasure of it."

"I'm in the pay of the Cheese Merchants Association of New York. They want you out of business. The head of the Association will be dropping me off every day on his way to work and he'll pick me up on his way home. The nightcat's name is Tom Fleetpaw, and he's just as tough as me. So you're as good as out of business, mouse."

"My name, Mr. O'Mouser, is Horace Tailington. *Mister* Tailington. Let's be reasonable about this. The Cheese Merchants Association and my family have worked side by side for generations. Our demands on their warehouses are small, and my firm does neat, efficient removal work. I have the best-organized, most careful group of cheese runners in the city. The Association wouldn't like it much if some messy, fly-by-night group of mice moved into the cheese trade—or worse, rats. No, Tailington Unlimited keeps the business orderly and respectable."

"Nevertheless, Tailington," said Rake with a twitch of his tail, "they've hired me and that's that."

"What do you get for the work, Mr. O'Mouser? In wages, I mean."

"A good feed every night when I get home—a bowl of milk and a plate of more or less fresh mackerel."

"I see. I see. If you'll just let me put the CLOSED TEMPO-RARILY sign up on the entrance, I'll clear out for now. I do believe this will be the first day I have failed to open Tailington Unlimited since I took over from my dear father all those years ago."

"That's the way it goes, Tailington. Now put up your sign and get out!"

Horace slipped nervously into his familiar office. The coal scuttle that stood by the potbellied stove was filled in case the spring weather should turn cold. His green eyeshade waited on the tall account desk. His morning edition of the *Squeak and Scurry* (a widely read newspaper among mice) was on the desk. But until he solved the problem of Rake O'Mouser he couldn't enjoy his familiar routine. With resignation Horace hung the CLOSED TEMPO-RARILY sign at the entrance. For the first time in his life, Horace Tailington was feeling nervous—and distinctly unorganized.

When he reached the sidewalk, Horace saw half a dozen of his loyal employees peeking out from behind the rear wheel of a big cart drawn up on the opposite side of the street.

"My compliments to you, Mr. O'Mouser," said Horace. "We'll meet again." Horace then tipped his hat to Rake, whose only response was an annoyed twitch of his slightly crumpled left ear.

"Life's not one big tea party, Tailington," commented the cat as an afterthought. "You'd better steer clear of me!"

"We'll see about that! We'll see," said Horace. He crossed the street to calm his employees.

"Oh, sir, we're out in the street," squeaked old Nibblehof, an elderly Limburger runner near retirement age.

"Now, now, Nibblehof," said Horace, "calm yourself. I'll settle this matter and we'll be back in business in no time at all."

Horace was not so sure of himself as he sounded. But he dried a few tears, patted a few backs, promised holiday pay for the time lost, and then hurried home.

The children were at school and Brie was out having a dress fitted at the local dressmaking establishment when Horace arrived home. He went directly into his study and began pacing up and down. And the more he paced, the fewer ideas he got and the more nervous and disorganized in his thinking he became. What could he do? What would become of them all? Would the children have to drop out of school? What if Tailington Unlimited should never, never open again? Would Brie be reduced to taking in washing? Would he have to peddle a few crumbs of cheese hole-to-hole through the neighborhood?

Horace poured himself a bracing glass of dandelion wine from a decanter that stood on the desk.

"Calm yourself, Horace," he said, addressing himself. "There is too much at stake here to behave wildly and thoughtlessly."

That cat's wages did seem meager. Oh, yes, cats did like fish and milk a good deal. But more-or-less fresh mackerel? That wouldn't be a treat to even the most debased feline taste. And only milk to wash it down with? No side dishes of liver or bits of salmon? No Hudson River shad? That O'Mouser chap was coarse, but he was no fool! Those weren't decent wages he was getting.

"I wonder . . .," thought Horace.

It was a difficult evening for Horace. He told Brie about his disaster at the office but said nothing in front of Daventry, Wensleydale, Stilton, and Cheshire. The less they knew about cats the better.

"You must not be so concerned, dear," said Brie when the children had been excused from the table to do their homework.

"But what will become of us? I feel completely disorganized for the first time in my life. In fact, the world is falling apart before my eyes!"

"You have connections in this city, my dear. Some friend will surely be able to help us."

For the first time in the course of an awful day, Horace's spirits lifted. He had thought of something. He had remembered an old —well, certainly not friend but—acquaintance.

"Sneerswell Rat!" exclaimed Horace aloud.

"Sneerswell Rat?" gasped Brie.

"The same."

"You mean that old scoundrel down in the fish market, the one that runs the Water Rat Brigade?"

"The same."

"But what ever in the world do you want with that villain?"

"Help," said Horace, "help, pure and simple. I'm going out, Brie. Don't wait up for me."

"But Horace—"

Before Brie could say anything more, Horace had left the room. Before she could recover from her amazement at Horace's odd behavior, he had selected a muffler and a tweed cap from the hall rack. Before she had a chance to protest, he was out the front door, down the front steps of the house, and on his way to catch a horsecar on Broadway. Horace Tailington was going to take drastic measures to solve a drastic problem.

It was very dark in the Fulton Fish Market when Horace got there. He had hopped off the horsecar at the corner of Broadway and Fulton Street and then scampered down Fulton toward the water. He was anxious not to be seen, so he scuttered around the edges of the pools of light thrown on the sidewalks by the gas street-lamps. He would never have believed he would be driven to this course of action—but there it was, grim necessity.

He knew just where he was going. Sneerswell Rat's organization, the more than a little notorious Water Rat Brigade, had its headquarters in one of the market district's most famous old restaurants. (It must remain nameless because it still exists.) Horace tapped on the old plank door. A panel in the center of the door slid open, and a rat's beady eyes and coarse whiskers could be seen inside.

"Whadda yez want?"

Not very good English, Horace thought to himself.

"Sneerswell Rat, if you please," said Horace in his boldest voice.

"So does yer Aunt Hortense, mouse! Beat it! Mr. Rat don't see no mice."

"He'll see *this* mouse," said Horace. "Tell Mr. Sneerswell Rat that Horace Tailington of Tailington Unlimited is here with a proposition of great common interest."

Evidently the magic name of Tailington was not unknown even among rats.

"OK, mouse, wait here."

The panel in the door snapped shut. Rough talk or not, the doorrat knew enough to go to his superiors.

It wasn't long before the door creaked open. Sneerswell himself stood there. A bigger, oilier, shiftier-looking rat never existed.

"My dear Tailington," said Sneerswell, "sorry you were held up by my doorrat. We never know who'll come tapping so late at night. Come in."

He bowed Horace into his office and offered him a chair. It was a nice enough office if you could ignore the rather disreputable-looking rats slouching in the dark corners of the room.

When Sneerswell saw Horace's alarm at the presence of his bodyguards, he sent them scurrying from the room.

"And now that we're alone, what may I do for you?" asked Sneerswell, settling into his big leather armchair.

"I want to make a business deal with you, Mr. Rat," said Horace.

"Ah, well, Tailington, it depends on what it is, doesn't it?"

"You rats buy a lot of cheese from my firm."

"Oh, yes indeed, Tailington, none of us could get by without Tailington Unlimited. Good yellow cheddar, a bit on the ripe and crumbly side, that's what we like, yes indeed."

"And you fellows deal in fish. You even sell it to cats, don't you, Mr. Rat?"

"Live and Let Live! That's the motto of the Water Rat Brigade." With this proclamation, Sneerswell Rat pointed to the row of framed photographs that hung above his desk. The photographs were rather formal views of the crack swimming and boating teams of the Water Rat Brigade—teams that were famous on the New York waterfront. And in each photograph, the Brigade's banner bearing the motto Live and Let Live was prominently displayed.

"Yes, yes, very handsome. Well, as I was saying—or perhaps I wasn't yet—I have a major cat problem. In fact my cat problem is so severe I'm in danger of being put out of business. But I think there is a solution to my problem that could benefit both of us."

"Go on, go on, Tailington, this interests me," said Sneerswell, his eyes glittering more brightly than usual.

"The Cheese Merchants Association of New York has hired cats to keep me out of my place of business. It's an outrage! I know of two cats they have on the job. The head cat seems to be a red tom called Rake O'Mouser."

"Yes, yes, we know him here. O'Mouser's been on the waterfront for many a year. He's a tough customer. But I take it you think you can buy him off in some way. That's not going to be easy."

"That's just where you come in, Mr. Rat. To begin with, I am, in return for your help, prepared to offer you the best deal on cheddar the Water Rat Brigade has ever had. And I'll throw in some of that Herkimer County cheese you love, free of charge."

"But for what 'help,' Tailington?"

"If you will supply a pound of shrimp and a fresh fillet of flounder to the guard cats who are locking me out, I will make the cheese deal with you. Actually, the seafood would come to me and I would then feed the guards into complacency. From what that O'Mouser fellow tells me, the Cheese Merchants Association pays very poor wages indeed—milk and half-spoiled mackerel. It shouldn't be hard to win the cats over to my side—with your help. They can just go right on patrolling to their heart's content, so long as they let me continue my business as usual. And the Cheese Merchants Association won't really be the wiser. People are not, as you no doubt have discovered yourself, Mr. Rat, very bright."

"Tailington, my dear fellow, you've got a nice little plan there. My dear old mother, Anaconda Rat, always said, 'Four legs is better than two, sonny,' bless her dear old heart."

"What do you say to my plan, Mr. Rat?" asked Horace.

"Well, of course, we must consider the exact figures involved as well as delivery dates of the merchandise to be exchanged and work out certain other particulars—but I say, Tailington, why not?" With this, Sneerswell was out of his chair and pumping one of Horace's forepaws heartily.

"Delighted, I'm sure," said Horace.

"After all, Tailington," said Sneerswell, "we must face facts. Rats have an undeserved bad reputation. You mice, for better or for worse, have a much better reputation and are even credited with taking thorns out of lions' paws and other such feats. A union between our two organizations couldn't really do either any harm, could it?"

"No harm at all, Mr. Rat," said Horace, forcing a little smile. He still didn't like or trust rats much, but nevertheless—.

"And if I may make a little suggestion, Tailington?"

"Yes, of course, Mr. Rat."

"When the final arrangements are made between us, let me and my organization distribute the fish to those wily felines. We're used to dealing with cats. We have, as you might say, the brawn. You mice have more delicate ways."

And with this remark Sneerswell bared his really quite astonishing fangs in a manner Horace would ordinarily have felt was ill-bred.

But Horace was so pleased that his deal had gone through that he was willing to forgive any breach of manners. He went home happy and told Brie the good news.

Within three days there was a new order at Tailington Unlimited. True, a cat still patrolled the main entrance day and night, Rake O'Mouser on the day shift, Tom Fleetpaw on the night. But it had all become quite different.

"Good morning, Mr. Tailington," said Rake, giving a smart salute with his tail.

"Good morning, Rake," said Horace, tipping his new derby hat. "And how are the wife and kittens?"

"All doing well, Mr. Tailington, thank you."

"Growing up big and strong, those kittens, on the shrimp and flounder, I daresay."

"Bigger every day."

"Fine. Fine. I know you don't care for that water rat who delivers the fish and shrimp, but 'Live and Let Live,' I always say."

"Yes, sir. That's what I say, too."

Horace went into his neatly ordered office, ready for a good day's work. If things continued to go as well as they had been going, he and Brie would leave the children with his sister and take a short sea voyage to Staten Island on one of the ferries. Sneerswell Rat had connections. Horace was once more an organized mouse.

"Live and Let Live," said Horace brightly to old Nibblehof, the Limburger runner.

"As you say, sir," said Nibblehof, who didn't look quite convinced.

POETRY

STONES

In all seasons,
in rain
or snow,
they wait
for you.

Bunched together,
apart,
they do not
mind
the weather.

Found,
they settle
in your hand
without moving.

ROSAMOND DAUER

FROG

Frog, frog,
Leap for me.
Scratch your back,
Tickle your feet,
Jump to the end
Of the line.

With bright eyes
Popping,
And silver skin
Shining,
Aim at the sun
And come down again.

ROSAMOND DAUER

THE EDGE

I kneel just inside the woods
in the sunshine filtered by gray birches
and beneath their bending
touch the deep mosses.
I hear the forest sounds
but look to see what might prowl
in that fringed darkness.

I will hurry home now.
I have remembered how my family fits,
five together like the pine needles.

CECILY CLARK

THE MECHANICAL LION

The mechanical lion raises his iron paw
to scratch a secret in the pavement
a message for us to read

what kind of message does a lion write
look down at the sidewalk
his words are in Latin
(lions read & write Latin)
he writes Latin with his right paw
& translates it with his left
it reads

>   Put a coin in my mouth
>   & I will tell your fortune

i put a nickel in his mouth (buffalo side up)
the lion answers on the pavement

>   You will soon be given a blue teapot.

WESLEY DAY

RED SHIRLEY

Shirley the poppy
    arches her neck
      like a swan.

When the day comes,
    throws back her head,
      laughs at the sun.

Foam-white and
    shelly-pink ones
      share the bed,

But Shirley the poppy
    flaunts her leaves,
      and laughs in red.
             ELISABETH MARGO

ARISTOTLE IN THE APPLE ORCHARD

We climbed the ladder in the apple orchard
each to see the moon thru a giant telescope
and then we saw the moon
and we saw the craters
and we saw why moonstones are called moonstones

we climbed the ladder to be closer to the moon
But what i remember is
    the air soaked with apples
    red moons
    green moons with a core
    cut them in half
for a white moon   a full white moon
    cut them in quarters
for a half moon

while we waited our turn to climb the ladder
we all ate apples
what i remember most is
the juicy taste of apples.
             WESLEY DAY

a cat's coming

a cat's coming a cat's coming a cat's coming
a cat to eat a rat, or me
a cat to sit in my lap, or not
a cat could do all of that
rap tap rap tap rap tap tap
oh, come in mistress cat
we have met before at another's house
won't you have a dish of silk or satin or milk
or, however you like to think of it
it's the best get together drink, i thought
you might like this room best
there's an afghan for sleeptime and a sandbox for
your convenience
strings and things for playtime
in the meantime
good mischief mistress cat
             WESLEY DAY

NORTH

The house is almost blind
to the north; blizzards pack
hard against the shingles.
The one window
gives but igloo light.

The dog barks unaccountably
in the night; we peer
for foxes in the moonlight
but do not see
what stalks the frosted side.
             CECILY CLARK

THE KITE

My kite is three feet broad, and six feet long;
    The standard straight, the bender tough and strong,
And to its milk-white breast five painted stars belong.

Grand and majestic soars my paper kite,
    Through trackless skies it takes its lofty flight:
Nor lark nor eagle flies to such a noble height.

As in the field I stand and hold the twine,
    Swift I unwind, to give it length of line,
Yet swifter it ascends, nor will to earth incline.

Like a small speck, so high I see it sail,
    I hear its pinions flutter in the gale,
And, like a flock of wild geese, sweeps its flowing tail.

ADELAIDE O'KEEFFE (1776–1855)

A GUINEA-PIG SONG

There was a little guinea-pig,
Who, being little, was not big;
He always walked upon his feet,
And never fasted when he eat.

When from a place he run away,
He never at the place did stay;
And while he run, as I am told,
He ne'er stood still for young or old.

He often squeaked, and sometimes violent,
And when he squeaked he ne'er was silent.
Though ne'er instructed by a cat,
He knew a mouse was not a rat.

One day, as I am certified,
He took a whim and fairly died;
And as I am told by men of sense,
He never has been living since.

ANONYMOUS (1773)

HYMN FOR SATURDAY

Now's the time for mirth and play,
Saturday's an holiday;
Praise to heaven unceasing yield,
I've found a lark's nest in the field.

A lark's nest, then your playmate begs
You'd spare herself and speckled eggs;
Soon she shall ascend and sing
Your praises to the eternal King.

CHRISTOPHER SMART (1722–1771)

WRITTEN IN THE ALBUM OF A CHILD

Small service is true service while it lasts;
Of friends, however humble, scorn not one:
The daisy, by the shadow that it casts,
Protects the lingering dew-drop from the sun.

WILLIAM WORDSWORTH (1770–1850)

PIED BEAUTY

Glory be to God for dappled things—
    For skies of couple-colour as a brinded cow;
        For rose-moles all in stipple upon trout that swim;
Fresh-firecoal chestnut-falls; finches' wings;
    Landscape plotted and pieced—fold, fallow, and plough;
        And áll trádes, their gear and tackle and trim.

All things counter, original, spare, strange;
    Whatever is fickle, freckled (who knows how?)
        With swift, slow; sweet, sour; adazzle, dim;
He fathers-forth whose beauty is past change:
                    Praise him.

GERARD MANLEY HOPKINS (1845–1889)

NIGHT CLOUDS

The white mares of the moon rush along the sky
Beating their golden hoofs upon the glass Heavens;
The white mares of the moon are all standing on their hind legs
Pawing at the green porcelain doors of the remote Heavens.
Fly, mares!
Strain your utmost,
Scatter the milky dust of stars,
Or the tiger sun will leap upon you and destroy you
With one lick of his vermilion tongue.

AMY LOWELL (1874–1925)

MOBY DICK—AN ANNIVERSARY

On May 1, 1976, the doors of a pleasant, white frame farmhouse called Arrowhead were opened to the public for the first time. Arrowhead is located near Pittsfield, Massachusetts. It has a fine view of the Greylock range of the Berkshire Hills. It is an attractive old farmhouse, perhaps a bit bigger than the average. But why has it become a museum when there are so many other old houses like it in New England? Because, in the opinion of many people, something that happened in this house marked a great leap forward in American literature. For it was at Arrowhead in 1850 that Herman Melville (1819–1891) wrote much of *Moby Dick,* his great epic of the sea. And 1976 is the 125th anniversary of the book's publication, in 1851.

There is little doubt today that *Moby Dick* is a masterpiece. It was certainly one of the first completely original works of fiction to be written in the United States.

Even after the American Revolution, American writers were strongly influenced by the British literary tradition and by the work of British writers. The English language shared by the two nations bound them more closely together than politics ever had. But Herman Melville saw himself as an American writer. And for Melville, as for many other people. the brave American seaman who sailed to the four corners of the earth became the symbol of the young nation. The United States had

become a major seafaring power. Melville himself had been to sea three times in youth and young manhood and had sailed on the whaler *Acushnet* in 1841. It was inevitable that Melville's masterpiece, *Moby Dick,* would be about a great adventure at sea.

In his quiet study at Arrowhead, with his wife Elizabeth and his young son Malcolm keeping a safe distance, Melville's memories of life at sea came flooding back to him. He used those memories in his gripping tale of a young man called Ishmael and his experiences aboard the *Pequod,* a whaler out of New Bedford, Massachusetts. The *Pequod* was skippered by the dark, brooding figure of the one-legged Captain Ahab. Ahab's sole mission in life was to pursue and kill the great white whale called Moby Dick. It was Moby Dick who had cost him his leg.

"There she blows! there! there! there! she blows! she blows!" That's the way the adventure described in this excerpt from *Moby Dick* begins. One of the sailors has sighted a school of whales. Young Ishmael, his friend Queequeg, and other members of the *Pequod*'s crew go off in whaleboats to pursue the whales —the first they have seen since setting sail. In a sudden squall Ishmael's boat becomes separated from the *Pequod* and the other whaleboats. The illustrations, the most famous ever created for the book, are by the American artist Rockwell Kent (1882–1971).

This is Arrowhead, the house where Herman Melville wrote *Moby Dick.*

It was a sight full of quick wonder and awe! The vast swells of
the omnipotent sea; the surging, hollow roar they made, as they
rolled along the eight gunwales, like gigantic bowls in a boundless
bowling-green; the brief suspended agony of the boat, as it would
tip for an instant on the knife-like edge of the sharper waves, that
almost seemed threatening to cut it in two; the sudden profound
dip into the watery glens and hollows; the keen spurrings and goad-
ings to gain the top of the opposite hill; the headlong, sled-like
slide down its other side;—all these, with the cries of the headsmen
and harpooneers, and the shuddering gasps of the oarsmen, with
the wondrous sight of the ivory Pequod bearing down upon her
boats with outstretched sails, like a wild hen after her screaming
brood;—all this was thrilling. Not the raw recruit, marching from
the bosom of his wife into the fever heat of his first battle; not the
dead man's ghost encountering the first unknown phantom in the
other world;—neither of these can feel stranger and stronger emo-
tions than the man does, who for the first time finds himself pulling
into the charmed, churned circle of the hunted Sperm Whale.

The dancing white water made by the chase was now becoming
more and more visible, owing to the increasing darkness of the dun
cloud-shadows flung upon the sea. The jets of vapor no longer
blended, but tilted everywhere to right and left; the whales seemed
separating their wakes. The boats were pulled more apart; Starbuck
giving chase to three whales running dead to leeward. Our sail was
now set, and, with the still rising wind, we rushed along; the boat
going with such madness through the water, that the lee oars could
scarcely be worked rapidly enough to escape being torn from the
row-locks.

Soon we were running through a suffusing wide veil of mist;
neither ship nor boat to be seen.

"Give way, men," whispered Starbuck, drawing still further aft
the sheet of his sail; "there is time to kill a fish yet before the squall
comes. There's white water again!—close to! Spring!"

Soon after, two cries in quick succession on each side of us de-
noted that the other boats had got fast; but hardly were they over-
heard, when with a lightning-like hurtling whisper Starbuck said:
"Stand up!" and Queequeg, harpoon in hand, sprang to his feet.
Though not one of the oarsmen was then facing the life and death

peril so close to them ahead, yet with their eyes on the intense countenance of the mate in the stern of the boat, they knew that the imminent instant had come; they heard, too, an enormous wallowing sound as of fifty elephants stirring in their litter. Meanwhile the boat was still booming through the mist, the waves curling and hissing around us like the erected crests of enraged serpents.

"That's his hump. *There, there,* give it to him!" whispered Starbuck.

A short rushing sound leaped out of the boat; it was the darted iron of Queequeg. Then all in one welded commotion came an invisible push from astern, while forward the boat seemed striking on a ledge; the sail collapsed and exploded; a gush of scalding vapor shot up near by; something rolled and tumbled like an earthquake beneath us. The whole crew were half suffocated as they were tossed helter-skelter into the white curdling cream of the squall. Squall, whale, and harpoon had all blended together; and the whale, merely grazed by the iron, escaped.

Though completely swamped, the boat was nearly unharmed. Swimming round it we picked up the floating oars, and lashing them across the gunwale, tumbled back to our places. There we sat up to our knees in the sea, the water covering every rib and plank, so that to our downward gazing eyes the suspended craft seemed a coral boat grown up to us from the bottom of the ocean.

The wind increased to a howl; the waves dashed their bucklers together; the whole squall roared, forked, and crackled around us like a white fire upon the prairie, in which, unconsumed, we were burning; immortal in these jaws of death! In vain we hailed the other boats; as well roar to the live coals down the chimney of a flaming furnace as hail those boats in that storm. Meanwhile the driving scud, rack, and mist, grew darker with the shadows of night; no sign of the ship could be seen. The rising sea forbade all attempts to bale out the boat. The oars were useless as propellers, performing now the office of life-preservers. So, cutting the lashing of the waterproof match keg, after many failures Starbuck contrived to ignite the lamp in the lantern; then stretching it on a waif pole, handed it to Queequeg as the standard-bearer of this forlorn hope. There, then, he sat, holding up that imbecile candle in the heart of that almighty forlornness. There, then, he sat, the sign and symbol of a man without faith, hopelessly holding up hope in the midst of despair.

Wet, drenched through, and shivering cold, despairing of ship or boat, we lifted up our eyes as the dawn came on. The mist still spread over the sea, the empty lantern lay crushed in the bottom of the boat. Suddenly Queequeg started to his feet, hollowing his hand to his ear. We all heard a faint creaking, as of ropes and yards hitherto muffled by the storm. The sound came nearer and nearer; the thick mists were dimly parted by a huge, vague form. Affrighted, we all sprang into the sea as the ship at last loomed

into view, bearing right down upon us within a distance of not much more than its length.

Floating on the waves we saw the abandoned boat, as for one instant it tossed and gaped beneath the ship's bows like a chip at the base of a cataract; and then the vast hull rolled over it, and it was seen no more till it came up weltering astern. Again we swam for it, were dashed against it by the seas, and were at last taken up and safely landed on board. Ere the squall came close to, the other boats had cut loose from their fish and returned to the ship in good time. The ship had given us up, but was still cruising, if haply it might light upon some token of our perishing,—an oar or a lance pole.

an excerpt from *Moby Dick* by HERMAN MELVILLE

This statue of Tom Sawyer (*left*) and Huck Finn stands in Hannibal, Missouri.

TOM SAWYER'S BIRTHDAY

It is hard to believe, but Tom Sawyer, one of the most famous boys in literature, celebrated his 100th birthday in 1976. For it was in 1876 that Samuel Langhorne Clemens, better known as Mark Twain, published *The Adventures of Tom Sawyer*.

The most cherished years of Mark Twain's boyhood were spent in the Mississippi River town of Hannibal, Missouri. And it is Hannibal and the great river that are the background for the adventures of Tom and his friends. In his introduction to the book, the author says, "Most of the adventures recorded in this book really occurred; one or two were experiences of my own, the rest those of boys who were schoolmates of mine . . . ."

But it doesn't matter whether the adventures are real or not—you'll never forget them. The excerpt that follows tells how Tom, Huckleberry Finn, and Joe Harper set up a pirate camp on an island in the river—and came face to face with the forces of nature.

The Pirate Crew

About midnight Joe awoke, and called the boys. There was a brooding oppressiveness in the air that seemed to bode something. The boys huddled themselves together and sought the friendly companionship of the fire, though the dull dead heat of the breathless atmosphere was stifling. They sat still, intent and waiting. The solemn hush continued. Beyond the light of the fire everything was swallowed up in the blackness of darkness. Presently there came a quivering glow that vaguely revealed the foliage for a moment and then vanished. By and by another came, a little stronger. Then another. Then a faint moan came sighing through the branches of the forest and the boys felt a fleeting breath upon their cheeks, and shuddered with the fancy that the Spirit of the Night had gone by. There was a pause. Now a weird flash turned night into day and showed every little grass-blade, separate and distinct, that grew about their feet. And it showed three white, startled faces, too. A deep peal of thunder went rolling and tumbling down the heavens and lost itself in sullen rumblings in the distance. A sweep of chilly air passed by, rustling all the leaves and snowing the flaky ashes broadcast about the fire. Another fierce glare lit up the forest, and an instant crash followed that seemed to rend the treetops right over the boys' heads. They clung together in terror, in the thick gloom that followed. A few big raindrops fell pattering upon the leaves.

"Quick, boys! go for the tent!" exclaimed Tom.

They sprang away, stumbling over roots and among vines in the dark, no two plunging in the same direction. A furious blast roared through the trees, making everything sing as it went. One blinding flash after another came, and peal on peal of deafening thunder. And now a drenching rain poured down and the rising hurricane drove it in sheets along the ground. The boys cried out to each other, but the roaring wind and the booming thunderblasts drowned their voices utterly. However, one by one they straggled in at last and took shelter under the tent, cold, scared, and streaming with water; but to have company in misery seemed something to be grateful for. They could not talk, the old sail flapped so furiously, even if the other noises would have allowed them. The tempest rose higher and higher, and presently the sail tore loose from its fastenings and went winging away on the blast. The boys seized each other's hands and fled, with many tumblings and bruises, to the shelter of a great oak that stood upon the riverbank. Now the battle was at its highest. Under the ceaseless conflagration of lightning that flamed in the skies, everything below stood out in clean-cut and shadowless distinctness: the bending trees, the billowy river, white with foam, the driving spray of spume-flakes, the dim outlines of the high bluffs on the other side, glimpsed through the drifting cloud-rack and the slanting veil of rain. Every little

while some giant tree yielded the fight and fell crashing through the younger growth; and the unflagging thunder-peals came now in ear-splitting explosive bursts, keen and sharp, and unspeakably appalling. The storm culminated in one matchless effort that seemed likely to tear the island to pieces, burn it up, drown it to the tree-tops, blow it away, and deafen every creature in it, all at one and the same moment. It was a wild night for homeless young heads to be out in.

But at last the battle was done, and the forces retired with weaker and weaker threatenings and grumblings, and peace resumed her sway. The boys went back to camp, a good deal awed;

but they found there was still something to be thankful for, because the great sycamore, the shelter of their beds, was a ruin now, blasted by the lightnings, and they were not under it when the catastrophe happened.

Everything in camp was drenched, the camp-fire as well; for they were but heedless lads, like their generation, and had made no provision against rain. Here was matter for dismay, for they were soaked through and chilled. They were eloquent in their distress; but they presently discovered that the fire had eaten so far up under the great log it had been built against (where it curved upward and separated itself from the ground), that a handbreadth or so of it had escaped wetting; so they patiently wrought until, with shreds and bark gathered from the under sides of sheltered logs, they coaxed the fire to burn again. Then they piled on great dead boughs till they had a roaring furnace, and were glad-hearted once more. They dried their boiled ham and had a feast, and after that they sat by the fire and expanded and glorified their midnight adventure until morning, for there was not a dry spot to sleep on, anywhere around.

As the sun began to steal in upon the boys, drowsiness came over them and they went out on the sand-bar and lay down to sleep. They got scorched out by and by, and drearily set about getting breakfast. After the meal they felt rusty, and stiff-jointed, and a little homesick once more. Tom saw the signs, and fell to cheering up the pirates as well as he could. But they cared nothing for marbles, or circus, or swimming, or anything. He reminded them of the imposing secret, and raised a ray of cheer. While it lasted, he got them interested in a new device. This was to knock off being pirates, for a while, and be Indians for a change. They were attracted by this idea; so it was not long before they were stripped, and striped from head to heel with black mud, like so many zebras —all of them chiefs, of course—and then they went tearing through the woods to attack an English settlement.

By and by they separated into three hostile tribes, and darted upon each other from ambush with dreadful war-whoops, and killed and scalped each other by thousands. It was a gory day. Consequently it was an extremely satisfactory one.

They assembled in camp toward supper-time, hungry and happy; but now a difficulty arose—hostile Indians could not break the bread of hospitality together without first making peace, and this was a simple impossibility without smoking a pipe of peace. There was no other process that ever they had heard of. Two of the savages almost wished they had remained pirates. However, there was no other way; so with such show of cheerfulness as they could muster they called for the pipe and took their whiff as it passed, in due form. . . . We will leave them to smoke and chatter and brag, since we have no further use for them at present.

an excerpt from *The Adventures of Tom Sawyer*
by MARK TWAIN

LOOKING AT BOOKS

It wasn't that everyone had suddenly forgotten how to read. It was just that 1976 was a remarkable year in the world of books for young people. Illustrations took on a new importance, and there were many fascinating picture books.

Left: This illustration is from *Underground*, an unusual new informational book. Author-illustrator David Macaulay explains with pictures and text the mazes of pipes, tunnels, conduits, and cables that lie beneath the streets of big cities.

Below: Martha Swope, a leading dance photographer, created *The Nutcracker*, a photo essay with lyrical pictures, like this one, of the New York City Ballet production of *The Nutcracker*, a dance treat for old and young alike.

British author Richard Adams, who wrote *Watership Down*, the popular adventure story about rabbits, has written an amazing new adventure about two Victorian tigers. It's called *The Tyger Voyage*. Adams collaborated with a talented new illustrator, Nicola Bayley. Illustrations like this one (*right*) glow with color, humor, and a sense of delightful mystery.

The winner of the Caldecott Medal in 1976 was *Why Mosquitoes Buzz in People's Ears*, a retelling by Verna Aarderma of a traditional West African tale. For it, Leo and Diane Dillon created illustrations like this one (*below*)—pictures that capture the colors and rhythms of African art.

THE STRONG VOICE

Once upon a time in Sweden in a river town some miles below a large lake, lived a small boy named Per. He was not very different from others of his age except for one thing and that was his voice. So weak was it that he was known by the nickname of "Peep, Peep, Peep." Even when he talked to his brothers and sisters they made fun of him. "We can't hear a word you're saying! Speak louder!" they cried. "Your voice sounds exactly like the squeaking of a mouse."

The older the boy grew, the more people teased him. When he was twelve years old he could stand it no longer, so he walked to the door of the schoolmaster who taught him reading and writing.

Little Per knocked timidly. Indeed, he did everything timidly, to match his little silly voice.

At once the door was thrown open and there stood his school-master with his spectacles far down on his nose and a goose-quill pen back of one ear. Under his left arm was a huge Book of Wisdom.

"So it's Peep, Peep, Peep!" cried he, chuckling at Per's droopy appearance.

"Sir Schoolmaster, since you know everything there is to know, kindly help me find for myself a voice that is loud enough to be heard and is not like the squeaking of a mouse!"

"Humph!" grunted the schoolmaster. "We shall see. Come in." With that he opened his Book of Wisdom and began to thumb over the pages.

Finally, he pushed up his spectacles, peered at a certain page, and read out loud: "If you want a voice that can be heard by everyone in the world, you must tell such wonderful news people forget their troubles." With that, the schoolmaster slammed both book and door right in Per's face, leaving the boy out in the cold and staring at the place where the schoolmaster had been.

The boy did not dare knock again and ask for further explanation, so he trudged away slowly, thinking over what the Book of Wisdom had told him.

"Where can I find such wonderful news that people will forget their troubles?" he kept asking himself.

The next day Per went into the market-place and began pulling at people's coattails. When they turned around and stared at him, he began in his tiny little voice: "I'll tell you some wonderful news. . . ." He really believed some wonderful news would flow from his lips if people would only look at him kindly, but no, they started laughing and shouting, "Oh, it's only Peep, Peep, Peep! We can't hear a single word you say for you sound exactly like a mouse!"

Very sad was little Per when he ran away in order not to hear the cruel words that fell on his ears like hail.

For a whole week, the boy wandered around, still trying to think of some wonderful news to tell people, but no inspiration came. At last, there was nothing to do but to go back to the schoolmaster's house.

"I can't find any wonderful news to tell for when people hear my squeaky voice they begin to laugh," sighed the boy when the schoolmaster stood before him.

"We'll look again in the Book of Wisdom," said the professor with his keen eyes sparkling behind his spectacles.

"To get people to listen to you," he read from the huge book, "you, yourself, must learn to listen."

With this strange remark, the professor slammed shut the book as before, and Per found himself on the steps of the house. Again Per walked home slowly, puzzling over what he had heard. For many days, he seemed to be wandering about in a fog—listening but understanding nothing. He was unhappy and he longed deeply to know the meaning of all living voices, so that in time miracles might begin to happen. Gradually he heard ants creeping and murmuring within their anthills. He knew where secret springs were bubbling beneath the surface of the earth. When birds twittered and chattered to each other, he came to know what they were saying. Trees whispering made little songs for him; and even the wind no longer sang a mysterious message.

One Sunday when people were coming out of church, Per stood near the door and began to pull at their coattails as before. When they turned and saw who it was, they scoffed: "Speak out like a real boy, not like a mouse. We can't hear a word you say!"

But "to speak out loud" was just what Per could *not* do, so he ran away as fast as his thin little legs would carry him. And they carried him straight to the door of the schoolmaster.

The schoolmaster gazed at him with a deep look and several times moved his spectacles up and down his nose. "Come in, Per, why are you waiting out there?" he said at last.

"Sir, I have been listening to birds and brooks and trees and wind, but when I open my lips to relate their wonderful stories to other folk, they won't listen, they just laugh."

Without a word, the old gentleman started thumbing over the pages of his Book of Wisdom. At last, he read out loud: "If you want people to turn to you, you must learn to do something which they can't do for themselves."

Once more Per found himself alone on the threshold of the professor's house, but even more puzzled and mystified than before. "What can I do that people can't do for themselves?" he thought sadly as he trudged home in the chilly evening.

Not long after this visit to the schoolmaster's a county fair was held in the river town where Per lived. Though rain had fallen for almost two weeks and people had said it looked as if it would never stop, on this day the sky was blue and clear.

Little Per was happy as he walked in and out among the stalls, and gazed at the bright peasant costumes, the little pets in cages, the white-painted booths laden with toys and goodies. On flagpoles fluttered yellow and pale blue flags of Sweden. The river at the end of the market-place sparkled and churned as if it wanted to overflow its banks for sheer joy.

Then, suddenly, as Per wandered there, he saw a magpie swoop down into a fluttering circle of doves. He listened when the magpie shrieked and he understood every word it said! "Doves, you'll soon have a visitor in this valley! That visitor is so angry he'll ruin everything. Even your nests will be washed away!"

"What visitor are you talking about?" cooed the doves in their soft, tender voices.

"The lake, of course! I've just flown over the dam; it won't last much longer."

At this dreadful news, Per stood stiff and still with fright, for destruction and death would come if the lake flooded down into the valley where he lived. As Per stood there listening, people began to stare at him. They noticed his face was white.

"Look at that foolish Peep, Peep, Peep! He's struck dumb. What's the matter, boy?" they cried.

Per did not answer; instead he dropped to his knees and put his ear to the ground. In a moment, he heard a stirring and rustling in the direction of the riverbank upstream. He heard and understood the waves of the lake as they grumbled and rumbled angrily. This is what they said: "We're going to break through the dam and be free. We'll travel down the valley . . . down . . . down . . ."

"What are you doing there with your ear glued to the ground?" people were crying. Per did not answer. Instead he leaped to his feet, and began to run just as fast as he could across the market and along the riverbank. He had but one thought: to reach the mill and get the miller to close the iron gates that strengthened the dam.

At once, people became so curious to learn what was happening to Peep, Peep, Peep that they rushed after him. Along the riverbank they went, pell-mell, hurry-burry, helter-skelter! Ahead of them was the little boy who had no voice to speak with, but who had fast little legs to run with and had a very good head on his shoulders.

At last, after much racing and panting, Per with the crowd streaking after him, arrived at the mill. Per dashed up to the great door of the mill and pounded as loudly as he could.

A servant boy with a prickly face stuck his nose out and shook his head even before Per could say a word: "The miller has gone to the fair. If he stays sober, he may get home tomorrow!"

Hopelessly, Per turned and stared at the dam. Louder than ever, the eddies were crying, "We are gnawing faster, deeper! Soon a hole will be eaten through; more holes; suddenly the lake will crash through. . . ."

He lost not another minute. He peeled off his jacket and, forgetting that he'd ever been known as the "Mouse," Per picked up two of the largest stones he could lift. With these in his arms he waded out into the churning stream. Suddenly it was clear to the people on the riverbank what Per was doing. They saw all at once what was happening to the dam. Per had no need of a voice! With one mind, men, women, and children started picking up logs, sticks, stones—anything and everything they could lift—and fearlessly they followed Per out into the surging waters.

Now all were busy, from graybeards to babes. It was wonderful how in a few hours the dam was made strong once again, stronger than it had ever been.

When night fell and at last Per was free to go to his home, the words of his schoolmaster kept running round and round in his head. "If you want people to listen to you, you must learn to do something they can't do for themselves."

But what was it he'd learned to do? He was far too sleepy to think this through, so he closed his eyes and fell into a deep sleep —and it was the best sleep he'd had for a very long time.

Next day when Per went to the market-place as usual, he noticed people following him and whispering to each other. When he met the dean of his school, this gentleman offered his hand in greeting, and then asked: "Don't you think our little hometown was most lucky in being saved from the flood?"

"Yes, it certainly was lucky, Sir," the boy replied, wondering if the dean knew in what manner and by whom the dam was saved from breaking.

When the dean left, Per heard the crowd whispering: "Friend Per thinks our town was *most* lucky in being saved from the flood!"

Presently, the general from a nearby fort came strutting across the market-place and when he saw the boy, he too offered his hand in greeting. "Friend Per, when are you going to honor us out at the fort? When will you pay us a visit?"

"Sir, I should like to go as soon as school is out," replied the boy at last, still in his tiny little voice.

"Fine! We'll expect you!" shouted the general as he wheeled around and marched away.

"Did you hear our friend Per is going to visit the fort?" repeated the crowd in the market-place. "The general asked him to go out there as soon as possible!"

Suddenly the crowd gathered around the boy and started asking him to visit their homes. Soon he had so many invitations thrust at him that he ran home to get away from them all.

But even in his own little house, wonders did not end. In his stuffy little sitting-room, the chief alderman was waiting for him.

"Friend," said he in his oily voice, "as you must know our town is about to elect a new mayor. The best mayor is he whose opinion counts most, whose voice carries furthest—we have nominated *you* to be mayor. Such is the will of our town's people."

One day after Per had moved down to the city hall, a knock came at his door. He opened, and there stood the schoolmaster with his spectacles far down on his nose, a goose-quill pen behind one ear, but no Book of Wisdom under his arm.

"My boy, what did I tell you? People will pay attention when you learn to do something for them they cannot do for themselves."

"But what is that?" queried Per, as he ushered his old friend into the mayor's room.

"You figure that out for yourself," replied the schoolmaster, his keen eyes twinkling.

a Swedish story from *Scandinavian Stories*
by MARGARET SPERRY

THE ANIMAL WORLD

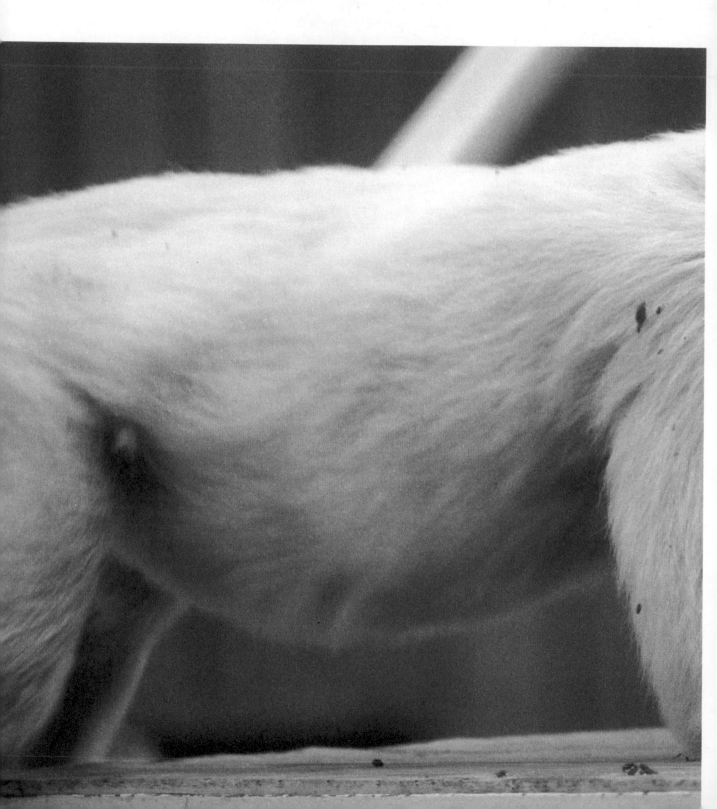

Albino animals are a rare sight. This albino, the vanilla gorilla, makes himself comfortable in his home in the zoo in Barcelona, Spain.

ANIMALS IN THE NEWS

This little fellow is taking his first cautious look at the world before coming completely out of the egg. He is a gavial, a relative of the crocodile, and among the first of his kind to be hatched in captivity—at a special hatchery in Orissa, India. Gavials are mostly found in India, and are an endangered species. The Indian Government is anxious to preserve them through a scientific conservation and breeding program.

If you'd just fallen off the top of one of the towers of New York City's World Trade Center, you'd have an odd expression on your face, too. In 1976 filmmakers created a new version of the 1933 film classic *King Kong*. Kong himself was bigger and better than ever. This huge Styrofoam, rubber, and horsehair dummy of Kong was used in filming his final, dramatic scene. But you have to see the film yourself to find out exactly what happened to the noble Kong—there's a lot of suspense.

A final portrait of a famous figure in the world of animals. This is Smokey Bear (*left*), the famous symbol of U.S. forest-fire prevention, who died at the National Zoo in Washington, D.C., in November. Smokey was 26 years old. He had retired from active duty in 1975.

These charming Australians (*below*) were a Bicentennial gift to the United States from Australia. They're koala bears and will live in the only koala bear colony in the United States—at the San Diego Zoo in California.

This is Zorro (*below*), Ken-L Ration's Dog Hero of the Year for 1976. Zorro, who is half German shepherd and half wolf, saved his master, Mark Cooper (whom he's playing with here), from drowning. He actually pulled Mark from a swirling whirlpool.

A print of the very first Westminster dog show—May 10, 1877.

WESTMINSTER'S 100TH DOG SHOW

"He's a really great show dog. . . . He's always in there trying," said the proud handler of a Lakeland terrier named Jo-Ni's Red Baron of Crofton. The terrier looked proud, too. It was no wonder. He had just been judged the top dog of the top dog show in the United States—the Westminster Kennel Club show. And it was an extra-special occasion. The February, 1976, show marked Westminster's 100th annual dog show.

The Westminster Kennel Club was formed by a group of sportsmen who met at the Westminster Hotel in New York to discuss their fine gundogs. They named their club after the hotel and held their first dog show in 1877.

That first Westminster show was a grand affair, with crowds of fashionably dressed people and more than 1,000 dogs. According to newspaper reports of the time, some of the dogs were "rigged up with ribbons, mats, cushions, bells, and lace collars." Among the dogs that made news were two Scottish deerhounds, Oscar and Dagmar, from the kennels of Queen Victoria of England. They were offered for sale at $50,000 each. Dash and Rex, two Irish water spaniels, also made news. They got into "a first-class dogfight . . . and were parted with difficulty."

The 100th Westminster dog show was as grand in its own way as the first Westminster. It attracted leading dog fanciers from the United States and other countries. They brought more than 3,000 dogs of 130 breeds and varieties. Many of the dogs had already earned the title of champion, and some had won roomfuls of trophies and ribbons. All the dogs had been clipped, snipped, brushed, and polished to perfection.

In the Westminster show, the dogs first

compete against others of their breed for Best of Breed awards. They are judged by standards that tell how each part of the dog's body should look and how the dog should gait, or move. Winners of Best of Breed awards then compete for Best of Group awards. (In a show where all recognized breeds are entered, the breeds are grouped into six categories: sporting dog, hound, working dog, terrier, toy, and nonsporting groups.) Finally the six Best of Group winners are judged for the top honor, Best in Show. And in 1976, it was Jo-Ni's Red Baron of Crofton who won Best in Show, the top dog of the 100th Westminster.

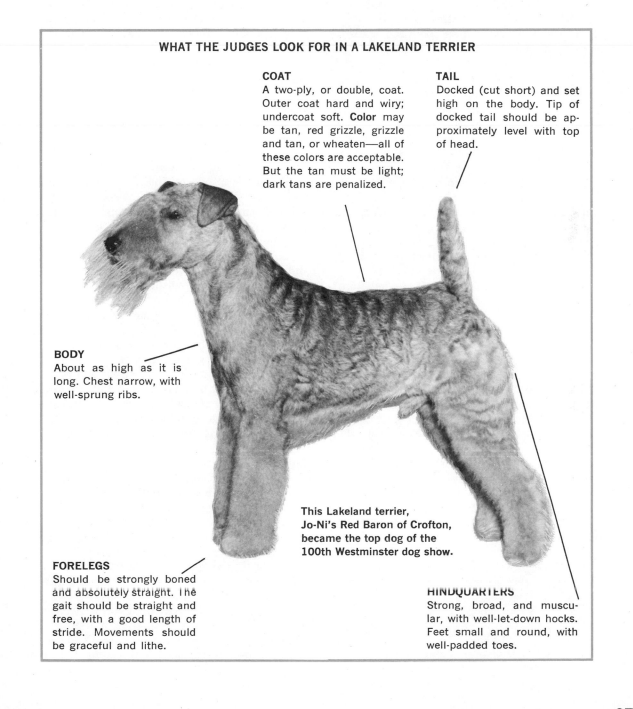

WHAT THE JUDGES LOOK FOR IN A LAKELAND TERRIER

COAT
A two-ply, or double, coat. Outer coat hard and wiry; undercoat soft. **Color** may be tan, red grizzle, grizzle and tan, or wheaten—all of these colors are acceptable. But the tan must be light; dark tans are penalized.

TAIL
Docked (cut short) and set high on the body. Tip of docked tail should be approximately level with top of head.

BODY
About as high as it is long. Chest narrow, with well-sprung ribs.

This Lakeland terrier, Jo-Ni's Red Baron of Crofton, became the top dog of the 100th Westminster dog show.

FORELEGS
Should be strongly boned and absolutely straight. The gait should be straight and free, with a good length of stride. Movements should be graceful and lithe.

HINDQUARTERS
Strong, broad, and muscular, with well-let-down hocks. Feet small and round, with well-padded toes.

A STRANGE LITTLE WHALE

One day in the 1500's, after returning from a difficult voyage to the Arctic, the explorer Martin Frobisher was ushered into the presence of England's Queen Elizabeth I. The voyage had been exhausting, but it had gathered valuable information about the coasts of northern Canada and Greenland. It had also brought back one valuable treasure: a narwhal horn. And this the proud seaman laid at the feet of his queen and patroness as he knelt before her.

The Queen was overjoyed, for she had not expected Frobisher to find such a rare treasure on his voyage. Wasn't the narwhal, after all, a magical sea beast, nearly as enchanting as the unicorn? And the long tapering ivory horn of both beasts—the narwhal and the unicorn—had mysterious powers to protect any person, even any nation, lucky enough to possess one. The Queen gave orders right away that the narwhal horn be taken to her castle at Windsor and placed on display.

What, you may ask, is a narwhal horn? And why did it have the power to make a great queen so happy? And were narwhals real animals, or were they imaginary, like the unicorn?

First, the narwhal horn is not really a horn, but a tooth, or tusk. And it extends forward from the upper left-hand jaw of a real animal. That animal is a gentle little whale called a narwhal. Once in a great while a narwhal will have two tusks, extending forward from either side of the jaw—a very strange-looking phenomenon. Only the males have the tusk, or tusks, which always spiral to the left and sometimes grow as long as 9 feet (nearly 3 meters). This length is remarkable because the narwhal's body never grows longer than 16 feet (4.9 m).

The word "narwhal" comes originally from Old Norse, an early Scandinavian language. No doubt the Vikings often saw—and possibly ate—narwhals as they journeyed the northern seas. There is some uncertainty about what "nar" refers to, but "whal," of course, means "whale." In Danish and Swedish the word for the animal is *narhval*.

Queen Elizabeth, or any other ruler who got hold of a narwhal tusk, was glad to have it because the narwhal had become mixed up with the ancient legend of the unicorn—and the horn of that horse-like beast was supposed to give virtue, strength, and protection to its owner. Both the narwhal tusk and the unicorn horn, it was said, would change color in the presence of poison—thus warning that an enemy was up to no good. And horn or tusk could be ground up, mixed with water, and drunk as an antidote if any poison had actually been swallowed.

Whalers would travel the Arctic waters in search of the little whale with the amazing tooth. On returning to Europe, some would claim that the narwhal tusks were "unicorn horns." The landlubber merchants paid outlandish prices, but they charged their royal customers much more. Emperor Charles V saved his realm by paying off a huge debt to the Margrave of Bayreuth with two narwhal tusks. Several royal treasuries boasted both a narwhal tusk and a unicorn horn, and no one seemed disturbed at how alike these treasures looked.

When the scientific age dawned and the mists of legend began to clear, people stopped trading fortunes for narwhal tusks and took a greater interest in the animal. If the narwhal was a real animal, and not just a "fabulous beast," then what exactly was it?

The narwhal is a whale, or, more scientifically put, a cetacean. We think of whales as huge, yet the narwhal is quite small. But then, the dolphins are technically whales too, and most of them are even smaller than the narwhals. As a matter of fact, the narwhals and the dolphins, as well as the much larger sperm whales (the species Moby Dick belonged to), are all members of a suborder of whales known as the Odontoceti, or "toothed whales." Indeed, you might say that the narwhal is the most "toothed" of all these creatures!

Theories abound as to what the narwhal's tooth is for—since it is surely not used for chewing! Because the females lack the tusk, and because the males are sometimes seen

Narwhals live in the Arctic seas north of Canada, Greenland, and Scandinavia. The male's long tusk, which is hollow, was thought in past times to have magic powers and was worth a fortune. Today scientists are trying to learn why the narwhal has its horn.

"fencing" with each other, it is thought possible that the tusk is for display in mating—that it plays the same role as a stag's antlers or a peacock's tail.

Another possibility is that the narwhals use their tusks to poke air holes in the ice that can so quickly form over their Arctic Ocean home. (All whales, which millions of years ago were land animals, breathe in air through lungs.) And yet another theory is mentioned by Herman Melville in *Moby Dick,* that greatest of all whaling yarns. Melville suggests that the tusk is used to rake the sea bottom and thus stir up a good fish dinner.

Someday scientists will learn more about the narwhal and solve some of the remaining mysteries—though it seems only fair that the little animal be allowed to keep some secrets. The reason narwhals may be studied more,

however, is that they are on the increase—a remarkable fact at a time when overhunting and other hazards are threatening nearly all the world's whales. The narwhals' good fortune rests on the ill fortune of another Arctic species, the great bowhead, or Greenland right, whale. This latter was so ardently hunted for its oil and whalebone that it reached the verge of extinction and became protected by law. The Arctic whalers were deprived of their best commercial catch by these laws and stopped fishing in the Arctic waters. This allowed the narwhal to increase in number. Now only the Eskimos hunt the narwhal, and ever-tighter restrictions are being placed on the Eskimos' catches. It seems that accidental circumstances have saved the narwhal. Or, is it a kind of miracle that has come to the aid of a miraculous beast?

275

Use your imagination! Almost anything can be used as a feeder. This snowman offers feathered friends suet, whole peanuts, and a choice of fruit slices.

This female cardinal has found a meal of sunflower seeds. It's easy to put food out on an upended log, but it's also an invitation to squirrels and chipmunks to stuff themselves.

This tropical bird feeder is made from two coconut halves. The upper half helps to keep the food dry and the hungry visitors shaded.

IT'S FOR THE BIRDS

More and more people are discovering the fun of indoor bird watching. Yes, *indoor*— if you set up a simple bird feeder outside your window. Stock the feeder with a mixture of wild-bird seed (available in most food stores); suet (beef fat); or peanut butter. People who live in the country will see more birds, but you can see a good many even if you live in the city or the suburbs. Once the birds learn to come to your feeder, they will depend on it, so keep it stocked with food. This is especially important when there is snow on the ground and it is difficult for the birds to find food.

A mesh bag for onions or oranges makes a good suet feeder. But don't be surprised if a hungry squirrel arrives on a feeder hung from a wire.

This downy woodpecker discovers a treasure of suet on an easily made feeder. Pull six wire hangers into a diamond shape, and wire or tie them together at the top, middle, and bottom. Hang it up and stock it with suet chunks.

High and dry, a chickadee inspects a store of seeds. You can make a feeder like this one. It is simply two salad bowls of different sizes, held together by a dowel.

James Walsh, a modern-day Noah, struggles with a two-toed sloth in a rain forest in Panama.

OPERATION NOAH

In eastern Panama, in one of the world's lushest and steamiest rain forests, the Noah's Ark story was acted out all over again during 1976. The flood in this case was caused by a dam, which created a new, man-made lake, whose waters were rapidly rising, covering even the treetops.

The animals in Panama did not have an actual ark to climb aboard. They were usually pulled into dugout canoes and small motorboats, which were weaving their way in and out among the top branches of the drowned trees, to which the animals were clinging. Nor did the animals line up quietly two by two waiting for rescue. They often bit and kicked and struggled as the members of the rescue team hauled them into the boats and took them to a safe, new life on higher ground.

The project was called Operation Noah II, and the leader of the team, the modern-day Noah, was James C. Walsh, of Boston. He works with the London-based International Society for the Protection of Animals (ISPA). His project, which is supported partly by dollars and quarters sent in by schoolchildren, is not the first such operation for the ISPA.

The organization saved animals as long ago as 1959 on Africa's Zambezi River in Operation Noah I. James Walsh's own skills were tested in 1965 in the South American country of Surinam, where he and his helpers pulled 10,000 animals from a man-made lake much like the one in Panama.

The goal in Panama was to save 5,000 animals—stranded in treetops or on tiny islands —from drowning or starvation. And the animals of this region are a precious group, for they include many curious, rare, and endangered species. Among these are big cats such as jaguars and pumas and the somewhat smaller ocelots, margays, and tiger cats. Other rare species endangered by the new lake were kinkajous; capuchin, squirrel, spider, and howler monkeys; sloths; anteaters; and tapirs (relatives of the rhinoceros).

But an animal did not have to be rare or odd to be a candidate for rescue. Every living creature in trouble, from fledgling birds, to deer, to poisonous snakes and scorpions, was helped to safety. The original Noah saved two of every species on earth. But John Walsh and his team, which included local Panamanians, rescued every animal they could get their hands on, whether or not the animal was poisonous, and whether or not the animal was grateful.

ALBINO ANIMALS

What color is a squirrel? A deer? A kangaroo? You would certainly never think of white, would you? Yet there are all-white deer, squirrels, and kangaroos. There are also some animals that are not all-white. These animals only have patches of white or are very light-colored. All such animals are commonly called albinos.

The word "albino" comes from a Latin word meaning "white." A true albino is all-white and has pink eyes. White-patched animals or very light-colored ones are partial albinos. Of course, not all white animals are albinos. Some animals are normally white, like polar bears and mountain goats. Others normally have white in certain places, like the white stripes down a skunk's back. An albino is an animal that is normally another color— it is white when it shouldn't be.

To understand how albinos get their strange whiteness, we must know how normally colored animals get their color. Special cells, called pigment cells, in the skin, hair, and eyes produce coloring matter, or pigment. One animal differs from another in color, depending on the amount and kind of pigment its pigment cells produce.

Now and then an animal is born whose pigment cells are unable to produce any coloring matter. Such an animal has pure white hair, and white skin with a very faint pink shade. The pink comes from the color of the blood vessels in the skin. The eyes are also pink, from the blood vessels in the eyes. An animal like this is a true albino.

The inability to produce pigment is an inherited trait. That is, it is one that is passed on by parents to their offspring in the living material called genes. The parents of an albino may be normally colored, yet each may have a gene for albinism (being albino). If there is such a gene in each of the two cells that unite to form the new individual, that individual will be an albino.

Peacocks are noted for their beautiful colors, but this beauty is all-white.

This albino gorilla has white fur and pink skin. He lives in the zoo in Barcelona, Spain. Here he enjoys a tussle with a normally colored friend.

Comfortably coiled in its cage at the Cincinnati, Ohio, zoo, an albino diamondback rattlesnake stares pink-eyed into the camera.

Three of a very rare kind. This albino kangaroo carries her twin babies in her pouch. Like the mother, the young kangaroos have white fur and pink eyes.

The stripes on this Indian tiger are normal, but the rest of its fur is white, rather than the usual golden brown.

Squirrels have big appetites, and this albino is no exception. Here it gets a firm hold on a nut before gnawing away at it.

Albinos, like this robin, may have special problems. For example, they may be able to spend only short periods of time in the sunlight.

This albino frog, like other albinos living in the wild, is at a disadvantage. Unlike many normally colored animals, albinos are easily seen by their enemies.

Why the Bear's Tail Is So Short

In the forest one day, Michael the fox was slinking along with a large fish in his teeth. Bruin the bear met him and asked, "What have you been doing today, Mister Fox?"

"Fishing" answered the fox, dropping the fish, but keeping one paw on it, for he trusted no one, not even the stupid, lumbering bear.

"Is fish good to eat like honey?" asked Bruin, sniffing the fish.

"Sweeter, and not full of bees," was the reply.

"If I want to go fishing, what do I do?" mumbled the bear.

"Go to the lake, cut a hole in the ice, and drop your tail into the water. Then wait!" The fox grinned.

"What for?" asked the big, brown bear in his big, bumbling way.

"Fish!" The fox smirked and took to his heels with his dinner once more tight in his teeth.

Now in those days all bears were said to have long tails, which they waved behind them like a bush.

So Bruin the bear, waving his tail hopefully, lumbered through the pine trees down to an inland lake that was frozen. With much hard work and trouble he cut a hole in the ice, sat down, and dropped his long tail through the hole into the icy water below.

Soon fish began to nibble on his tail.

"Each bite on *me* means more bites on *you* when I eat you for supper!" burbled the bear.

The small fish did not answer.

A larger fish bit on the bear's tail.

"Are you herring or eel?" asked the bear.

Suddenly came a long, strong pull.

"What are you?" roared the bear with tears in his eyes. "Are you dolphin or whale?"

Neither dolphin nor whale answered.

The bear was cold. The bear was sleepy. He slept. He forgot the fox, and the fish, and even his tail in the ice.

Suddenly the scream of a sea gull woke him. "Go home! Go home! While there is still time!"

Bruin woke up with a start and tried to jump to his feet; but alas, he was frozen tight.

"No matter," he thought, "When I get loose I'll have enough fish to give me dinners for a month of Sundays."

With a great tug he pulled himself loose and turned to look round. What did he find? No fish and no tail, for many fish had bitten his long bushy tail; and they had swum away with pieces of it down into the deep waters where he could never find them.

And that is why, to this very day, bears of every size and shape, and in every land, have but a very small stub for a tail.

There ends my tale because the bear has so little.

a Norwegian fable from *Scandinavian Stories*
by MARGARET SPERRY

THE IBISES OF BIRECIK

Spotting a rare bird in your backyard can be quite a thrill. So just imagine how the people living in Birecik in Turkey must feel— they have a whole flock of rare birds nesting right in the middle of their town. The birds are members of the ibis family, a group of birds related to the storks.

The particular kind of ibis found in Birecik is known to scientists as *Geronticus eremita* (roughly, "the old hermit"); its common names include hermit ibis and bald ibis. It is about the size of a goose, and has long red legs, a long curved beak, and a ruff or crest of longer feathers at the back of the head. This ibis is an extremely rare bird. The only nesting colonies known to exist in the wild are the one in Turkey and another in Morocco.

Hermit ibises nest on the narrow ledges of cliffs. The 60-foot (18-meter) cliff they nest on at Birecik is right in the middle of the town. And the ibises are surrounded on all sides by houses and cave dwellings. (In Turkey a cliff is a good place to build a house. Houses cut into cliffsides are cool in summer.)

In 1972, three scientists visited Birecik and saw that the ibises were in trouble. They noticed that the ledge of the cliff was very narrow—so narrow that when the adult birds

These ibis chicks and their parents (*left*) have a better chance of surviving, thanks to the work of the World Wildlife Fund.

landed or flew away from their nests, they would often knock their eggs and chicks over the edge by accident. The scientists also saw that the town was growing, and people were building houses closer and closer to the ibises' nesting ledge. Furthermore, there were people living on top of the cliff who were throwing garbage down onto the nesting ledge. All these things endangered the ibises.

The three scientists went to work to do something to help. The mayor of Birecik became concerned and ordered that no more houses should be built near the nesting site. He has since tried to persuade the people who live closest to the ledge to move away so their houses can be torn down. He has even offered them free land elsewhere.

People throughout the world who were concerned with wildlife preservation focused their attention on Birecik. The World Wildlife Fund granted money to one of the scientists so he could help the ibises of Birecik. He widened the nesting ledge while the ibises were wintering in Africa. When the ibises returned in the spring of 1973, they had more room for their nests. As a result, 21 new chicks left with the flock on the fall migration to Africa; in 1972 there had been only 9 chicks that had survived from the eggs laid that spring.

The decline in the birds' numbers had thus been slowed, at least temporarily. But the future of this rare ibis—which has survived for millions of years—is still in doubt. Only with continued conservation efforts and great care can we hope to keep them from disappearing from the face of the earth.

This is the cliff in the middle of Birecik in Turkey where the rare hermit ibises (*circled*) nest each spring.

Beehives in Poland may
be carved figures
of people . . .

or animals . . .

The bees enter their hive through an opening in
the front; beekeepers remove the wax and honey
through a much larger opening in the back.

286

. . . or they may be modern.

THE BEEHIVES OF POLAND

Bees are useful creatures. They give us honey and wax. Honey is a delicious sweetener, and wax is used in many things, including candles, which were very necessary before electricity was discovered. But bees are also strange and fascinating creatures. Their organized social behavior and uncanny instincts have made them objects of wonder.

Many authors have mentioned bees in their writings. Shakespeare, in *Henry V*, compares the social order observed among bees with that of "a peopled kingdom"; and Sir Arthur Conan Doyle had his great detective Sherlock Holmes retire to the country to keep bees. Many legends and traditions about bees have also sprung up. One of the most interesting bits of bee lore is the tradition of "telling the bees." According to this custom, a household that keeps bees must be sure to tell the bees of any important events in the family's life. If they don't, the bees will fly away. Bees are also believed to like peacefulness. It is said that they will not stay with people who quarrel.

In the wild, bees make wax nests in hollow trees or logs; they store honey and raise their young in these nests. When people began to keep bees, they built structures, called hives, for the bees to make their nests in. Many early hives were simply hollow logs, such as the bees were used to in the wild. Later, more elaborate structures were built. In western Europe dome-shaped hives of coiled wicker or straw, called skeps, became popular. Skeps were a common sight on many farms, especially if the farmer had an orchard. (Some trees cannot bear fruit if there aren't bees around to pollinate the flowers.) This kind of hive was also common in colonial America. Still later, beekeeping became a specialized, large-scale part of agriculture. Bees were kept on special bee farms, or apiaries. Efficient, very plain, rectangular wooden hives became popular.

But these are not the only kinds of hives. In eastern Europe, and especially in Poland, people have long made special hives that are truly works of art. These hives are made out of wood, but the wood is carved into figures of people or animals. Sometimes there is just a face carved into the side of the upright log that forms the body of the hive. Sometimes the whole hive is a carved wooden statue. Even the more modern rectangular hives are painted in colorful designs.

The Poles are very proud of this unique form of folk art, and several museums in Poland have collections of these beehives. In some towns the hives are kept in outdoor museums, with sweet-smelling flowers growing all around. And bees still live in these beehives, going about their age-old task of making "sweetness and light."

In some Polish towns, hives are kept in outdoor museums, in the midst of gardens of flowers.

REIGNING CATS AND DOGS

Pet dogs and cats are members of the family in more than half of all American households. To celebrate the 200th birthday of the United States, let's combine pets and history as an interesting Bicentennial topic and talk about the pets of some American presidents.

Most historians have written about U.S. presidents in their role as chief executive. But a more intimate picture of their lives is seen in their man-dog relationships.

. . .An austere Jefferson, living alone in the unfinished White House, with his favorite gundog beside him . . . Gaunt Lincoln, turning from the anguish of civil war to a jolly romp with the White House dogs . . . Fiery, high-booted Jackson, unbending from affairs of state to play gently with his hound's litter of puppies . . .

The statue *The Hoosier Youth* shows Abraham Lincoln with his favorite foxhound, Jip.

▶ WASHINGTON AND THE AMERICAN FOXHOUND

This side of George Washington's life will probably surprise you because it's not in most history books. But he was "one of the most noted dog breeders in United States history" and has been called the developer of the American foxhound, according to the American Kennel Club (AKC).

The AKC's famous collection of dogdom history has fascinating accounts of Washington's hobby of dog breeding. That hobby stemmed from his great devotion to foxhunting, or riding to hounds. It was a popular outdoor sport among Virginia country gentlemen.

Proud of his foxhounds, which came from Britain, Washington started to develop an American foxhound strain. His diaries are filled with accounts of breeding his hounds. Some of the names he chose for his hounds were Mopsey, Taster, Tipler, Cloe, Lady, Forester, Captain, Sweetlips, Vulcan, Searcher, and Rover.

Washington's breeding program is credited with having followed scientific principles, as they were then known. And he kept what may have been one of the earliest studbooks in the United States.

During the American Revolution, when Washington commanded the U.S. Army, an incident took place that reveals his understanding of the anguish a dog suffers when it is separated from its master. A strange dog had wandered into the American encampment, lost and frightened. When Washington was notified of it, he examined the dog and noticed that its collar was inscribed "General Howe." He had the lost pet returned to the enemy general under a flag of truce.

▶ LINCOLN'S PETS

Abraham Lincoln's childhood pet was nothing fancier than a young pig. It must have been a smart pig because little Abe soon taught it to play hide and seek. And when fully grown, the pig was so big that Lincoln rode it like a pony.

Years later, as a young lawyer, Lincoln rescued a struggling pig stuck in the mud alongside the road. Dismounting from his horse, he waded into the mud and carried the squealing porker to solid ground. As it ambled away, we can imagine Lincoln smiling over a childhood memory rather than worrying about his muddy clothes.

Lincoln was a teenager when he acquired an American foxhound. Accounts differ, but most refer to that hound as his favorite, named Jip.

This was the foxhound immortalized with the President in the Paul Manship statue in Fort Wayne, Indiana. Called *The Hoosier Youth,* the statue shows the dog leaning trustfully against Lincoln's thigh, the President's hand resting gently on the dog's head.

Fido, a mongrel, was the family dog during the years in Springfield, Illinois. It had to be left behind with neighbors when the Lincolns made the long trip to Washington as the first family.

The grim Civil War years left President Lincoln little time for pets. But there were ponies, dogs, and pet goats and rabbits for the Lincoln boys, Tad and Willy.

Then came the shocking assassination. At Lincoln's burial ceremony back in Springfield, Fido was still there. But a year later Fido, too, was assassinated—by a knife-wielding drunk. Fido is buried in the back garden of Lincoln's home.

▶ TR'S "ZOO"

Unforgettable to anyone visiting the White House grounds during Theodore Roosevelt's presidency was the surprising number of pets found there. Roosevelt started an entirely new chapter in the history of White House pets when, at the beginning of the 20th century, he became the nation's youngest president at age 42. He ushered in a period in which the executive mansion was thrown open to pets of all kinds.

Roosevelt's pets included nine riding horses; two carriage horses; Algonquin, his son Archie's calico pony; Pete, a bull terrier; Sailor Boy, a Chesapeake retriever; Jack, his son Kermit's terrior; Manchu, his daughter Alice's spaniel; Skip, a mongrel; Rollo, a Saint Bernard; Josiah, a badger; two cats; raccoons; assorted guinea pigs; and his son Quentin's collection of pet snakes. And the family's

Teddy Roosevelt had so many pets, that it sometimes seemed as if he were in the middle of a zoo.

summer home at Oyster Bay, Long Island, harbored an animal world resembling a zoo. The zoo included a lion, a hyena, a wildcat, a coyote, a zebra, five bears, kangaroos, and various other small animals, reptiles, and birds.

Sailor Boy, the retriever, liked to go boating with the children. If they forgot to take him, he'd jump into the water, swim to the boat, and clamber aboard.

Rollo, the Saint Bernard, was the children's favorite dog. The good nature of this big fellow was a White House legend. The youngsters could do almost anything with him, and he joined joyously in their games.

Another favorite was Skip, the bright little mongrel. Skip and his pony friend, Algonquin, developed a trick that always delighted the family. The pony would canter around the lawn and suddenly Skip would run up and leap on the pony's back. Algonquin would stop and try in vain to shake the dog off his back. But everyone knew he was just pretending to be annoyed; otherwise why did he always slow down when Skip came running toward him?

▶ HARDING'S LADDIE BOY

A number of presidential pets have achieved more than a footnote in White House history. The first to become internationally famous was Laddie Boy, a purebred Airedale and President Warren G. Harding's beloved companion.

When the Hardings settled into the White House in 1921, Laddie Boy arrived as a gift from a friend in Ohio. With his friendly ways, Laddie Boy quickly became the number one White House dog.

Newsboys donated the money for this bronze statue of President Harding's Laddie Boy.

This Airedale also had natural poise, dignity, and a presence befitting the White House life-style. Let a delegation come calling on the President, and the dog was always out on the front step to assist in the greetings. And at VIP meetings, he literally sat beside the President in his own special chair.

Laddie Boy had a knack of getting in the papers, often and favorably. A favorite subject for the Washington press corps, he became a national celebrity as they pictured him attending cabinet meetings, delivering Harding's daily papers, and skillfully retrieving lost balls during the President's frequent golf games.

A bronze statue of Laddie Boy is in the Smithsonian Institution, paid for by thousands of penny donations by newsboys. It's a fitting memorial to a newspapermen's friend.

▶ SILENT CAL'S DOGS

The Calvin Coolidge years were noted for tranquility and for White House dogs that were almost as famous as Laddie Boy.

Silent Cal and the First Lady loved pets. They had many varieties, including songbirds, a donkey, cats, a raccoon, and the Coolidge dogs, which attracted the frequent attention of news photographers. Best known were Rob Roy, a white Scotch collie; Prudence Prim, another white collie; Peter Pan, a wirehaired terrier; and Paul Pry, an Airedale half brother of Laddie Boy.

Rob Roy was known as Oshkosh before becoming a Coolidge family dog. Mrs. Coolidge was so impressed by his magnificent appearance that she renamed him Rob Roy, after a character in a Sir Walter Scott novel.

Rob Roy was fond of coffee. Sometimes, at social gatherings, the President would calmly pour some coffee into his saucer while his guests watched in astonishment—until they realized he was pouring it for Rob Roy.

Prudence Prim, the beautiful female white collie, had finer, more graceful lines than Rob Roy. A favorite companion of the First Lady, she was so elegant that photographers pleaded for poses with her mistress. Prudy's manners were equally elegant. At the Coolidges' frequent garden parties, she accepted everyone's admiration, mingling with guests as graciously as the hostess.

Calvin Coolidge and his wife were always surrounded by animals.

Peter Pan was a pedigreed terrier who was a little too nervous to cope with all the people and activities of a busy environment. He took his guard duties too seriously and would nip at the heels of workmen and other strangers around the grounds. Eventually, he was given to a family friend where the home life was more to his liking.

Paul Pry also came to the Coolidges with a different name, Laddie Buck, but Mrs. Coolidge decided to call him Paul Pry. She is said to have chosen that name because the young Airedale always had his nose in everybody's business. However, he grew too enthusiastic and was given a more fitting home as a Marine Corps mascot.

▶ FDR'S FAMOUS FALA

One of the most famous White House dogs was Fala, a purebred Scottish terrier who received countless fan letters as the famous companion of Franklin Delano Roosevelt during his last years as president.

To millions of Americans during World War II, Fala and FDR were symbols of cour-

age. If the war reports were grim, a news photo of Fala, briskly vigilant beside his master, was sure to lift everyone's spirits and make everyone smile.

Born on April 7, 1940, Fala was the son of an exceptional pair of Scotties. For FDR and Fala, it was love at first sight. The President named him after Fallahill, a Scottish estate of Roosevelt relatives.

As a member of the family, Fala slept on a navy blanket in FDR's bedroom. It is said that no President and his dog shared a deeper affection. They became almost inseparable.

At official meetings, press conferences, and state affairs, Fala was usually there. On trips to the family estate at Hyde Park, New York, or to Warm Springs, Georgia, where the President exercised his paralyzed legs, there was Fala beside him.

One memorable occasion involved a top-secret meeting at sea, where FDR and British Prime Minister Winston Churchill signed the Atlantic Charter on the USS *Augusta*. Later, when pictures were released around the world, sure enough there was Fala.

President Franklin Roosevelt and Fala were nearly inseparable.

Another famous photo was taken during the "war dog" funds drive. With the President beside him, Fala made front-page news becoming an "Army Private" by donating a dollar. Other dogs of other owners followed suit and donated money.

After Roosevelt's death in 1945, Fala lived at Hyde Park with Mrs. Roosevelt. Fala died seven years later and is buried in the rose garden, where he rests, as usual, near his master.

▶ KENNEDY'S PETS GALORE

Few White House families had a greater affection for pets than the family of John F. Kennedy.

The children were pet-oriented from early childhood. Jacqueline Kennedy grew up with horses and hounds. An accomplished horsewoman, she taught the children to ride soon after they learned to walk. Scenes with the pony, Macaroni, were a favorite subject of news photographers, when permitted.

There were pets galore in the Kennedy family: Charlie, their daughter Caroline's Welsh terrier; Tom Kitten, a cat; Robin, a canary; Bluebell and Maybell, parakeets; the ponies Tex, Leprechaun, and Macaroni; a colony of hamsters; Sardar, Mrs. Kennedy's horse; Zsa Zsa, a trained rabbit; Clipper, a German shepherd; Wolf, a wolfhound; and Pushinka, and her pups by Charlie: Butterfly, White Tips, Streaker, and Blackie.

When Robin died, it was buried ceremoniously on the South Lawn. A few days later, when Mrs. Kennedy was about to give the visiting Empress of Iran a White House tour, Caroline solemnly requested that she be shown the canary's grave.

Pushinka, a gift of Nikita Khrushchev, was a daughter of Strelka, one of the Russian Sputnik space dogs. For Pushinka and Charlie, it was love at first sight and Russian-American puppies resulted.

The activities of the children and their play-school companions, with pets in the midst of everything, made this side of the White House a happy place for Jack and Jacqueline Kennedy. To the President, working in the Oval Office, it was something more. Whenever he needed a brief respite, he had only to step outside on the lawn and clap his hands. Within seconds the children, laughing and chattering, and the pets would arrive. And once more the President would be grinning his famous grin.

▶ JOHNSON'S HIM, HER, AND YUKI

In America's history, no public act by any president has provoked such worldwide outrage as Lyndon B. Johnson's innocently pulling the ears of the White House beagles, Him and Her.

It happened while he was strolling on the grounds with some visiting bankers, accompanied by reporters and photographers. Him and Her romped up for some doggy treats President Johnson always carried in his pocket. Photographers pleaded for a pose with the dogs doing a trick. When that didn't work, LBJ playfully lifted Him, and then Her, upright by their ears as flash bulbs popped. The photos made the front page and angry letters, calls, and telegrams flooded the White House.

The President was hurt far more than the dogs; from his boyhood on, he had always cherished beagles as pets. And one keeper of the White House doghouse called him "possibly the greatest pet lover of all our presidents."

Him and Her, born in June, 1963, had arrived during Johnson's vice-presidency. They were a gift to his daughter Luci. Johnson became devoted to them. Like so many other presidents, he could "talk" and unwind with the pets as a relaxation from the heavy burdens of state.

Her died suddenly in November, 1964, after swallowing a stone she was playing with. And in June, 1966, Him was killed by a car while chasing a squirrel. Both deaths were tragic blows to the Johnsons.

Then along came Yuki, an abandoned little white mongrel rescued by Luci at a gas station and brought home. Bright and lovable, Yuki filled an empty place in President Johnson's heart for many years. Asked how he could become so fond of a mutt, LBJ is reported to

Lyndon Johnson with Him and Blanco, a white collie that was another White House pet.

have replied "Because he speaks with a Texas accent and he likes me."

When Johnson decided not to seek re-election, the dogs, including some of Him's puppies, went home with the family to Texas. But only Yuki traveled with his master aboard Air Force One, the presidential jet.

▶ FORD'S LIBERTY

When the Ford family moved into the White House in the summer of 1974, something was missing: a family dog. People wondered whether, unlike most other presidents, this one would be dog-less.

Happily, their misgivings ended a few months later when Liberty arrived at the White House. A frisky young golden retriever, she was a gift to the President from his daughter Susan and White House Photographer David Hume Kennerly. And the public learned the Fords were a doggy family after all, having had two other goldens before.

To introduce the newest member of the first family, a press conference was held on the South Lawn. For the benefit of photographers, President Ford tossed a tennis ball for Liberty to recapture. Instead, she ran to make friends with the reporters, entangling herself in legs and camera equipment. The President laughed and exclaimed, "Hey, I thought you were a retriever."

Some would-be White House dogs have been unable to cope with the sometimes hectic life there. Throngs of visitors and bustling activities can place a strain on a dog's nervous system. So it takes a dog with an easygoing temperament to get along there—and Liberty had it. She was not the least bit nervous.

Liberty adjusted calmly to the demands of any situation. She posed agreeably for news photographers and visitors, greeted delegations and dignitaries with her master, and made friends with everyone. One friendship eluded her: that of Shan, Susan Ford's Siamese cat. But both slept in Susan's bedroom.

Camp David weekends, with the family together, were special treats for Liberty. She loved walks in the woods with Betty Ford and swims in the pool with the President. Obviously, Mr. Ford enjoyed these light moments. And whatever keeps the President of the United States smiling must be good for the country.

TED KAVANAUGH
Director, ALPO Pet News Bureau

President Ford and his golden retriever, Liberty.

Susan Ford and Shan.

Amy Carter and Misty.

▶ THE WHITE HOUSE CATS

History has recorded that several of our presidents had cats in the executive mansion. Abraham Lincoln was the first U.S. President to have a cat. He loved cats, saying that they were his "hobby." He would get down on the floor and play with his son's cat, Tabby. Pets and children (young Willy and Tad) kept the first family in a constant flurry of activity. One of the most hectic days in the White House was the day that President Lincoln's dog had puppies within minutes of the arrival of a litter of kittens from Tabby!

Siamese fanciers will be interested to know that President Rutherford B. Hayes was the proud recipient of the first Siamese ever sent to America from Thailand. Appropriately named Siam, she was brought from Bangkok in 1878 by the U.S. Consul, and became a White House favorite.

President Theodore Roosevelt was a lover of all animals, wild and domesticated. Among his menagerie of pets, he had two cats in the White House. Slippers, a silver female, made history by refusing to move from her comfortable position in the middle of the White House floor, causing President Roosevelt to escort a party of distinguished foreign dignitaries out and around the sleeping beauty. Slippers, a wanderer, was also unusual in that she was a polydactyl—she had six toes.

Slippers' counterpart, Tom Quartz, was an aggressive black male who used to chase Jack, the Roosevelts' dog, around the White House. Kermit, young son of President Roosevelt, was especially fond of Tom Quartz.

The next president to have cats at 1600 Pennsylvania Avenue was Calvin Coolidge. He was owned by a pair of felines—Tiger and Blacky. President Coolidge and especially Mrs. Coolidge adored cats. Tiger, a gray striped male wanderer, would drape himself in a snake-like manner around the President's neck. Blacky, a jet black, furry male, was sent to the Coolidges by a Waverly, Massachusetts, nurse. As Blacky grew older, his hunting and bird-catching instincts resulted in his frequent banishment to the White House guardhouse. Tiger and Blacky wore green and red collars, respectively, with the words, "The White House" imprinted on them.

Tom Kitten, who grew up to become Tom Terrific, was counted among the number of pets of the Kennedy White House. One of Caroline's favorite pets, Tom was jet black and served as an appropriate accessory to her witch costume as she and John-John went trick-or-treating one Halloween. Since President Kennedy developed an allergy to cats, Tom Terrific was later given to the President's secretary, Mary Gallagher.

Under President Ford the White House was once again blessed with the presence of a feline face—that of Shan, a seal point Siamese female. The particular pet of President Ford's daughter, Susan, Shan was given full run of the executive mansion's living quarters.

And President Jimmy Carter has continued the tradition. A male seal point Siamese named Misty Malarky Ying Yang, the pet of his young daughter Amy, is the most recent cat in the White House.

MARIBETH ECHARD
Cat Fanciers' Federation

WORLD OF SPORTS

Closing ceremonies of the 1976 Olympic Summer Games, held in Montreal, Canada.

Champion skier Rosi Mittermaier was one of the stars of the Winter Olympic Games.

The luge event is one of the most exciting of the Winter Games. The race-course is the same as for the bobsled, but with more steeply inclined starting ramps. Small wooden sleds are used, and speed is the name of the game. The racers lie on their backs and steer with their feet, zooming at 90 mph (145 kph).

THE 1976 OLYMPIC GAMES

The Games of the XII Winter Olympiad were held in Innsbruck, Austria, from February 4 to 15. Some 1,100 athletes from 36 countries competed under ideal winter conditions, and rewrote the record book as they skated faster and ski-jumped farther than ever.

▶ **THE WINTER WINNERS**

The Alpine skier is usually the glamor performer in this festival on snow and ice. The heroine of the 1976 Games was Rosi Mittermaier, a 25-year-old West German. Mittermaier captured the downhill and special slalom events, but just missed a third gold medal when she was beaten by 12/100 second in the giant slalom by an 18-year-old Canadian, Kathy Kreiner. Kreiner, who lives in Timmins, Ontario, was clocked in 1:29.13, Mittermaier in 1:29.25.

On the ice, the star was Dorothy Hamill, a brown-haired 19-year-old from Connecticut. She leaped, spun, and glided over the ice in an almost flawless exhibition that earned her the gold medal in figure skating. Hamill's performance was the latest in a long line of dazzling triumphs by U.S. Olympic figure-skating champions, such as Peggy Fleming, Carol Heiss, and Tenley Albright.

In the speed-skating events, Sheila Young of Michigan gained another gold for the United States when she won the 500-meter event. She set an Olympic record of 42.76 in the process, finishing just ahead of Cathy Priestner of Canada. Young, who is also a world bicycle-racing champion, returned to the United States with a total of 3 medals. She won the silver medal in the 1,500-meter event and the bronze in the 1,000 meters. It was the first time a U.S. competitor had won 3 medals in any Winter Olympic Games.

The Soviet Union's athletes enjoyed their greatest success on the ice, with a total of 12 medals, of which 6 were gold. They took golds in the men's 500-meter speed-skating event and in the women's 1,000-, 1,500-, and 3,000-meter events. In figure skating, the pairs title was won by the husband-and-wife team of Irina Rodnina and Alexander Zaitsev,

and the ice dancing by Ludmila Pakhomova and Alexander Gorshkov.

The Soviet hockey team gave Russia another medal on the ice when it won a 4–3 decision over Czechoslovakia in the final.

East Germany swept the competition on sleds, capturing the gold medals in the luge and bobsled races.

For the native Austrian spectators, there were thrills at the start and finish of the Games. Franz Klammer captured the opening event, the men's downhill skiing, and Karl Schnabl won the closing event, the 90-meter ski jump.

Dorothy Hamill glided over the ice to a gold medal.

The Soviet Union had collected the most medals by the time the Winter Games were over. The Russians won 27 medals in the 37 events—13 gold, 6 silver, and 8 bronze. East Germany was the runner-up with a total of 19 —7 gold, 5 silver, and 7 bronze. The U.S. squad ended up with 10 medals—3 gold, 3 silver, and 4 bronze. It was the best showing for a U.S. team since the 1952 Winter Games in Norway.

▶ THE SUMMER GAMES

The Summer Games of the XXI Olympiad were held in Montreal, Canada, from July 17 to August 1. Queen Elizabeth II formally opened the festival by delivering the ceremonial speech in French and English. The traditional flame-lighting ceremony was a special one. The Olympic torch made an electronic journey. It began on the Plains of Olympia in Greece, where the flame was lighted by the rays of the sun and carried by relay runners

With four golds, John Naber (second from the bottom) was a star of the Summer Games.

to Athens. In Athens the flame was converted into electric impulses, which were then transmitted by satellite to Ottawa, where they activated a laser beam. The laser beam kindled a torch, which was again given over to relay runners. The torch was carried into the Montreal stadium by two runners instead of the usual one—by Stephane Prefontaine, 15, of Montreal, and Sandra Henderson, 16, of Toronto. Together the boy and girl lit the Olympic flame. And the athletes were ready to play.

But there were large gaps in the ranks of the athletes. By the time the competition began, some 32 countries—mostly African, Asian, and Caribbean—had withdrawn. They were protesting the presence of New Zealand athletes at the Games—and, indirectly, South Africa's racial policy of apartheid. South Africa is not allowed to play in the Olympics, but a New Zealand rugby team had played a series of exhibition games in South Africa.

The Taiwanese athletes were also absent. They were barred by the Canadian Government, which did not want Taiwan to compete under its name, the Republic of China. And there was still another problem: construction strikes had left the main stadium unfinished. Luckily, there was enough of it built to be played in.

Despite the problems, nearly 8,000 athletes from the farthest corners of the earth took part and performed great feats of speed and strength.

Water Sports

Glory in the swimming and diving competition was shared equally by two groups, the U.S. men and the East German women. The American males captured 13 of the 15 gold medals, and the East German girls fell just a little short of that spectacular achievement with 11 victories in the 15 events. World records were set in 22 of the 26 swimming races.

John Naber was the "Mark Spitz" of this Olympiad. While Naber failed to match Spitz's hoard of 7 golds, he did reach the winner's stand four times. Naber lowered the world records in his individual triumphs in the 100- and 200-meter backstroke events, and he was a member of the winning 400-meter medley and 800-meter freestyle relay teams.

Together Sandra Henderson of Toronto and Stephane Prefontaine of Montreal light the Olympic flame in a special opening ceremony.

Bruce Jenner puts the shot. This is one of the ten events in the decathlon competition, which Jenner won, setting a world record in the process.

Nadia Comaneci, the 14-year-old Rumanian gymnast, was awarded perfect scores seven times. No gymnast in the history of the Olympics had ever before received a score of 10.

Alberto Juantorena races to victory in the 800-meter run. He also won the 400-meter run, a rare double triumph.

Among the many record breakers, Jim Montgomery of Wisconsin supplied the outstanding performance when he shattered the 50-second barrier in the 100-meter freestyle with a 49.99 clocking. The only non-American winners were David Wilkie of Scotland, representing Britain, in the 200-meter breaststroke, and Klaus Dibiasi of Italy, in the platform diving.

Over the years, American girls have been equally successful in Olympic swimming. But in this Olympiad the dominant position was taken by an East German squad that had never before produced a gold medalist. Led by 17-year-old Kornelia Ender, the East Germans saw their flag hoisted to the top 11 times. Ender captured 4 gold medals, in the 100-meter butterfly, 100- and 200-meter freestyle, and as a member of the winning 400-meter medley relay team. Only once before had a woman won 4 golds—in the London Olympics in 1948. Ender also won a silver in the 400-meter freestyle relay, the event in which the Americans won their only gold medal. Shirley Babashoff of California, regarded as the American most likely to succeed, was forced to settle for 4 silver medals.

East German men won 5 of the 8 rowing events, including the highly prized one for the eight-oar competition, once the particular province of U.S. oarsmen. The East Germans also took 4 of the 6 gold medals in the women's rowing.

Track and Field

Individual stars in the track competition were Lasse Viren of Finland and Alberto Juantorena of Cuba. Viren repeated his 1972 victories in the 5,000- and 10,000-meter runs, and then made an unsuccessful bid in the marathon. Juantorena scored a rare twin triumph, in the 400- and 800-meter runs.

The major performer for the Americans was Bruce Jenner, a part-time insurance salesman from California. He gave an awesome two-day performance in the ten-event decathlon, and not only captured the gold medal, but scored 8,618 points, surpassing the old world record by 164 points.

The glamor event of the track competition, the metric mile (1,500 meters), was won by John Walker of New Zealand, but his principal rival, Filbert Bayi, was missing, because his country, Tanzania, had withdrawn.

In the women's competition, the East Germans overwhelmed the opposition. They won the gold medals in 9 of the 14 events. They collected 19 medals in all, ahead of the Soviet Union's 8.

Basketball

Memories of Munich and their controversial 51–50 defeat by the Soviet Union haunted the U.S. basketball players as they drove through the round robin tournament to the gold medal. In 1972, the last three seconds of the contest had been played three times before the Russians won by 1 point. But the U.S. victory at Montreal wasn't exactly revenge, because the Soviet team had been eliminated in the semifinal by Yugoslavia.

The Americans won 6 games on the way to the championship, defeating Yugoslavia, 95–74, in the last game. Of the 71 games played since basketball was added to the Olympic program in 1936, the Munich final remains the only game ever lost by a U.S. men's squad.

In 1976, women's basketball was included for the first time, and the Soviet team led by 6-foot 11-inch (210.8-cm), 280-pound (127-kilo) Yuliana Semenova outclassed the other five entrants. The U.S. team, beaten by the Russians, 112–77, took the silver medals.

Gymnastics

The darling of the Olympics was a 14-year-old, 86-pound (39-kilo) Rumanian girl, Nadia Comaneci. The roars of approval from the 19,000 spectators in the Montreal Forum even surpassed the reception given the remarkable Russian gymnast Olga Korbut four years earlier. Never before had the Olympic judges given a perfect score of 10 to a gymnast, but Comaneci was awarded that supposedly impossible score 7 times as she won 3 gold medals—in the all-around competition, on the balance beam, and on the uneven bars—plus a silver in the team event and a bronze for floor exercises.

Other Competitions

The United States has always been dominant in professional boxing. But rarely have American amateur pugilists had the success they enjoyed in the 1976 Olympics. The 5 gold medalists matched the individual performances of the U.S. squad in 1952, but this time a silver and a bronze were added to the haul. And for the first time ever, two brothers were gold medalists: Leon Spinks in the light heavyweight division, and the younger Mike in the middleweight.

The equestrian events at Bromont, Quebec, attracted more than customary interest because Princess Anne of Britain was a competitor. But the big surprise was the victory of Edmund Coffin of Vermont in the three-day individual event. He was the first American ever to capture the gold in that event.

Like the equestrian competitions, the shooting events have men and women competing against each other. The small-bore rifle three-position event developed into a tense struggle between U.S. Army Capt. Lanny Bassham and Margaret Murdock of Kansas, the first woman to represent the United States in Olympic shooting. Bassham and Murdock ended the competition with the same score—1,162 points. It took the judges 3½ hours to decide to award the gold to Bassham. Bassham insisted that Murdock join him on the top pedestal during the medal ceremony, "since we were virtually tied." Murdock went home with the silver, and became the first woman to win a medal in Olympic shooting.

The world's strongest man, 345-pound (156-kilo) Vasili Alekseyev, repeated his 1972 triumph in weight lifting, super heavyweight division, as he led four other Soviet weight lifters to the gold medalist's pedestal.

When the games ended on August 1, the Soviet Union had won the most gold medals, 47, and the most medals altogether, 125. The United States had a total of 94 medals, including 34 golds. A surprisingly strong group from East Germany had finished with 90 medals, and had surpassed the Americans in individual glory with 40 gold medals.

Despite the problems that had threatened the cancellation of the Summer Games, they had been held on schedule and played to capacity audiences. The athletes left Canada with the hope that "they leave politics out of it" when they meet in Moscow in 1980.

HY GOLDBERG
NBC Sports

304

FINAL MEDAL STANDINGS

Winter Games—Innsbruck, Austria

Country	Gold	Silver	Bronze	Total
Soviet Union	13	6	8	27
East Germany	7	5	7	19
United States	3	3	4	10
Norway	3	3	1	7
West Germany	2	5	3	10
Finland	2	4	1	7
Austria	2	2	2	6
Switzerland	1	3	1	5
Netherlands	1	2	3	6
Italy	1	2	1	4
Canada	1	1	1	3
Britain	1	0	0	1
Czechoslovakia	0	1	0	1
Liechtenstein	0	0	2	2
Sweden	0	0	2	2
France	0	0	1	1

Summer Games—Montreal, Canada

Country	Gold	Silver	Bronze	Total
Soviet Union	47	43	35	125
East Germany	40	25	25	90
United States	34	35	25	94
West Germany	10	12	17	39
Japan	9	6	10	25
Poland	7	6	11	24
Bulgaria	6	7	9	22
Cuba	6	4	3	13
Rumania	4	9	14	27
Hungary	4	5	12	21
Finland	4	2	0	6
Sweden	4	1	0	5
Britain	3	5	5	13
Italy	2	7	4	13
France	2	2	5	9
Yugoslavia	2	3	3	8
Czechoslovakia	2	2	4	8
New Zealand	2	1	1	4
South Korea	1	1	4	6
Switzerland	1	1	2	4
Jamaica	1	1	0	2
North Korea	1	1	0	2
Norway	1	1	0	2
Denmark	1	0	2	3
Mexico	1	0	1	2
Trinidad & Tobago	1	0	0	1
Canada	0	5	6	11
Belgium	0	3	3	6
Netherlands	0	2	3	5
Portugal	0	2	0	2
Spain	0	2	0	2
Australia	0	1	4	5
Iran	0	1	1	2
Mongolia	0	1	0	1
Venezuela	0	1	0	1
Brazil	0	0	2	2
Austria	0	0	1	1
Bermuda	0	0	1	1
Pakistan	0	0	1	1
Puerto Rico	0	0	1	1
Thailand	0	0	1	1

1976 OLYMPIC GOLD MEDAL WINNERS

WINTER GAMES—INNSBRUCK, AUSTRIA

SPORT	EVENT	WINNER
Biathlon	Individual	Nikolai Kruglov, U.S.S.R.
	Relay	U.S.S.R.
Bobsledding	Two-Man	East Germany
	Four-Man	East Germany
Hockey	Team	U.S.S.R.
Luge	Men's Singles	Detlef Guenther, East Germany
	Men's Doubles	East Germany
	Women's Singles	Margit Schumann, East Germany
Alpine Skiing, Men	Downhill	Franz Klammer, Austria
	Giant Slalom	Heini Hemmi, Switzerland
	Special Slalom	Piero Gros, Italy
Alpine Skiing, Women	Downhill	Rosi Mittermaier, West Germany
	Giant Slalom	Kathy Kreiner, Canada
	Special Slalom	Rosi Mittermaier, West Germany
Nordic Skiing, Men	15-kilometer Cross-Country	Nikolai Bazhukov, U.S.S.R.
	30-kilometer Cross-Country	Sergei Savelyev, U.S.S.R.
	50-kilometer Cross-Country	Ivar Formo, Norway
	40-kilometer Cross-Country Relay	Finland
	Combined	Ulrich Wehling, East Germany
	70-meter Jump	Hans-Georg Aschenbach, East Germany
	90-meter Jump	Karl Schnabl, Austria
Nordic Skiing, Women	5-kilometer Cross-Country	Helena Takalo, Finland
	10-kilometer Cross-Country	Raisa Smetanina, U.S.S.R.
	20-kilometer Cross-Country Relay	U.S.S.R.
Figure Skating	Men's Singles	John Curry, Britain
	Women's Singles	Dorothy Hamill, U.S.
	Pairs	Irina Rodnina/Alexander Zaitsev, U.S.S.R.
	Dance	Ludmila Pakhomova/Alexander Gorshkov, U.S.S.R.
Speed Skating, Men	500-meter	Yevgeni Kulikov, U.S.S.R.
	1,000-meter	Peter Mueller, U.S.
	1,500-meter	Jan Egil Storholt, Norway
	5,000-meter	Sten Stensen, Norway
	10,000-meter	Piet Kleine, Netherlands
Speed Skating, Women	500-meter	Sheila Young, U.S.
	1,000-meter	Tatyana Averina, U.S.S.R.
	1,500-meter	Galina Stepanskaya, U.S.S.R.
	3,000-meter	Tatyana Averina, U.S.S.R.

SUMMER GAMES—MONTREAL, CANADA

SPORT	EVENT	WINNER
Archery	Men	Darrell Pace, U.S.
	Women	Luann Ryon, U.S.
Basketball	Team, men	U.S.
	Team, women	U.S.S.R.
Boxing	Light Flyweight	Jorge Hernandez, Cuba
	Flyweight	Leo Randolph, U.S.
	Bantamweight	Yong Jo Gu, North Korea
	Featherweight	Angel Herrera, Cuba
	Lightweight	Howard Davis, U.S.
	Light Welterweight	Ray Leonard, U.S.
	Welterweight	Jochen Bachfeld, East Germany
	Light Middleweight	Jerzy Rybicki, Poland
	Middleweight	Michael Spinks, U.S.
	Light Heavyweight	Leon Spinks, U.S.
	Heavyweight	Teofilo Stevenson, Cuba
Canoeing, Men	500-meter Kayak Singles	Vasile Diba, Rumania
	500-meter Kayak Doubles	East Germany
	1,000-meter Kayak Singles	Rudiger Helms, East Germany
	1,000-meter Kayak Doubles	U.S.S.R.
	1,000-meter Kayak Fours	U.S.S.R.
	500-meter Canadian Singles	Alexander Rogov, U.S.S.R.
	500-meter Canadian Doubles	U.S.S.R.
	1,000-meter Canadian Singles	Matija Ljubek, Yugoslavia
	1,000-meter Canadian Doubles	U.S.S.R.
Canoeing, Women	500-meter Kayak Singles	Carola Zirzow, East Germany
	500-meter Kayak Doubles	U.S.S.R.
Cycling	Road Race	Bernt Johansson, Sweden
	Team Road Race	U.S.S.R.
	Pursuit	Gregor Braun, West Germany
	Team Pursuit	West Germany
	Sprint	Anton Tkac, Czechoslovakia
	1,000-meter Time Trial	Klaus-Jürgen Grunke, East Germany
Equestrian	3-Day Event	Edmund Coffin, U.S.
	Team 3-Day Event	U.S.
	Dressage	Christine Stueckelberger, Switzerland
	Team Dressage	West Germany
	Jumping	Alwin Schockemoehle, West Germany
	Team Jumping	France
Fencing, Men	Epee	Alexander Pusch, West Germany
	Team Epee	Sweden
	Foil	Fabio Dal Zotto, Italy
	Team Foil	West Germany
	Saber	Viktor Krovopovskov, U.S.S.R.
	Team Saber	U.S.S.R.

SPORT	EVENT	WINNER
Fencing, Women	Foil	Ildiko Schwarczenberger, Hungary
	Team Foil	U.S.S.R.
Field Hockey	Team	New Zealand
Gymnastics, Men	All-Around	Nikolai Andrianov, U.S.S.R.
	Team	Japan
	Floor Exercises	Nikolai Andrianov, U.S.S.R.
	Horizontal Bar	Mitsuo Tsukahara, Japan
	Long Horse Vault	Nikolai Andrianov, U.S.S.R.
	Parallel Bars	Sawao Kato, Japan
	Rings	Nikolai Andrianov, U.S.S.R.
	Side Horse	Zoltan Magyar, Hungary
Gymnastics, Women	All-Around	Nadia Comaneci, Rumania
	Team	U.S.S.R.
	Balance Beam	Nadia Comaneci, Rumania
	Floor Exercises	Nelli Kim, U.S.S.R.
	Side Horse Vault	Nelli Kim, U.S.S.R.
	Uneven Parallel Bars	Nadia Comaneci, Rumania
Handball	Team, men	U.S.S.R.
	Team, women	U.S.S.R.
Judo	Lightweight	Hector Rodriguez, Cuba
	Light Middleweight	Vladimir Nevzorov, U.S.S.R.
	Middleweight	Isamu Sonoda, Japan
	Light Heavyweight	Kazuhiro Ninomiya, Japan
	Heavyweight	Sergei Novikov, U.S.S.R.
	Open	Haruki Uemura, Japan
Modern Pentathlon	Individual	Janusz Pyciak-Peciak, Poland
	Team	Britain
Rowing, Men	Single Sculls	Pertti Karppinen, Finland
	Double Sculls	Norway
	Quadruple Sculls	East Germany
	Coxed Pairs	East Germany
	Coxless Pairs	East Germany
	Coxed Fours	U.S.S.R.
	Coxless Fours	East Germany
	Eights	East Germany
Rowing, Women	Single Sculls	Christine Scheiblich, East Germany
	Double Sculls	Bulgaria
	Quadruple Sculls	East Germany
	Coxless Pairs	Bulgaria
	Coxed Fours	East Germany
	Eights	East Germany
Shooting	Free Pistol	Uwe Potteck, East Germany
	Rapid-Fire Pistol	Norbert Klaar, East Germany
	Small-Bore Rifle, prone	Karlheinz Smieszek, West Germany
	Small-Bore Rifle, 3-position	Lanny Bassham, U.S.
	Rifle, running-game target	Alexander Gazov, U.S.S.R.
	Shotgun, trapshooting	Don Haldeman, U.S.
	Shotgun, skeetshooting	Josef Panacek, Czechoslovakia

SPORT	EVENT	WINNER
Soccer	Team	East Germany
Swimming, Men	100-meter Backstroke	John Naber, U.S.
	200-meter Backstroke	John Naber, U.S.
	100-meter Breaststroke	John Hencken, U.S.
	200-meter Breaststroke	David Wilkie, Britain
	100-meter Butterfly	Matt Vogel, U.S.
	200-meter Butterfly	Mike Bruner, U.S.
	100-meter Freestyle	Jim Montgomery, U.S.
	200-meter Freestyle	Bruce Furniss, U.S.
	400-meter Freestyle	Brian Goodell, U.S.
	800-meter Freestyle Relay	U.S.
	1,500-meter Freestyle	Brian Goodell, U.S.
	400-meter Medley	Rod Strachan, U.S.
	400-meter Medley Relay	U.S.
	Platform Diving	Klaus Dibiasi, Italy
	Springboard Diving	Phil Boggs, U.S.
Swimming, Women	100-meter Backstroke	Ulrike Richter, East Germany
	200-meter Backstroke	Ulrike Richter, East Germany
	100-meter Breaststroke	Hannelore Anke, East Germany
	200-meter Breaststroke	Marina Koshevaya, U.S.S.R.
	100-meter Butterfly	Kornelia Ender, East Germany
	200-meter Butterfly	Andrea Pollack, East Germany
	100-meter Freestyle	Kornelia Ender, East Germany
	200-meter Freestyle	Kornelia Ender, East Germany
	400-meter Freestyle	Petra Thumer, East Germany
	400-meter Freestyle Relay	U.S.
	800-meter Freestyle	Petra Thumer, East Germany
	400 meter Medley	Ulrike Tauber, East Germany
	400-meter Medley Relay	East Germany
	Platform Diving	Elena Vaytsekhovskaya, U.S.S.R.
	Springboard Diving	Jenni Chandler, U.S.
Track and Field, Men	100-meter Dash	Hasely Crawford, Trinidad
	200-meter Dash	Don Quarrie, Jamaica
	400-meter Run	Alberto Juantorena, Cuba
	400-meter Relay	U.S.
	800-meter Run	Alberto Juantorena, Cuba
	1,500-meter Run	John Walker, New Zealand
	1,600-meter Relay	U.S.
	5,000-meter Run	Lasse Viren, Finland
	10,000-meter Run	Lasse Viren, Finland
	20,000-meter Walk	Daniel Bautista, Mexico
	110-meter Hurdles	Guy Drut, France
	400-meter Hurdles	Edwin Moses, U.S.
	3,000-meter Steeplechase	Anders Gaerderud, Sweden
	Marathon	Waldemar Cierpinski, East Germany
	Discus Throw	Mac Wilkins, U.S.
	Hammer Throw	Yuri Sedyh, U.S.S.R.
	High Jump	Jacek Wszola, Poland
	Javelin Throw	Miklos Nemeth, Hungary
	Long Jump	Arnie Robinson, U.S.
	Pole Vault	Tadeusz Slusarski, Poland
	Shot Put	Udo Beyer, East Germany
	Triple Jump	Viktor Saneyev, U.S.S.R.
	Decathlon	Bruce Jenner, U.S.

SPORT	EVENT	WINNER
Track and Field, Women	100-meter Dash	Annegret Richter, West Germany
	200-meter Dash	Baerbel Eckert, East Germany
	400-meter Run	Irena Szewinska, Poland
	400-meter Relay	East Germany
	800-meter Run	Tatyana Kazankina, U.S.S.R.
	1,500-meter Run	Tatyana Kazankina, U.S.S.R.
	1,600-meter Relay	East Germany
	100-meter Hurdles	Johanna Schaller, East Germany
	Discus Throw	Evelin Schlaak, East Germany
	High Jump	Rosemarie Ackermann, East Germany
	Javelin Throw	Ruth Fuchs, East Germany
	Long Jump	Angela Voigt, East Germany
	Shot Put	Ivanka Christova, Bulgaria
	Pentathlon	Siegrun Siegl, East Germany
Volleyball	Team, men	Poland
	Team, women	Japan
Water Polo	Team	Hungary
Weight Lifting	Flyweight	Alexander Voronin, U.S.S.R.
	Bantamweight	Norair Nurikyan, Bulgaria
	Featherweight	Nikolai Kolesnikov, U.S.S.R.
	Lightweight	Zbigniew Kaczmarek, Poland*
	Middleweight	Yordan Mitkov, Bulgaria
	Light Heavyweight	Valeri Shary, U.S.S.R.
	Middle Heavyweight	David Rigert, U.S.S.R.
	Heavyweight	Valentin Khristov, Bulgaria*
	Super Heavyweight	Vasili Alekseyev, U.S.S.R.
Wrestling, Freestyle	Paperweight	Khassan Issaev, Bulgaria
	Flyweight	Yuji Takada, Japan
	Bantamweight	Vladimir Yumin, U.S.S.R.
	Featherweight	Jung-Mo Yang, South Korea
	Lightweight	Pavel Pinigin, U.S.S.R.
	Welterweight	Jiichiro Date, Japan
	Middleweight	John Peterson, U.S.
	Light Heavyweight	Levan Tediashvili, U.S.S.R.
	Heavyweight	Ivan Yarygin, U.S.S.R.
	Super Heavyweight	Soslan Andiyev, U.S.S.R.
Wrestling, Greco-Roman	Paperweight	Aleksei Shumakov, U.S.S.R.
	Flyweight	Vitali Konstantinov, U.S.S.R.
	Bantamweight	Pertti Ukkola, Finland
	Featherweight	Kazimier Lipien, Poland
	Lightweight	Suren Nalbandyan, U.S.S.R.
	Welterweight	Anatoli Bykov, U.S.S.R.
	Middleweight	Momir Petkovic, Yugoslavia
	Light Heavyweight	Valeri Rezantsev, U.S.S.R.
	Heavyweight	Nikolai Bolboshin, U.S.S.R.
	Super Heavyweight	Alexander Kolchinski, U.S.S.R.
Yachting	Finn	East Germany
	Flying Dutchman	West Germany
	470 Class	West Germany
	Soling	Denmark
	Tempest	Sweden
	Tornado	Britain

*Later disqualified for drug use; first place officially declared vacant.

They're for the birds! Especially if they're the fans who love Detroit's star pitcher Mark ("The Bird") Fidrych and Sesame Street's Big Bird. With his pitching skill and strange ways, Fidrych became an overnight sensation in 1976.

BASEBALL

The 1976 baseball season had a nostalgic touch—the New York Yankees reached the World Series after a lapse of twelve years. But that was as far as it went. The Cincinnati Reds had the talent. Indeed, they reminded many of past Yankee teams that had been baseball's undisputed champions. The Reds swept the Yankees in four straight games in the World Series. It was the second consec-

utive Series triumph for the Reds. And those two Series wins were the first back-to-back victories by a National League pennant winner in 54 years. (The last were by the New York Giants, in 1921 and 1922.)

Only the second game of the Series was even a close contest, and the Reds scored the winning run in the ninth inning for a 4–3 decision. Over-all, the Reds piled up 22 runs in the four games, and the Yankees, 8.

Johnny Bench became the Most Valuable Player in the World Series, although he had had only a mediocre season. The catcher's .533 average (8 hits in 15 at bats) was the fourth highest in World Series history. On the losing side, Yankee catcher Thurman Munson delivered nine hits for a .529 mark. During the regular season he had batted .302, second on his team to Mickey Rivers' .312.

Cincinnati's sweep of the Yankees followed a similar success in the playoff for the pennant, in which the Reds eliminated the Philadelphia Phillies, leaders in the National League East, in three straight engagements. And that same superiority had been displayed throughout the season, in every area except pitching. Four of the top ten batters in the league wore Cincinnati uniforms: Ken Griffey, Pete Rose, Joe Morgan, and Cesar Geronimo. Their averages ranged from Griffey's .336 down to Geronimo's .307. Rose led the league in total hits (215), runs scored (130), and two-base hits (42).

Bill Madlock of the Cubs retained his National League batting crown with .339 and a three-point edge over Griffey. John Denny of St. Louis had the lowest earned run average among pitchers with 2.52.

The Yankees won the American League East title on the fire power of Rivers, Munson, Chris Chambliss, Roy White, and Graig Nettles (League home run leader with 32), plus the pitching of Ed Figueroa, Dock Ellis, Catfish Hunter, and Ken Holtzman.

The Kansas City Royals won the American League West title. The Royals were sparked by league batting king George Brett (.333) and runner-up Hal McRae (.332). With their help, the Royals fought the Yankees through five games before Chambliss walloped a ninth-inning homer for a 7–6 triumph, and the pennant for the Yankees.

In World Series action, Yankee Thurman Munson scores past Cincinnati catcher Johnny Bench. Cincinnati swept the championship 4–0, with Bench winning MVP honors for Series play.

Brett was the American League's batting king, replacing Rod Carew, the Minnesota hitter who had led for four consecutive campaigns. Rookie Mark Fidrych of Detroit had the lowest earned run average among pitchers, 2.34.

The two World Series teams supplied the Most Valuable Players (MVP) in the two leagues. Joe Morgan, the Reds' second baseman, won the award in the National, and Thurman Munson, the Yankee catcher, won in the American. Morgan had won the MVP title in 1975, too, and only one other National Leaguer had ever done that before, Ernie Banks of the Cubs in 1958 and 1959.

One of the two Cy Young Awards, for the outstanding pitchers in the two leagues, also had a repeat winner—Jim Palmer of the Baltimore Orioles, with a 22–13 record. Palmer became the first three-time winner of this award in the American League. The National League choice was Randy Jones of the San Diego Padres, with a 22–14 mark.

1976 WORLD SERIES RESULTS

		R	H	E	Winning/Losing Pitcher
1	Cincinnati	5	10	1	Gullett
	New York	1	5	1	Alexander
2	Cincinnati	4	10	0	Billingham
	New York	3	9	1	Hunter
3	Cincinnati	6	13	2	Zachry
	New York	2	8	0	Ellis
4	Cincinnati	7	9	2	Nolan
	New York	2	8	0	Figueroa

FINAL MAJOR LEAGUE BASEBALL STANDINGS

AMERICAN LEAGUE

Eastern Division

	W	L	Pct.	GB
*New York	97	62	.610	—
Baltimore	88	74	.543	10½
Boston	83	79	.512	15½
Cleveland	81	78	.509	16
Detroit	74	87	.460	24
Milwaukee	66	95	.410	32

Western Division

	W	L	Pct.	GB
Kansas City	90	72	.556	—
Oakland	87	74	.540	2½
Minnesota	85	77	.525	5
California	76	86	.469	14
Texas	76	86	.469	14
Chicago	64	97	.398	25½

NATIONAL LEAGUE

Eastern Division

	W	L	Pct.	GB
Philadelphia	101	61	.623	—
Pittsburgh	92	70	.568	9
New York	86	76	.531	15
Chicago	75	87	.463	26
St. Louis	72	90	.444	29
Montreal	55	107	.340	46

Western Division

	W	L	Pct.	GB
*Cincinnati	102	60	.630	—
Los Angeles	92	70	.568	10
Houston	80	82	.494	22
San Francisco	74	88	.457	28
San Diego	73	89	.451	29
Atlanta	70	92	.432	32

*pennant winners

MAJOR LEAGUE LEADERS

AMERICAN LEAGUE

Batting
(top 10 qualifiers)

	AB	H	R	Pct.
Brett, Kansas City	645	215	94	.333
McRae, Kansas City	527	175	75	.332
Carew, Minnesota	605	200	97	.331
Bostock, Minnesota	474	153	75	.323
LeFlore, Detroit	544	172	93	.316
Lynn, Boston	507	159	76	.314
Rivers, New York	590	184	95	.312
Carty, Cleveland	552	171	67	.310
Munson, New York	616	186	79	.302
Garr, Chicago	527	158	63	.300

NATIONAL LEAGUE

Batting
(top 10 qualifiers)

	AB	H	R	Pct.
Madlock, Chicago	514	174	68	.339
Griffey, Cincinnati	562	189	111	.336
Maddox, Philadelphia	531	175	75	.330
Rose, Cincinnati	665	215	130	.323
Morgan, Cincinnati	472	151	113	.320
Garvey, Los Angeles	631	200	85	.317
Montanez, Atlanta	650	206	74	.317
Parker, Pittsburgh	537	168	82	.313
Watson, Houston	585	183	76	.313
Geronimo, Cincinnati	486	149	59	.307

Pitching
(top 5 qualifiers, based on ERA)

	W	L	ERA
Fidrych, Detroit	19	9	2.34
Blue, Oakland	18	13	2.35
Tanana, California	19	10	2.44
Torrez, Oakland	16	12	2.50
Palmer, Baltimore	22	13	2.51

Pitching
(top 5 qualifiers, based on ERA)

	W	L	ERA
Denny, St. Louis	11	9	2.52
Rau, Los Angeles	16	12	2.57
Seaver, New York	14	11	2.59
Koosman, New York	21	10	2.70
Zachry, Cincinnati	14	7	2.74

Home Runs

	HR
Nettles, New York	32
Bando, Oakland	27
Jackson, Baltimore	27
Hendrick, Cleveland	25
May, Baltimore	25
Rice, Boston	25
Tenace, Oakland	22

Home Runs

	HR
Schmidt, Philadelphia	38
Kingman, New York	37
Monday, Chicago	32
Foster, Cincinnati	29
Morgan, Cincinnati	27
Cey, Los Angeles	23
Murcer, San Francisco	23

Masaru Mizuki slides home, scoring one of Tokyo's 10 runs in the final game of the Series.

LITTLE LEAGUE BASEBALL

In 1974, the officials of Little League Baseball announced that they would no longer allow foreign teams to play in the Little League World Series. The reason eventually given for the ban was that foreign teams were chosen from much wider geographical areas than were the U.S. teams. The action received much criticism in the United States. Nevertheless, in 1975 only U.S. teams played in the Little League World Series.

In 1976, however, the ban was lifted. The league authorities said that the foreign teams had agreed to limit player selection to population areas of 15,000 people. And so the 1976 Little League World Series, played in Williamsport, Pennsylvania, was once again international. The championship final pitted the team from Tokyo, Japan, against the team from Campbell, California. Tokyo emerged the winner of the Series.

The Japanese had arrived in Williamsport with two spectacular pitchers. Each pitched a

no-hit game on the way to the final. In Tokyo's opening triumph, an overwhelming 25–0 victory over Kaiserslautern of West Germany, Kiyoshi Tsumura pitched a perfect game (no batter reached first base). Tsumura also struck out 15 batters and hit a grand slam homer. The second Tokyo hurler, Daisuki Araki, pitched a 4–0 no-hitter against the Puerto Nuevo team, from Puerto Rico, to bring Tokyo into the final. He wasn't quite perfect, however. He walked a batter in the first inning.

In the championship game, Tsumura returned to the mound for Tokyo and limited the Californians to three hits. The Japanese batters made their pitcher's task easy by scoring seven runs by the third inning. He was also helped by the California team, which made five fielding errors and a combination of nine wild pitches and passed balls. Tokyo won that decisive engagement 10–3.

In the two games he pitched, Tsumura struck out a total of 24 batters. In the three victories, he contributed 5 hits and drove in 6 runs. The Japanese scored a total of 39 runs on 37 hits in their three winning games.

The Phoenix Suns take on the powerful Boston Celtics in an NBA championship playoff game.

BASKETBALL

The Boston Celtics have been professional basketball's dominant team in this generation. In the 1975–76 season, they continued their superiority by capturing their 13th National Basketball Association (NBA) championship in the last 20 years.

Boston's victory over the Phoenix Suns, 4 games to 2, in the final playoff series, wasn't too surprising. What was surprising was the presence of the Suns in the title round. The Suns had had a mediocre season record and

had placed third in the league's Pacific Division. They reached the championship series by eliminating the 1975 champions, the Golden State Warriors.

As was expected, the Phoenix squad ultimately lost to the experience and skill of Boston veterans Jo Jo White, John Havlicek, Charlie Scott, and Dave Cowens. But Phoenix enjoyed at least one shining hour. In the fifth contest, with the playoff series deadlocked, 2 games to 2, the Suns carried the Celtics into three overtime periods before Boston gained the 128–126 decision. That exhausting battle was called "the greatest basketball game ever played." After that, the Celtic triumph in the sixth and final game was anti-climactic. White, the offensive star throughout the series, earned the Most Valuable Player (MVP) award.

In the American Basketball Association (ABA), the New York Nets won the title for the second time in three years by defeating the Denver Nuggets in a 6-game series.

This championship round matched the two best teams in the standings—Denver and New York—and the two best players—David Thompson of the Nuggets and Julius Erving of the Nets. In the final game, Thompson scored 42 points, and the Nets were forced to overcome a 22-point third-quarter deficit. But in the end, Erving and the Nets won, 112–106. Erving was voted MVP.

When the 1976–77 season opened in late October, the long-rumored merger of the NBA and the ABA had taken place. The NBA absorbed four teams, the New York Nets, Denver Nuggets, San Antonio Spurs, and Indiana Pacers. Three ABA teams—the Kentucky Colonels, St. Louis Spirits, and Virginia Squires—were disbanded, and their best players went to clubs in the expanded NBA. There was one startling development in the shuffling: Julius Erving, the star player for the New York Nets when they won the ninth—and last—ABA championship, was traded to the Philadelphia 76ers.

The National Collegiate Athletic Association (NCAA) championship tournament resulted in a triumph for Indiana University, which scored an 86–68 victory over the University of Michigan in the finale. The Hoosiers became one of the few major college teams ever to go through a basketball season with a perfect record—32 victories, no defeats. In the tournament semifinals, Indiana had eliminated UCLA, winner in 11 of the last 13 years.

The University of Kentucky won the National Invitation Tournament, the oldest of the college basketball post-season competitions. In this, the 39th tournament, the Wildcats outscored the University of North Carolina–Charlotte, 71–67.

FINAL NBA STANDINGS

EASTERN CONFERENCE

Atlantic Division

	W	L	Pct.
Boston	54	28	.659
Philadelphia	46	36	.561
Buffalo	46	36	.561
New York	38	44	.463

Central Division

	W	L	Pct.
Cleveland	49	33	.598
Washington	48	34	.585
Houston	40	42	.488
New Orleans	38	44	.463
Atlanta	29	53	.354

WESTERN CONFERENCE

Midwest Division

	W	L	Pct.
Milwaukee	38	44	.463
Detroit	36	46	.439
Kansas City	31	51	.378
Chicago	24	58	.293

Pacific Division

	W	L	Pct.
Golden State	59	23	.720
Seattle	43	39	.524
Phoenix	42	40	.512
Los Angeles	40	42	.488
Portland	37	45	.451

NBA Championship: Boston Celtics

FINAL ABA STANDINGS

	W	L	Pct.
Denver	60	24	.714
New York	55	29	.655
San Antonio	50	34	.595
Kentucky	46	38	.548
Indiana	39	45	.464
St. Louis	35	49	.417
Virginia	15	68	.181

ABA Championship: New York Nets

COLLEGE BASKETBALL

Conference	Winner
Atlantic Coast	Virginia
Big Eight	Missouri
Big Ten	Indiana
Ivy League	Princeton
Mid-American	Western Michigan
Missouri Valley	Wichita State
Pacific Eight	UCLA
Southeastern	Alabama
Southern	Virginia Military
Southwest	Texas Tech
West Coast Athletic	Pepperdine
Western Athletic	Arizona
Yankee	Massachusetts

NCAA: Indiana

National Invitation Tournament: Kentucky

Phil Hubbard moves the ball past Kent Benson, but by the end of the game, Indiana had beaten Michigan 86–68 for the NCAA title.

Pittsburgh Steeler John Stallworth leaps to catch a pass in the AFC championship game with the Oakland Raiders.

FOOTBALL

The teams that have dominated the National Football League (NFL) in recent years continued to do so during 1976, with one exception. The New England Patriots changed their 1975 record of 3–11 into a 1976 record of 11–3. This gave the Patriots a tie with the Baltimore Colts for the Eastern Division title in the American Conference.

Both those teams reached the post-season playoffs, along with the Oakland Raiders (13–1) and the Pittsburgh Steelers (10–4) in the American Conference. In the National Conference the entries were the Dallas Cowboys (11–3), the Washington Redskins (10–4), the Minnesota Vikings (11–2–1), and the Los Angeles Rams (10–3–1).

The most spectacular effort during the regular season had been the late surge by the Steelers. After losing four of their first five contests, they won nine in a row to gain the division title. Pittsburgh entered the playoffs with the hope of eventually setting a Super Bowl record—three consecutive triumphs.

They made it ten straight wins with a 40–14 playoff victory over the Colts. But with Franco Harris and Rocky Bleier, their two 1,000-yard rushers, on the sidelines with injuries, the Steelers bowed to Oakland, 24–7, in the American Conference championship game. Minnesota captured the National Conference crown in a 24–13 battle with Los Angeles.

And that's how it ended up. When all eight teams had completed their playoff skirmishing, it was Oakland against Minnesota in the Super Bowl. Neither team had ever won a Super Bowl before, although the Raiders had played in one and the Vikings in three. The Bowl ended with Minnesota crushed by Oakland, 32–14— a failure for yet a fourth time.

Individually, O. J. Simpson of the Buffalo Bills was football's star again. He gained his fourth league rushing title in five years with 1,503 yards, 113 more than the surprising Walter Payton of the Chicago Bears.

Two new teams, Tampa Bay and Seattle, increased the NFL roster to 28. While Seattle managed two victories, Tampa Bay was the first club in NFL history to lose all 14 contests.

Jack Youngblood of the Los Angeles Rams grabs Minnesota Viking quarterback Fran Tarkenton, who is trying to launch a pass, in the NFC championship game.

In the 1977 Cotton Bowl, a Houston defensive back hurdles a Maryland fullback in a vain effort to block a punt. Houston won the Bowl.

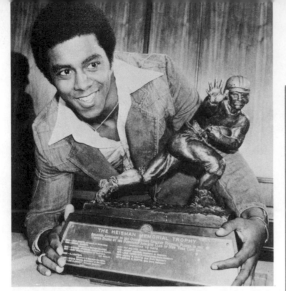
Heisman Trophy winner Tony Dorsett, of the University of Pittsburgh.

In the Canadian League, the Ottawa Rough Riders captured the Grey Cup by defeating the Saskatchewan Roughriders.

▶ **COLLEGE PLAY**

Led by Heisman Trophy winner Tony Dorsett, the University of Pittsburgh gained top rank among the nation's college football teams with an 11–0 record. Dorsett completed his four years of varsity competition by breaking or tying 18 college records; these included 6,082 yards rushing in a career, 1,948 yards rushing in a season, and 356 points and 59 touchdowns in a career.

COLLEGE FOOTBALL

Conference	Winner
Atlantic Coast	Maryland
Big Eight	Colorado; Oklahoma; Oklahoma State (tied)
Big Ten	Michigan; Ohio State (tied)
Ivy League	Brown; Yale (tied)
Mid-American	Ball State
Pacific Eight	Southern California
Southeastern	Georgia
Southern	East Carolina
Southwest	Houston; Texas Tech (tied)
Western Athletic	Brigham Young; Wyoming (tied)
Yankee	New Hampshire

Cotton Bowl: Houston 30, Maryland 21
Gator Bowl: Notre Dame 20, Penn State 9
Orange Bowl: Ohio State 27, Colorado 10
Rose Bowl: Southern California 14, Michigan 6
Sugar Bowl: Pittsburgh 27, Georgia 3

Heisman Trophy: Tony Dorsett, Pittsburgh

FINAL NFL STANDINGS

AMERICAN CONFERENCE

Eastern Division

	W	L	T	Pct.	PF	PA
Baltimore	11	3	0	.786	417	246
New England	11	3	0	.786	376	236
Miami	6	8	0	.429	263	264
Jets	3	11	0	.214	169	383
Buffalo	2	12	0	.143	245	363

Central Division

	W	L	T	Pct.	PF	PA
Pittsburgh	10	4	0	.714	342	138
Cincinnati	10	4	0	.714	335	210
Cleveland	9	5	0	.643	267	287
Houston	5	9	0	.357	222	273

Western Division

	W	L	T	Pct.	PF	PA
Oakland	13	1	0	.929	350	237
Denver	9	5	0	.643	315	206
San Diego	6	8	0	.429	248	285
Kansas City	5	9	0	.357	290	376
Tampa Bay	0	14	0	.000	125	412

Conference Champion: Oakland Raiders

NATIONAL CONFERENCE

Eastern Division

	W	L	T	Pct.	PF	PA
Dallas	11	3	0	.786	296	194
Washington	10	4	0	.714	291	217
St. Louis	10	4	0	.714	309	267
Philadelphia	4	10	0	.286	165	286
Giants	3	11	0	.214	170	250

Central Division

	W	L	T	Pct.	PF	PA
Minnesota	11	2	1	.821	305	176
Chicago	7	7	0	.500	253	216
Detroit	6	8	0	.429	262	220
Green Bay	5	9	0	.357	218	299

Western Division

	W	L	T	Pct.	PF	PA
Los Angeles	10	3	1	.750	351	200
San Francisco	8	6	0	.571	270	190
Atlanta	4	10	0	.286	172	312
New Orleans	4	10	0	.286	253	346
Seattle	2	12	0	.143	229	429

Conference Champion: Minnesota Vikings

1977 SUPER BOWL WINNER: Oakland Raiders

Having just won the U.S. Open, a jubilant Jerry Pate tosses his golf ball to the gallery.

Ray Floyd coaxes in a birdie putt during the Masters tournament—which he won.

GOLF

PROFESSIONAL		AMATEUR	
	Individual		**Individual**
Masters	Raymond Floyd	**U.S. Amateur**	Bill Sander
U.S. Open	Jerry Pate	**U.S. Women's Amateur**	Donna Horton
Canadian Open	Jerry Pate	**British Amateur**	Dick Siderowf
British Open	Johnny Miller	**British Women's Amateur**	Cathy Panton
PGA	Dave Stockton	**Canadian Amateur**	Jim Nelford
World Series of Golf	Jack Nicklaus	**Canadian Ladies Amateur**	Debbie Massey
U.S. Women's Open	JoAnne Carner		
Ladies PGA	Betty Burfeindt		
	Team		**Team**
World Cup	Spain	**Curtis Cup**	United States

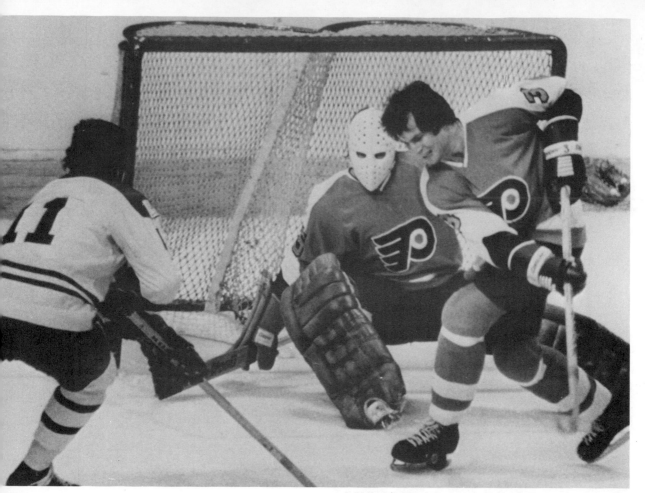

A Philadelphia defenseman scoops the puck as the Flyers and the Canadiens battle it out for the Stanley Cup.

HOCKEY

In sports, so-called dynasties—teams that keep winning for many years—do not occur often. In hockey it is no different. In 1974 and 1975, the Philadelphia Flyers had won the Stanley Cup, the championship trophy of the National Hockey League (NHL). It seemed certain that the exuberant young Flyers would continue to keep a tight hold on the cup in the immediate future.

But skaters in old, familiar uniforms—those of the Montreal Canadiens—came roaring down the ice in 1976 to frustrate the Flyers' bid for a third straight crown. And the Canadiens did it in the shortest possible time, with a four-game sweep in the best-of-seven series for the trophy.

For the Canadiens, it was their 18th Stanley Cup triumph since the National Hockey League was organized. And rarely had their superiority been so unchallenged. During the regular season, the Canadiens compiled the best record in the league, 58 victories, 11 defeats, and 11 ties, for a total of 127 points, an all-time high. Then they swept through the post-season competition with twelve triumphs in thirteen engagements—winning four straight from the Chicago Black Hawks, losing only one of five to the New York Islanders, and conquering the Philadelphia Flyers in four straight.

The Canadiens achieved their spectacular success with a combination of offense and defense. Guy Lafleur captured the Ross Trophy as the league's individual high scorer. And Montreal goalie Ken Dryden was awarded the

Vezina Trophy as the best at that defensive position. Lafleur scored 56 goals and, with assists, finished with 125 points. Dryden had the lowest average yield of goals per game, 2.03.

Philadelphia's only consolation was Reggie Leach's winning the award for the most valuable player in the Stanley Cup competition. His 19 goals during the playoffs gave him a total of 80 for the season, erasing Phil Esposito's former record of 79.

▶ WHA PLAY

In the World Hockey Association (WHA), the championship series also resulted in a swift triumph, and also ended a two-year reign. Playing for the Avco Cup, the Winnipeg Jets defeated the Houston Aeros in four straight games. The finale was a crushing 9–1 defeat for the Aeros, who had won the title in 1974 and 1975.

Winnipeg became the first Canadian winner of the Avco trophy. New England had captured it in the WHA's first season, 1973. For 36-year-old veteran Bobby Hull of the Jets, it was a particularly satisfying success. The year before, Hull had scored 77 goals and been the WHA's most valuable player, but Winnipeg had failed to reach the playoffs. In 1976, Marc Tardif of the Quebec Nordiques was the scoring leader, with 71 goals, and also earned the MVP prize. Hull didn't take an individual honor in 1976, but he was happy sipping the winning team's champagne. He hadn't been part of a victory party since 1961, when he had participated in the Chicago Black Hawks' Stanley Cup triumph.

▶ THE CANADA CUP

The Canada Cup competition was founded in the hope of establishing world supremacy in hockey. In 1976 the round robin tournament attracted six countries—Canada, Czechoslovakia, Sweden, Finland, the Soviet Union, and the United States. Team Canada won the Cup with a two-game sweep over the Czechoslovakian National Team in the best-of-three final series. But it definitely wasn't as easy as it sounds.

The Czechs reached the finals with victories over the Soviets, Finland, and Canada; a 4–4 tie with the United States; and a 2–1 defeat

In the WHA championship final, Ulf Nilsson of the Jets is about to take a slap shot as Gordie Howe of the Aeros tries to check him.

A Czech defenseman and a Canadian center fight for the puck in Canada Cup play.

321

by Sweden. The Canadians, in the round robin contests, defeated Finland, the United States, Sweden, and Russia, and lost in their early skirmish with the Czechs.

Then came the final series of play. After a 6–0 triumph in the opening game at Toronto, the Canadians finished the Czechs at Montreal with a 5–4 victory in overtime. Darryl Sittler of the Toronto Maple Leafs scored the decisive goal after 11 minutes 33 seconds of the "sudden death" overtime period.

Bobby Orr, now a member of the Chicago Black Hawks, was chosen the most valuable player in the tournament. In the final series, he scored two goals in the first game and had a total of six assists in the two engagements.

FINAL NHL STANDINGS

CAMPBELL CONFERENCE

Patrick Division

	W	L	T	Pts.
Philadelphia	51	13	16	118
N.Y. Islanders	42	21	17	101
Atlanta	35	33	12	82
N.Y. Rangers	29	42	9	67

Smythe Division

	W	L	T	Pts.
Chicago	32	30	18	82
Vancouver	33	32	15	81
St. Louis	29	37	14	72
Minnesota	20	53	7	47
Kansas City	12	56	12	36

WALES CONFERENCE

Norris Division

	W	L	T	Pts.
Montreal	58	11	11	127
Los Angeles	38	33	9	85
Pittsburgh	35	33	12	82
Detroit	26	44	10	62
Washington	11	59	10	32

Adams Division

	W	L	T	Pts.
Boston	48	15	17	113
Buffalo	46	21	13	105
Toronto	34	31	15	83
California	27	42	11	65

Stanley Cup: Montreal Canadiens

FINAL WHA STANDINGS

East Division

	W	L	T	Pts.
Indianapolis	35	39	6	76
Cleveland	35	40	5	75
New England	33	40	7	73
Cincinnati	35	44	1	71

West Division

	W	L	T	Pts.
Houston	53	27	0	106
Phoenix	39	35	6	84
San Diego	36	38	6	78

Canadian Division

	W	L	T	Pts.
Winnipeg	52	27	2	106
Quebec	50	27	4	104
Calgary	41	35	4	86
Edmonton	27	49	5	59
Toronto	24	52	5	53

Avco Cup: Winnipeg Jets

OUTSTANDING PLAYERS

Scorer	Marc Tardif, Quebec
Rookie	Mark Napier, Toronto
Goalie	Michael Tion, Indianapolis
Most Valuable Player	Marc Tardif, Quebec
Sportsmanship	Vaclav Nedomansky, Toronto
Defenseman	Paul Shmyr, Cleveland
Avco Cup play	Ulf Nilsson, Winnipeg

OUTSTANDING PLAYERS

Ross Trophy (scorer)	Guy Lafleur, Montreal
Calder Trophy (rookie)	Bryan Trottier, N.Y. Islanders
Vezina Trophy (goalie)	Ken Dryden, Montreal
Hart Trophy (most valuable player)	Bobby Clarke, Philadelphia
Lady Byng Trophy (sportsmanship)	Jean Ratelle, Boston
Norris Trophy (defenseman)	Denis Potvin, N.Y. Islanders
Conn Smythe Trophy (Stanley Cup play)	Reggie Leach, Philadelphia

Outstanding NHL players: Conn Smythe Trophy winner Reggie
Leach (*above*) and Norris Trophy winner Denis Potvin (*below*).

ICE SKATING

FIGURE SKATING

World Championships

Men	John Curry, Britain
Women	Dorothy Hamill, U.S.
Pairs	Irina Rodnina/
	Alexander Zaitsev, U.S.S.R.
Dance	Ludmila Pakhomova/
	Alexander Gorshkov, U.S.S.R.

United States Championships

Men	Terry Kubicka
Women	Dorothy Hamill
Pairs	Tai Babilonia/Randy Gardner
Dance	Colleen O'Connor/Jim Millns

SPEED SKATING

World Championships

Men	Piet Kleine, Netherlands
Women	Sylvia Burka, Canada

Randy Gardner and Tai Babilonia, dazzling skaters who won the U.S. Pairs Championship.

World Cup ski champ Ingemar Stenmark.

SKIING

WORLD CUP CHAMPIONSHIPS

Men	Ingemar Stenmark, Sweden
Women	Rosi Mittermaier, West Germany

CANADIAN-AMERICAN TROPHY SERIES

Men

Downhill	Eric Wilson, U.S.
Slalom	John Teague, U.S.
Giant Slalom	Ron Fuller, U.S.
Overall	Eric Wilson, U.S.

Women

Downhill	Jeanette Zanier, Canada
Slalom	Christin Cooper, U.S.
Giant Slalom	Viki Fleckenstein, U.S.
Overall	Viki Fleckenstein, U.S.

U.S. ALPINE CHAMPIONSHIPS

	Men	Women
Downhill	Greg Jones	Susie Patterson
Slalom	Cary Adgate	Cindy Nelson
Giant Slalom	Geoff Bruce	Lindy Cochran
Combined	Cary Adgate	Viki Fleckenstein

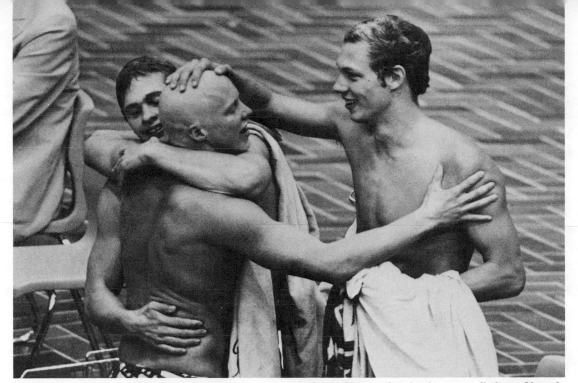

Billy Forrester, Mike Bruner, and Steve Gregg, after having won all three Olympic medals in the 200-meter butterfly. Bruner set a world record in the process.

SWIMMING

WORLD SWIMMING RECORDS SET IN 1976

EVENT	HOLDER	TIME
Men		
100-meter freestyle	Jonty Skinner, South Africa	0:49.44
200-meter freestyle	Bruce Furniss, U.S.	1:50.29
400-meter freestyle	Brian Goodell, U.S.	3:51.93
1,500-meter freestyle	Brian Goodell, U.S.	15:02.40
100-meter backstroke	John Naber, U.S.	0:55.49
200-meter backstroke	John Naber, U.S.	1:59.19
100-meter breaststroke	John Hencken, U.S.	1:03.11
200-meter breaststroke	David Wilkie, Britain	2:15.11
200-meter butterfly	Mike Bruner, U.S.	1:59.23
400-meter individual medley	Rod Strachan, U.S.	4:23.68
Women		
100-meter freestyle	Kornelia Ender, E. Germany	0:55.65
200-meter freestyle	Kornelia Ender, E. Germany	1:59.26
400-meter freestyle	Petra Thumer, E. Germany	4:09.89
800-meter freestyle	Petra Thumer, E. Germany	8:37.14
100-meter backstroke	Ulrike Richter, E. Germany	1:01.51
200-meter backstroke	Brigit Treiber, E. Germany	2:12.47
100-meter breaststroke	Hannelore Anke, E. Germany	1:10.86
200-meter breaststroke	Marina Koshevaya, U.S.S.R.	2:33.35
100-meter butterfly	Kornelia Ender, E. Germany	1:00.13
200-meter butterfly	Rosemarie Gabriel, E. Germany	2:11.22
200-meter individual medley	Kornelia Ender, E. Germany	2:17.14
400-meter individual medley	Ulrike Tauber, E. Germany	4:42.77

One of Björn Borg's most popular triumphs was over Ilie Nastase, in the U.S. Open semifinals.

TENNIS

Tennis continued to be one of the most popular sports throughout the world in 1976. Jimmy Connors of the United States and Björn Borg of Sweden shared honors among the men competitors, and Chris Evert of the United States was the undisputed queen—worldwide.

Connors captured the U.S. Open at Forest Hills in September after Borg had become the Wimbledon champion in July. It was fitting that the top-seeded performers, Connors and Borg, met in the final at Forest Hills. Connors emerged with the trophy and the $30,000 first prize after a blistering match that lasted more than three hours. The scores were 6–4, 3–6, 7–6, 6–4. Borg had come into the final the winner of 19 consecutive matches. His wins had included a very popular semifinal triumph over the Rumanian player Ilie Nastase, who had angered the huge Forest Hills crowd by his behavior in an earlier contest.

For Connors it was the first major success since his sweep of the top tournaments in 1974. Otherwise, it was Borg's year. At Wimbledon, the 20-year-old Borg became the youngest winner in 45 years as he swept through the final against Nastase, 6–4, 6–2, 9–7. This 90th Wimbledon tournament was marked by a spectacular series of upsets. Among those eliminated in early rounds were Connors; Arthur Ashe, the 1975 winner; and Adriano Panatta, who had won the Italian and French championships earlier in the year. Borg's other triumphs included the World Championship Tennis competition at Dallas, Texas, with a first prize of $50,000. In Hawaii, Nastase took home the Avis Challenge Cup and $100,000, the largest single prize in tennis history.

The 21-year-old Chris Evert was the victor in both the Wimbledon and U.S. Open tournaments. She regained the Wimbledon crown after having lost it for one year, and won her second straight U.S. Open title. The victim in the final in both tournaments was Evonne Goolagong Cawley of Australia. The scores at Wimbledon were 6–3, 4–6, 8–6, and at Forest Hills 6–3, 6–0. This last triumph was Evert's 101st consecutive success on the clay courts.

TOURNAMENT TENNIS

	Australian Open	French Open	Wimbledon	U.S. Open
Men's Singles	Mark Edmondson, Australia	Adriano Panatta, Italy	Björn Borg, Sweden	Jimmy Connors, U.S.
Women's Singles	Evonne Goolagong Cawley, Australia	Sue Barker, Britain	Chris Evert, U.S.	Chris Evert, U.S.
Men's Doubles	John Newcombe/Tony Roche, Australia	Fred McNair/Sherwood Stewart, U.S.	Brian Gottfried, U.S./ Raul Ramirez, Mexico	Marty Riessen, U.S./ Tom Okker, Netherlands
Women's Doubles	Evonne Goolagong Cawley/Helen Gourlay, Australia	Fiorella Bonicelli, Uruguay/Gail Lovera, France	Chris Evert, U.S./ Martina Navratilova, Czechoslovakia	Linky Boshoff/ Ilana Kloss, South Africa

Davis Cup Winner: Italy

Miklos Nemeth hurls the javelin to a world record 310' 4½", winning the gold medal at the 1976 Olympics.

TRACK AND FIELD

WORLD TRACK AND FIELD RECORDS SET IN 1976

EVENT	HOLDER	TIME, DISTANCE, OR POINTS
	Men	
800-meter run	Alberto Juantorena, Cuba	1:43.5
2,000-meter run	John Walker, New Zealand	4:51.4
20,000-meter run	Jos Hermens, Netherlands	57:24.2
3,000-meter steeplechase	Anders Gaerderud, Sweden	8:08.0
50,000-meter walk	Berndt Kannenberg, W. Germany	3:56.52
400-meter hurdles	Edwin Moses, U.S.	0:47.64
High Jump	Dwight Stones, U.S.	7' 7¼"
Pole Vault	Dave Roberts, U.S.	18' 8¼"
Shot Put	Alexander Baryshnikov, U.S.S.R.	72' 2¼"
Discus	Mac Wilkins, U.S.	232' 6"
Javelin	Miklos Nemeth, Hungary	310' 4½"
Decathlon	Bruce Jenner, U.S.	8,618 points
	Women	
100-meter run	Annegret Richter, W. Germany	0:11.01
400-meter run	Irena Szewinska, Poland	0:49.29
800-meter run	Tatyana Kazankina, U.S.S.R.	1:54.94
1,000-meter run	Nikolina Shtereva, U.S.S.R.	2:33.8
1,500-meter run	Tatyana Kazankina, U.S.S.R.	3:56.0
3,000-meter run	Ludmila Bragina, U.S.S.R.	8:27.1
High Jump	Rosemarie Ackermann, E. Germany	6' 5¼"
Long Jump	Siegrun Siegl, E. Germany	22' 11¼"
Discus	Faina Melnik, U.S.S.R.	231' 3"
Javelin	Ruth Fuchs, E. Germany	226' 9¼"
Shot Put	Helena Fibingerova, Czechoslovakia	72' 1¾"

THE CREATIVE WORLD

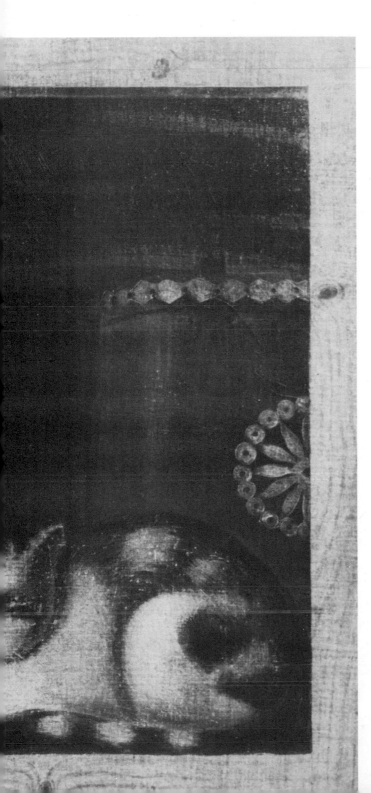

Haven't you walked along a street and felt that someone was watching you? And when you looked up at the nearest house you saw a cat, settled comfortably on a windowsill, watching you and the rest of the world go by. This painting, called *Cat in Window*, was done by an unknown artist in the 19th century. It was exhibited as part of one of the most charming art shows of 1976—The Cat in American Folk Art.

GREAT MUSIC FOR YOU

In order to appreciate great literature, you have to be able to read. If a book you are interested in is written in a language you don't understand, you have to find a good translation of it—or give up the idea of reading it. But anyone can listen to music and hear exactly what the composer has to say. You don't need special education to appreciate good music. You just need an open mind and open ears. Music really is a universal language, understandable to anyone who wants to listen.

Composers have always written music for young people to listen to and perform. Some composers have written for young people just because they like them—as people and as an audience. Other composers have written pieces for their young music students. These pieces are intended to teach techniques of playing a specific instrument. They are also intended to teach basic lessons about musical structure and theory. And some composers have written for young audiences because they will become older audiences when they grow up. A composer who is writing music that is considered unusual or experimental may feel that he has to "educate" his audience. He may

feel he has a better chance if he begins with young people. Artists of all kinds believe that young people are open-minded and that they are a good audience for new ideas.

There has been so much important music written for young people that it is impossible to discuss it all. Here are some favorite works you may have been listening to for years, without knowing they were written just for you.

▶ **OLD MASTERS**

The German composer Johann Sebastian Bach (1685–1750) knew a lot about young people. At various times in his long career he was a music teacher and choir master and worked with young singers and instrumentalists. And he had 20 children of his own. Some of his children became musicians, too.

Since Bach wrote a great deal of choral music for use in churches, some of his work naturally included childrens' voices. Many churches had childrens' choirs, especially boys' choirs. However, some of Bach's best-known work specifically intended for young people was keyboard music. In many cases it was music written for his own children to per-

Two members of the Vienna Boys' Choir, in costume as the hero and heroine of Mozart's *Bastien et Bastienne*, outside Vienna's beautiful Hofburg palace.

form. There was rarely a time in the Bach household when someone was not taking music lessons. If you take piano lessons, it's possible that you have played some of the study pieces the Bach children played while their father looked on. In the period of his career lasting from 1717 to 1723, Bach wrote a number of keyboard pieces for his two eldest children. They included the first volume of his famous keyboard studies called *The Well-Tempered Clavier* and the collection called *Little Preludes, Inventions and Symphonies*.

Bach's study pieces are never boring. Since he had worked so much with young musicians, he had great respect for their skill and intelligence. Bach's music for young keyboard performers was meant to exercise the mind as well as the fingers. These pieces are unique, in that they teach you how to "think" music as well as play it.

If you know anything about his life, it won't surprise you to learn that Wolfgang Amadeus Mozart (1756–1791) wrote music for young people. He began his own career as a performer and composer when he was still a small child. And like many great artists, Mozart never lost his child's vision of the world. His famous fairy-tale opera *The Magic Flute* can be enjoyed equally by young people and adults. It has even been performed as a puppet show, with puppet performers acting out the roles while live or recorded singers provide the voices. But Mozart also wrote music especially suited to young people.

In 1768, when he was 12 years old, Mozart wrote a delightful short opera about a pair of young lovers called *Bastien et Bastienne*. This little opera has been enormously popular with young people. It is still in the repertoire of the well-known choral group the Vienna Boys' Choir. These Austrian youngsters often perform *Bastien et Bastienne* on their world concert tours.

▶ THE 20TH CENTURY

Composers of the 20th century have been especially interested in writing music for young people. The modern French composers Camille Saint-Saëns (1835–1921), Claude Debussy (1862–1918), and Maurice Ravel (1875–1937) all wrote delightful music for children. Saint-Saëns' orchestral suite called *Carnival of the Animals* has been very popular with young people. The modern American poet Ogden Nash wrote a humorous narration in verse to accompany the piece. It is frequently performed in English-speaking countries, with an actor reading the Nash narration.

Benjamin Britten (1913–1976), the British composer who died in 1976, had a special gift for working with young performers and audiences. Britten grew up in the Anglican church tradition of childrens' choirs and congregational singing of hymns. He never lost his love of childrens' voices.

Many of Britten's works are actually designed to be performed in churches. But most of them do not fall into the traditional categories of music written to accompany religious services. Britten's church music is often music to delight, instruct, and even amuse a congregation—all the while giving a religious message. And Britten had another, very clever reason for wanting his works performed in churches. He could get true audience participation that way. Many of Britten's religious works include his own settings of the traditional hymns sung in many churches. By making these hymns part of a new composition, he could get the young people and adults in the congregation to participate in his creation. And if you have participated in singing a new musical work, you are more likely to understand and appreciate it.

In 1946, Britten wrote a piece based on a musical theme by the 17th-century British composer Henry Purcell. The piece was called *The Young Person's Guide to the Orchestra*. It is, in fact, the most delightful possible teaching guide to the instruments of a large symphony orchestra. A narrator describes each group of instruments as they begin playing. Later a ballet was created, using the Britten music and narration and adding dancers. The dancers provide a visual representation of the groups of instruments as the orchestra members play them.

In 1948, Britten wrote a cantata called *Saint Nicholas*. It is scored for soloists, childrens' choirs, an adult choir, percussion instruments, and congregational singing. The story of the cantata is the life and works of Saint Nicholas of Myra, a 4th-century bishop who was one of the most popular saints of the

The violins dance, in the New York City Ballet's production of *Fanfare*, the ballet based on Benjamin Britten's *The Young Person's Guide to the Orchestra*.

Middle Ages and famous as a patron of children. In fact, our modern idea of Santa Claus grew up around the old legends of Saint Nicholas of Myra. This cantata—to the delight of children and adults—is often performed on or near Saint Nicholas' Day (December 6).

Britten again turned to audience participation when he wrote *Let's Make an Opera*. It was first produced in 1949. It is a work in which young singers go through all the stages of producing their own opera. And as they put their opera together, they invite the audience to join them by singing the part of the opera chorus. The opera the young people perform—the opera within an opera—is called *The Little Sweep*. It is based on one of William Blake's *Songs of Innocence,* "The Chimney Sweeper."

One of Britten's most popular works for young people was first performed in 1958 and continues to be performed frequently. It is called *Noye's Fludde* ("Noah's Flood," in modern English) and is taken from a medie-val English mystery play based on the Biblical story of Noah, his ark, and the Great Flood. The work is full of parts for children of all ages—including a remarkable, funny chorus of singing animals. The squeaking of very small children singing the roles of mice usually "brings down the house." *Noye's Fludde* is a production young people have always loved to watch—and to be in.

▶ THE WINNERS

But for all the popularity of the music we have discussed previously, there are two 20th-century composers who have contributed the most popular music of all for young people. They are Sergei Prokofiev (1891–1953), a famous Russian composer, and Gian Carlo Menotti (1911–   ), an Italian-born American composer. Prokofiev's orchestral piece *Peter and the Wolf* and Menotti's Christmas opera *Amahl and the Night Visitors* have become true classics in the repertoire of music written especially for young people. A closer

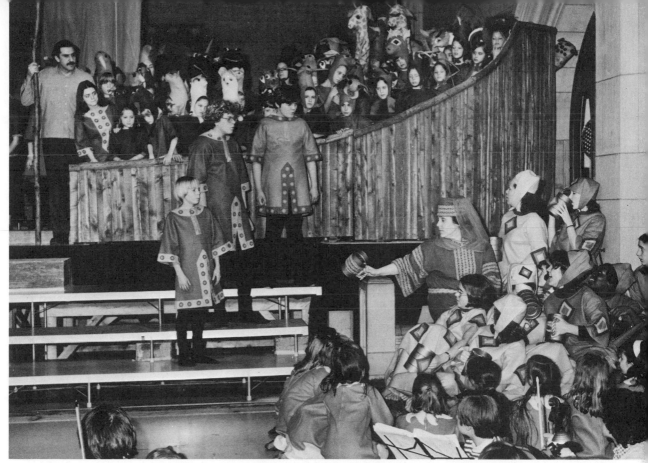

A rehearsal of a church production of Britten's opera *Noye's Fludde*. Noah *(upper left)* and a number of the animals are already aboard the ark. His sons *(center)* try to persuade their mother, Mrs. Noah *(lower right)*, to join them.

Mrs. Edward Kennedy, wife of the Massachusetts senator, is narrator in a Boston Pops performance of Prokofiev's *Peter and the Wolf*, conducted by Arthur Fiedler.

look at the Prokofiev and Menotti works may explain why they have been so popular.

Sergei Prokofiev wrote several pieces for children. But there is no doubt that his best-known work is the "symphonic fairy tale" that he called *Peter and the Wolf.* Prokofiev wrote both the music and the words in less than a week. He conducted the first performance of *Peter,* in Moscow, on May 2, 1936.

Peter and the Wolf was not just popular with audiences. Prokofiev himself had a special affection for the work. He conducted it for American children on a visit to Boston in 1937, during the last trip he made out of the Soviet Union. Since that time, it has become a favorite of millions of young people all over the world, through both recordings and live performances. *Peter and the Wolf* uses a narrator who tells the story of Peter. Many well-known people—actors, politicians, teachers, and others—have read the part of the narrator. One of the best-known actors to read the narrator's part was the master of the horror film, Boris Karloff!

The work is written for a full symphony orchestra and narrator. Like Britten's *Young Person's Guide to the Orchestra,* it provides a delightful way of learning to recognize the sounds of the various instruments.

In the story, each character is represented by a different instrument and is assigned a special, distinctive tune, or theme. Peter, the hero, is portrayed by a cheerful melody in the strings (violins, violas, cellos, and basses). The twittering of his friend the bird is heard in the chirping of the flute. The oboe represents the quacking duck. The staccato melody of the clarinet's low register portrays the stalking cat. And Peter's stern grandfather is depicted by the huffing and puffing bassoon. The brass instruments of the orchestra (trumpet, three French horns, and trombone) make the ferocious snarls of the hungry wolf. The guns of the hunters are represented by the noisy thunder of kettledrums.

"Petya," as Peter is called by Prokofiev in Russian (we would say "Pete" in English), is a brave Soviet boy who disregards his grandfather's warning that there is a wolf lurking in the nearby forest. No sooner does Peter's grandfather leave him, than a big gray wolf comes out of the forest. But Peter is unafraid.

While his friend the bird distracts the wolf by fluttering about—and the cat watches the bird and everything else from the safety of a tree-top—the resourceful Peter climbs a tree and lassoes the angry wolf by the tail. And just at that moment a band of hunters comes by and takes the wolf off to the zoo in a happy procession. But the ending is not altogether happy. The wolf did manage to swallow the slow-footed duck—whole and quacking. In fact, the mournful quacking of an oboe describes the duck's sad end in musical terms.

Not only is *Peter and the Wolf* delightful music, it makes the process of learning some useful information about music and the orchestra fun.

Gian Carlo Menotti, who wrote the other musical winner, was born in Cadegliano, Italy. He composed his very first opera when he was ten. He came to the United States when he was sixteen to study music at Curtis Institute, in Philadelphia, Pennsylvania, one of America's leading conservatories of music. He has made America his home since then. Although he has written many instrumental works, including a violin and a piano concerto, he is most famous for his operas. He frequently writes the words, or librettos, for his operas as well as the music. Many people consider Menotti the world's leading modern opera composer.

Menotti has a special love for children. He also has a special ability to speak to them in a verbal and musical language that is both simple and direct.

Menotti's famous opera for young people, *Amahl and the Night Visitors,* was the first opera written especially for television. It was first seen on NBC-TV on Christmas Eve, 1951. Since then it has become a regular Christmas feature in many parts of the world. It is still done on television, but it is also done in live stage productions.

All of the action of *Amahl and the Night Visitors,* even the characterization of the adults in the story, is presented from the point of view of Amahl, the hero. Amahl is a crippled beggar. He is twelve, and he supports both himself and his mother by begging. They live in a crude shepherd's hut, and sometimes they both go to bed hungry at night. One evening, three kings knock at the door of their

Amahl is center stage in a production of Menotti's *Amahl and the Night Visitors*.

hut, seeking shelter for the night. They are following a brilliant star that has appeared in the eastern sky. They tell Amahl and his mother that the star has a flaming tail that floods the heavens with its glowing radiance. In the richness of their robes and jewels, the kings are like a child's dream come true. Stately King Melchior carries a coffer of gold. King Balthazar, who is black, bears an urn filled with incense. And King Kaspar, who is slightly deaf, has brought a golden cup, or chalice, filled with myrrh, a precious spice. They are accompanied by their page, an Oriental slave.

After Amahl's strange visitors fall asleep, Amahl's mother decides that she must steal some of King Melchior's gold. "All that gold for a child they do not even know!" she sings, remembering that the kings had told her they were seeking a mysterious child who had been born. When the page awakens and catches Amahl's mother in the act of stealing gold,

Amahl defends her. The kings explain that they are bringing their gifts to the long-awaited Christ Child. This so impresses Amahl that he offers his own crutch as a gift. "He may need it," Amahl sings, "and this one I made myself." At that very moment a miracle occurs. Amahl can walk perfectly well without his crutch. After a happy, tender farewell to his mother, he dances off with the kings to greet the newborn Prince of Peace. The first miracle of Christmas has taken place.

Reading the story is not the best way of learning about *Amahl*. The music that goes with the story is filled with pure joy and wonder. Not only is *Amahl and the Night Visitors* the most popular opera ever written for young people, it is one of the best of all short modern operas written for people of any age. Young people can be proud it was dedicated to them.

JOEL HONIG
Contributor to *Opera News*

A beautifully dressed Cuna woman sews a mola.

MAGIC IN MOLAS

Throughout the centuries, people all over the world have created folk art. From the earliest times, men and women have looked around them and found materials of all kinds to use in making useful and often beautiful objects. Traditional folk arts and crafts are not learned in an art school. They are passed down from parent to child. You have probably seen many examples of folk art without realizing that it was called that. You may well have seen African wood carvings, American Indian pottery and beadwork, or colorful hand-woven fabrics from many parts of the world.

One of the most exciting and distinctive examples of a true folk art being produced today is made of brightly colored cloth. It is the mola. Molas are unusual pieces of cut-

work embroidery made by the Cuna Indian women.

The Cuna live in the San Blas, or Mulatas, Islands, an archipelago off the Caribbean coast of the Republic of Panama. It would take only a few minutes to fly from Panama City to the islands. But the trip would take you back centuries. People there live much as they did before the Europeans came to Latin America in the 15th and 16th centuries. Although they are Panamanian citizens, the Cuna live by their own traditional laws and speak their own language. They live in small village communities headed by chiefs. They raise most of their own food—and hunt, fish, and trap for what they don't raise.

The molas created by the Cuna are different from every other type of handwork. The designs are cut down through many layers of cloth, each one of a different color. A little bit of each layer and of each color shows when the design is finished. The technique the Cuna women use is almost like sculpture in cloth.

Molas are usually made in rectangular panels. Frequently, colorful blouses are made using molas—a panel on the front and a panel on the back of a blouse. But molas are also used as wall hangings or are framed and displayed like pictures. They are true works of art.

The design of each mola reflects the tastes and interests of the artist who makes it. The Cuna are an ancient people, and they have many traditional designs that have been passed down for centuries. They often use these designs in molas. Many of the traditional designs are of fantastic sea creatures and jungle beasts. But the Cuna use modern designs as well. A mola might represent a baseball game or an event in the news or a magazine illustration. And a new mola design may become so popular that it is passed down over a period of years, just like the ancient designs. The Cuna now find man's first landing on the moon a topic of great interest. They do not quite understand what the event means—they're not even sure they believe it ever happened—but they love to include moon landings in mola designs.

The Cuna women are famous for their clothes. Many people consider their outfits among the most beautiful of Latin-American Indian costumes. A typical outfit includes a

A mola decorated with simple leaf and plant designs and geometric figures.

blouse decorated with molas, a sarong-style skirt, a gold nose ring, ear disks, and strings of beads worn around the neck, wrists, and ankles.

The Cuna people have been making molas as we know them for about a hundred years. No one is sure how the tradition began. One story says that Christian missionaries were responsible for them, in an odd way. The Cuna women originally wore little clothing, but painted their bodies with traditional designs. When the missionaries suggested that they wear more clothing, so the story goes, the Cuna women began creating garments that had the same designs as the ones they had originally painted on their bodies. However, there is no proof that the story is true. It is more likely that the Cuna invented molas when European traders began bringing scissors, needles, thread, and cotton cloth to the islands.

SYLVIA ROSENTHAL
Editor, *Disney's It's a Small World* encyclopedia

An imaginary whiskered sea creature stares straight out at you from this mola.

THE MUSIC SCENE

Paul Simon. Still crazy after all these years.

"Pop music is in a terrible state right now," said singer-composer Paul Simon, who was sporting a brand-new, bushy black moustache. "Only a handful of people are doing something good." And that just about summed up 1976 as far as popular music was concerned.

Simon won two Grammy Awards—for Album of the Year and Best Male Pop Vocal Performance—with *Still Crazy After All These Years*. The album contained "My Little Town," for which he was briefly reunited with his former partner, Art Garfunkel. Simon's real number-one single, however, was "Fifty Ways to Leave Your Lover," a delightful bit of romantic nonsense. But it was hardly a song that fitted into Simon's own category of "something good."

That's the kind of year it was. That was what record buyers wanted. And that's what ex-Beatle Paul McCartney gave them in his smash, overly sweet serenade, "Silly Love Songs." Grace Slick and her Jefferson Air-

Bob Dylan in concert.

plane, now known as The Jefferson Starship, followed in the same pattern. As their album *Red Octopus* was being applauded by rock critics, and selling over 2,000,000 copies, Slick said "Now we're back on top because we're doing love songs instead of political harangues."

Curtis Mayfield, who was once known for his "meaningful" songs that brought an "awareness" to his listeners, agreed with Slick. "People are not buying social commentary," he said. "People want to hear about romance," which just happened to be the subject of his *Give, Get, Take, Have* album. "And," Mayfield added, "they are dancing more."

▶ THE DISCO BEAT

And indeed they were dancing more. The popularity of "Disco Duck," "Shake Your Booty," and "Disco Lady," among other singles, proved that the disco craze was continuing to grow in 1976. Even "The Hustle" remained at the top of the list. Emphasizing the happy sound of an overpowering dance beat, disco songs relied on a few words relentlessly repeated over and over again. "More, More, More" by the Andrea True Connection, "That's the Way I Like It" by K. C. and the Sunshine Band, "Fly, Robin, Fly" and "Get Up and Boogie" by the Silver Convention were just a few records with the happy disco beat.

▶ TV'S GIFTS TO THE MUSIC SCENE

Television's contribution to the crop of "escapist" hit records was important. TV themes were very popular with the record-buying public. The themes from *S.W.A.T., Baretta, Happy Days,* and *Laverne and Shirley* shot to the top of the charts. The most excitement, however, was caused by the theme from *Welcome Back, Kotter,* written by John Sebastian. "Welcome Back" made a singing idol of John Travolta, who plays Vinnie Barbarino in the popular TV series.

▶ AND THE BEAT GOES ON

Some of the giants of rock continued to make music, but several of them began to fall into disfavor with the critics, and perhaps the record buyers too. The Rolling Stones' *Black and Blue* and the Led Zeppelin's *Presence* left

John Travolta tapes "Welcome Back, Kotter."

some reviewers far from satisfied. One critic wrote: "Instead of creating new sounds, they have merely recycled old ones." Popular Elton John also came in for some criticism and bad reviews. Despite them, Elton went to the top of the album charts with *Rock of the Westies*. He also had a hit single, "Don't Go Breaking My Heart," sung with Kiki Dee.

Neil Diamond continued to receive praise. At the peak of his performing career, he had sellout performances in Las Vegas at the new Aladdin Theatre of the Performing Arts. He also appeared for a week at the Greek Theatre in Hollywood, California. Diamond described his latest best-selling album, *Beautiful Noise,* as "remembrances of a time in the early 60's when a young songwriter set out to make his way in the beautiful but noisy streets of New York's Tin Pan Alley." In his new album, Diamond not only used song forms of the pre-rock era, but gave his work a glitter and theatricality that suggested a Broadway musical.

Bob Dylan continued his spectacular career. His *Basement Tapes,* made with The Band at Big Pink several years ago, was formally released by Columbia Records. Another new album release of his, *Desire,* climbed to the top

Willie Nelson—a "country outlaw" who hit the top.

of the charts. The biggest news of 1976, however, was Dylan's Rolling Thunder Revue, a series of concerts that brought him together again with Joan Baez and several other recording stars. The Revue traveled through 50 states, playing small halls as well as large ball parks. There were crowds wherever they played. At the end of his tour, Dylan appeared in his first TV special, *Hard Rain*.

Paul McCartney celebrated the American Bicentennial year with a grand tour of his own. While he and his group, Wings, were on the road, their album *Wings at the Speed of Sound* and the hit single "Silly Love Songs" traveled to the top on all the best seller lists. As if McCartney's popularity weren't enough to keep the memory of Beatlemania alive, England experienced a Beatles blitz in which 23 of their old records appeared at the same time in the Top 100.

The sound of the classics had an echo in pop music in two new recordings. One of the recordings let the public see another side of an established star. Barbra Streisand struck a new note in her career with *Classical Barbra,* an album of songs by Schumann, Handel, Debussy, and Carl Orff.

In the second recording, Ludwig van Beethoven made it to the top—in the form of Walter Murphy and the Big Apple, that is. Their rock version of the opening theme of Beethoven's Symphony No. 5, called "A Fifth of Beethoven," pleased young record buyers.

Another established star, Linda Ronstadt, continued to amaze her fans. She made her debut as a composer on her latest LP, *Hasten Down the Wind*. Her smash single of the year was a revival of "That'll Be the Day," the Buddy Holly hit of the 50's.

As the year ended, Stevie Wonder came out with *Songs in the Key of Life,* a brilliant two-record album. The title song was also released as a single. Displaying Wonder's amazing versatility as songwriter, singer, arranger, producer, and performer on numerous instruments, the album was hailed by the critics as "monumental." It combined beautiful music with a social message. Stevie gave rich expression to his feelings about many things and, most of all, about the troubled society in which we live.

NASHVILLE REVISITED

It was a good year for the so-called Outlaws of Country Music. Willie Nelson of Austin, Texas, found acceptance after 20-year struggle against the Nashville country sound. Nelson's battle with the typical country-music formula resulted in his winning a Grammy for the Best Male Country Vocal Performance of the year. His success was not a complete departure from the Nashville style, however. Nelson's award-winning song, "Blue Eyes Crying in the Rain," was a revival of a ballad by the late Fred Rose, one of Nashville's founders.

Jerry Jeff Walker, another "country outlaw," made some noise with his hit single, "It's a Good Night for Singing."

Nashville itself has also undergone a change. Many of the old-time performers are not happy with the new artists, styles, and sounds coming from the Tennessee city. They feel it has stopped being the capital of grassroots country music and has been transformed into a city of slick, commercial recording and a confusion of sounds.

NEWLY ARRIVED

ZZ Top, a Texas band that won't tell the source of its strange name, made a hit album without recording a hit single. Some reports say that the band was a bigger draw in Nashville than Elvis Presley, and that it broke Led Zeppelin attendance records in New Orleans. Playing a rocking brand of boogie blues, the three-man group produced a best-selling LP called *Fandango*.

Aerosmith, another unusual group, were dismissed as "primitives" by reviewers. But Aerosmith fans were not listening to the criticism. They were buying Aerosmith records by the millions, earning the group four platinum LP's. *Rocks,* their latest album, was one of those hitting the million mark. In the hard rock tradition of the Yardbirds, Led Zeppelin, and Kiss, Aerosmith played in a loud, ferocious style that was described as "bionic rock." With his bizarre clothes and strange mannerisms, lead singer Steve Tyler reminded many admirers of a young Mick Jagger.

A newcomer whose arrival met with a less than enthusiastic reception was Keith Carradine. Keith is the son of movie star John Carradine, and brother of TV and motion-picture actor David Carradine. Keith won fame for his performance in the film *Nashville,* and also won an Academy Award for his composition "I'm Easy." The hit record was dismissed by some country singers as uninspired, but that did not stop it from making the charts.

Frampton Comes Alive! was the perfect title of an album that became a number-one best seller and turned Peter Frampton, the former

Peter Frampton sang his way to a top prize in the Rock Music Awards.

Patti Smith—"rock's new poet laureate."

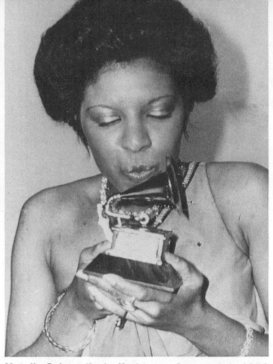

Natalie Cole walked off with two Grammys in 1976.

Humble Pie London guitarist, into a headliner. Frampton came out ahead of both Bob Dylan and Bruce Springsteen and won the Best Male Singer designation in the annual Rock Music Awards.

"I'm trying to put new thinking in people's minds," said newcomer Patti Smith, a 28-year-old performer from New Jersey. Her first album, *Horses,* was well received by young record buyers. Patti has been called "the biggest new media celebrity since Springsteen," and "rock's new poet laureate." She traces her roots to black music and claims that when she first heard Little Richard, she felt as if she'd "been shocked by lightning."

Two other female singers fired electrical charges into the rock atmosphere. Adopting a disco beat in "Young Hearts Run Free," soul singer Candi Staton produced a disc that went to number one on soul charts in the United States.

Nat "King" Cole's daughter, Natalie Cole, walked off with the Grammy Award for Best Female Vocal Rhythm and Blues Performer with "This Will Be." It was the first time since the Rhythm and Blues category was established in 1967 that gospel singer Aretha Franklin did not win.

▶ OUT OF THE PAST

Singers from the 1950's returned to the limelight in 1976. British rock 'n' roller Cliff Richard, remembered for "Living Doll" and "Moving On," came back with his recording of "Devil Woman." A hit record was not Richard's only claim to renewed fame. He completed a very successful tour of the Soviet Union, with sellout concerts in Moscow and Leningrad.

The Beach Boys, who were responsible for the surfing craze of an earlier decade, returned with *15 Big Ones,* an album whose title was inspired by the length of their career.

The earlier "comebacks" of Paul Anka, Frankie Valli, Bobby Vinton, and Neil Sedaka seemed to have an effect on Frankie Avalon. The star of all the "Beach Party" films of the '60's, Frankie came back with a revival of his 1959 hit, "Venus."

The many comebacks helped to fill the spot left by the breakup of several important groups. Despite the enthusiastic reception of their new album, *Native Sons,* folk-rockers Kenny Loggins and Jim Messina decided to separate. Equally disturbing to its large following was the breakup of the Allman Brothers Band.

▶ **THE SOUND OF JAZZ**

Jazz fans applauded the appearance of their favorite kind of music on the pop charts. Chick Corea's *The Leprechaun* and John McLaughlin & the Mahavishnu Orchestra's *Inner Worlds* were welcome additions to the popular music scene. The continued popularity of Latin salsa, a blend of Afro-Cuban rhythms and big band jazz, also gave jazz fans something to shout—and dance—about. When George Benson's album *Breezin'* hit the Top Pop 5, jazz lovers were convinced that their kind of music was moving toward a popular revival. "Ten years ago, rock was the creative force. Not anymore," said the manager of KBCA-FM, Los Angeles' only all-jazz station. "I'm convinced that now the most creative work being done in music is in jazz."

Pioneer bluesman Huddie Ledbetter was the subject of a controversial full-length film, *Leadbelly.* Some historians argued that the treatment of Leadbelly's life was not factual. They claimed that it failed to portray the violence and bitterness that made his music great. The film's director, Gordon Parks, answered his critics by suggesting that *"Leadbelly* speaks for every black who's catching hell."

▶ **STILLED MUSIC**

The most upsetting news to hit the folk and rock world was the death of Phil Ochs. Ochs was one of the most influential writer-performers of the protest rock movement of the 1960's. His hit single "I Ain't Marching Any More" became a theme song of that troubled decade. Ochs' death at the age of 35 marked the end of a superb talent.

ARNOLD SHAW
Author, *Honkers and Shouters:*
The Rhythm and Blues Years; The Rockin' 50's

1976 GRAMMY AWARDS

Record of the Year	*Love Will Keep Us Together*	The Captain and Tennille, artists
Album of the Year	*Still Crazy After All These Years*	Paul Simon, artist
Song of the Year	*Send In the Clowns*	Stephen Sondheim, songwriter
New Artist of the Year		Natalie Cole
Pop Vocal Performance—female	*At Seventeen*	Janis Ian, artist
Pop Vocal Performance—male	*Still Crazy After All These Years*	Paul Simon, artist
Rhythm and Blues Vocal Performance—female	*This Will Be*	Natalie Cole, artist
Rhythm and Blues Vocal Performance—male	*Living for the City*	Ray Charles, artist
Country Vocal Performance—female	*I Can't Help It*	Linda Ronstadt, artist
Country Vocal Performance—male	*Blue Eyes Crying in the Rain*	Willie Nelson, artist
Original Score for a Motion Picture	*Jaws*	John Williams, composer
Score from an Original Cast Show	*The Wiz*	Charlie Smalls, composer
Classical Album	*Beethoven: Symphonies*	Sir Georg Solti conducting the Chicago Symphony Orchestra
Recording for Children	*The Little Prince*	Richard Burton, Jonathan Winters, Billy Simpson, et al.

George Burns (best supporting actor) and Walter Matthau in *The Sunshine Boys*.

1976 ACADEMY AWARDS

CATEGORY	WINNER
Picture	*One Flew over the Cuckoo's Nest*
Actor	Jack Nicholson (*One Flew over the Cuckoo's Nest*)
Actress	Louise Fletcher (*One Flew over the Cuckoo's Nest*)
Supporting Actor	George Burns (*The Sunshine Boys*)
Supporting Actress	Lee Grant (*Shampoo*)
Director	Milos Forman (*One Flew over the Cuckoo's Nest*)
Foreign Language Film	*Dersu Uzala* (U.S.S.R.)
Song	"I'm Easy" (*Nashville*)
Documentary Feature	*The Man Who Skied down Everest*
Documentary Short	*The End of the Game*
Cinematography	John Alcott (*Barry Lyndon*)

Jack Nicholson (best actor) in *One Flew over the Cuckoo's Nest.*

Goldie Hawn and Lee Grant (best supporting actress) in *Shampoo.*

ANIMALS IN ART

Animals have always fascinated artists. Prehistoric painters made pictures of wild game on the walls of their caves. The monks of the Middle Ages used many animals in their illuminations of manuscripts. Traditional Japanese printmakers over the centuries have recorded the antics of rabbits, cats, mice, and other creatures. Human artists, it seems, never tire of drawing the animals with whom they share their world.

First, let's look at work by three famous artists—Albrecht Dürer, George Stubbs, and Thomas Eakins. Dürer helped bring the ideals of Italian Renaissance art to Germany in the 16th century. Stubbs painted the world of the English country gentry of the 18th century. Thomas Eakins was a pioneer in American realist painting and in photography in the late 19th and early 20th centuries. If you were to hang typical works by each of these men on the same wall of the same museum, you might find it hard to believe that they had anything at all in common—except great talent. But these men, each one quite different from the other, shared something else. The three of them loved animals. And they each had a special —and similar—regard for the animals who appeared in their work. For these artists, animals were not just attractive or decorative figures to add interest to their work. These men saw animals as important living beings with unique beauty and charm.

▶ YOUNG HARE

This watercolor of a young hare, painted in 1502, is probably the best-known representation of an animal in all of Western art. The hare—a close relative of the rabbit—gives no evidence of knowing how famous he is. For this is a real hare, sitting exactly as any alert animal would sit if he knew an artist was close by, painting him. The texture and pattern of his fur have been captured exactly. The set of his handsome ears (alert but not frightened) is perfect. His eyes are also alert and aware of everything that is going on. And you can see his powerful legs with their real and business-like nails (good for digging and for self-defense).

Dürer's animals were always real—hares, owls, squirrels alike. This is no pretty bunny with long eyelashes—the sort you see on boxes of Easter candy. This is a real animal who is truly beautiful because he is real.

Albrecht Dürer (1471–1528), who painted the *Young Hare,* was born in Nuremberg, Germany. His father was a skilled artisan, a master goldsmith. As a young man, Dürer went to Italy to study the techniques and ideas of the artists there who were caught up in the free and inquisitive spirit of the time. We now call that spirit, and that time, the Renaissance. Dürer learned many things in Italy and on the long journeys that took him there. One lesson seemed especially important to him. The lesson was that the people, creatures, and things of earth have a beauty and dignity that is always present to be captured by the skillful and truthful artist.

Albrecht Dürer was, in many ways, one of Europe's first "modern" painters. The artists

of the Renaissance, Dürer among them, had a strong interest in science and natural history. They wanted to know exactly how the human body was constructed so that they could draw it accurately as well as beautifully. They also wanted to know exactly how the birds and the animals looked so that they could represent them better, too. And they wanted to know about botany so that they could draw perfect trees, plants, and flowers. Dürer became a master at drawing the human body, at sketching animals, and at making scientifically accurate studies of flowers and grasses.

But the *Young Hare* shows more than scientific interest. This hare is a kind of pioneer animal in art—for he is fulfilling a new role. The hare is looking out at us from the page for his own sake. He is the one and only subject of a very exceptional and sensitive painting. Dürer was familiar with the illuminated manuscripts of the Middle Ages. These manuscripts were often richly decorated with paintings of animals and flowers that often represented or symbolized ideas and even human qualities. Although Dürer sometimes used animals to represent human qualities in his paintings—the owl might represent wisdom—he went beyond this. Animals, for Dürer, were too important to be used as decoration and symbol alone. They were important for their own sakes.

The *Young Hare* is a real animal, looking out at us from the past. And he is a link with the past. For this hare's many, many times great-grandchildren look much the same as he did, and are with us today. Many of the beautiful things of earth do endure. Dürer's *Young Hare* reminds us of this.

▶ CREAM PONIES

George Stubbs (1724–1806) was fascinated by animals, especially horses. He was largely self-taught as a painter. But early in his life he decided to become the best possible painter of horses. So he set out to learn not only good painting techniques from the work of English masters but the details of animal anatomy as well. Many people now feel that Stubbs did achieve his ideal, that he really did become the best horse painter of his day or any other day. And a great many people also feel he attained an even higher goal—that of being a great painter in every way.

The full name of *Cream Ponies* is thoroughly descriptive, to say the least. It is called *Park Phaeton with a Pair of Cream Ponies in Charge of a Stable-Lad with a Dog.* ("Phaeton" is the name of the type of carriage the ponies are hitched to.) It was painted between 1780 and 1785. *Cream Ponies* shows us Stubbs at work doing all of the things he knew and liked best.

There is never any doubt about what interests Stubbs in any one of his paintings. He is a direct painter. In any Stubbs painting that includes horses, you can always assume the painting is about horses. There is no doubt that *Cream Ponies* is about the perfectly matched pair hitched to the elegant phaeton. Cream-colored ponies were rare, and their owner was undoubtedly proud of them. And Stubbs found them beautiful. Like Dürer, Stubbs wished to paint animals with the greatest scientific accuracy and attention to detail. Unlike Dürer's wide-ranging interests, Stubbs's main interest in art was animals—specifically horses. Horses summed up his highest ideals of grace and beauty.

Even if we were not immediately drawn to the cream ponies themselves because they are so unusual, Stubbs has made sure our eyes will focus on them. They are at the center of the painting. The phaeton, to the left, and the boy and his dog, to the right, are interesting in themselves—but they are there, primarily, to draw our eyes to the ponies. The curves of the phaeton lead in to the ponies. The boy and his frisking dog also point in toward the ponies. And the dark trees of the background make the light color of the ponies leap forward. To make absolutely sure our eyes travel

from the boy and dog to the horses (for the stableboy and his dog really are lively), Stubbs has painted the browbands of the ponies the same color as that in the stripes of the stableboy's elegant jacket.

Elegance is probably the key word to use in describing *Cream Ponies*. Park phaetons were elegant vehicles a country squire would use to drive around the gravel drives of his estate. And if you owned two such fine ani-

mals as these, you would never hitch them to a common cart, anyway. The phaeton is a tribute to their beauty. And the stableboy is dressed up for the sake of the ponies, too. It is quite unlikely that he dressed like this while currying horses in the stable. In fact, the picture has a sense of waiting about it. The horses and the boy and the dog are waiting for the owner of the phaeton to come out of his house, all ready to go for a brisk drive.

Stubbs also had a sense of humor. And he is almost as good at painting dogs as he is at painting horses. The dog in *Cream Ponies* has seen the stableboy (who is probably his master) and the ponies in far less formal situations. He's not about to be impressed by their dressed-up finery. He's ready to play. It wouldn't be hard to imagine him, running alongside the phaeton as it goes through the park, dodging the ponies' prancing hoofs.

Thomas Eakins (1844–1916) was an American painter who was surrounded by animals for most of his life. There wasn't a time when he didn't have a collection of dogs, cats, horses, and even monkeys. The dogs and cats wandered around his house at will—the cats often outnumbering the other animals.

In addition to being a fine painter, Eakins was a pioneer in the use of photographs as the basis for paintings, in place of or in addition to the traditional pencil or charcoal sketches. It was only natural for Eakins to photograph animal models as well as human models. Animals were very much a part of his life. In fact, some specific animal models became especial favorites of his. He photographed a spaniel called Harry again and again.

But there was a unique quality to Eakins' photographs of animals, just as there was a unique quality to his photographs of people. Despite the fact that photography was by no means an advanced art when he took many of his photographs (in the 1880's and 1890's), a surprising number of them proved to be works of art in themselves.

We do not know this cat's name. In fact, the photograph is simply entitled *Cat*. We do not know exactly when it was taken. It is assumed that it was taken later in the artist's photographic experiments, perhaps in the 1890's, because it is very sophisticated and accomplished. We do not know if this cat was one of the family's battalion of cats. It may have belonged to a neighbor. It seems likely, because of the wall and vines in the background, that the cat was photographed in the garden of Eakins' house in Philadelphia, where many of the photographs were taken. But there is no doubt at all that the subject of *Cat* is a very special animal. For of all of Eakins' photographs of animals, this is one of the most charming and it is, without a doubt, an accomplished work of art.

The pattern of the vines against the wall forms a rich, dark background for the white cat. And this surely must be one of the best possible cat models. If you have a cat, you have probably seen it box with its forepaws at a passing insect or at an object—something tantalizing like a feather—that you pass in front of it, just out of reach. This cat is ready for anything. We will never know what Eakins did to capture the cat's attention. "Look at the birdie!" would have been enough to do it.

Eakins' attitude toward animals is different from that of Dürer or Stubbs. For Dürer, animals were a side or facet of nature, a part of the natural world he wanted to study and admire in careful, almost scientific detail, a part of the great web of creation. For Stubbs, animals, especially horses, were the focus of his whole attention as an artist. Horses were, to Stubbs, the most beautiful and fascinating of creatures and, therefore, his art was concentrated on depicting them. But for Eakins, animals were a part of the total world he experienced as a man and as an artist. They were as common in his world as sunshine or wind or air. He photographed, drew, and painted animals because they were part of his everyday life and he was an artist and painter of the real.

However, the unique qualities of this special white cat did not escape Eakins. Many of Eakins' most famous paintings show movement or activity—rowing, diving, sailing, for instance. He was, in fact, a master at capturing moving objects on canvas at just the right moment. Undoubtedly the cat in this photograph, caught in the midst of activity, provided a perfect subject for Eakins. The painter had always admired feline movements. *Cat* is not a study of a beautiful animal posed like an ancient Egyptian cat carved in stone. This is a portrait of a real cat on the verge of getting into a great deal of mischief. But this cat is also balanced delicately, its paws at rest and yet ready, its eyes focused with full attention on whatever object it is watching. The cat's concentration, in fact, is what Eakins has captured.

But *Cat* stands by itself as a work of art. It is as perfectly designed as a fine Japanese print. The texture of the vines is contrasted with the regularity of the fur and of the design in the rug on which the cat is sitting. And the cat's collar is made more interesting by the single bell, put there to warn unwary birds of a very clever animal's approach. If we had never seen a cat before, this photograph would go a long way in explaining what a cat is really like.

This humorous cat is a modern creation in iron and was meant to be used as a doorstop. To judge by its expression, it's trying to see who's coming and who's going—at the same time.

HUNDREDS OF CATS

Everywhere you looked, there were cats. There were dignified family portraits of cats; there were pictures of people with their cats (or cats with their people, however you want to look at it); there were toys shaped like cats, a cat-head nutcracker, cat weathervanes —there were a lot of cats!

And they were all at the Museum of American Folk Art in New York City. In 1976 a remarkable exhibition called The Cat in American Folk Art was held at the museum. There were representations of cats from colonial times to the 20th century. It was a great success. Oh, a few mice, birds, and dogs may have objected, but people of all ages loved it.

Everyone who saw the show was impressed by what good artist's models cats have always been. It's probably because cats have always been confident about how beautiful they are.

Tom Cat, portrait of cat drawn in 1850. Tom must have ended up as president of a bank!

The lively cat on this weathervane is running straight into the wind.

Kittens liked to help, even in 1845. This painting is called *Picking Flowers.*

A charioteer drives his prancing horses in this bronze relief from ancient Greece.

HORSES IN ART

Horses have been important to people for a very long time. Fossils of ancient horses have been found on all the earth's continents except Australia. As people used horses more and more, they also recorded this use in drawing and painting and sculpture. Actually, the artists of the world have made a contribution to modern science. Scientists can estimate the age of horse fossils, but they cannot tell us much about the animal's beauty and grace. However, loving and accurate drawings, paintings, and carvings can give us a very clear idea of what a breed of horses might have looked like at a given time in history.

▶ THE ANCIENT WORLD

The earliest known pictures of horses were drawn by prehistoric people on the walls of caves. Famous examples of these drawings are found in the caves of Lascaux, in France, and Altamira, in Spain. We know that the cave dwellers hunted horses for meat. Piles of horse bones have been found in prehistoric caves.

No one knows who first tamed or rode a horse. Early Babylonian writings on clay tablets (made between 3000 and 2000 B.C.) mention horses living in the mountains bordering the Black and Caspian seas. And early Assyrian relief carvings show riders on horse-back and two-wheeled chariots drawn by pairs of horses.

Many historians believe that the custom of using horses to draw chariots spread from Assyria to Egypt and Greece. They base this belief, at least in part, on evidence from art. There are horses drawing two-wheeled chariots in a number of early Egyptian wall paintings. A fresco painted on the wall of a palace at Tiryns, Greece, about 1300 B.C., shows a whole procession of horse-drawn chariots.

In the early period of ancient Greek art, stylized horse figures were used as a decoration on pottery; stylized bronze statuettes of horses were also made. By the 5th century B.C., the Greeks were drawing and sculpting more realistic horses. Beautiful horses and horses' heads were made: some were life-size and larger than life-size, and carved from stone; others were miniatures, cut into precious or semiprecious stones to make seals or jewelry.

Art has even taught us something about the history of the saddle. Many of the ancient Greek statues of men on horseback indicate that they rode bareback. The first saddles were probably blankets wrapped around the horse's middle for the greater comfort of horse and rider. In Assyrian carvings, horses are shown with saddles. These saddles were elaborate and had fringes of tassels. Eventually saddles became works of art in themselves.

There is no doubt that the peoples of the Italian peninsula had horses. There are many horses shown in the art of the Etruscans and, later, of the Romans.

We know that the Romans liked chariot racing, because Roman writers have left accounts of the sport. Since many Roman wall paintings have been destroyed, our knowledge of Roman horses comes mostly from sculpture, mosaic floors, and coins. We also know that the famous gladiators of ancient Rome sometimes rode into the arena on horseback.

▶ THE EAST

The rulers and nobles of ancient China had their household animals—including their horses—killed and buried with them when they died. However, by the time of the Han dynasty (202 B.C.–A.D. 220) that wasteful practice had gone out of fashion. Instead, important people were buried with figures of their animals made of bronze, jade, or pottery. These little tomb figures became real works of art in the hands of skilled craftsmen. The representations of horses were especially beautiful.

The T'ang dynasty of old China (618–906) was famous for its pottery. The pottery figures of horses from this period were exceptional. They were often glazed and colored. And these pottery horses are detailed. We can even learn from T'ang horse figures that Chinese women enjoyed playing polo. There is

A pottery horse from China's T'ang dynasty.

actually a figure of a woman polo player on horseback!

Another form of Chinese art in which horses were a favorite theme was painting on silk. Silk paintings of horses were made under many dynasties, but those made in the Sung dynasty (960–1279) are especially fine.

In Japan, horses have been a favorite theme in art since the earliest times. Horses appear

Detail from a 16th-century Persian miniature painting of horses in battle.

in Japanese scroll paintings, on Japan's famous decorative screens, and later in prints by the country's 18th- and 19th-century printmakers.

The people of the Indian subcontinent were always great horse lovers. The beautiful miniatures painted in India during the Mogul period (1526 to about 1800) often had horses and riders as themes. And Persian miniature paintings, showing both Chinese and Indian influence, often included lively scenes filled with horses and riders.

▶ THE WELL-DRESSED HORSE

European art has always been filled with horses. Horses carried the knights of the Middle Ages into battle and horses pulled the plows in farmers' fields. And when the great cities were built, carts drawn by horses brought food and other supplies into the cities. People traveled from one city to another on

Bronco Buster, **by Frederic Remington.**

horseback or in wagons and carriages drawn by horses. In many ways, European civilization from the Middle Ages to the development of the automobile was built on the use of horses. And since horses were everywhere and were a vital part of everyone's life, they became an important subject for painters and sculptors.

Horses appeared in the illustrations of books, in frescoes on the walls of churches and palaces, and, especially during the Renaissance, in panel paintings. Because they were medieval or Renaissance horses, they were remarkably well dressed. When the knights of the Middle Ages rode into battle in elaborate suits of armor, their horses often wore armor, too. And the horses' armor was just as likely to be decorated by skilled artists as the knights' was. But besides armor to protect them in battle, medieval horses also wore brightly colored cloth trappings, called caparisons, to make them look fine on festive occasions.

During the Renaissance, the artists of Europe continued to paint horses, but they also made excellent drawings and engravings of them. Bronze statues of horses and riders, many of them even bigger than life-size, were created by sculptors to put in the squares of great cities. Kings and emperors often had themselves painted on horseback.

Ownership of horses was always considered a matter of prestige in Europe. The owners of fine racehorses and carriage horses wanted portraits of their animals. One of the most famous English horse painters, George Stubbs (1724–1806), was so serious a student of

The exciting painting of a horserace (*left*) was done in the early 19th century by the French painter Théodore Géricault. He was recapturing a wonderful day he had spent at the famous Epsom Downs racecourse while he was visiting England. The painting is beautiful—but it's inaccurate. Like everyone of his generation, Géricault believed that when fast-running horses left the ground, their legs stretched out, front and back. It was not until a pioneer photographer named Eadweard Muybridge made motion studies of animals in the 1870's that everyone discovered the truth. These photographs (*above*) prove that a galloping horse tucks its legs under it when it leaves the ground.

the anatomy of horses that he produced a detailed book of horse anatomy that is still appreciated.

French painters liked horses, too. Théodore Géricault (1791–1824) painted horses often —on the racecourse, on the battlefield, and in many other places as well. And both Edgar Degas (1834–1917) and Henri de Toulouse-Lautrec (1864–1901) found great beauty and style in horses—especially racehorses.

The painters who used racehorses as models later in the 19th century had one secret the early horse painters hadn't had. They knew what horses really looked like when they were running. Since horses run very fast, the artist's eye cannot really see their legs clearly in action. Before the invention of photography, artists, even very good artists, often pictured running horses in very strange positions. For instance, a horse might have both front legs stretched out in front of it, and both hind legs stretched out in back—and all four feet off the ground at once. No doubt that is what the artists thought they saw when they looked at a running horse. But in the 1870's they learned something surprising. An English photographer, Eadweard Muybridge, went to California and made a series of consecutive photographs of horses performing various gaits. These photographs proved that a horse did sometimes have all four feet off the ground at once (some people had maintained that it never did). But his photographs also showed that this never occurred when the front and hind legs were stretched out before and behind the horse, in the way they were so often shown in paintings. In fact, it became obvious

that horses previously painted by some of the most famous artists of all time would have fallen flat on their faces if they had really run the way they were shown running.

▶ AMERICAN HORSES

Americans inherited a love of horses from the British. They also followed the European custom of portraying great national leaders on horseback. Many American cities have statues of George Washington and other American heroes on horseback. And in the 19th century, pioneer printmakers like Currier & Ives published many prints showing famous racehorses and trotters.

But the great theme of American horse painters was found in the West. Here, in the vast spaces of the new land, both Indians and, later, ranchers and settlers practically lived on horseback. George Catlin (1796–1872) did many paintings and sketches of western horses. Perhaps the most famous of all American horse painters was Frederic Remington (1861–1909), who captured American cowboys and Indians so successfully that he gave the whole world an image of what the West was like. He was also a talented sculptor, and his bronze statues of bucking horses and riders capture the motion of the horse's body.

Horses are graceful and beautiful animals. Even though we no longer depend on them for transportation, we do not stop being awed by their beauty. And their beauty remains a fitting and exciting subject for artists of every sort.

MARION B. WILSON
Artist and writer

FANCY DUDS

Young people have rebelled—and their rebellion has been creative. They have grown tired of wearing clothes that someone else has designed. In a way, they're designing their own clothes and, in so doing, they have invented a whole new art form. You might say that these young artists are wearing their personal art galleries on their backs—and on other parts of their anatomies as well.

One of the most popular "canvases" for these creative young people is blue denim. Inexpensive denim blue jeans, shirts, and jackets have become material for self-expression. Someone discovered that the familiar faded blue color of traditional denim makes an ideal background for fantastic designs of all kinds. Some of the designs are embroidered directly on the denim in colored cotton thread. Other designs are cut out of brightly colored materials and sewn on the denim like patches. The important thing is how beautiful and how personal the designs are. Young people who never before displayed any interest in needlework are suddenly asking their grandmothers for sewing and embroidery lessons—boys as well as girls!

The other basic piece of clothing that has come in for creative decoration is the basic T-shirt. This familiar garment—worn by millions of American servicemen in World War II and popular thereafter—used to be white. Just plain white. Plain white T-shirts now almost seem to be a thing of the past. You can now buy T-shirts in all the colors of the rainbow. But young people are no longer content with expressing themselves in color alone. You can now have anything you choose printed on your T-shirt—many shops will do it for you. And many shops offer a selection of designs that can be applied to the shirts in a variety of ways. There are familiar advertising slogans, cartoon figures, animals—everything imaginable and a few things not. You can even have your own photograph put on your T-shirt. Nothing could be more personal and individual than that!

INTERNATIONAL STATISTICAL SUPPLEMENT
(as of December 31, 1976)

NATION	CAPITAL	AREA (in sq mi)	POPULATION (estimate)	GOVERNMENT
Afghanistan	Kabul	250,000	19,300,000	Mohammed Daud Khan—president
Albania	Tirana	11,100	2,500,000	Enver Hoxha—communist party secretary Mehmet Shehu—premier
Algeria	Algiers	919,593	16,800,000	Houari Boumédienne—president
Angola	Luanda	481,351	6,800,000	Agostinho Neto—president
Argentina	Buenos Aires	1,072,158	25,400,000	Jorge Rafael Videla—president
Australia	Canberra	2,967,900	13,600,000	Malcolm Fraser—prime minister
Austria	Vienna	32,374	7,600,000	Rudolf Kirchschläger—president Bruno Kreisky—chancellor
Bahamas	Nassau	5,380	200,000	Lynden O. Pindling—prime minister
Bahrain	Manama	240	260,000	Isa bin Sulman al-Khalifa—head of government
Bangladesh	Dacca	55,126	77,000,000	Abu Sadat Mohammed Sayem—president
Barbados	Bridgetown	166	250,000	J. M. G. Adams—prime minister
Belgium	Brussels	11,781	9,800,000	Baudouin I—king Leo Tindemans—premier
Benin (Dahomey)	Porto-Novo	43,483	3,100,000	Mathieu Kerekou—president
Bhutan	Thimbu	18,147	1,200,000	Jigme Singye Wangchuk—king
Bolivia	La Paz Sucre	424,163	5,600,000	Hugo Banzer Suárez—president
Botswana	Gaborone	231,804	700,000	Sir Seretse Khama—president
Brazil	Brasília	3,286,478	107,000,000	Ernesto Geisel—president
Bulgaria	Sofia	42,823	8,700,000	Todor Zhivkov—communist party secretary Stanko Todorov—premier
Burma	Rangoon	261,789	31,300,000	U Ne Win—president U Sein Win—prime minister
Burundi	Bujumbura	10,747	3,800,000	Jean-Baptiste Bagaza—president
Cambodia (Kampuchea)	Pnompenh	69,898	8,100,000	Khieu Samphan—head of state
Cameroon	Yaoundé	183,569	6,400,000	Ahmadou Ahidjo—president
Canada	Ottawa	3,851,809	23,000,000	Pierre Elliott Trudeau—prime minister
Cape Verde	Praia	1,557	300,000	Aristides Pereira—president
Central African Republic	Bangui	240,535	2,600,000	Jean Bedel Bokassa—president
Chad	N'Djemena	495,754	4,000,000	Félix Malloum—head of government

NATION	CAPITAL	AREA (in sq mi)	POPULATION (estimate)	GOVERNMENT
Chile	Santiago	292,257	10,300,000	Augusto Pinochet Ugarte—president
China	Peking	3,705,396	839,000,000	Hua Kuo-feng—communist party chairman Li Hsien-nien—premier
Colombia	Bogotá	439,736	24,000,000	Alfonso López Michelsen—president
Comoros	Moroni	838	310,000	Ali Soilih—head of state
Congo	Brazzaville	132,047	1,400,000	Marien Ngouabi—president
Costa Rica	San José	19,575	2,000,000	Daniel Oduber Quirós—president
Cuba	Havana	44,218	9,100,000	Osvaldo Dorticós Torrado—president Fidel Castro—premier
Cyprus	Nicosia	3,572	640,000	Archbishop Makarios III—president
Czechoslovakia	Prague	49,370	14,900,000	Gustáv Husák—communist party secretary and president Lubomír Štrougal—premier
Denmark	Copenhagen	16,629	5,100,000	Margrethe II—queen Anker Jorgensen—premier
Dominican Republic	Santo Domingo	18,816	4,700,000	Joaquín Balaguer—president
Ecuador	Quito	109,483	6,700,000	Alfredo Poveda Burbano—president
Egypt	Cairo	386,660	38,000,000	Anwar el-Sadat—president Mamdouh Salem—premier
El Salvador	San Salvador	8,260	4,000,000	Arturo Armando Molina—president
Equatorial Guinea	Malabo	10,830	310,000	Francisco Macías Nguema—president
Ethiopia	Addis Ababa	471,777	28,000,000	military government
Fiji	Suva	7,055	580,000	Ratu Sir Kamisese Mara—prime minister
Finland	Helsinki	130,120	4,700,000	Urho K. Kekkonen—president Martti J. Miettunen—premier
France	Paris	211,207	53,000,000	Valéry Giscard d'Estaing—president Raymond Barre—premier
Gabon	Libreville	103,346	530,000	Albert B. Bongo—president
Gambia	Banjul	4,361	520,000	Sir Dauda K. Jawara—president
Germany (East)	East Berlin	41,768	16,900,000	Erich Honecker—communist party secretary Willi Stoph—premier
Germany (West)	Bonn	95,976	62,000,000	Walter Scheel—president Helmut Schmidt—chancellor
Ghana	Accra	92,099	9,900,000	Ignatius K. Acheampong—head of government
Greece	Athens	50,944	9,100,000	Constantine Tsatsos—president Constantine Caramanlis—premier

NATION	CAPITAL	AREA (in sq mi)	POPULATION (estimate)	GOVERNMENT
Grenada	St. George's	133	100,000	Eric M. Gairy—prime minister
Guatemala	Guatemala City	42,042	5,600,000	Kjell Laugerud García—president
Guinea	Conakry	94,926	4,400,000	Sékou Touré—president Lansana Beavogui—premier
Guinea-Bissau	Bissau	13,948	530,000	Luiz de Almeida Cabral—president
Guyana	Georgetown	83,000	800,000	Arthur Chung—president Forbes Burnham—prime minister
Haiti	Port-au-Prince	10,714	4,600,000	Jean-Claude Duvalier—president
Honduras	Tegucigalpa	43,277	3,000,000	Alberto Juan Melgar Castro—head of state
Hungary	Budapest	35,919	10,600,000	János Kádár—communist party secretary György Lazar—premier
Iceland	Reykjavik	39,768	220,000	Kristján Eldjárn—president Geir Hallgrimsson—prime minister
India	New Delhi	1,266,598	600,000,000	Fakhruddin Ali Ahmed—president Indira Gandhi—prime minister
Indonesia	Jakarta	735,269	131,000,000	Suharto—president
Iran	Teheran	636,294	33,000,000	Mohammed Reza Pahlavi—shah Amir Abbas Hoveida—premier
Iraq	Baghdad	167,925	11,100,000	Ahmed Hassan al-Bakr—president
Ireland	Dublin	27,136	3,100,000	Patrick Hillery—president Liam Cosgrave—prime minister
Israel	Jerusalem	7,992	3,400,000	Ephraim Katzir—president Yitzhak Rabin—prime minister
Italy	Rome	116,303	56,000,000	Giovanni Leone—president Giulio Andreotti—premier
Ivory Coast	Abidjan	124,503	6,800,000	Félix Houphouet-Boigny—president
Jamaica	Kingston	4,232	2,000,000	Michael N. Manley—prime minister
Japan	Tokyo	143,750	112,000,000	Hirohito—emperor Takeo Fukuda—premier
Jordan	Amman	37,738	2,700,000	Hussein I—king Mudar Badran—premier
Kenya	Nairobi	224,959	13,400,000	Jomo Kenyatta—president
Korea (North)	Pyongyang	46,540	15,900,000	Kim Il Sung—president Pak Sung Chul—premier
Korea (South)	Seoul	38,022	34,700,000	Park Chung Hee—president
Kuwait	Kuwait	6,880	1,000,000	Sabah al-Salim al-Sabah—head of state
Laos	Vientiane	91,429	3,300,000	Souphanouvong—president Kaysone Phomvihan—premier
Lebanon	Beirut	4,015	2,900,000	Elias Sarkis—president Selim al-Hoss—premier

NATION	CAPITAL	AREA (in sq mi)	POPULATION (estimate)	GOVERNMENT
Lesotho	Maseru	11,720	1,000,000	Moshoeshoe II—king Leabua Jonathan—prime minister
Liberia	Monrovia	43,000	1,700,000	William R. Tolbert—president
Libya	Tripoli	679,360	2,500,000	Muammar el-Qaddafi—president Abdul Salam Jallud—premier
Liechtenstein	Vaduz	61	24,000	Francis Joseph II—prince
Luxembourg	Luxembourg	999	360,000	Jean—grand duke Gaston Thorn—premier
Madagascar (Malagasy Republic)	Tananarive	226,657	7,500,000	Didier Ratsiraka—president
Malawi	Lilongwe	45,747	5,000,000	H. Kamuzu Banda—president
Malaysia	Kuala Lumpur	127,316	11,900,000	Yahaya Putra ibni al-Marhum—paramount ruler Hussein Onn—prime minister
Maldives	Male	115	120,000	Ibrahim Nasir—president
Mali	Bamako	478,765	5,700,000	Moussa Traoré—president
Malta	Valletta	122	320,000	Sir Anthony Mamo—president Dom Mintoff—prime minister
Mauritania	Nouakchott	397,954	1,300,000	Moktar O. Daddah—president
Mauritius	Port Louis	720	900,000	Sir Seewoosagur Ramgoolam—prime minister
Mexico	Mexico City	761,602	61,000,000	José López Portillo—president
Monaco	Monaco-Ville	0.4	25,000	Rainier III—prince
Mongolia	Ulan Bator	604,248	1,500,000	Yumzhagiyn Tsedenbal—communist party secretary
Morocco	Rabat	172,413	17,300,000	Hassan II—king Ahmed Osman—premier
Mozambique	Maputo	302,329	9,200,000	Samora Machel—president
Nauru	—	8	8,000	Bernard Doniyogo—president
Nepal	Katmandu	54,362	12,600,000	Birendra Bir Bikram Shah Deva—king Tulsi Giri—prime minister
Netherlands	Amsterdam	15,770	13,700,000	Juliana—queen Joop den Uyl—premier
New Zealand	Wellington	103,736	3,100,000	Robert D. Muldoon—prime minister
Nicaragua	Managua	50,193	2,200,000	Anastasio Somoza Debayle—president
Niger	Niamey	489,190	4,600,000	Seyni Kountche—head of government
Nigeria	Lagos	356,668	63,000,000	Olusegun Obasanjo—head of government
Norway	Oslo	125,181	4,000,000	Olav V—king Oddvar Nordli—prime minister
Oman	Muscat	82,030	800,000	Qabus ibn Said—sultan

NATION	CAPITAL	AREA (in sq mi)	POPULATION (estimate)	GOVERNMENT
Pakistan	Islamabad	310,403	71,000,000	Chaudri Fazal Elahi—president Zulfikar Ali Bhutto—prime minister
Panama	Panama City	29,209	1,700,000	Omar Torrijos Herrera—head of government
Papua New Guinea	Port Moresby	178,260	2,800,000	Michael Somare—prime minister
Paraguay	Asunción	157,047	2,600,000	Alfredo Stroessner—president
Peru	Lima	496,223	15,900,000	Francisco Morales Bermúdez—president
Philippines	Manila	115,830	43,000,000	Ferdinand E. Marcos—president
Poland	Warsaw	120,724	34,200,000	Edward Gierek—communist party secretary Piotr Jaroszewicz—premier
Portugal	Lisbon	35,553	8,800,000	António Ramalho Eanes—president Mário Soares—premier
Qatar	Doha	4,000	150,000	Khalifa bin Hamad al-Thani—head of government
Rhodesia	Salisbury	150,803	6,300,000	John Wrathall—president Ian D. Smith—prime minister
Rumania	Bucharest	91,700	21,300,000	Nicolae Ceauşescu—communist party secretary Manea Manescu—premier
Rwanda	Kigali	10,169	4,200,000	Juvénal Habyalimana—president
São Tomé and Príncipe	São Tomé	372	80,000	Manuel Pinto da Costa—president
Saudi Arabia	Riyadh	829,997	9,000,000	Khalid bin Abdul-Aziz—king
Senegal	Dakar	75,750	4,100,000	Léopold Senghor—president
Seychelles	Victoria	107	58,000	James Mancham—president
Sierra Leone	Freetown	27,700	2,800,000	Siaka P. Stevens—president
Singapore	Singapore	224	2,300,000	Benjamin H. Sheares—president Lee Kuan Yew—prime minister
Somalia	Mogadishu	246,200	3,200,000	Mohammed Siad Barre—head of government
South Africa	Pretoria Cape Town	471,444	25,500,000	Nicolaas Diederichs—president B. John Vorster—prime minister
Spain	Madrid	194,897	35,500,000	Juan Carlos I—king Adolfo Suárez González—premier
Sri Lanka (Ceylon)	Colombo	25,332	14,000,000	William Gopallawa—president Sirimavo Bandaranaike—premier
Sudan	Khartoum	967,497	17,800,000	Gaafar al-Numeiry—president
Surinam	Paramaribo	63,037	420,000	Henck A. E. Arron—prime minister
Swaziland	Mbabane	6,704	500,000	Sobhuza II—king
Sweden	Stockholm	173,732	8,200,000	Carl XVI Gustaf—king Thorbjörn Fälldin—prime minister

NATION	CAPITAL	AREA (in sq mi)	POPULATION (estimate)	GOVERNMENT
Switzerland	Bern	15,941	6,400,000	Kurt Furgler—president
Syria	Damascus	71,586	7,400,000	Hafez al-Assad—president Abdel Rahman Khleifawi—premier
Taiwan	Taipei	13,885	16,000,000	C. K. Yen—president Chiang Ching-kuo—premier
Tanzania	Dar es Salaam	364,898	15,200,000	Julius K. Nyerere—president
Thailand	Bangkok	198,456	42,000,000	Bhumibol Adulyadej—king Thanin Kraivichien—premier
Togo	Lomé	21,622	2,200,000	Étienne Eyadema—president
Tonga	Nuku'alofa	270	100,000	Taufa'ahau Tupou IV—king Prince Tu'ipelehake—prime minister
Trinidad & Tobago	Port of Spain	1,980	1,100,000	Eric Williams—prime minister
Tunisia	Tunis	63,170	5,800,000	Habib Bourguiba—president
Turkey	Ankara	301,381	39,200,000	Fahri Korutürk—president Suleyman Demirel—premier
Uganda	Kampala	91,134	11,600,000	Idi Amin—president
U.S.S.R.	Moscow	8,649,512	255,000,000	Leonid I. Brezhnev—communist party secretary Aleksei N. Kosygin—premier Nikolai V. Podgorny—president of presidium
United Arab Emirates	Abu Dhabi	32,278	220,000	Zayd bin Sultan—president
United Kingdom	London	94,226	56,000,000	Elizabeth II—queen James Callaghan—prime minister
United States	Washington, D.C.	3,615,123	215,000,000	James Earl Carter, Jr.—president Walter F. Mondale—vice-president
Upper Volta	Ouagadougou	105,869	6,100,000	Sangoulé Lamizana—president
Uruguay	Montevideo	68,536	3,100,000	Aparicio Méndez—president
Venezuela	Caracas	352,143	12,000,000	Carlos Andrés Pérez—president
Vietnam	Hanoi	128,402	44,000,000	Le Duan—communist party secretary Ton Duc Thang—president Pham Van Dong—premier
Western Samoa	Apia	1,097	150,000	Malietoa Tanumafili II—head of state
Yemen (Aden)	Madinat al-Shaab	112,000	1,700,000	Salem Ali Rubaya—head of state Ali Nasir Mohammed—prime minister
Yemen (Sana)	Sana	75,290	5,300,000	Ibrahim al-Hamidi—head of government
Yugoslavia	Belgrade	98,766	21,500,000	Josip Broz Tito—president Dzemal Bijedić—premier
Zaïre	Kinshasa	905,565	24,900,000	Mobutu Sese Seko—president
Zambia	Lusaka	290,585	4,900,000	Kenneth D. Kaunda—president

INDEX

A

Aarderma, Verna, American writer
  Why Mosquitoes Buzz in People's Ears, African story, picture 261
Academy Awards, motion pictures 344–45
Adams, Brock, U.S. public official 35
Adams, John, U.S. president 43
Adams, Richard, British writer
  Tyger Voyage, The, book, picture 261
Adventures of Tom Sawyer, The, novel by Mark Twain 256–59
Aeronautics
  National Air and Space Museum 90–93
Aerosmith, American music group 341
Afghanistan 360
Africa
  Angola 61
  Namibia 72
  Seychelles 62–63
  southern African crisis 68–69
Agriculture
  beekeeping 287
  Indochina 64
Agustinianos, ancient people, South America 119
Air and Space Museum, Washington, D.C. 90–93
Airplanes see Air transportation
Air pollution
  Venice, Italy 158; picture 161
Air transportation
  Canadian airline pilots' strike 23
  hijacking of airplanes 73–75
  MiG-25, Soviet fighter 28
  National Air and Space Museum 90–93
  supersonic aircraft 21, 101
Akhnaton, Egyptian pharaoh 118
Aksenov, Vladimir V., Soviet cosmonaut 29
Alaska
  U.S. Geological Survey's new map 122
  Willow South chosen for new capital 32
Albania 360
Alberta, province, Canada
  aurora borealis, picture 102
  Boy Scout Jamboree 220
Albino animals 279–82
Alekseyev, Vasili, Soviet athlete 304
Algeria 360
Alhambra, palace-fortress, Granada, Spain 192
Amahl and the Night Visitors, opera by Menotti 332, 334–35
Amerasinghe, Hamilton Shirley, Sri Lankan diplomat 29
American Basketball Association 314, 315
American foxhound, dog 288, 289
American Indians see Indians, American
American Kennel Club 288
American League, baseball 310–12
American Legion convention, Philadelphia, Pennsylvania 27

American Museum, England 59
American Museum of Natural History, New York City
  Hall of Minerals and Gems 112–15
American Revolution see Revolutionary War
Amerigo Vespucci, Italian ship 55
Andrew Doria, U.S. ship 128
Andrus, Cecil D., U.S. public official 35
Angel Sounding a Trumpet, statue, Ste. Anne de Beaupré, Canada, picture 181
Angola 61, 360
  Rhodesian crisis 69
  United Nations membership 23, 34
Animals
  albino animals 279–82
  animals in the news, pictures 270–71
  asexual reproduction 96–99
  Boy Scout conservation program 221
  Operation Noah, rescue project 278
  pets of U.S. presidents 288–95
  stamps 149
  See also Animals in art; and specific kinds of animals
Animals in art 346–51
  Cat, photograph by Eakins 350; picture 351
  Cat in American Folk Art, exhibition, New York City 352; pictures 328–29, 353
  Chinese rose quartz dog, picture 115
  Cream Ponies, painting by Stubbs 348–49
  Haida totem poles 156–57
  horses 354–57
  Japanese rock crystal elephant, picture 115
  Young Hare, painting by Dürer 346–47
Anne, British princess 304
Anne, Saint, mother of the Virgin Mary 181
Apartheid, South Africa's segregation policy 68, 69
Apiaries, bee farms 287
Apollo 11, spacecraft 90; picture 91
Araki, Daisuki, Japanese athlete 313
Archeology 118–19
  Bronze Age artifacts found in Thailand 108–9
  Egyptian mummy, identification of 120
  horses in art 354
Archery, sport
  Olympic Games 306
Architecture
  fountains 192–95
Arctic regions
  whales 274–75
Argentina 360
  Operation Sail 54, 55
  Perón, Isabel Martínez de, deposed 17
Argo Merchant, tanker 34
Arithmetic
  calculators 94
Arkansas
  Invitational Canoe Races, Scout events 223
Armstrong, Anne, U.S. ambassador to Britain 13
Arrowhead, Herman Melville's home, Massachusetts 252
Art
  beehives of Poland 286–87
  Bicentennial exhibitions 57, 58, 59
  Byzantine art, Cappadocia, Turkey 165; picture 164
  Calder, Alexander, death of 32

Cat, photograph by Eakins 350; picture 351
Cat in American Folk Art, exhibition, New York City 352; pictures 328–29, 353
Chinese altar vase, picture 115
Chinese rose quartz dog, picture 115
Cream Ponies, painting by Stubbs 348–49
fountains 192–95
Haida totem poles 156–57
Here Fell Custer, painting, picture 199
horses in art 354–57
Japanese rock crystal elephant, picture 115
Medici Chapel, Florence, Italy 154
molas, Cuna Indian embroidery 336–37
ojo de Dios, Indian design 136–38
Pomegranate, mobile by Calder, picture 33
posters 182–89
Space Mural—A Cosmic View, The, mural by McCall, picture 91
Sun, The, sculpture by Lippold, picture 92
tapestry, picture 124–25
Young Hare, painting by Dürer 346–47
Arts and crafts see Hobbies, handicrafts, and projects
Asexual reproduction, biology 96–99
Asia
China 66
earthquakes 116
Indochina 64–65
Atmosphere
ozone layer 101
Atomic energy see Nuclear energy
Aton, Egyptian sun god 118
ATS-6, communications satellite 121
Aurora australis or **Southern lights** 102
Aurora borealis or **Northern lights** 102
Austin, Texas
National Explorer Olympics winner 223
Australia 360
Boy Scout meeting 220
Olympic Games 304
Rockefeller's visit 59
Australian Open, tennis tournament 326
Austria 360
coins 129
Olympic Games 299, 304, 14
stamps 149
Automobiles
CB radio 106
Avalon, Frankie, American singer 343
Avco Cup, hockey trophy 321
Awards see Prizes and awards

B

Bach, Johann Sebastian, German composer 330–31
Bad News Bears, The, motion picture, picture 207
Baez, Joan, American singer 340
Bagaza, Jean-Baptiste, Burundi president 32
Bahamas 360
Boy Scout scuba-diving program 223
Bahrain 360
Bald ibis, bird 284–85
Bali, island, Indonesia
earthquake 25
Ballet
Cheri, photograph by Clark Federer 200–1
Fanfare, picture 332
Nutcracker, The, book by Martha Swope, picture 260
Ball lightning 87
Ban Chiang, Thailand
Bronze Age artifacts found 108; picture 109
Bangladesh 360
Barbados 360

Barcelona, Spain
albino gorilla in zoo, pictures 268–69, 280
Bark, ship 55
Barkentine, ship 55
Barnum & Bailey Circus poster, picture 186
Baseball, sport 310–12
Little League 313
Basketball, sport 314–15
Olympic Games 303, 306
Basques, people 74; picture 75
Bassham, Lanny, American athlete 304
Bastien et Bastienne, opera by Mozart 331; picture 330
Battersby, Peter, American photography contest winner, picture 216
Bayley, Nicola, British illustrator
Tyger Voyage, The, book, picture 261
Beardsley, Aubrey, English artist
posters 184
Bears, animals
Smokey Bear, picture 271
Beavers, Canadian Boy Scouts, picture 221
Bee, insect 287
Beehives, structures for bees' nests 286–87
Beirut, Lebanon 77
Belgium 360
Canadian Rangers, picture 227
Olympic Games 304
Bell, Alexander Graham, Scottish-American inventor
commemorative stamps 146
Bell, Griffin B., U.S. public official 35
Bellow, Saul, American writer 31
Bench, Johnny, American athlete 310; picture 311
Benin or **Dahomey** 360
Benson, Kent, American athlete, picture 315
Bergland, Bob S., U.S. public official 35
Berlinguer, Enrico, Italian Communist leader, picture 67
Bermuda
Olympic Games 304
Bernhardt, Sarah, French actress
poster by Alphonse Mucha, picture 183
Bhutan 360
Biathlon, sport
Olympic Games 305
Bicentennial, United States
Boy Scouts 220, 221
coins 128
Girl Scouts 226, 227
observances by other nations 56–59
Operation Sail 54–55
posters 187
re-enactment of famous events, pictures 46–49
stamps 146
two-dollar bills 18
U.S. history 42–45
Bicentennial Bell 57
Bicentennial Children's Museum, Fairfield, Connecticut, picture 49
Bicentennial Diamond Necklace, picture 115
Bicentennial Wagon Train, picture 48
Big Bird, television character, picture 310
Biofeedback, medical technique 107
Bird feeders 276–77
Birds
albino peacock, picture 279
albino robin, picture 282
bird feeders, pictures 276–77
cardinal, picture 276
carrier pigeon 155
chickadee, picture 277
Chinese enamel birds, picture 52
downy woodpecker, picture 277
gannet 103
ibis 284–85
oil spill 35
whooping crane 99; picture 98

Birecik, Turkey
  ibises, birds 284–85
Black opal, mineral, picture 113
Blumberg, Baruch S., American scientist 31
Blumenthal, W. Michael, U.S. public official 35
Boats
  CB radio 106
Bobsledding, sport
  Olympic Games 305
Bolivia 360
Bonaventure Island, Quebec, Canada 103
Book cover
  instructions for making 140–41
Bordaberry, Juan María, Uruguayan president 22
Borg, Björn, Swedish athlete 326
Borge, Victor, Danish-American pianist and comedian 59
Boston Celtics, basketball team 314, 315
Boston Pops Orchestra, picture 333
Botanical Gardens, Denver, Colorado 214
Botany see Plants
Botswana 360
Boxing, sport
  Olympic Games 303–4, 306
Boy Scouts 220–23
Bradley, Will, American artist
  posters 184
Brazil 360
  Girl Guide literacy project, picture 225
  Olympic Games 304
Bremerton, Washington
  colonial classroom, picture 47
Brett, George, American athlete 310, 311, 312
Brezhnev, Leonid, Soviet public official
  nuclear explosions treaty with U.S. 21
British Columbia, province, Canada
  Habitat conference, Vancouver 22
  Haida Indians 156
  totem pole, picture 157
  Vancouver 105
Britten, Benjamin, British composer 34
  music for young people 331–32
Bronco Buster, sculpture by Remington, picture 356
Bronze Age, archeology 108–9
Brown, Edmund G., U.S. governor 37
Brown, Harold, U.S. public official 35
Bruner, Mike, American athlete 325
Buddha, founder of Buddhism 119
Buddhism, religion 119
  Chinese altar vase, picture 115
Bulgaria 360
  Olympic Games 304
Burma 360
Burns, George, American comedian 344
Burundi 360
  Micombero deposed 32
Butz, Earl L., U.S. public official 30
Bykovsky, Valeri F., Soviet cosmonaut 29
Byzantine art
  Cappadocia, Turkey 165; picture 164

C

Cabinet of the United States 35
  Butz, Earl L., resignation of 30
  Usery, Willie Julian, Jr., appointment of 13
Calculators 94
Calcutta, India
  Mother Teresa 196
Caldecott Medal, picture book award
  Why Mosquitoes Buzz in People's Ears, African story, picture 261

Calder, Alexander, American artist 32
  Pomegranate, mobile, picture 33
Calder Trophy, hockey 322
Califano, Joseph A., Jr., U.S. public official 35
California
  Campbell's Little League baseball team 313
  landsailing 203, 204; picture 205
  modern pioneers 170–73
  San Diego Zoo's koala bears, picture 271
  Temple City's National Explorer Olympics winner 223
Callaghan, James, British prime minister 16
Cambodia 65, 64, 360
  Khieu Samphan named chief of state 19
Cameroon 360
Campbell, California
  Little League World Series 313
Canada 360
  airline pilots' strike 23
  Boy Scouts 220; picture 221
  coins 129
  Communications Technology Satellite 13
  football 318
  Girl Guides 227
  Haida Indians 156
  hockey 320–22
  Landsat's photographs of border 123
  Lévesque elected premier of Quebec 33
  Montreal's Château Ramezay 174–75
  natural wonders 102–5
  Olympic Games 300, 304
  Ste. Anne de Beaupré 181
  ships of Lake Huron 176–80
  stamps 146, 149
  Trudeau's visit to Latin America 13
  Trudeau's visit to the United States 58
  Upper Canada Village, Ontario 162–63
Canada Cup, hockey trophy 321
Canadian-American Trophy, skiing 324
Canadian Provincial Jamboree, Boy Scouts 220
Canoeing, sport
  Olympic Games 306
Cape Verde 360
Capital punishment
  Supreme Court ruling 24
Cappadocia, area, Turkey 164–65
Cardinal, bird, picture 276
Carl XVI Gustaf, Swedish king
  United States, visit to 58
Carnival of the Animals, composition by Saint-Saëns 331
Carradine, Keith, American actor and composer 341
Cars
  CB radio 106
Carter, Amy, daughter of President Carter 41; picture 295
Carter, James Earl, Jr., U.S. president 41, 32
  cabinet 35
  elections 36–40
  electoral votes, map 40
Carter, Lillian, mother of President Carter 41
Carter, Rosalynn, wife of President Carter 41; pictures 36, 295
Cartography, science of making maps 122–23
Castro, Fidel, Cuban premier, picture 13
Cat, animal
  Eakins' photograph 350; picture 351
  folk art exhibition, New York City 352; pictures 328–29, 353
  pets of U.S. presidents 295
Catholic Church, Roman see Roman Catholic Church
Cat in the Window, painting, picture 328–29
Catlin, George, American artist 357
Cave dwellings
  Cappadocia, Turkey 165; pictures 164
Caxton, William, English printer
  commemorative stamps 149

Cayman Islands
    stamps 146
CB radio or **Citizens Band radio** 106
Centennial, United States 43–45
Centennial Exposition, 1876, Philadelphia, Pennsylvania
    50–53, 44–45
Central African Republic 360
Ceylon see Sri Lanka
Chad 360
Château Ramezay, Montreal, Canada 174–75
Chemistry, Nobel prize in 31
Chéret, Jules, French artist 183
Chess, game
    Korchnoi seeks asylum in Netherlands 25
    stamps 149
Cheyenne Indians
    Custer's Last Stand 197–99
Chiang Ching, widow of Mao Tse-tung 66
Chicago, Illinois
    Daley, Richard J., death of 35
Chickadee, bird, picture 277
Children Headed West, story by Elisabeth Margo 230–39
Children's Book Week poster, picture 188
Children's Express, magazine 38
Chile 361
    Operation Sail 55
China 66, 11, 361
    Chou En-lai, death of 12
    earthquake 116, 25
    Mao Tse-tung, death of 28
    Nixon's visit 15
Chinese art
    altar vase, picture 115
    dog, picture 115
    enamel birds, picture 52
    horses 355
    statue of Kuan-yin, goddess of mercy, picture 114
Chou En-lai, Chinese premier 12, 66
Christianity
    Cappadocia, Turkey 165
    Lebanon 76, 77
    Mother Teresa 196
    Northern Ireland 70–71
    Ste. Anne de Beaupré, Quebec, Canada 181
    women, ordination of 28
Christian Radich, Norwegian ship 55
Christie, Dame Agatha, British writer 12
Church, Frank, U.S. senator 37
Cincinnati Reds, baseball team 310–12
Circus poster, picture 186
Citizens Band radio 106
Clemens, Samuel Langhorne, American writer
    Adventures of Tom Sawyer, The, novel 256–59
Cloning, reproduction from a single body cell 97–99;
    picture 96
Clothing
    Cuna Indians 336–37
    young people's designs 358–59
Coffin, Edmund, American athlete 304
Coin collecting 128–29
Cole, Natalie, American singer 342
Colombia 361
    archeology 119
    Operation Sail 55
Colombo, Sri Lanka
    conference of nonaligned nations 26
Colorado
    Denver's community garden 211
    National Explorer Olympics, Scout events, Fort Collins
    223; pictures 222
Comaneci, Nadia, Rumanian athlete 210, 26, 303; picture
    302
Comer, Sherri, American landsailing champion 203, 204;
    picture 202

Communications satellites
    ATS-6 121
    Communications Technology Satellite 13
Communism
    Indochina 64–65
    Italy 67, 22
Comoros 361
Computers
    map making, use in 123
Concorde, supersonic transport plane 101, 21
Conference of nonaligned nations, Colombo, Sri Lanka 26
Conference on Human Settlements see Habitat
Congo 361
Congress of the United States 32
Connecticut
    Fairfield University's Bicentennial Children's Museum,
        picture 49
    Hartford's re-enactment of march of French troops,
        picture 49
Connor, Lee, American photography contest winner
    Encased, photograph 219
Connors, Jimmy, American athlete 326
Conn Smythe Trophy, hockey 322
Conservation of wildlife
    Boy Scouts 221
    gavials of India, picture 270
    ibises of Birecik, Turkey 285
    whales 275
Continental Congress, U.S. history 42
Conventions, Political 37; pictures 38
Cook Islands
    coins 128
Coolidge, Calvin, U.S. president
    pets 290–91, 295
Copper, metal, picture 112
Corliss steam engine 51
Cosmic Laser Concert 84–86; picture 80–81
Costa Rica 361
Cotton Bowl, football game 318
Country music 341
Crafts see Hobbies, handicrafts, and projects
Crazy Horse, American Indian leader 199
Cream Ponies, painting by George Stubbs 348–49
Crime
    terrorism 73–75
Cuba 361
    Olympic Games 304
Cub Scouts 221–22
Cuna Indians
    molas, embroidery 336–37
Curtis Cup, golf trophy 319
Custer, George Armstrong, U.S. soldier 197–99
Custer Battlefield National Monument, Montana 197
Custer's Last Stand or **The Battle of the Little Bighorn**
    197–99
Cycling, sport
    Olympic Games 306
Cyprus 361
Cy Young Awards, baseball 311
Czechoslovakia 361
    hockey 321
    Olympic Games 304

D

Dahomey see Benin
Daley, Richard J., U.S. mayor 35
Dams
    Teton Dam, Idaho 22
    Venice, Italy, picture 161
Dance see Ballet

Danmark, Danish ship 55
Dar Pomorza, Polish ship 55
Davis Cup, tennis trophy 326
Death penalty
    Supreme Court ruling 24
Debates, Political 39–40
Debussy, Claude, French composer 331
Declaration of Independence, painting by Trumbull 146
Declaration of Independence, U.S. 43
    200th anniversary celebrated 24
Deerfield, Massachusetts 166–69
Degas, Edgar, French artist 357
Democratic Party, U.S. 36–40
    convention, picture 38
Denim, cloth 358; pictures 359
Denmark 361
    Fourth of July Festival 59
    Girl Guide literacy projects 226
    Margrethe II's visit to the United States 58
    Olympic Games 304
    Operation Sail 55
    stamps 146
Denver, Colorado
    community garden 214
Denver Nuggets, basketball team 314, 315
Diamond, mineral, pictures 114, 115
Diamond, Neil, American musician and composer 339
Dillon, Leo and Diane, American illustrators
    Why Mosquitoes Buzz in People's Ears, African story,
      picture 261
Disco music 339
Diving, sport
    Olympic Games 300
Dog, animal
    Chinese carving, picture 115
    Cream Ponies, painting by George Stubbs 349
    pets of U.S. presidents 288–94
    Westminster Kennel Club show 272–73
    Zorro, picture 271
Dole, Robert J., U.S. senator 37
Dominican Republic 361
Dorsett, Tony, American athlete 318
Douglas DC-3, airplane 93
Drought
    Great Britain 117
    Kansas wheat field, picture 18
Dryden, Ken, Canadian athlete 320
Dryer, Ivan, American filmmaker 84
Dublin, Ireland
    Ewart-Biggs, assassination of 71
Duff, Larkin, American photography contest winner, pic-
    ture 217
Dürer, Albrecht, German artist 346
    Young Hare, painting 346–47
Dylan, Bob, American musician and composer 339;
    picture 338

E

Eagle, bird
    totem pole, picture 157
Eagle, U.S. bark 55
Eagle Scouts 221, 223
Eakins, Thomas, American artist and photographer 346
    Cat, photograph 350; picture 351
Eanes, António Ramalho, Portuguese president 23
Earthquakes 116
    China 25
    Guatemala 14; picture 15
    Indonesia 25
    Italy 20

    Philippines 26
    Turkey 33
East Germany see German Democratic Republic
Ebla, ancient kingdom, Syria 118
Economics, Nobel prize in 31
Ecuador 361
    Rodríguez Lara deposed 12
Education
    calculators 94
    Girl Scout and Girl Guide literacy projects 226
    television programs, India 121
Egypt 361
    archeology 118
    Sinai desert territory 15
Egypt, Ancient
    horses in art 354
    mummies and tombs 120
Elections
    Italy 67, 22
    Mexico 24
    Portugal 78, 19, 23
    Quebec 33
    Sweden 67
    United States 36–40
Electoral votes, U.S. election, map 40
Elephant, animal
    Japanese carving, picture 115
Elizabeth, British queen mother 149
Elizabeth I, queen of England
    narwhal horn 274
Elizabeth II, queen of United Kingdom
    Olympic Games 300
    United States, visit to 56, 57
Ellis Island, New York 21
El Salvador 361
    Girl Guide literacy project 226–27
Embroidery
    clothing decorations by young people 358;
      pictures 359
    molas 336–37
    tapestry, picture 124–25
Emerald, mineral, picture 114
Endangered species of wildlife
    cloning as a method of preservation 98
    commemorative coins 128
    commemorative stamps 149
    gavial, reptile, picture 270
    ibis, bird 284–85
    whales 275
Ender, Kornelia, East German athlete 303, 325;
    picture 209
Energy
    game 143
    nuclear energy 87
England see Great Britain
Entebbe airport, Uganda 24, 73, 74
Enterprise, space shuttle 88
Environment
    air pollution, Venice, Italy 158; picture 161
    effect on human development 99
    supersonic aircrafts' damage to atmosphere 101
    See also Endangered species of wildlife
Episcopal Church
    ordination of women 28
Equatorial Guinea 361
Equestrian events
    Olympic Games 304, 306
Erving, Julius, American athlete 314
Esmeralda, Chilean barkentine 55
Ethiopia 361
Evert, Chris, American athlete 326
Ewart-Biggs, T. E., British ambassador 71
Exhibitions
    Bicentennial exhibitions 57, 58, 59

cat in folk art 352; pictures 328–29, 353
Centennial Exposition, 1876 50–53
INTERPHIL 76, stamps 146
Explorer I, American satellite 93
Explorer Scouts 222, 223
Project SOAR 221

F

Fairfield University, Connecticut
Bicentennial Children's Museum, picture 49
Fala, President Franklin D. Roosevelt's dog 291–92
Fälldin, Thorbjörn, Swedish prime minister 29;
picture 67
Fanfare, ballet, picture 332
Farming see Agriculture
Federer, Clark, American photography contest winner
Cheri, photograph 200–1
Fencing, sport
Olympic Games 306
Ferdinand, Joan, American winner of Soap Box Derby,
picture 209
Festivals
American Folklife, Washington, D.C. 58
Community Medieval Festival, New York City 206
Fidrych, Mark, American athlete 311, 312; picture 310
Fiedler, Arthur, American conductor, picture 333
Field hockey, sport
Olympic Games 307
Figure skating, sport 324
Hamill, Dorothy 211
Olympic Games 299, 305
Fiji 361
Films see Motion pictures
Finland 361
Olympic Games 304
Finn, Huckleberry, literary character 256
Flagg, James Montgomery, American artist
poster, picture 186
Fletcher, Louise, American actress 344
Floods
Idaho 22
Panama 278
Philippines 116
Venice, Italy 158–61
Florence, Italy
fountains 193
Medici Chapel 154
Flu, disease
swine influenza vaccination campaign 17, 35
Flute, musical instrument
shakuhachi 172–73
Flyer, airplane 90
Fokker T-2, airplane 93
Folk art
beehives of Poland 286–87
cat in folk art 352; pictures 328–29, 353
molas, Cuna Indian embroidery 336–37
ojo de Dios, Indian woven design 136–38
Food
recipes for supper 144–45
Football, sport 316–18
Ford, Gerald R., U.S. president 13, 15
elections 36–40
electoral votes, map 40
nuclear explosions treaty with U.S.S.R. 21
pets 294, 295
swine influenza vaccination campaign 17
Ford, Jack, son of President Ford 38
Ford, Susan, daughter of President Ford
Shan, Siamese cat 294, 295

Forest Hills, New York
tennis tournament 326
Forest of the Statues, archeological site, Colombia 119
Fort Wayne, Indiana
Hoosier Youth, The, statue of Lincoln 289;
picture 288
Fountains 190–95
Fourth of July, U.S. holiday 42–45
Operation Sail 54–55
Foxbat, Soviet airplane 28
Foxhound, dog 288, 289
Frampton, Peter, British musician 341–42
France 361
Concorde, supersonic transport plane 101
fountains 193–94
Giscard's visit to United States 57
Indochina 64
Lascaux cave drawings 354
Malraux, André, death of 33
Olympic Games 304
posters 183; pictures 182, 185
Revolutionary War television series 59
Franco, Francisco, Spanish dictator 79
Franklin, Benjamin, U.S. statesman
commemorative stamps 146
French Open, tennis tournament 326
Friedman, Milton, American economist 31
Frobisher, Martin, English explorer 274
Frog, amphibian
albino frog, picture 282
cloning 97; picture 96
Fukuda, Takeo, Japanese premier 35
Fundy, Bay of, North America
Tidal Bore 105; picture 104
Fusion, Nuclear, physics
lightning 87

G

Gabon 361
Gajdusek, D. Carleton, American scientist 31
Gall, American Indian leader 199
Gálvez, Bernardo de, Spanish commander 57
statue, picture 58
Gambia 361
Games 212–213
Gannet, bird 103
Gardens
community gardens 214–15
Girl Scout and Girl Guide projects 224, 226;
picture 227
Moorish gardens of Spain 192
Gator Bowl, football game 318
Gavial, reptile, picture 270
Gazela Primeiro, U.S. barkentine 55
Geller, Arnold, American photography contest winner
Autumn Rest, photograph 218
Gemini 4, spacecraft 90
Gems
Hall of Minerals and Gems, American Museum of Natural History 112–15
General Assembly, United Nations 29
Genetics
albino animals 279
gene, material that transmits inherited
characteristics 96, 97
Geneva Conference on Rhodesia 69
Geography
map making 122–23
Geology
earthquakes 116

Georgia
  Plains, President Carter's home 41
Géricault, Théodore, French artist 357
  painting by, picture 356
German Democratic Republic or **East Germany** 361
  Olympic Games 304, 14
Germany, Federal Republic of or **West Germany** 361
  Olympic Games 304
  Operation Sail 54, 55
  Schmidt's visit to the United States 58
Ghana 361
  Girl Guide, picture 224
Girl Scouts and Girl Guides 224–27
Giscard d'Estaing, Valéry, French president
  United States, visit to 57
Gloria, Colombian bark 55
Goddard, Robert H., American physicist 100
Goddard Space Flight Center, Greenbelt, Maryland 100
Golf, sport 319
Gorch Fock, German bark 54, 55
  poster, picture 189
Gorilla, animal
  albino gorilla, pictures 268–69, 280
Grammy awards, music 343
Granada, Spain
  fountains 192; picture 190
Grant, Lee, American actress 344; picture 345
Grant, Ulysses S., U.S. president 51, 52
Great Britain or **United Kingdom of Great Britain
  and Northern Ireland** 365, 11
  Bicentennial exhibitions 59
  Britten, Benjamin, death of 34
  Christie, Dame Agatha, death of 12
  Concorde, supersonic transport plane 101
  drought 117
  Elizabeth II's visit to United States 56, 57
  Liverpool's Tilting Fountain 194–95
  Montgomery, Field Marshal Viscount, death of 17
  Northern Ireland 70–71
  Olympic Games 304
  Operation Sail 55
  posters 184
  Reuters news agency 155
  stamps 149
  Wilson, Harold, resignation of 16
Greece 361
  horses in art 354
  springs and fountains 191–92
  stamps 149
Greenland
  stamps 149
Grenada 362
Griffon, ship 176–77
Guadeloupe, island, Caribbean
  La Soufrière, volcano 27, 116; picture 26
Guatemala 362
  earthquake 14, 116; picture 15
Guerrilla activities, undercover warfare
  Rhodesia 69
Guinea 362
Guinea-Bissau 362
Gullager, Christian, Danish painter 58
Guyana 362
Gymnastics, sport
  Comaneci, Nadia 210
  Olympic Games 303, 307

H

Habitat or **Conference on Human Settlements,**
  Vancouver, Canada 22

  commemorative stamps 149
  Girl Guides 227
Haida Indians 156–57
Haiti 362
  coins 128
Hall of Minerals and Gems, American Museum of
    Natural History, New York City 112–15
Hamill, Dorothy, American athlete 211, 299
Hancock-Clarke house, Lexington, Massachusetts,
    picture 46
Handball, sport
  Olympic Games 307
Handicrafts see Hobbies, handicrafts, and projects
Hanoi, Vietnam 24, 64
Harald, Norwegian crown prince
  United States, visit to 58
Harding, Warren G., U.S. president
  Laddie Boy, Airedale dog 290
Hare, animal
  Young Hare, painting by Albrecht Dürer 346–47
Harris, Fred, U.S. senator 37
Harris, Patricia R., U.S. public official 35
Hartford, Connecticut
  re-enactment of march of French troops, picture 49
Hawaii
  U.S. Geological Survey's new map 122
Hayes, Rutherford B., U.S. president
  Siamese cat 295
Hearst, Patricia, American kidnap victim 16
Heisman Trophy, football 318
Henrik, Danish prince
  United States, visit to 58
Her, President Lyndon B. Johnson's beagle 293
Here Fell Custer, painting, picture 199
Hijacking of airplanes 73–75
  Entebbe airport rescue operation, Uganda 24
Him, President Lyndon B. Johnson's beagle 293
Hobbies, handicrafts, and projects
  cooking supper, menu and recipes for 144–45
  energy game 143
  gift-wrapping paper 133
  literary quiz 139
  Loch Ness monster maze 127
  making a bird feeder 276–77
  making a book cover 140–41
  making giant dice 126
  making an ojo de Dios 136–38
  making pencil holders 134–35
  making a pomander 130
  making a rock necklace 142
  making a wood collage painting 132
  printing from nature 150–51
Hockey, sport 320–23
  Olympic Games 299, 305
Honduras 362
Hoosier Youth, The, statue of Lincoln 289; picture 288
Hopkins, Gerard Manley, English poet
  Pied Beauty, poem 251
Horses in art 354–57
  Cream Ponies, painting by George Stubbs 348–49
Howe, Gordie, Canadian athlete, picture 321
Hua Kuo-feng, Chinese premier 66
  Nixon's visit 15
Hubbard, Phil, American athlete, picture 315
Hughes, Howard, American industrialist 18
Hull, Bobby, Canadian athlete 321
Human Settlements, Conference on see Habitat
Humphrey, Hubert, U.S. senator 37
Hungary 362
  Olympic Games 304
Huron, Lake, Canada–United States
  ships 176–80
Hyde Park, New York
  Franklin D. Roosevelt's home 291, 292

Hydrogen, element
   nuclear fusion 87

I

Ibis, bird 284–85
Ice hockey, sport 320–23
   Olympic Games 299, 305
Iceland 362
Ice skating, sport 324
   Hamill, Dorothy 211
   Olympic Games 299, 305
Idaho
   flood 22
Ikhnaton, Egyptian pharaoh 118
Immunization, medicine
   swine influenza vaccination campaign 17, 35
Independence Day see Fourth of July
Independence Hall, Philadelphia, Pennsylvania,
   picture 45
Independence National Historical Park, Philadelphia,
   Pennsylvania 57
Independence Square, Philadelphia, Pennsylvania
   Liberty Bell 12
India 362
   archeology 119
   educational television 121
   gavial, reptile, picture 270
   horses in art 356
   Mother Teresa of Calcutta 196
   Pakistan, diplomatic relations with 20
   Ranger literacy campaign 226
   stamps 149
Indiana
   Fort Wayne statue of Lincoln, *The Hoosier Youth* 289;
     picture 288
Indians, American
   Cuna Indians 336–37
   Custer's Last Stand 197–99
   Deerfield Massacre 166
   Haida totem poles 156–57
   ojo de Dios, woven design 136–38
Indochina 64–65
Indonesia 362
   earthquake 25, 116
Influenza, disease
   swine influenza vaccination campaign 17, 35
Innsbruck, Austria
   Olympic Games 299, 14
Insects
   bees 287
International statistical supplement 360–65
INTERPHIL 76, international philatelic exhibition,
   Philadelphia, Pennsylvania 146
I.R.A. or **Irish Republican Army** 71
Iran 362
   Olympic Games 304
Iraq 362
Ireland 362
   Northern Irish conflict 71
Irian Jaya, province, Indonesia
   earthquake 25
Irish Republican Army 71
Israel 362
   Entebbe airport rescue operation 24, 73, 74
   Palestine Liberation Organization, U.N. debate with
     16; picture 17
   Scout Friendship Caravan 220
   Sinai desert territory returned to Egypt 15
Italy 67, 11, 362
   coin shortage 129
   earthquake 20, 116
   elections 22
   fountains 192, 193; pictures 190, 191
   Medici Chapel, Florence 154
   Olympic Games 304
   Operation Sail 55
   Venice 158–61
Ivory Coast 362

J

Jackson, Henry, U.S. senator 37
Jackson, Randy, American landsailing champion 203
Jade, mineral, picture 114
Jadeite, mineral, picture 115
Jamaica 362
   Olympic Games 304
Japan 362
   Fukuda, Takeo, becomes premier 35
   horses in art 356
   Little League World Series 313
   Olympic Games 304
   Operation Sail 54, 55
   rock crystal elephant, picture 115
Japanese flute, musical instrument 172–73
Jazz, music 343
Jeans, clothing 358; picture 359
Jefferson, Thomas, U.S. president
   Declaration of Independence 43
Jefferson Starship, The, American music group 339
Jenner, Bruce, American athlete 303, 327; picture 301
Jewelry
   Bicentennial Diamond Necklace, picture 115
   rock necklaces 142
Jip, Lincoln's foxhound 289
   Hoosier Youth, The, statue by Paul Manship,
     picture 288
John, Elton, British musician-composer 339
Johnson, Lyndon B., U.S. president
   pets 293
Jones, Randy, American athlete 311
Jo-Ni's Red Baron of Crofton, Lakeland terrier dog
   272, 273
Jordan 362
J particle, physics 31
Juan Carlos I, Spanish king 79
   United States, visit to 57
Juan Sebastian de Elcano, Spanish schooner 55
Juantorena, Alberto, Cuban athlete 303, 327;
   picture 302
Judo, sport
   Olympic Games 307
Juneau, capital of Alaska 32

K

Kampuchea see Cambodia
Kangaroo, animal
   albino kangaroo, picture 281
Kansas
   wheat field affected by drought, picture 18
Kansas City, Missouri
   Republican Convention 37
Kansas City Royals, baseball team 310, 312
Kapilvastu, ancient city, India 119
Kennedy, Mrs. Edward, wife of U.S. senator, picture 333
Kennedy, John F., U.S. president
   pets 292–93, 295

Kent, Rockwell, American artist 252
  Moby Dick, pictures 253–55
Kenya 362
Khieu Samphan, Cambodian chief of state 19
Khmer Republic see Cambodia
Kidnapping 74
King Kong, motion picture, picture 270
King Tut or **Tutankhamen,** Egyptian king 120
Kleiman, Mark, American mathematics student,
    picture 207
Knight, Donald, American photography contest winner
  Multiple Horseman, photograph 219
Koala bear, animal, picture 271
Korchnoi, Viktor, Russian chess grandmaster 25
Korea, Democratic People's Republic of or **North
    Korea** 362
  Olympic Games 304
Korea, Republic of or **South Korea** 362
  Olympic Games 304
Kosciusko, Thaddeus, Polish soldier 128
Kreiner, Kathy, Canadian athlete 299
Kreps, Juanita M., U.S. public official 35
Kruzenshtern, Soviet bark 54, 55
Kuwait 362

L

Laddie Boy, President Harding's dog 290
Lady Byng Trophy, hockey 322
Lafleur, Guy, Canadian athlete 320
Lakeland terrier, dog 272; picture 273
Lander, robot used in Viking missions to Mars 24, 83
Landsailing, sport 202–5
Landsat, artificial satellite 123
Laos 65, 362
Laser, physics 84
Laserium: The Cosmic Laser Concert 84–86; picture
    80–81
La Soufrière, volcano, Guadeloupe 27, 116; picture 26
Leach, Reggie, Canadian athlete 321; picture 323
Lebanon 76–77, 362
Legion fever, mystery disease of American Legion
    conventioneers 27
Leningrad, U.S.S.R., picture 195
Let's Make an Opera, composition by Britten 332
Lévesque, René, Canadian premier of Quebec 33
Levinson, Ron, American photography contest winner
  Carnival Excursion, A, photograph 216
Lexington, Massachusetts
  re-enactment of Paul Revere's ride, picture 46
Liberia 363
  Girl Guides 224
Libertad, Argentine ship 54, 55
Liberty, President Ford's dog 294
Liberty Bell 12, 57
Liberty nickel, U.S. coin 129
Libya 363
Liechtenstein 363
  Olympic Games 304
Lightning 87
Lincoln, Abraham, U.S. president
  assassination reported by Reuters news agency 155
  pets 288–89, 295
Lippold, Richard, American sculptor
  Sun, The, sculpture, picture 92
Lipscomb, William N., Jr., American chemist 31
Liquid-fueled rockets 100, 88–89
Literacy
  Girl Guide and Girl Scout projects 226
  Soviet literacy-campaign poster, picture 187

Literature
  Christie, Dame Agatha, death of 12
  Malraux, André, death of 33
  Nobel prize 31
  quiz 139
  See also Young people's literature
Little Bighorn, Battle of the 197–99
Little League Baseball 313
Little Preludes, Inventions and Symphonies,
    compositions by Bach 331
Little Sweep, The, composition by Britten 332
Live and Let Live, story 240–47
Liverpool, England
  Tilting Fountain 194–95
Loch Ness monster 110–11
Loch Ness monster maze 127
London, England
  Reuters news agency 155
López Portillo, José, Mexican president 24
Louisiana
  New Orleans' National Explorer Sailing
    Championship 223
Lovejoy Plaza, Portland, Oregon 195; picture 194
Lowell, Amy, American poet
  Night Clouds, poem 251
Luanda, capital of Angola 61
Luge, sport
  Olympic Games 305
Luxembourg 363

M

Maass, Clara, American nurse
  commemorative stamp 149
Macaulay, David, British-American writer and illustrator
  Underground, book, picture 260
Madagascar or **Malagasy Republic** 363
Madlock, Bill, American athlete 310, 312
Magic Flute, The, opera by Mozart 331
Magna Carta, English charter of liberties 56
Magnetic Hill, New Brunswick, Canada 105; picture 104
Malagasy Republic see Madagascar
Malawi 363
Malaysia 363
Maldives 363
Mali 363
Malraux, André, French writer and political leader 33
Malta 363
Mammal, animal
  cloning 97–98
Mammoth, animal
  cloning 99
Manship, Paul, American sculptor
  Hoosier Youth, The, statue of Lincoln 289; picture 288
Mao Tse-tung, Chinese Communist Party chairman 66,
    28; picture 29
Maps 122–23
Margrethe II, Danish queen
  Denmark's Fourth of July Festival 59
  United States, visit to 58
Mars, planet 82–83
  Viking I landing 24
  Viking II landing 28
Marshall, F. Ray, U.S. public official 35
Maryland
  Goddard Space Flight Center, Greenbelt 100
Massachusetts
  Arrowhead, Melville's home 252
  Deerfield 166–69
  oil spill 34
  re-enactment of Paul Revere's ride, picture 46

Mathematical Olympiad
Kleiman, Mark, winner, picture 207
Mathematics
calculators 94
Matthau, Walter, American actor, picture 207
Mauritania 363
Mauritius 363
Mayfield, Curtis, American musician and composer 339
McCall, Robert, American painter
Space Mural—A Cosmic View, The, mural, picture 91
McCarthy, Eugene, U.S. political leader 36
McCartney, Paul, British musician and composer 338, 340
Medici Chapel, Florence, Italy 154
Medicine
American Legion conventioneers' illness 27
biofeedback 107
Nobel prizes 31
organ transplants 99
swine influenza vaccination campaign 17, 35
Melbourne, Australia
Boy Scout meeting 220
Melville, Herman, American writer
Moby Dick 252–55
Memorial Hall, Philadelphia, Pennsylvania
Bicentennial birthday cake, picture 47
Méndez, Aparicio, Uruguayan president 22
Menotti, Gian Carlo, Italian-American composer 332, 334
Mesopotamia
Bronze Age 108–9
Metropolitan Museum of Art, New York City
Cloisters' Medieval Festival 206
Mexico 363
election 24
Olympic Games 304
Michelangelo, Italian artist 154
Micombero, Michel, Burundi president 32
Middle Ages
Community Medieval Festival, New York City 206
fountains 192
horses in art 356
Middle East 76–77
Lebanon 76–77
Sinai desert territory returned to Egypt 15
MiG-25, Soviet airplane 28
Miki, Takeo, Japanese premier 35
Minerals
Hall of Minerals and Gems, American Museum of Natural History 112–15
Minnesota Vikings, football team 316, 318
Mircea, Rumanian bark 55
Missouri
Republican Convention, Kansas City 37
Mittermaier, Rosi, German athlete 299; picture 298
Mobile, sculpture 32; picture 33
Moby Dick, novel by Herman Melville 252–55
narwhal tusk 275
Modern pentathlon, sport
Olympic Games 307
Mohammed, Murtala Ramat, Nigerian head of state 14
Mola, Cuna Indian embroidery 336–37
Monaco 363
Mondale, Joan, wife of U.S. vice-president, picture 36
Mondale, Walter F. ("Fritz"), U.S. vice-president 32, 37, 38; picture 36
Money
coin collecting 128–29
two dollar bills 10
Mongolia 363
Olympic Games 304
Montana
Custer's Last Stand 197–99
Montgomery, Bernard Law, British field marshal 17
Montgomery, Jim, American athlete 303

Montreal, Canada
Château Ramezay 174–75
Olympic Games 300
Montreal Canadiens, hockey team 320, 322
Moors, North African people
art and architecture 192; picture 190
Morgan, Joe, American athlete 311, 312
Morocco 363
Mother Teresa, Albanian missionary in India 196
Motion pictures
Academy Awards 344–45
Bad News Bears, The, picture 207
King Kong, picture 270
To Fly, film of airborne tour of the U.S. 93
Movies see Motion pictures
Mozambique 363
Rhodesian crisis 69
Mozart, Wolfgang Amadeus, Austrian composer 331
Mucha, Alphonse, Czech artist
posters 183–84
Mummy, preserved body 120
Munson, Thurman, American athlete 310, 311, 312
Murdock, Margaret, American athlete 304
Murphy, Walter, American musician 340
Museum of American Folk Art, New York City
Cat in American Folk Art, exhibition 352; pictures 328–29, 353
Museums
Arrowhead, Melville's home 252
Bicentennial exhibitions 57, 58, 59
Cloisters, New York City 206
Deerfield, Massachusetts 166, 169
Hall of Minerals and Gems, American Museum of Natural History 112–15
Museum of American Folk Art, New York City 352
National Air and Space Museum, Washington, D.C. 90–93
Music 338–43
Bicentennial performances 58
Britten, Benjamin, death of 34
Laserium show 84–86
Robeson, Paul, death of 13
shakuhachi, Japanese flute 172–73
young people's music 330–35
Muslims, followers of the Islamic religion
Lebanon 76, 77
Muybridge, Eadward, Anglo-American photographer 357

N

Naber, John, American athlete 300, 325
Namibia or South West Africa 72
Nancy, ship 177–78
Nantucket Island, Massachusetts
oil spill 34
Narwhal, whale 274–75
NASA or National Aeronautics and Space Administration
space shuttle 88–89
Nash, Ogden, American poet 331
Nastase, Ilie, Rumanian athlete 326
National Aeronautics and Space Administration
space shuttle 88–89
National Air and Space Museum, Washington, D.C. 90–93
National Basketball Association 314, 315
National Collegiate Athletic Association 314
National Football League 316, 318
National Hockey League 320, 322
National Invitation Tournament, basketball 315
Nationalists, Spanish political faction 79
National League, baseball 310–12
National Maritime Museum, Greenwich, England 59

National Portrait Gallery, Washington, D.C.
  Bicentennial exhibition 58
National Zoo, Washington, D.C.
  Smokey Bear, picture 271
NATO or **North Atlantic Treaty Organization**
  Strausz-Hupe, Robert, U.S. ambassador 15
Nauru 363
Needlework
  embroidered designs on clothes 358; pictures 359
  molas, Cuna Indian embroidery 336–37
  tapestry, picture 124–25
Nelson, Willie, American musician 341; picture 340
Nemeth, Miklos, Hungarian athlete 327
Nepal 363
Ness, Loch, lake, Scotland 110–11
Netherlands 363
  Olympic Games 304
Netherlands Antilles
  coins 128
Neto, Agostinho, president of Angola 61
New Brunswick, province, Canada
  Magnetic Hill 105; picture 104
  tidal bore 105; picture 104
New Jersey
  Explorer Scouts, picture 221
  Operation Sail 54–55
New Orleans, Louisiana
  National Explorer Sailing Championship 223
New York, state
  Girl Scout gardening project, Suffolk County 225–26;
    picture 227
  Hyde Park home of Franklin D. Roosevelt 291, 292
  Oyster Bay home of Theodore Roosevelt 289
  See also New York City
New York City, New York
  Community Medieval Festival 206
  Democratic Convention 37
  Ellis Island re-opened 21
  Hall of Minerals and Gems, American Museum of
    Natural History 112–15
  National Council of the Boy Scouts of America 223
  Operation Sail 54–55
  posters, picture 182
  tapestry depicting skyline, picture 124–25
New York City Ballet, pictures 260, 332
New York Nets, basketball team 314, 315
New York Yankees, baseball team 310–12
New Zealand 363
  Olympic Games 300, 304
NFL or **National Football League** 316, 318
Nicaragua 363
  coins 128
  stamps 149
Nicholas, Saint, bishop of Myra 331–32
Nicholson, Jack, American actor 344; picture 345
Niger 363
Nigeria 363
  Mohammed, Murtala Ramat, assassination of 14
Nippon Maru, Japanese bark 54, 55
Nixon, Richard M., former U.S. president
  China, visit to 15
Noah, Operation, animal-rescue project 278
Nobel prizes 31
Noise
  supersonic aircraft 101
Nonaligned nations, Conference of, Colombo, Sri Lanka
  26
Norodom Sihanouk, Cambodian chief of state 19
Norris Trophy, hockey 322
North Atlantic Treaty Organization
  Strausz-Hupe, Robert, U.S. ambassador 15
Northern Ireland 70–71, 11
  terrorism 74
  See also Great Britain

Northern lights or **Aurora borealis** 102
North Korea see Korea, Democratic People's Republic of
Norway 363
  Harald and Sonja's visit to the United States 58
  Olympic Games 304
  Operation Sail 55
Noye's Fludde, composition by Britten 332
  church production, picture 333
Nuclear energy
  production by fusion 87
Nuclear explosions treaty, U.S.–U.S.S.R. 21
Numismatics or **Coin collecting** 128–29
Nutcracker, The, book by Martha Swope, picture 260
Nutrition
  Girl Guide projects 224, 225

O

Oakland Raiders, football team 316, 318
Obasanjo, Olusegun, Nigerian head of state 14
Ochs, Phil, American musician-composer 343
Ohio
  albino rattlesnake in Cincinnati zoo, picture 280
Oil spill
  Argo Merchant 34
Ojos de Dios, Indian woven designs 136–38
O'Keeffe, Adelaide, British poet
  Kite, The, poem 250
Olga, Typhoon 21, 116
Olympic Games 298–309, 14, 26
  Boy Scouts 223
  closing ceremonies, picture 296–97
  coins 128, 129
  Comaneci, Nadia 210
  Hamill, Dorothy 211
  posters 187; picture 189
  stamps 149
  terrorism at 1972 Games 74
Oman 363
O'Neal, Tatum, American actress, picture 207
One Flew over the Cuckoo's Nest, motion picture 344;
    picture 345
Ontario, province, Canada
  Olympiad for the Physically Disabled 149
  Upper Canada Village 162–63
Opal, mineral, picture 113
Operation Noah, animal-rescue project 278
Operation Sail 54–55
  posters 187; picture 189
Orbiter, space shuttle component 88, 89
Orange Bowl, football game 318
Oregon
  Portland's Lovejoy Plaza 195; picture 194
Orr, Bobby, Canadian athlete 322

P

Painting see Art
Pakistan 364
  Girl Guides 225
  India, diplomatic relations with 20
  Olympic Games 304
  stamps 149
Palestine Liberation Organization or **PLO**
  Israel's U.N. debate with 16; picture 17
  Lebanon 77; picture 76
Palestinian refugees
  Lebanon 77

Palme, Olof, Swedish prime minister 29
Palmer, Arnold, American golfer
  around-the-world jet flight 20
Palmer, Jim, American athlete 311, 312
Panama 364
  Cuna Indians 336–37
  Girl Guides 225
  Operation Noah, animal-rescue project 278
Papua New Guinea 364
  Girl Guide educational project 226
Paraguay 364
Paris, France
  fountains 193
  posters on kiosk, picture 182
Park Phaeton with a Pair of Cream Ponies in Charge
    of a Stable-Lad with a Dog, painting by George
    Stubbs 348–49
Parrish, Maxfield, American artist
  posters 184
Pathet Lao, Laotian Communists 65
Peacock, bird
  albino peacock, picture 279
Peking, China 116; picture 25
Penfield, Edward, American artist
  posters 184
Pennsylvania
  Bicentennial Wagon Train, picture 48
  Williamsport's Little League World Series 313
  Woodward Township School, picture 48
  See also Philadelphia
Pentathlon, sports
  Olympic Games 307
Perón, Isabel Martínez de, Argentine president 17
Persian art
  horses 356; picture 355
  Moorish courts of Spain 192
Peru 364
Peter I or Peter the Great, Russian Czar
  Leningrad's fountain, picture 195
Peter and the Wolf, composition by Prokofiev 332, 334;
    picture 333
Petitcodiac River, New Brunswick, Canada
  tidal bore 105; picture 104
Pets of U.S. presidents 288–95
Phaeton, carriage 348
Philadelphia, Pennsylvania
  American Legion conventioneers' illness 27
  Bicentennial birthday cake, picture 47
  Centennial Exposition, 1876 51, 44–45
  Elizabeth II's visit 56, 57
  first Fourth of July 42–43
  Independence Hall, picture 45
  INTERPHIL 76, philatelic exhibition 146
  Liberty Bell 12
  presidential candidates' debate 39
Philadelphia Flyers, hockey team 320, 322
Philadelphia Phillies, baseball team 310, 312
Philately see Stamp collecting
Philip, Prince, husband of Queen Elizabeth II of Britain
  United States, visit to 57
Philippines 364
  earthquake 26
  tsunami or tidal wave 116
  typhoon 21, 116
Phoenix Suns, basketball team 314, 315
Photography
  Eakins, Thomas 350; picture 351
  Landsat's photographs of earth 123
  Muybridge's horse photographs 357
  Nutcracker, The, book by Martha Swope, picture 260
  posters 184; picture 152–53
  Scholastic Photography Awards, pictures 200–1,
    216–19
  underwater 110–11

Physics, Nobel prizes in 31
Physiology or medicine, Nobel prizes in 31
Piazza San Marco, Venice, Italy, picture 159
Picking Flowers, folk painting, picture 353
Picture books 228–29, 260–61
Pioneers
  Children Headed West, story 230–39
  modern pioneers 170–73
Pittsburgh Steelers, football team 316, 318
Pittsfield, Massachusetts
  Arrowhead, Melville's home 252
Plains, Georgia 41
Planetarium
  National Air and Space Museum 93
Plants
  asexual reproduction 96–97
  community gardens 214–15
  stamps 149
Plasma, state of matter
  ball lightning 87
PLO see Palestine Liberation Organization
Ploughboy, ship 179; picture 178
Pnompenh, capital of Cambodia 65
Pocumtuck Indians 166
Poetry 248–51
Poirot, Hercule, fictional character 12
Poland 364
  beehives 286–87
  coins 128, 129
  Olympic Games 304
  Operation Sail 55
Pollution
  Venice, Italy 158; picture 161
Polo, sport
  ancient China 355
Pomander, scented ball 130
Pomegranate, mobile by Calder, picture 33
Pompeii, Italy
  fountains 192; picture 191
Pony, animal
  Cream Ponies, painting by George Stubbs 348–49
Popular Movement for the Liberation of Angola 61
Portland, Oregon
  Lovejoy Plaza 195; picture 194
Portugal 78, 11, 364
  Angola 61
  elections 19, 23
  Olympic Games 304
  Operation Sail 54, 55
Postage stamps see Stamp collecting
Posters 182–89
  Belgian poster of 1896, picture 152–53
Pottery
  Bronze Age pottery found in Thailand 108–9
  Chinese 355
Presidents of the United States
  elections of 1976 36–40
  pets 288–95
Primary elections, United States 37
Printing
  posters 183
  stamps 149
Printing from nature 150–51
Prizes and awards
  Academy Awards, motion pictures 344
  baseball 310, 311
  basketball 314
  football 318
  golf 319
  Grammy awards, music 343
  hockey 322
  landsailing 203
  Nobel prizes 31
  Olympic Games 304

photography 200–1, 216–19
  skiing 324
  tennis 326
  Westminster Kennel Club show 272–73
Prokofiev, Sergei, Russian composer 332–34
Protestantism
  Northern Ireland 70–71
Psi particle, physics 31
Puerto Rico
  Olympic Games 304
Pulaski, Casimir, Polish soldier 128

Q

Qatar 364
Quartz, mineral, picture 115
Quebec, province, Canada
  Bonaventure Island 103
  Lévesque, René, elected premier 33
  Montreal's Château Ramezay 174–75
  Ste. Anne de Beaupré 181
  Venturers, Boy Scouts, picture 220
Queen Charlotte Islands, Canada
  Haida Indians 156
Queen Elizabeth Park, Vancouver, British Columbia, Canada 105
Quizzes
  literature 139
  well-known parents and children 131

R

Radio
  CB or Citizens Band 106
Ramezay, Château, Montreal, Canada 174–75
Ramezay, Claude de, French governor of Montreal, Canada 174
Rangers, Girl Scouts, picture 227
  literacy project, India 226
Rattlesnake, reptile
  albino diamondback, picture 280
Ravel, Maurice, French composer 331
Reagan, Ronald, U.S. political leader 37, 38, 40
Recipes 144–45
Refugees
  Indochina 64
  Palestinian refugees in Lebanon 77
Religion
  Buddha's ashes found 119
  Lebanon 76, 77
  Mother Teresa 196
  Northern Ireland 70–71
  rock churches, Cappadocia, Turkey 165; picture 164
  Ste. Anne de Beaupré, Quebec, Canada 181
  women, ordination of 28
Remington, Frederic, American artist 357
  Bronco Buster, sculpture, picture 356
Renaissance art and architecture
  Dürer, Albrecht 346–51
  fountains 192–94
  horses 356
Reproduction, biology 96–99
Republican Party, U.S. 36–40
  convention, picture 38
Reuter, Paul Julius, German-born founder of Reuters news agency 155
Revere, Paul, American patriot and silversmith
  re-enactment of ride, picture 46

Revolutionary War, U.S. history
  commemorative stamps 146
  re-enactments, pictures 46, 49
Rhodesia 69, 68, 11, 364
  blacks named to Cabinet 19
Richard, Cliff, British musician 342
Richter, Burton, American physicist 31
Rines, Robert H., American scientist 110
Robeson, Paul, American actor and singer 13
Robin, bird
  albino robin, picture 282
Rochambeau, Comte de, French general
  re-enactment of Revolutionary War march, picture 49
Rock crystal, mineral, picture 115
Rockefeller, Nelson A., U.S. vice-president
  Australia, visit to 59
Rockets 100
  National Air and Space Museum 93; picture 92
  space shuttle launching 88–89
Rock formations
  Cappadocia, Turkey 165; pictures 164
Rodríguez Lara, Guillermo, president of Ecuador 12
Rojtman Diamond, gem, picture 114
Rolling Thunder Revue, concert series 340
Roman Catholic Church
  Mother Teresa 196
  Northern Ireland 70–71
  Ste. Anne de Beaupré, Quebec, Canada 181
Rome, Italy
  fountains 192, 193; picture 190
  horses in ancient Rome 355
Ronstadt, Linda, American singer 340
Roosevelt, Franklin Delano, U.S. president
  Fala, Scottish terrier 291–92
Roosevelt, Theodore, U.S. president
  pets 289–90, 295
Rose Bowl, football game 318
Rose quartz, mineral, picture 115
Ross Trophy, hockey 320
Rowing, sport
  Olympic Games 303, 307
Rumania 364
  Comaneci, Nadia 210
  Olympic Games 304
  Operation Sail 55
Russia see Union of Soviet Socialist Republics
Rwanda 364

S

Sager, Catherine ("Katy"), American pioneer 230–39
Sagres II, Portuguese bark 54, 55
Sailboat regatta, Quebec, picture 220
Sainte Anne de Beaupré, Canada 181
Saint Nicholas, cantata by Britten 331–32
Saint-Saëns, Camille, French composer 331
Salsa, music 343
Salyut 5, Soviet space station 27
San Agustín, Colombia 119
San Diego Zoo, California
  koala bears, picture 271
San Francisco, California
  presidential candidates' debate 39–40
San Lorenzo, Church of, Florence, Italy 154
San Marco, Piazza, Venice, Italy, picture 159
San Salvador, capital of El Salvador
  Girl Guide literacy project 227
Santa Claus 332
Santiago, Panama
  Girl Guide nutrition project 225
São Tomé and Príncipe 364

Sapphire, mineral, pictures 113, 114
Sarkis, Elias, Lebanese president 76, 77
Satellites, Artificial
 ATS-6 121
 Communications Technology Satellite 13
 Landsat 123
 National Air and Space Museum 93
 Salyut 5, Soviet space station 27
 space shuttle 88–89
Saudi Arabia 364
Savannah, Seige of, 1779
 commemorative coins 128
Sawyer, Tom, literary character 256–59
Schmidt, Helmut, German chancellor
 United States, visit to 58
Schnepf, Jim, American photography contest winner
 Break Thru, photograph 219
Scholastic Photography Awards 216; pictures 200–1, 216–19
Schroeder, Becky J., American student and inventor, picture 208
Scotland
 Loch Ness monster 110–11
 See also Great Britain
Scranton, William W., U.S. representative to the United Nations 15
Scuba diving, sport
 Boy Scouts 223
Sculpture *see* Art
SEATO or **Southeast Asia Treaty Organization** 15
Security Council, United Nations
 Israel-PLO debate 16; picture 17
Segregation
 South Africa 68, 69
Semenova, Yuliana, Soviet athlete 303
Semitic languages
 Eblaites, ancient people 118
Senegal 364
Seni Pramoj, Thai premier 30
Sesame Street, television program
 Big Bird, picture 310
Sexual reproduction, biology 96
Seychelles 62–63, 23, 364
Shakuhachi, Japanese flute 170–73
Shan, Susan Ford's Siamese cat 294, 295
Ships
 Andrew Doria 128
 Argo Merchant's oil spill 34
 Griffon, La Salle's ship 176–77
 Nancy, Canadian schooner 177–78
 Operation Sail 54–55; picture 189
 Ploughboy, Canadian steamer 179; picture 178
 stamps 146
 Sylvia L. Ossa 30
 Waubuno, Canadian steamer 180; picture 179
Shoemaker, Scott, American photography contest winner
 Indianapolis at Night, photograph 217
Shooting events, sports
 Olympic Games 304, 307
Siamese cat 295
Sierra Leone 364
Sihanouk, Norodom, Cambodian chief of state 19
Silver dollar, Canadian coin 129
Silver dollar, U.S. coin 129
Simon, Paul, American singer and composer 338
Simpson, O. J., American athlete 316
Sinai, region, Middle East 15
Singapore 364
Sioux Indians
 Custer's Last Stand 197–99
Sir Winston Churchill, British ship 55
SITE or **Satellite Instructional Television Experiment,** India 121

Sitting Bull, American Indian leader 199
Sittler, Darryl, Canadian athlete 322
Skating 324
 Hamill, Dorothy 211
 Olympic Games 299, 305
Skiing, sport 324
 Olympic Games 299, 305, 14
Skylab Orbital Workshop 93
Sloth, animal, picture 278
Smart, Christopher, English poet
 Hymn for Saturday, poem 250
Smith, Ian, Rhodesian prime minister 19
Smith, Patti, American musician 342
Smithsonian Institution, Washington, D.C.
 Bicentennial exhibitions 53, 57, 58
 National Air and Space Museum 90–93
 statue of Laddie Boy, Harding's dog 290
Smokey Bear, picture 271
Snake, reptile
 albino rattlesnake, picture 280
Soap Box Derby
 Ferdinand, Joan, winner, picture 209
Soares, Mário, Portuguese premier 19, 23, 78
Soccer, sport
 National Explorer Olympics, picture 222
 Olympic Games 308
Social Democratic Party, Sweden 29, 67
Socialist Party, Portugal 78
Solar system, picture 95
Solid-fueled rockets 100
 space shuttle 88–89
Somalia 364
Sonar, system for sending and receiving underwater sound 111
Sonja, Norwegian crown princess
 United States, visit to 58
Sophia, Spanish queen, picture 79
 United States, visit to 57
Soufrière, La, volcano, Guadeloupe 27, 116; picture 26
South Africa 69, 68, 364
 Namibia 72
 Transkei 30
Southeast Asia
 Indochina 64–65
Southeast Asia Treaty Organization 15
Southern lights or **Aurora australis** 102
South Korea *see* Korea, Republic of
South West Africa *see* Namibia
South West Africa People's Organization 72
Soviet Union *see* Union of Soviet Socialist Republics
Soweto, South Africa 69; picture 68
Soyuz 21, Soviet spacecraft 27
Soyuz 22, Soviet spacecraft 29
Space exploration, picture 95
 Communications Technology Satellite 13
 National Air and Space Museum 90–93
 rockets 100
 space shuttle 88–89
 U.S.S.R. 27, 29
 Viking missions to Mars 24, 28, 83
Space Mural—A Cosmic View, The, mural by McCall, picture 91
Space shuttle, spacecraft 88–89
Space station
 U.S.S.R.'s Salyut 5 27
Spain 79, 78, 364
 Altamira cave drawings 354
 Barcelona zoo's albino gorilla, pictures 268–69, 280
 Basques 74; picture 75
 Juan Carlos I's visit to United States 57
 Moorish architecture 192; picture 190
 Olympic Games 304
 Operation Sail 55
Spanish Civil War, 1936–1939 79

Special Birthday, A, book by Symeon Shimin, picture 228–29
Speed skating, sport 324
   Olympic Games 299, 305
Spirit of St. Louis, airplane 90
Spirit of '76, The, painting by Willard 146
Sports
   baseball 310–12
   basketball 314–15
   football 316–18
   golf 319
   hockey 320–23
   ice skating 324
   landsailing 202–5
   Little League baseball 313
   National Explorer Olympics, Scout events 223
   Olympic Games 298–309
   posters 187
   skiing 324
   stamps 149
   swimming 325
   tennis 326
   track and field 327
Sputnik I, Soviet satellite 93
Squirrel
   albino squirrel, picture 282
Sri Lanka or **Ceylon** 364
   conference of nonaligned nations 26
   Girl Guide sewing class, picture 226
SST or **Supersonic transport,** aircraft 21, 101
Stabile, sculpture 32
Stamp collecting 146–49
Stanley Cup, hockey trophy 320
Star of India, sapphire, picture 114
Statistics, International 360–65
Statues, Forest of the, archeological site, Colombia 119
Steamships 178–79
Stories
   Adventures of Tom Sawyer, The, novel by Mark Twain 256–59
   Children Headed West 230–39
   Live and Let Live 240–47
   Moby Dick, novel by Melville 253–55
   Strong Voice, The 262–67
   Why the Bear's Tail Is So Short 283
Strausz-Hupe, Robert, U.S. ambassador to NATO 15
Streisand, Barbra, American singer and actress 340
Strong Voice, The, Swedish story 262–67
Stubbs, George, English painter 346, 356
   Cream Ponies, painting 348–49
Subatomic particles, physics
   psi or J particle 31
Sublette, Kansas
   wheat field affected by drought, picture 18
Sudan 364
Sugar Bowl, football game 318
Sun, The, sculpture by Lippold, picture 92
Sung dynasty, China 355
Super Bowl, football game 316, 318
Supersonic transport, aircraft 21, 101
Supreme Court, U.S.
   capital punishment upheld 24
Surinam 364
Surrender of Lord Cornwallis, The, painting by Trumbull 146
Swaziland 364
Sweden 67, 11, 364
   Carl XVI Gustaf's visit to United States 58
   elections 29
   Olympic Games 304
Swimming, sport 325
   Olympic Games 300, 308
Swine influenza, disease
   vaccination campaign 17, 35

Switzerland 365
   Olympic Games 304
   toy exhibition in the United States 58; picture 59
Swope, Martha, American photographer
   Nutcracker, The, book, picture 260
Sylvia L. Ossa, cargo ship 30
Syria 365
   Ebla, ancient kingdom 118
   Lebanese civil war, intervention in 77

T

Taiwan or **Nationalist China** 365
   Olympic Games 300
Tall Ships
   Operation Sail 54–55
Tangshan, China
   earthquake 25, 116
Tanzania 365
Tapestry
   New York City skyline, picture 124–25
Tardiff, Marc, Canadian athlete 321
Team Canada, hockey team 321
Television
   Amahl and the Night Visitors, opera by Menotti 334
   France's Revolutionary War series 59
   India's educational programs 121
   music 339
   political debates 39–40
Tennis, sport 326
Teresa, Mother, Albanian missionary in India 196
Terrorism 73–75
   Northern Ireland 70–71
Teton Dam, Idaho 22
Texas
   Austin's National Explorer Olympics winner 223
Thailand 365
   Bronze Age artifacts found in Ban Chiang 108–9
   Indochinese refugees 64
   military coup 30
   Olympic Games 304
Thanin Kraivichien, Thai premier 30
Thebes, Egypt
   archeology 118
Thompson, David, American athlete 314
Thunderstorms
   lightning 87
Tidal bore, Bay of Fundy 105; picture 104
Tiger, animal
   albino tiger, picture 281
Tilting Fountain, Liverpool, England 194–95
Ting, Samuel C. C., American physicist 31
Tiy, Egyptian queen 120
Togo 365
Tokyo, Japan
   Little League World Series 313
Tom Sawyer, The Adventures of, novel by Mark Twain 256–59
Tonga 365
Totem poles 156–57
Toulouse-Lautrec, Henri de, French artist 357
   posters 183
Tovarishch, Soviet bark 55
Toys
   Swiss exhibition in the United States 58; picture 59
Track and field, sports 327
   Olympic Games 303, 308–9
Transceiver, radio set 106
Transkei 30, 69
Transportation, U.S. Department of
   Concorde controversy 101

Travolta, John, American singer and actor 339
Trevi fountain, Rome, Italy, picture 190
Trinidad and Tobago 365
  Boy Scouts 220
  Olympic Games 304
Trudeau, Pierre Elliott, Canadian prime minister
  Latin America, visit to 13
  United States, visit to 58
Trumbull, John, American artist
  Bicentennial stamps 146
Tsumura, Kiyoshi, Japanese athlete 313
Tsunami or **Tidal wave** 116
TU-144, Soviet airplane 101
Tunisia 365
Turkey 365
  Cappadocia 165; pictures 164
  earthquake 33
  Girl Guide literacy programs 226
  ibises of Birecik 284–85
Turks and Caicos Islands
  coins 128
Tutankhamen or **King Tut,** Egyptian king 120
Twain, Mark, American writer
  Adventures of Tom Sawyer, The, novel 256–59
Two-dollar bill, U.S. money 18, 129
Two-toed sloth, animal, picture 278
Tyger Voyage, The, book by Richard Adams, picture 261
Typhoon Olga
  Philippines 21, 116

U

Udall, Morris, U.S. congressman 37
Uganda 365
  Entebbe airport rescue operation 24, 73, 74
Ulster see Northern Ireland
U.N. see United Nations
Underground, book by David Macaulay, picture 260
Underground nuclear explosions treaty, U.S.–U.S.S.R. 21
Underwater photography
  Loch Ness monster 110–11
UNESCO see United Nations Educational, Scientific and
    Cultural Organization
Unicorn, mythical animal 274
Union of Soviet Socialist Republics 365
  fountain, Leningrad, picture 195
  MiG-25, jet fighter plane 28
  nuclear explosions treaty with U.S. 21
  Olympic Games 304, 14
  Operation Sail 54, 55
  posters 187
  Rhodesian crisis 69
  space exploration 27, 29
  TU-144, Soviet airplane 101
United Arab Emirates 365
United Kingdom see Great Britain
United Nations
  Angola 23, 34
  General Assembly session 29
  Girl Scouts and Girl Guides 224
  Habitat or Conference on Human Settlements 22
  Israel–Palestine Liberation Organization debate 16;
    picture 17
  Namibia or South West Africa 72
  Scranton, William W., U.S. representative 15
  stamp 149
  Western Samoa 34
  Young, Andrew J., Jr., U.S. representative 35
**United Nations Educational, Scientific and Cultural Or-
ganization**
  Cooperative Action Programme 224

United States 365, 11
  Bicentennial observances by other nations 56–59
  cabinet selected by Carter 35
  Carter, James Earl, Jr. 41
  Centennial Exposition 50–53
  coins 129
  Custer's Last Stand 197–99
  elections 36–40
  Fourth of July celebrations 42–45
  Girl Scouts 225–26, 227
  important events of 1976 12–35
  Indochinese refugees 64
  map making 122–23
  Olympic Games 304
  posters 184, 187; pictures 182, 186, 188, 189
  Rhodesian crisis 69
  stamps 146, 149
  Vietnam 64
United States Alpine Championships, skiing 324
United States Open, tennis tournament 326
Upper Canada Village, Ontario 162–63
Upper Volta 365
Uruguay 365
  Bordaberry removed from office 22
Usery, Willie Julian, Jr., U.S. public official 13
U.S.S.R. see Union of Soviet Socialist Republics

V

Vaccination, medicine
  swine influenza immunization campaign 17, 35
Valley Forge, Pennsylvania
  Bicentennial Wagon Train, picture 48
Vance, Cyrus R., U.S. public official 35
Vancouver, British Columbia, Canada 105
  Habitat conference 22
  totem pole, picture 157
Venezuela 365
  Olympic Games 304
Venice, Italy 158–61
Venturers, Canadian Boy Scouts, picture 220
Versailles, palace, France
  fountains 193–94
Vezina Trophy, hockey 321
Victoria, capital of Seychelles 62, 63
Victoria and Albert Museum, London, England 59
Videla, Jorge, Argentine president 17
Vienna Boys' Choir 331; picture 330
Vietnam 64–65, 365
  north and south reunited 24
Viking I, spacecraft 24, 83
Viking II, spacecraft 28, 83
Vin Fiz, airplane 93
Viren, Lasse, Finnish athlete 303
Volcano
  La Soufrière, Guadeloupe 27, 116; picture 26
Volleyball, sport
  National Explorer Olympics, picture 222
  Olympic Games 309
Volynov, Boris, Soviet cosmonaut, picture 27

W

Wales see Great Britain
Walker, John, New Zealand athlete 303, 327
Wallace, George C., U.S. governor 37
Walsh, James C., American leader of Operation Noah
  278

Washington, state
    Bremerton's colonial classroom, picture 47
Washington, D.C.
    American Bicentennial Parade, picture 46
    Bicentennial exhibitions 57, 58
    Eagle Scout Bicentennial Celebration 221
    National Air and Space Museum 90–93
    National Zoo's Smokey Bear, picture 271
    Smithsonian's re-creation of the Centennial Exposition
      53
Washington, George, U.S. president
    foxhounds 288
Washington Crossing the Delaware, painting by Leutze
    146
Washington Reviewing His Ragged Army at Valley Forge,
    painting by Trego 146
Water fountains 190–95
Water polo, sport
    Olympic Games 309
Waubuno, ship 180; picture 179
Weaving
    ojo de Dios, Indian design 136–38
Weight lifting, sport
    Olympic Games 304, 309
Well Tempered Clavier, The, compositions by Bach 331
Western Samoa 365
    coins 128, 129
    United Nations, admission to the 34
West Germany see Germany, Federal Republic of
Westminster Kennel Club show 272–73
Whales
    great bowhead or Greenland right whale 275
    narwhal 274–75
    totem pole, picture 157
Wheelchair Olympics or Olympiad for the Physically Dis-
    abled, Etobicoke, Canada 149
White, Jo Jo, American athlete 314
Whooping crane, bird 99; picture 98
Why Mosquitoes Buzz in People's Ears, African story,
    picture 261
Why the Bear's Tail Is So Short, Norwegian fable 283
Wildlife conservation see Conservation of wildlife
Williamsburg, Virginia
    presidential candidates' debate 40
Williamsport, Pennsylvania
    Little League World Series 313
Willow South, Alaska 32
Wilson, Harold, British prime minister 16
Wimbledon, England
    tennis tournament 326
Winnipeg Jets, hockey team 321, 322
Women, Education of
  Girl Scout and Girl Guide literacy projects 226
Women, Ordination of 28
Wonder, Stevie, American musician 340
Wood carving
    beehives of Poland 286–87
    totem poles 156–57
Wood collage painting
    instructions for making 132
Woodpecker, bird, picture 277
Woodward Township School, Pennsylvania, picture 48
Wordsworth, William, English poet
    Written in the Album of a Child, poem 251
World Association of Girl Guides and Girl Scouts 224

World Cup, golf trophy 319
World Cup, skiing trophy 324
World Hockey Association 321, 322
World Series, baseball 310, 311
    Little League 313
World Wildlife Fund
    commemorative coins 128
    ibises of Birecik, Turkey 285
Wrestling, sport
    Olympic Games 309
Wright, Orville, American inventor 90

X Y

X-1, airplane 93

Yachting, sport
    Olympic Games 309
Yemen (Aden) 365
Yemen (Sana) 365
Yost, Edward, American balloonist 30
Young, Andrew J., Jr., U.S. representative to the United
    Nations 35
Young, Sheila, American athlete 299
Young Hare, painting by Albrecht Dürer 346–47
Young people's literature
    Adventures of Tom Sawyer, The, novel by Mark Twain
      256–59
    book illustrations, pictures 260–61
    Children Headed West, story 230–39
    Live and Let Live, story 240–47
    Moby Dick, novel by Melville 252–55
    poetry 248–51
    quiz 139
    Strong Voice, The, Swedish story 262–67
    Why the Bear's Tail Is So Short, Norwegian fable 283
Young people's music 330–35
Young Person's Guide to the Orchestra, The, composition
    by Britten 331
    Fanfare, ballet based on composition, picture 332
Youth organizations
    Boy Scouts 220–23
    Girl Scouts and Girl Guides 224–27
Yugoslavia 365
    Olympic Games 304

Z

Zaïre 365
Zambia 365
Zholobov, Vitali, Soviet cosmonaut, picture 27
Zoology see Animals
Zoos
    Barcelona zoo's albino gorilla, pictures 268–69, 280
    Cincinnati zoo's albino rattlesnake, picture 280
    National Zoo's Smokey Bear, picture 271
    San Diego zoo's koala bears, picture 271
Zorro, dog, picture 271
ZZ Top, American music group 341

The following list credits or acknowledges, by page, the source of illustrations and text excerpts used in THE NEW BOOK OF KNOWLEDGE ANNUAL. Illustration credits are listed illustration by illustration—left to right, top to bottom. When two or more illustrations appear on one page, their credits are separated by semicolons. When both the photographer or artist and an agency or other source are given for an illustration, they are usually separated by a dash. Excerpts from previously published works are listed by inclusive page numbers.

12 Courtesy of Philadelphia Convention and Visitors Bureau
13– UPI
23
24 NASA
25 Wide World
26 A.F.P.—Pictorial Parade
27 Tass—Sovfoto
28 UPI
29 Wide World
30– UPI
32
33 Collection of Whitney Museum of American Art, N.Y.
34 Wide World
36 Wide World
38– UPI
39
41 Charles M. Rafshoon
42 Dan Budnik—Woodfin Camp
44– The Bettmann Archive
45
46 Michael Philip Manheim—Photo Researchers; Wide World
47 Wide World
48 Jane Latta; Vannucci—Leo de Wys, Inc.
49 UPI; Ken Heyman
50 Brown Brothers
51 Robert C. Lautman
52 Robert C. Lautman; Robert C. Lautman—The Metropolitan Museum of Art, gift of Mrs. Amos L. Beaty, 1961
53 Robert C. Lautman
54 George Holton—Photo Researchers
55 Courtesy The East New York Savings Bank, Brooklyn, N.Y.
56 Wide World
57 UPI
58 Wide World; E. C. Johnson—Leo de Wys, Inc.
59 Smithsonian Institution
61 A.F.P.—Pictorial Parade
63 George Buctel
65 Matthew Naythons—Sipa/Liaison
66 Max Scheler—Stern/Black Star
67 UPI; Bertil Reijbrandt—Swedish Information Service
68 UPI
70 Leif Skoogfors—Woodfin Camp
72 P. Frankel—United Nations
73 Yismach, by permission of Keter Publishing House, Ltd., from 90 Minutes at Entebbe, by William Stevenson, Bantam Books, Inc.
75 Michal Heron—Photo Researchers
76 Cameron—Sygma
78 Alain DeJean—Sygma
79 Viamonte—Gamma-Liaison
80– Courtesy Laser Images, Inc.
81
82 Jet Propulsion Laboratory; NASA
84– Courtesy Laser Images, Inc.
86
87 The New York Public Library Picture Collection
88 Wide World
89 NASA
90 Smithsonian Institution
91 J. Kelly Beatty—Sky and Telescope
92 J. Kelly Beatty—Sky and Telescope; Smithsonian Institution
93 Smithsonian Institution
94 Courtesy Texas Instruments
95– George Buctel
96
98 Allan D. Cruickshank—National Audubon Society/Photo Researchers

100 NASA
101 Courtesy British Aircraft Corp.
102 Courtesy Canadian Consulate
103 Robert C. Hermes—National Audubon Society/Photo Researchers
104 Annan Photo Features
105 Bernard Wolf—DPI
106 Courtesy Pearce-Simpson, Gladding Corp.
107 Merrim—Monkmeyer
108 George Buctel
109 University Museum, Philadelphia, Pa.
110 Paul Hosefros—The New York Times
111 Wide World
112 American Museum of Natural History
113 John Cubito—American Museum of Natural History; John Cubito—American Museum of Natural History; Henry Janson—American Museum of Natural History
114 John Cubito—American Museum of Natural History; American Museum of Natural History; American Museum of Natural History; John Cubito—American Museum of Natural History
115 American Museum of Natural History; John Cubito—American Museum of Natural History; John Cubito—American Museum of Natural History; John Cubito—American Museum of Natural History
117 UPI
118 The New York Times
119 George Holton—Photo Researchers; UPI
120 UPI
121 Baldev—Transworld
122 Joan Forbes—The Christian Science Monitor, © 1975 The Christian Science Publishing Society
123 Eros Data Center
124– Jane Latta
125
126 Adapted from Working With Odds and Ends, © 1972 Santillana, S.A. de Ediciones. English translation © 1973 Mac-Donald & Co. (Publishers) Ltd. By permission of Franklin Watts, Inc.
127 Jacques Chazaud

128– Courtesy Krause Publications, Inc.
129
130 Rob Downey
131 Reprinted by permission from The Christian Science Monitor, © 1976 The Christian Science Publishing Society. All rights reserved.
132– Reprinted and adapted with permission
133 of Macmillan Publishing Co., Inc., from Let's Make More Presents, by Esther Hautzig. Illustrations © 1973 by Macmillan Publishing Co., Inc.
134– Adapted from String, Raffia, & Material
135 © 1969 Santillana, S.A. de Ediciones. English translation © 1970 MacDonald & Co. (Publishers) Ltd. By permission of Franklin Watts, Inc.
136– Sybil C. Harp
138
140– Adapted from String, Raffia, & Material
141 © 1969 Santillana, S.A. de Ediciones. English translation © 1970 MacDonald & Co. (Publishers) Ltd. By permission of Franklin Watts, Inc.
142 © 1976, Highlights for Children, Inc., Columbus, Ohio
143 © 1976, Highlights for Children, Inc., Columbus, Ohio. Answers: The TV is on and no one is watching; more lights are on than the man needs for reading; the open window, broken pane, and open curtains are all wasting heat; the thermostat is higher than necessary; there is a piece of furniture blocking the radiator; and somebody has left the car motor running, wasting gasoline.
144 Ann Hagen Griffiths—DPI
151 Sybil C. Harp
152– Courtesy William E. Shapiro
153
154 Dmitri Kessel
155 Culver Pictures
156– Robert W. Kelley
157
158 Z. Haber—Photo Trends
159 UPI
160 George Buctel
161 UPI; UPI; David Lees—Fortune magazine © Time Inc.
162– Courtesy Ontario Industry and Tourism
163
164 Roland and Sabrina Michaud—Rapho/Photo Researchers; Rowan—Photo Researchers; Rowan—Photo Researchers
167– Richard Tedeschi
168
170 Lynn Earley
172– Lynn Earley
173
174– Courtesy Armour Landry
175
176– Metropolitan Toronto Library Board
179
181 J. Deschenes—Fauvea Photo Inc.
182 Susanne F. Stevens—Lincoln Center; Courtesy French Government Tourist Office
183 The New York Public Library Picture Collection
184– Courtesy William E. Shapiro
185
186 Courtesy Circus World Museum, Baraboo, Wis.; The New York Public Library Picture Collection
187 Sovfoto
188 Poster by Uri Shulevitz for 1976 Children's Book Week, sponsored by The Children's Book Council, N.Y.

189 Courtesy Canadian Consulate; Courtesy T.S.L. & Associates
190 Ulf Sjostedt—F.P.G.; H. Muller-Brunke—F.P.G.
191 Rapho/Photo Researchers
193 Courtesy French Government Tourist Office
194 Courtesy Bureau of Parks and Recreation, Portland, Oreg.; Bandphoto
195 Bob and Ira Spring—Alpha
196 Jean Pierre Laffont—Sygma
197 GAF Corporation
198 Library of Congress
199 Painting by Eric von Schmidt
200– Courtesy Scholastic Photography Awards,
201 conducted by Scholastic Magazines, Inc., and sponsored by Eastman Kodak Company
202 Michele and Tom Grimm
205 Michele and Tom Grimm
206 Courtesy The Metropolitan Museum of Art, The Cloisters
207 Wide World; Neal Boenzi—*The New York Times*
208 *The New York Times;* Wide World
209 Wide World; UPI
210 UPI
211 Ken Regan—Camera 5
212– Courtesy New Games Foundation
213
214– Text adapted from "Dig In!," by Madeleine Livaudais, © 1976, *Ranger Rick's*
215 *Nature Magazine,* published by The National Wildlife Federation. By permission of the publisher. Photos by Duffy White.
216– Courtesy Scholastic Photography Awards,
219 conducted by Scholastic Magazines, Inc., and sponsored by Eastman Kodak Company
220 Boy Scouts of Canada
221 Boy Scouts of America; Boy Scouts of Canada
222– Boy Scouts of America
223
224– Girl Scouts of the U.S.A.
226
227 Girl Scouts of the U.S.A.; Girl Guides of Canada
228– Illustrations © 1976 by Symeon Shimin,
229 *A Special Birthday,* published by McGraw-Hill Book Company
230 Chicago Historical Society
232 Museum of Science and Industry, Chicago
236 Oregon Historical Society
240 Charles McVicker
245 Charles McVicker
252 Courtesy Walter Scott, Berkshire County Historical Society
253 The Rockwell Kent Legacies
255 The Rockwell Kent Legacies
256 Courtesy Missouri Division of Tourism
258 Susan Swan
260 From *Underground,* by David Macaulay © 1976 by David Macaulay, published by Houghton Mifflin Company, Boston,

1976; Martha Swope, from *The Nutcracker,* by Martha Swope, Dodd, Mead & Company, Inc.
261 From *The Tyger Voyage,* by Richard Adams, illustrated by Nicola Bayley © 1976 by Nicola Bayley. Reprinted by permission of Alfred A. Knopf, Inc.; Illustration from *Why Mosquitos Buzz in People's Ears: A West African Tale,* illustrations © 1975 by Leo and Diane Dillon. Reprinted by permission of The Dial Press.
262– From *Scandinavian Stories,* by Margaret
267 Sperry. Illustrations by Jenny Williams. Illustrations © 1971 by Franklin Watts, Inc. Used by permission.
268– Tom McHugh—Photo Researchers
269
270 H. R. Bustard—F.A.O.; UPI
271 UPI; Courtesy The Quaker Oats Company; UPI
272 Culver Pictures
273 Evelyn M. Shafer
275 Courtesy George Luther Schelling—*Audubon* magazine
276 J. A. Hancock—Photo Researchers; Russ Kinne—Photo Researchers; Fritz Henle—Photo Researchers
277 George H. Harrison; Herman Gantner; George H. Harrison
278 Alan Riding—*The New York Times*
279 Ted Eckhart—Photo Researchers
280 Tom McHugh—Photo Researchers
281 Douglass Baglin—Rapho/Photo Researchers; S. Nagendra—Photo Researchers
282 Karl H. Maslowski—Photo Researchers; Karl and Steve Maslowski—Photo Researchers; Tom McHugh—Photo Researchers
283 From *Scandinavian Stories,* by Margaret Sperry. Illustrations by Jenny Williams. Illustrations © 1971 by Franklin Watts, Inc. Used by permission.
284– Udo Hirsch
285
286 Robert Scott Milne
287 Eastfoto
288 Courtesy Lincoln National Life Foundation, Fort Wayne, Ind.
289 Courtesy Theodore Roosevelt Collection, Harvard College Library
290 Smithsonian Institution
291 Culver Pictures
292– UPI
293
294 The White House
295 UPI; Charles M. Rafshoon
296– Depardon—Uzan/Liaison
297
298 Herbert Sundhöfer; Courtesy Austrian National Tourist Office
299 Tony Triolo—*Sports Illustrated* © Time Inc.
300 Wide World
301 Gerry Cranham—Photo Researchers; Wally McNamee—Woodfin Camp

302 Neil Leifer—*Sports Illustrated* © Time Inc.; Alain DeJean—Sygma
310 UPI
311 Daniel S. Baliotti
313 UPI
314 Bob Kingsbury—Focus Productions
315 Wide World
316 UPI
317 UPI; Wide World
318 UPI
319 UPI; Wide World
320– UPI
321
323 Daniel S. Baliotti; Joe DiMaggio/Jo Anne Kalish—Peter Arnold
324– Wide World
325
326 Bruce Curtis—Peter Arnold
327 UPI
328– Courtesy Museum of American Folk
329 Art, Private Collection
330 Courtesy Austrian Tourist Office, N.Y.C.
332 Martha Swope
333 J. Kellum Smith; Wide World
335 © Beth Bergman
336 J. Alex Langley—DPI
337 Jane Latta; Joyce Deyo
338 Courtesy Columbia Records; © Chuck Pulin
339 UPI
340 Courtesy Columbia Records; Courtesy CBS Records
341 © Chuck Pulin
342 © Chuck Pulin; UPI; Courtesy Reprise Records
344 From the MGM release *The Sunshine Boys* © 1975 Metro-Goldwyn-Mayer Inc.
345 © 1976 N. V. Zwaluw, distributed by United Artists Corp; © Columbia Pictures
347 Graphische Sammlung, Albertina, Vienna
348– From the collection of Mr. & Mrs. Paul
349 Mellon
351 Hirshhorn Museum and Sculpture Garden, Smithsonian Institution
352 Museum of American Folk Art, Collection of Burton and Helaine Fendelman; Museum of American Folk Art, Collection of Mr. and Mrs. Kenneth Milne; Museum of American Folk Art, Collection of Mr. and Mrs. Burton E. Purmell
353 New York State Historical Association, Cooperstown
354 Giraudon, Paris
355 Belzeaux—Rapho/Photo Researchers; The Metropolitan Museum of Art, Gift of Arthur A. Houghton, Jr., 1970
356 Giraudon, Paris; Remington Art Museum, Ogdensburg, N.Y., all rights reserved.
357 Gernsheim Collection Humanities Research Center, The University of Texas, Austin
358 Ann Hagen Griffiths—DPI
359 Courtesy Levi's Denim Art Contest